Jacques Lacan and the Freudian Practice of Psychoanalysis

Jacques Lacan's work has become a standard reference in gender, women's and cultural studies. Yet despite its popularity is frequently being overlooked as a paragon of post-modernism by scientists and literary scholars alike.

Jacques Lacan and the Freudian Practice of Psychoanalysis paints a completely new picture of the man and his ideas. Situating Lacan's contributions firmly within the Freudian tradition of clinical psychoanalysis, the book succeeds in showing how his ideas can become more accessible, and re-evaluates his significance within the field of psychodynamic psychotherapy.

The book is structured thematically around five key issues: diagnosis, the analyst's position during the treatment, the management of transference, the formulation of interpretations, and the organisation of analytic training. For each of these issues, Lacan's entire work, both published and unpublished material, has been taken into account and theoretical principles have been illustrated with clinical examples. The book also contains the first complete bibliography of Lacan's works in English.

Clear, detailed, and wide ranging, *Jacques Lacan and the Freudian Practice of Psychoanalysis* will prove essential reading, not only for professionals and students within the fields of psychology and psychiatry, but for all those keen to discover a new Lacan.

Dany Nobus is a Lecturer in Psychology and Psychoanalytic Studies at Brunel University. He is the Chair of the Universities Association for Psychoanalytic Studies (UAPS).

The Makers of Modern Psychotherapy
Series editor: Laurence Spurling

This series of introductory, critical texts looks at the work and thoughts of key contributors to the development of psychodynamic psychotherapy. Each book shows how the theories examined affect clinical practice, and includes biographical material as well as a comprehensive bibliography of the contributor's work.

The field of psychodynamic psychotherapy is today more fertile but also more diverse than ever before. Competing schools have been set up, rival theories and clinical ideas circulate. These different and sometimes competing strains are held together by a canon of fundamental concepts, guiding assumptions and principles of practice.

This canon has a history, and the way we now understand and use the ideas that frame our thinking and practice is palpably marked by how they came down to us, by the temperament and experiences of their authors, the particular puzzles they wanted to solve and the contexts in which they worked. These are the makers of modern psychotherapy. Yet despite their influence, the work and life of some of these eminent figures is not well known. Others are more familiar, but their particular contribution is open to reassessment. In studying these figures and their work, this series will articulate those ideas and ways of thinking that practitioners and thinkers within the psychodynamic tradition continue to find persuasive.

Laurence Spurling

Also in this series:
John Bowlby and Attachment Theory Jeremy Holmes
Frances Tustin Sheila Spensley
Michael Fordham: Innovations in Analytical Psychology James Astor
Heinz Kohut and the Psychology of the Self Allen Siegel
The Clinical Thinking of Wilfred Bion Joan and Neville Symington
Harry Stack Sullivan: Interpersonal Theory and Psychotherapy F. Barton
Evans III
R. D. Laing and the Paths of Anti-Psychiatry Zbigniew Kotowicz
Anna Freud: A View of Development, Disturbance and Therapeutic Techniques
Rose Edgcumbe

Jacques Lacan and the Freudian Practice of Psychoanalysis

Dany Nobus

London and Philadelphia

First published 2000 by Routledge
11 New Fetter Lane, London EC4P 4EE

Simultaneously published in the USA and Canada by
Taylor & Francis Inc
325 Chestnut Street, 8th Floor, Philadelphia PA 19106

Routledge is an imprint of the Taylor & Francis Group

© 2000 Dany Nobus

Typeset in Times by Keystroke, Jacaranda Lodge, Wolverhampton
Printed and bound in Great Britain by TJ International Ltd,
Padstow, Cornwall

British Library Cataloguing in Publication Data
A catalogue record for this book is available from the British Library

Library of Congress Cataloging in Publication Data
Nobus, Dany.
    Jacques Lacan and the Freudian practice of psychoanalysis / Dany Nobus.
        p.   cm. – (Makers of modern psychotherapy)
    Includes bibliographical references and index.
    1. Psychoanalysis. 2. Lacan, Jacques, 1901– I. Title. II. Series.
    RC506 .N63 2000
    616.89'17 – dc21   00–025501

ISBN 0–415–17961–0 (hbk)
ISBN 0–415–17962–9 (pbk)

To the Memory of my Father, Marcellus Josephus
Nobus, 1926–1986

Contents

Acknowledgements

It is a Lacanian commonplace to claim that every subject is in debt to the symbolic. Although I do not want to dispute the validity of this assertion – after all, I could not have written this book if language and speech had not been given to me – producing this text has made me feel that I am also indebted to a cornucopia of friends, colleagues and students. Some of these debts may be imaginary, to the extent that I may just have wished for some of these people to assist me, yet most of them are very real and therefore difficult to confront. Moreover, since my expressions of gratitude in these acknowledgements are purely symbolic, my imaginary and real debts to them are doomed to remain uncleared.

First of all, I wish to thank all those people who have given me the opportunity to test some of the ideas included in this book by inviting me into their seminars. Thanks to Alison Hall and Alan Rowan I have been able to present parts of Chapter 1 at Leeds Metropolitan University and Enfield Hospital in North London. Thanks to Russell Grigg I had the chance to discuss my interpretation of Lacan's scattered ideas on perversion with the members of his group at Deakin University in Melbourne. Thanks to Jennifer Rutherford the same section on perversion was subsequently discussed at Macquarrie University in Sydney and, also in Sydney, Eleanor Sebel gave me the opportunity to present my account of Lacan's theory of psychosis in the comfortable atmosphere of her reading group. Sections of Chapter 2 were first presented at the Institute of Contemporary Arts in London during a conference on 'Lacan and History' organized by Yannis Stavrakakis and Dylan Evans. They know how grateful I am for having been asked to participate in this thought-provoking event. The central part of Chapter 3, on the relationship between love and knowledge, was the subject of a talk at the 5th Lacan Symposium in Melbourne, organized by the Australian Centre for Psychoanalysis in the Freudian Field. Thank you Leonardo Rodríguez, Silvia Rodríguez, and Carmela Levy-Stokes. Vicente Mira, who decided to accompany me on my Australian travels, proved not only an excellent companion and an expert guide on single malt whiskies, but also a most stimulating intellectual sparring partner. Parts of Chapter 3 and Chapter 4 were presented at the Centre for Freudian Analysis and Research (CFAR) in London, which has become one of my preferred arenas for talking about my work. My thanks to Bernard Burgoyne, Vivien Bar, Alan Rowan, Gerry Sullivan and all the CFAR regulars. Thanks also to Liz Reid and Audrey Cantlie for giving me the opportunity to present a first version of Chapter 5 at a meeting of The Higher Education Network for Research and Information in Psychoanalysis (THERIP) in London. The text of my lecture was subsequently published as 'Splitting Images: Lacan, Institutional Politics and the Social Authorization of Psychoanalysis' in *P/S: Journal of the Universities Association for Psychoanalytic Studies*, 1998, 1(1), pp. 53–67.

Outside the public eye I have had numerous discussions (both imaginary and real) about the topic of this book with interlocutors in various parts of the world. Perhaps they do not realize the impact they have had on the shaping of my ideas, but I could not have formulated a consistent argument without the input of Parveen Adams (despite our clashes), David F. Allen (from Paris to Brionne), Eric Corijn (despite the virtues of leisure), Sadhvi Dar (I have been your student too), Dylan Evans (despite evolutionary psychology), Bruce Fink (your book was first), Katrien Libbrecht (despite the Little Potato), Kenneth Reinhard (you wanted this book), Harry Stroeken (from Utrecht to Gent), Laurence Spurling (a brilliant series editor) and Paul Verhaeghe (teachers can become friends). Manya Steinkoler allowed me to sit in on Alice's Kitchen Seminar, the most exciting intellectual high to come from a Southern Californian kitchen in years, which has given me unprecedented creative energy and the courage to carry on writing. Let's hope Alice's seminar finds a publisher soon. As always, Katrien Libbrecht's tender care, intellectual scope, and unwavering belief in my abilities proved invaluable for completing the manuscript.

Finally, I wish to thank all those people who have contributed, in one way or another, to the creation of what is meant to be the first comprehensive bibliography of Lacan's writings in English. Without the help of David F. Allen, Josefina Ayerza, Dirk De Schutter, Russell Grigg, Richard G. Klein and Megan Williams, I would definitely have given up the enterprise altogether. For his truly amazing bibliographic skills and his willingness to share his precious materials with impatient academics like me, I am especially grateful to Richard G. Klein. I hope my contribution to his collection will partly pay off my intellectual debts.

London, 23 November 1999

PERMISSIONS

Preface

At the close of this century, and nearly twenty years after his death, the figure of Jacques Lacan (1901–1981) continues to spark fierce controversy. Worshipped by a pleiad of followers in France, Spain, Italy and large parts of South America, Lacan has grown into a thoroughbred Western Zen-master whose thought-provoking statements ('Loving is to give what one does not have', 'Woman does not exist', 'There is no such thing as a sexual relationship') provide many scholars with theoretical tools to dissect the insecurities of contemporary society and their pathological effects. People are often drawn to Lacan's ideas because their enigmatic, provocative and uncompromising character is strangely appealing, and many students engage with Lacan's works following the principle 'I haven't got a clue, but I like it', simultaneously hoping to derive some universal wisdom from the opaque texts. From another angle, Lacan has been perceived by hard-nosed scientists as the ultimate paragon of post-modern discourse. They see him alternatively as a highly unpalatable character who fluttered and flaunted without saying anything sensible, or a pretentious shrink suffering from the delusion that he was a genius. For who else but a madman would have the nerve to pontificate at the prestigious Massachusetts Institute of Technology that human beings think with their feet (and sometimes with their forehead muscles), rather than with their brains?

The turmoil created by Lacan's idiosyncratic viewpoints, not to mention his eccentric life-style, has often overshadowed the fact that he was essentially a practising psychoanalyst who devoted his entire career to the redemption and development of Freud's clinical insights. Discussions surrounding Lacan's works have mainly focused on the theoretical contents of his *Ecrits*, a massive collection of contrived texts stemming from seminars or conference presentations, and to a far lesser extent on his clinical contributions. Likewise, it has often been overlooked that Lacan's *Séminaire*, which ran for almost thirty years, was initially part of an institutionalized programme designed to train new analysts. An even lesser known fact is that Lacan alternated this *Séminaire* with clinical case-presentations, a practice which has now become largely obsolete but which was widespread within psychiatric training hospitals during Lacan's lifetime. Rather than a forum for Lacan's masterly messages, these presentations of psychiatric patients functioned as an open laboratory in which the analyst could be contemplated as a researcher who was trying to make sense of what the patients were teaching him. Working within a Freudian paradigm, the only data that mattered to Lacan were the patients' verbal productions, yet he gathered them in an extremely meticulous fashion, and often surprised his audience by claiming not to understand words and relationships which seemed child's play to everybody else. Despite the prevailing image of Lacan as a guru or charlatan, clinical experience thus informed all of his theorizations and much of their obscurity (whether prophetic or nonsensical) dissolves when this clinical breeding-ground is taken into account.

For material rather than intellectual reasons, evaluating Lacan's clinical work is an onerous task in its own right. With two exceptions (Lacan 1980a[1976]; 1998c[1976]) the minutes of his case-presentations have not been published and he himself did not produce any extensive case-studies. Alternatively, patient-accounts of Lacan's analytic procedures could be consulted (Schneiderman 1983; Rey 1989; Godin 1990; Giroud 1990), yet these often strongly fictionalized testimonies lack reliability owing to the patients' emotional ties with their analysts and the singularity of their experiences. Lacan did devote some of his papers to broad clinical issues such as the nature of psychosis and the direction of the treatment, and many of his ostensibly philosophical texts did include discussions of psychoanalytic practice. Yet it is not always easy to extract the clinical juice from Lacan's abstract, seemingly philosophical discourse, as any reader of the *Ecrits* will have experienced.

Since Lacan remained adamant throughout his career that his practice was situated strictly within the boundaries delineated by Freud, it seemed to me that Freud's psychoanalytic apparatus – comprising the nosological categories of neurosis and psychosis, and the techniques of free association, interpretation and transference – constitutes the most appropriate tool to distill these clinical ideas. Using a Freudian lever, I have thus tried to reopen Lacan's seminars and writings in order to revalue their taste within a clinical (rather than structuralist, philosophical or post-modernist) setting. Clinical as well as Freudian, this book proceeds from a double vantage point, which is reflected in its title, *Jacques Lacan and the Freudian Practice of Psychoanalysis*. In reference to the various aspects of Freud's treatment model, I have adopted Lacan's motto of the 'return to Freud' in order to scrutinize his own texts and to extract their significance for practising psychoanalysts and 'modern psychotherapists'.

My itinerary through Lacan's *œuvre* has also taught me that, by contrast with other 'makers of modern psychotherapy' such as Bion, Winnicott, Laing and Kohut, the importance of his contributions for the broad contemporary tradition of psychodynamic psychotherapy hinges less on some innovative concept or key proposition, and more on his overarching exploration of the effects of speech and language on the human condition. This idea was partly fuelled by my observation that it is virtually impossible to isolate Lacan's concepts and propositions from their global theoretical framework. It is for example extremely arduous to elucidate his notion of the mirror-stage without referring to his triad of the symbolic, the imaginary and the real, whereas any explanation of these three categories in turn requires an exposition of the distinction between the Other and the other, and by extension between the signifier and the signified.

Due to his tightknit and austere conceptual idiom, Lacan has sometimes been vilified for transforming clinical practice into an abstract, pseudo-metaphysical discourse. When researching this book I have often felt sympathy for the detractors, especially when confronted with Lacan's dense arguments, his elliptic style and his convoluted prose. Yet, at the same time, I have discovered that even more than the Freudian inspiration of his trajectory, Lacan's self-acknowledged intention to explain the relationship between the subject, speech and language serves as an excellent springboard for overcoming the difficulties of his work. And indeed, the centrality of this relationship in his texts should make them worthwhile for all practitioners working within therapeutic paradigms that are based on the power of speech, and should suffice as a guarantee for their lasting significance within the entire tradition of modern psychotherapy.

As a result, it is perhaps not even necessary to rely on a clinical Freudian framework to grasp the value of Lacan's musings or to benefit from his approach. Since Lacan's theory of Freudian analytic treatment is predicated upon the idea that speech constitutes its only source of power, anybody who is willing to spend some time listening to what other people have to say or what they are unable to say, should find something of interest in Lacan's works. This simple effort of inviting the other to speak and listening to what is being said, forms in Lacan's view the linchpin of psychoanalytic treatment and therefore the nucleus of his *œuvre*. In a sense, both those who hail Lacan like a Messiah and those who scorn him as a demon have probably never really bothered listening to what people in their immediate environment have to say about themselves and others. But when a mere 'effort of listening' can be a possible starting-point for broaching Lacan's ideas, his works should become potentially accessible to all those people in the possession of ears that are willing to hear – not merely the entire community of 'modern psychotherapists', but a substantial section of the public at large. From a 'Lacan for the Lacanians' to a 'Lacan for everybody'!

Introduction

Reacting against the discipline of ego-psychology, the prevalent psychoanalytic paradigm during the 1950s, Lacan took pride in placing his own project under the aegis of 'a return to the meaning of Freud' (1977f[1955]:117). Lest this meaning be obfuscated, he called upon psychoanalysts to regauge Freud's concepts by unearthing their historical origins and by accounting their subjective value. According to Lacan (1977e[1953]:37–38), both Freud's *œuvre* and the clinical practice of psychoanalysis were on the verge of losing their cutting edge, owing to the fact that some of the most influential analysts and notably the Americanized troika called Hartmann, Kris and Loewenstein had become more interested in current affairs than in history, and more concerned with engineering conforming behaviours in the individual than with laying bare his psychic singularities.[1]

Lacan's main ambition during the 1950s consisted in the recovery of the roots of psychoanalysis, in order to tailor its contemporary practice to the sphere of the subject. This was initially realized through a detailed re-reading of Freud's case-studies and his papers on technique (Lacan 1988b[1953–54]).[2] Since Lacan's early assertions on psychoanalysis were thus based on a scrupulous reconsideration of the Freudian canon, they are surely less 'deviant' than was acknowledged by the psychoanalytic establishment and than is generally assumed. They only appear as eccentric if 'mainstream' psychoanalysis is considered representative of Freud's discovery, and lose much of their revolutionary character when situated within their proper Freudian context. Lacan himself did not hesitate to denounce the reigning conceptions within the International Psychoanalytic Association (IPA) as the true anti-Freudian diversions, and to designate his own views as strictly loyal to the Freudian enterprise (Lacan 1977i[1958]:226). For instance, when writing an article on the variations of the psychoanalytic standard treatment during the early 1950s

(Lacan 1966b[1955]), Lacan felt obliged to explain to what extent the prevailing standard treatment was in itself a 'deviation' from the Freudian model.

Lacan's reclaimed Freudian inspiration pervades almost every aspect of his clinical theory. It is recognizable in his distinctions between the various psychic structures, in his suggested techniques of interpretation, in his proposed strategies for the handling of transference, and even in his reflections upon the analyst's position within the treatment. Lacan's commitment to the Freudian letter went so far that in January 1980, at the age of seventy-eight, he used it as an argument to dissolve his own school, which he scorned for its resemblance to a church and its harbouring of too many Lacanians and not enough Freudians (Lacan 1990e[1980]).[3]

In the present book I have tried to remain truthful to this pervasive, self-acknowledged Freudian inspiration of Lacan's itinerary by showing how most of his views on psychoanalytic practice originate in one or another aspect of Freud's works. Even where Lacan did not explicitly mention his indebtedness to Freud when formulating a particular principle, I have tried to retrace its origins in the Freudian corpus, thus re-establishing a theoretical and historical continuity. In this way I hope that Lacan's ideas, even some of the most controversial ones, will become more acceptable to those practising psychoanalysts who are still convinced that he was simply a recalcitrant, idiosyncratic charlatan.

In choosing to clarify Lacan through Freud, I have also taken a stance that is radically opposed to that which is more or less common within Lacanian circles, and which consists in the re-discovery of Freud through Lacan. To me, Freud's works do not require a Lacanian framework to be comprehensible, and I am not interested in demonstrating how the father of psychoanalysis had already foreshadowed some of the masterly insights of his son. My purpose is simply to explain Lacan's clinical theory in a way accessible to the informed layperson, and to show that the bulk of his propositions is rooted in one or another aspect of Freud's œuvre. Hoping that the resulting picture of Lacan will be less disturbing than the predominant one, I anticipate that for his ardent followers Lacan will lose much of his originality and creativity through this procedure. Yet inasmuch as this decomposition of the 'great Lacan' myth may pose an insuperable problem to some admirers, I nevertheless believe that my strategy to give Lacan a proper place in the history of psychoanalysis and modern psychotherapy will prove more valuable for the future of Lacan studies than a strategy which refuses to contextualize the man and his ideas.

Of course, Lacan also elaborated, specified and often radicalized Freudian theory, borrowing notions from linguistics, anthropology, ethology, philosophy, cybernetics and mathematics (to name only a few disciplines), an integrative process which became ever more visible as the years progressed. Indeed, it would be inaccurate and unfair to claim that Lacan's works display but an amalgam of Freudian principles couched in highbrow (post-)structuralist language. Much more than that, they contain practical solutions to various Freudian problems (such as the antagonism between repetition and remembering), innovative decompositions of Freudian notions (as exemplified in Lacan's distinction between the imaginary, the symbolic and the real father), the deployment of entirely new concepts (such as jouissance and the object *a*), the radical replacement of major Freudian systems by others (such as the substitution of language for constitution), and the displacement of fairly marginal Freudian insights towards the centre of psychoanalytic theory and practice (such as the idea of *Verwerfung* as the causal mechanism of psychosis). To represent this dialectical relationship between Freudian and Lacanian doctrine, this book not only highlights Lacan's ongoing engagement with Freud's *œuvre*, but also his eagerness to carve out new slabs of theory from the Freudian rock, and his fearlessness in contradicting and correcting the father of psychoanalysis.

Each of the five chapters in this book revolves around an issue which spans the entire field of psychodynamic psychotherapy and to which every practitioner working within this field will be able to relate. As such, the reader will successively learn about diagnostic criteria, the position of the analyst within the treatment, the handling of transference, techniques of interpretation, and the organization of analytic training. Proceeding from these issues, I have outlined the Lacanian approach in keeping with its Freudian inspiration and its dialectical relationship with the Freudian canon. Rather than a chronological take on the procedures of Lacanian psychoanalysis – describing the treatment from the initial contact between the analyst and the patient to its logical end – I have adopted a thematic stratification of the materials, mainly because every attempt to present a detailed chronological account of a psychoanalytic process is doomed to come short of the huge diversity of clinical situations. As Freud underscored in the opening paragraph of 'On Beginning the Treatment' (1913c:123), the technical explanation of psychoanalytic practice encounters the same limits as those imposed on the description of chess strategies: the endless variety of possible moves after the play has started forces the writers of manuals to restrict themselves to an account of the openings and end-games. Faced with the task of writing a monograph on Lacanian practice, I have embraced this standpoint wholeheartedly, yet instead of fixing myself on the commencement and the termination of the treatment I have chosen to canvas, in a non-hierarchical sequence, crucial factors of the analyst's involvement with the patient that operate simultaneously throughout the course of an analysis.

Unlike a traditional 'operating manual', this book does not include the answers to frequently asked questions, much less a series of dos and don'ts about Lacanian psychoanalysis. Here too I have followed one of Freud's remarks in 'On Beginning the Treatment', namely that the diversity of relevant psychic constellations, the plasticity of the psychic processes and the wealth of determining factors with which analysts are confronted in their practice preclude the formulation of standard instructions (ibid.:123). At best some broad guidelines or recommendations can be formulated which the analyst is held to apply flexibly, creatively and knowledgeably. The layperson or professional who expects to learn from this book what a Lacanian analyst is supposed to do or say in particular situations will thus be seriously disappointed. Yet I firmly believe that this disappointment will be less disturbing and easier to overcome than that which occurs whenever one tries to apply formal rules of thumb to complex clinical realities.

Finally, I have also tried to avoid writing a clinical text that is at once a simplification of Lacanian psychoanalysis. Although the level of sophistication in Lacan's own works and in the lion's share of the existing Lacanian publications is much higher than that which I have sustained in the present book, I have endeavoured to write a correct and accurate account of Lacanian practice within the constraints of the series in which this book is being published. As Einstein loved to say, we should make things as simple as possible, but not simpler, which is exactly what I have attempted to do. Of course, this maxim does not guarantee that the contents of the book will be comprehensible to everyone, and neither does it warrant the completeness of its survey of Lacanian practice. Whereas I take full responsibility for any remaining bits of esotericism – something which can only be explained by the fact that I have not made things simple enough – the incompleteness of the project follows from its envisaged accuracy. For it is only possible to render Lacan's ideas accurately by endorsing their incompleteness, a feature which he himself attributed to the essentially unfinished state of language.

NOTES

1   In order to avoid the annoying 'he or she' I will use 'he' and 'she' alternatively to refer to the gender of the analyst or the analysand. The reader should therefore take into account that whenever I use a particular gender,

this does not mean that the principle or example only applies to female or male analysts (or analysands).

2   Between 1950 and 1953, Lacan conducted seminars on Freud's case-studies of Dora (Freud 1905e[1901]), the Wolf Man (Freud 1918b[1914]) and the Rat Man (Freud 1909d) at his house in Paris, the text of which remains unpublished except for a small excerpt from the Wolf Man seminar in Italian (Lacan 1989c[1951–52]). Lacan's seminar on Dora did provide the backdrop for his 1951 paper 'Intervention on Transference' (1982a[1951]), and his seminar on the Rat Man informed his 1953 text 'The Neurotic's Individual Myth' (1979[1953]).

3   See also Lacan's final seminar (the so-called 'Caracas Seminar'), in which he proclaimed: 'If you [my audience] want it is your turn to be Lacanians. I am Freudian' (1981b:104).

Chapter 1

Diagnosis via speech and transference

WHY DIAGNOSIS?

Throughout his works, Lacan insisted on the differences between various mental organizations, on the analyst's need to recognize these differences, and on the mandatory adoption of a differential treatment approach in the light of the psychic economy the analyst has acknowledged in the patient. The 'Lacanian analyst' has to bear in mind some basic nosological categories and is held to diagnose patients at the earliest stage of the clinical process, because her position within the treatment should differ according to the psychic structure of the patient. Hence, the initial assessment of the patient is not merely a matter of registration, due to the fact that it has major clinical consequences.

Like so many other aspects of Lacan's clinical theory, the importance of a correct diagnosis prior to the beginning of psychoanalytic treatment is rooted in Freud's papers on technique. In 'On Beginning the Treatment' (Freud 1913c), Freud argued in favour of a trial period (*Probezeit*, *Erprobung*, *Sondierung*) of one or two weeks before the start of the treatment, for which he adduced the necessary, yet laborious diagnostic procedure as one of the main reasons. Until the end of his career, Freud remained convinced that the standard method of psychoanalysis was of no use to people suffering from paraphrenia – or some other form of psychosis – which prompted him to demand that the analyst recognize this contraindication during the trial period (ibid.:124).[1] Failure to do so, or making a diagnostic mistake, would be disastrous as some patients (neurotics wrongly diagnosed as paraphrenics) would be unjustly excluded from treatment, whereas others (paraphrenics erroneously qualified as neurotics) would be unjustly admitted.

Compared to Freud's dual opposition of neurosis and psychosis, Lacan's nosological framework is slightly more sophisticated and its categories more mutually exclusive. Whereas Freud also designated the psychoses as narcissistic neuroses (and the neuroses proper as transference neuroses) (Freud 1916–17a[1915–17]:420), Lacan defined neurosis and psychosis as fundamentally different psychic structures with separate causalities. To the Freudian neurosis/psychosis dualism he also added the distinct psychic structure of perversion, which Freud chiefly addressed on a purely phenomenological level – as sadism, masochism, exhibitionism, voyeurism, etc. Indeed, Freud never sharply discriminated between psychosis and perversion, and his only formal distinction between perversion and neurosis resides in his thesis that the latter is the negative of the former, which he defended for example in 'Three Essays on the Theory of Sexuality' (1905d:165). Lacan rationalized and systematized Freud's diagnostic categories, ultimately constructing the triptych of neurosis, psychosis and perversion, in which each of the terms represents a separate clinical entity.

Furthermore, the clinical impact of these categories within Lacanian analysis no longer concerns the patient's possible entry to the treatment, but rather the analyst's prescribed position within the treatment and his preferable handling of transference. Unlike Freud, Lacan did not regard psychotics as unsuitable candidates for analysis. This does not imply that for Lacan the Freudian dispositions remain valid under all circumstances, but that the clinical premises of Freudian psychoanalysis can and should be modified, without therefore losing their vigour, to accommodate different types of patients.

DIAGNOSTIC CRITERIA

So how does the analyst actually arrive at a diagnosis? In 'On Beginning the Treatment', Freud was not very forthcoming about how to distinguish practically neurosis from psychosis, yet he did warn his readers about the deceitfulness of the clinical picture:

> Often enough, when one sees a neurosis with hysterical or obsessional symptoms, which is not excessively marked and has not been in existence for long – just the type of case, that is, that one would regard as suitable for treatment – one has to reckon with the possibility that it may be a preliminary stage of what is known as dementia praecox ('schizophrenia', in Bleuler's terminology; 'paraphrenia', as I have proposed to call it), and that sooner or later it will show a well-marked picture of that affection.
>
> (Freud 1913c:124)

Freud contended that ostensibly neurotic symptoms (such as elusive bodily pains and compulsive behaviours) should not be taken as unambiguous signs of an underlying neurotic illness, however conspicuous they may be. A psychosis can hide under the mask of a neurosis, and the analyst should not be misled by the colours of the clinical guise.[2] To many of his contemporaries, Freud's admonition must have seemed odd, used as they were in privileging strict relationships between certain symptoms and certain disorders. Yet it may also surprise those contemporary clinicians who still believe that hallucinations are sufficient for diagnosing psychosis or that persistent offending is pathognomonic for psychopathy. None the less, Freud's first, negative diagnostic rule read that one should not take symptoms at face value. Mental organization had to be dislodged from observable phenomena, and analysts were urged to suspend their judgement and to look for more reliable criteria.

Defining such criteria proved more onerous than exposing the misleading ones though. Freud was adamant that the psychoanalytic process is unpredictable and that the analyst's initial diagnosis can always be disproved by the vicissitudes of the treatment, in which case analysts should be willing to change their minds about the patient's psychic economy. Paradoxically, the most correct analytic diagnosis would be that which the analyst is able to formulate at the end of the treatment, which is unfortunately a point of no return. The whole diagnostic enterprise reminded Freud (1933a[1932]:155) of the medieval ordeal by water, albeit with the analyst rather than the patient in the position of the victim.

Despite these problems, and despite his advocacy of a 'dynamic diagnosis', Freud did suggest at least two positive diagnostic criteria. The first criterion can be inferred from his alternative tabulation of neuroses and psychoses as transference neuroses and narcissistic neuroses respectively. On the one hand, Freud classified anxiety hysteria (phobia), conversion hysteria and obsessional neurosis as transference neuroses, because the emotional tie connecting the patient to the analyst acquires in these cases an 'extraordinary, and for the treatment, positively central, importance' (Freud 1916–17a[1915–17]:445). On the other hand, patients suffering from a narcissistic neurosis – dementia praecox, paranoia or melancholia – 'have no capacity for transference or only insufficient residues of it' (ibid.:447). When faced with the task of distinguishing between neurosis and psychosis, the analyst should thus investigate whether the patient is capable of developing and maintaining an emotional tie, the absence of such an ability indicating psychosis and giving the analyst enough reason to rule out psychoanalytic treatment. Here Freud exchanged the objective diagnosis based on 'symptoms interpreted as signs' for an intersubjective diagnosis, resting on the evaluation of a relationship.

However, transference was not the only and perhaps not even the most significant criterion Freud employed to discriminate between neurosis and psychosis. In his metapsychological paper 'The Unconscious' (1915e), he opposed schizophrenia to hysteria and obsessional neurosis on no other grounds than the patient's speech. According to Freud, a schizophrenic patient's speech bears witness to a remarkable meticulousness, with expressions often displaying a degree of artificiality, sentences becoming disorganized and words getting strangely mixed up with the body. Schizophrenic patients appear to be using 'condensed speech', because whole series of thoughts find an outlet in single words, which consequently acquire massive meaning and become linked to a bodily organ or process.[3] Freud attributed these extraordinary schizophrenic speech characteristics to the prevalence of word-connections over thing-connections in psychosis. In psychotic patients, the relationship between what Freud called 'word-presentations' (*Wortvorstellungen*) and 'thing-presentations' (*Sachvorstellungen*) has been severed, resulting in a closed circuit of symptomatic word-connections. Patients are no longer concerned about the actual 'things' that words represent in a particular language; they merely relate to their verbal content.[4]

A clear illustration of this radical inertia of thing-presentations in psychosis is offered by a girl who complains that her eyes have been twisted – an example Freud borrowed from Victor Tausk (1919) – because her lover is a genuine eye-twister (*Augenverdreher*). In German, an *Augenverdreher* is an arrant deceiver, and although the woman is aware of this meaning (the thing-presentation), she is unable to assimilate it. She can only relate to the literal meaning (the word-presentation) of *Augenverdreher*, through which she is forced to conclude that her lover has twisted her eyes physically.[5] The woman's conviction that she is suffering from twisted eyes (her symptom) is determined by the broken connection between the word-presentation and the thing-presentation. Although she knows the thing-presentation, it is impossible for her to use this meaning in order to relativize the literal one.

Another example of this linguistic mechanism, reported to me by a colleague, concerns a man who threatens to sabotage the central heating of the psychiatric clinic where he was based, and even to set the whole building on fire, in order to take revenge on those members of staff who have left him out in the cold. Like the female patient, this man is incapable of assimilating the thing-presentation of the expression 'to be left out in the cold', i.e. to be left behind, although he is perfectly aware of it. To him, 'to be left out in the cold' means that some people have tried to lower his body temperature, and therefore he feels that these scoundrels deserve tit for tat.

On the surface, neurotic patients can suffer from the same kinds of symptoms (twisted eyes, physical coldness) as psychotics, which is exactly what Freud intended to demonstrate, but the neurotic symptoms respond to an entirely different psychic economy. In neurosis, the word-presentation has not been cut off from the thing-presentation, but the word-presentation has been repressed. It has been driven out of the patient's consciousness into the unconscious. The upshot is that the word-presentation exercises its influence without the patient being aware of what has produced the symptoms. In neurosis, symptoms are determined by a repressed, unconscious representation and it is the analyst's task to bring the patient to the point where this hidden factor can be retrieved. Put differently, neurotic patients somehow suffer from a 'lacking word', which the analytic process can help to recover. In psychosis, matters are completely different. Although symptoms are also determined by word-presentations, the latter are not repressed and neither are the thing-presentations. Whereas a neurotic patient fails to find the building blocks of her symptoms, a psychotic patient has nothing to hide. All the materials are out in the open. This is why Freud, talking about the schizophrenic woman, observed: 'The patient's comments . . . have the value of an analysis . . . They throw light at the same time on the meaning and the genesis of schizophrenic word-formation' (Freud 1915e:198). Of course, the drama is that in psychosis the 'analytic' value of the patient's utterances has no bearing whatsoever on the destabilization of the symptoms.

Freud's considerations on differential diagnostics form the nucleus of Lacan's distinctions between neurosis, psychosis and perversion. Within a Lacanian orientation, psychic structures do not differ as far as the clinical picture is concerned, but on the basis of speech and language, and with respect to the subject's relationships with his peers, family members, colleagues, lovers, therapists, etc. Lacan had already drawn attention to both these criteria in his earliest writings on paranoia (Lacan 1975a[1931]; 1975b[1932]; 1988d[1933]), but they did not start to gain momentum until the 1950s, as part of his 'return to Freud' and his aspiration to restore the value of speech and language in psychoanalysis. Perhaps as a result of his own training as a clinical psychiatrist working with psychotic patients, Lacan detailed these criteria most emphatically for the psychic structure of psychosis and he was least explicit concerning perversion. Moreover, in his discussion of the various psychic structures he usually highlighted the speech and language features, the nature of the transference being regarded as an effect of these characteristics.

In the subsequent sections of this chapter, I will follow a similar trajectory, from psychosis to neurosis and perversion, and from speech to transference. As Lacan's comments on perversion are less elaborated and coherent than those on psychosis and neurosis, the section on perversion will necessarily be more tributary to others' and my own interpretations of Lacan's works than the preceding ones.

PSYCHOTIC COMMUNICATION

In his so-called 'Rome Discourse' (1977e[1953]), Lacan set out to revalue the function of speech within psychoanalytic treatment. Observing that psychoanalysis was drifting away towards some kind of enlightened behaviourism, he argued that psychoanalysts urgently needed to acknowledge that their clinical practice was invented as a 'talking cure' and that its salutary effects were predicated upon the power of speech. To Lacan, the truly Freudian revolution lay in the discovery that words have the potential to precipitate, perpetuate and eradicate both physical and mental symptoms, a conclusion which psychoanalysts were more and more neglecting in favour of pre-verbal, 'behavioural engineering'. Redeeming Freud's legacy, Lacan asserted that the power of speech is nothing magical, but a quality derived from the fact that a human being's law is the law of language (ibid.:61). The symbolic structure of language presides over human beings, who not only derive their speech but their entire 'humanity' from it, including their specific problems.

This being the kernel of Lacan's 1953 discourse and his main argument for reorganizing psychoanalysis around speech and language, he at once pointed out that not every human being integrates these structuring components in the same manner. Lacan even went so far as to say that the relation between speech and language can sometimes be outright paradoxical in particular subjects (ibid.:68). As a first example of this, he adduced the general clinical category of madness (*folie*). Here, the paradox is that people can talk freely about what bothers them, that they use language flexibly in order to construct extremely sophisticated delusional systems, and play with words uninhibitedly, whilst at the same time completely disowning their own language. Lacan indicated that in psychosis radical freedom of speech is paired with an absence of the spoken word, because the latter no longer addresses itself to somebody else: 'the subject, one might say, is spoken rather than speaking' (ibid.:69).

As Lacan had already underscored in a 1946 discussion with Henri Ey, psychotic people are in a sense the most free individuals one can imagine, yet for this radical freedom they have to pay with their bodies and souls (Lacan 1966a[1946]:176; Miller 1987:143).[6]

It was not until 1955–56, when Lacan embarked on an investigation of the memoirs of President Schreber (Schreber 1988[1903]) and Freud's analysis of the book (Freud 1911c[1910]), that he further specified the singular nature of speech and language in psychosis. At the start of *Seminar III*, Lacan maintained that speech generally addresses itself to others (interlocutors and addressees, including oneself), yet immediately adding that beyond these others, speech also involves the Other (Lacan 1993[1955–56]:36–38). The Other is nothing but the dimension of the others that remains unknown to the speaker, because he approaches them via language. Language erects a wall between the addressor and the addressee, as a result of which the others become partly unfathomable (Lacan 1988c[1954–55]:244–247). Put differently, the other represents the addressee in so far as she is recognized and known (as another self, an alter ego) by the speaker, whereas the Other entails the recognized, yet never fully ascertained aspect of this addressee.

To illustrate this, Lacan referred to a message such as 'You are my master', transmitted by an individual to a known other (the 'you' in the sentence) without the sender being able to know for sure whether this other person really is or wants to be a master (Lacan 1993[1955–56]:37–38). Here, communication is not a simple process of two comparable agencies (senders and receivers) exchanging information, but a threefold interaction between two (or more) individuals and the Other, in which assumptions are being made and agreements being sought. Indeed, the wall imposed by language between the speaker and her interlocutors requires people to set limits in order to define and control each other's positions. The wall does not merely bar access to the complete other; it also urges people to make arrangements about each other's specific contributions in the interaction, and to engage themselves in the establishment of symbolic pacts.

Applying this dynamics to what is happening with psychotics, Lacan arrived at the key insight that in psychosis the Other is excluded (ibid.:52–53). This does not mean that language and speech disappear – indeed, psychotics can be very loquacious, and when they do remain silent, it is often because they are invaded by highly eloquent voices – but that communication has lost its dimension of the unknown. For a psychotic person, nothing is unsure within what is being transmitted; sentences are unidimensional, a word does not carry any other meaning than that which is presented by the word itself. This evidently brings to mind Freud's example of the woman with the twisted eyes, for whom it was impossible to assimilate that *Augenverdreher* (also and primarily) means 'deceiver'. Lacan reformulated this mechanism saying that 'the signifier itself (and not that which it signifies) . . . is the object of the communication', which entails fundamental modifications of the entire language structure (the symbolic code) (Lacan 1977h[1957–58]:184).

This altered psychotic language system demonstrates a number of peculiarities. According to Lacan, one of the most salient phenomena of the psychotic 'neo-code' concerns its containment of new linguistic formations, 'expressions that are neological in form . . . and usage' (ibid.: 184). Schreber's designation for his own 'neo-code', the *Grundsprache* (basic language) is an example of a formal neologism, because it does not belong as such to a shared linguistic domain. His notion of *Seelenmord* (soul murder) could be termed a neologism of usage, because it was transferred from an already existing discourse to a delusional context.[7] Both types of neologism convey nothing more than their 'nominal' meaning. Lacan stated that 'for the subject this high voltage of the signifier drops' (ibid.:185), that is to say, the signifier is being discharged to the point where but one meaningful unit remains. Consequently, expressions impose themselves on the psychotic patient as refrains in a popular song; they reappear time and again in the same fashion. For people are evidently only driven to use different words and phrases when they feel that their previous expressions have not adequately conveyed the intended meaning, or when there is a risk that the others will understand them incorrectly. When there is no such risk because ambiguity has been excluded, different words are unnecessary.

Apart from these alterations of the language system, psychotics also manifest idiosyncrasies on the level of the message. Relying on examples reported by Schreber in his memoirs, Lacan pointed out that psychotic messages always include a challenge between the involved partners. Schreber for instance described how divine figures tormented him day and night by uttering unfinished sentences such as 'Now I will myself . . . ' and 'You ought to . . . ', which he was then forced to complete with the appropriate endpart, respectively ' . . . face the fact that I am an idiot' and ' . . . be exposed as the negator of God and as given up to dissolute sensuality, not to mention other things'.

A first salient characteristic of these messages, on Lacan's account, is that the sending agency, in stopping just before the part of the sentence that would make the content of the message clear, reduces the message to a grammatical form of address. The only meaning the fragmented sentences uttered by Schreber's voices still have is the meaning of 'message' as such.

The interrupted messages mean nothing except for the grammatically determined fact that they are being addressed to somebody. A second distinguishing feature of these messages is that Schreber has to add his own part on the basis of his knowledge of the code – every beginning has its proper ending – in order to restore their communicative value. The messages are, in Lacan's words, 'a hallucinatory provocation' (ibid.:186) because they incite and coerce Schreber to produce what he knows. In addition, Schreber cannot refrain from retorting and his reply does not silence the voices. Neither the divine interventions nor Schreber's own answers are subject to his individual control, which confirms Lacan's idea that the psychotic is spoken rather than speaking.

THE CAUSE OF PSYCHOSIS

In *Seminar III*, Lacan did not content himself with describing the principal features of psychotic communication – the exclusion of the Other, the semantic 'shallowness' of language, a code that has become message and a message that has been reduced to its code, and the compulsory nature of the exchange – he also tried to delineate the cause of these features.

Assuming that the dimension of the Other and the possibility to define positions within a particular exchange are due to the wall imposed by language, Lacan had to conclude that in psychosis this wall has somehow not been erected. In psychotic patients, language has not been anchored. Rather than a firmly embedded, solid structure, it is a free-floating, flat and permeable screen. Implicitly referring to Freud's idea that in psychosis the link between the word-presentation and the thing-presentation has been severed, Lacan defined this non-embedment of language as a lack of 'quilting points' (*points de capiton*) between the signifier and the signified (Lacan 1993[1955–56]:268–270), for which he in turn held the foreclosure (*forclusion*) of the Name-of-the-Father responsible (Lacan 1977h[1957–58]:215).[8]

In the final session of *Seminar III* Lacan proposed 'foreclosure' as the best translation of Freud's term *Verwerfung* (Lacan 1993[1955–56]:321). In Freud's works, *Verwerfung* can hardly lay claim to conceptual status – there are very few passages in which the term appears – and it is not really elaborated as the specific cause of psychosis.[9] In conceptualizing *Verwerfung* as a distinct mechanism for psychosis, Lacan took his main lead from Freud's formula in his case-study of the Wolf Man that a 'repression [*Verdrängung*] is something very different from a condemning judgement [*Verwerfung*]' (Freud 1918b[1914]:79–80). Between 1954 and

1956, he then tried to define *Verwerfung* in opposition to repression, but also in relation to the mechanisms of *Verneinung* (negation) and *Bejahung* (affirmation), which Freud had discussed in his paper 'Negation' (1925h). Eventually, Lacan reached the conclusion that *Verwerfung* and *Verdrängung* differ with regard to their effects:

> What comes under the effect of repression returns, for repression and the return of the repressed are just the two sides of the same coin. The repressed is always there, expressed in a perfectly articulate manner in symptoms and a host of other phenomena. By contrast, what falls under the effect of *Verwerfung* has a completely different destiny . . . [W]hatever is refused in the symbolic order, in the sense of *Verwerfung*, reappears in the real.
>
> (Lacan 1993[1955–56]:12–13)

The meaning Lacan gave to *Verwerfung* here – a process through which something reappears (as a hallucination) in the real – tallies with Freud's description of the mechanism of psychotic symptom formation in his Schreber study. A paranoid patient suffering from hallucinations or persecutory delusions was in Freud's opinion subject to a process whereby 'an internal perception is suppressed, and . . . its content enters consciousness in the form of an external perception' (Freud 1911c [1910]:66). Initially, Freud called this process 'projection', but owing to the fact that people regularly attribute their mental states to external rather than internal causes – which also deserves to be called projection – he came to question his own designation: 'It was incorrect to say that the perception which was suppressed internally is projected outwards; the truth is rather . . . that what was abolished internally returns from without' (ibid.:71). Lacan must have noticed that Freud was looking in vain for an appropriate denominator to grasp the psychic mechanism of psychosis, which prompted him to designate the mechanism as *Verwerfung*, bearing in mind that Freud himself had conceived *Verwerfung* as radically different from repression.

In ultimately choosing to translate *Verwerfung* as foreclosure, Lacan re-emphasized the linguistic nature of the psychotic mechanism. Indeed, whereas foreclosure is a juridical term expressing the expiration of a person's assigned rights (for instance, the legal access to one's children after a divorce) when he does not exercise them, Lacan took it from a paper on the nature of French negations by Damourette and Pichon (1928). With French negations generally consisting of two parts – as in *ne . . . pas* and *ne . . . jamais* – Damourette and Pichon redefined the first part as the discordant component and the second one as the foreclosure, observing that the latter part is more akin to the rough logical negation than the former, which can in some cases even be omitted without the meaning of the sentence being lost. They also considered foreclosure to be the linguistic index of a desire to exclude the possibility that a certain event exists or happens again, a phenomenon which they compared to the excision (scotomization) of a perception from the field of vision.[10] Without restricting himself to this particular structure of French negation, Lacan substituted foreclosure for other translations of *Verwerfung*, because in his view the operation epitomized the exclusion of a linguistic element (a signifier) rather than an 'internal perception'. As to the exact nature of this signifier, he explored various avenues throughout *Seminar III*, finally designating it as the Name-of-the-Father from his 1957–58 text on psychosis onwards.

Lacan had introduced the concept of the Name-of-the-Father in a 1953 lecture on the neurotic's individual myth, in order to separate the real father, a flesh and blood man, from the symbolic 'function of the father', which he interpreted as the culturally determined regulation of the natural order of things (Lacan 1979[1953]:422–423). In the contemporaneous 'Rome Discourse', he further specified that 'in the *name of the father* . . . we must recognize the support of the symbolic function which, from the dawn of history, has identified his person [the person of the father] with the figure of the law (Lacan 1977e[1953]:67).[11] Hence, in Lacan's theory of the 1950s the signifier of the Name-of-the-Father bears a striking resemblance to how the Jewish God Yahweh was understood by Freud in his *Moses and Monotheism* (1939a[1937–39]). Yahweh is an upholding, yet demanding agency which never reveals its true face. An immaterial, yet speaking creature which promises redemption in exchange for a strict obeyance to the divine law, whose first indication is the act of circumcision, it is an abstract intangible principle imposing an alternative, symbolic order onto the people of Israel, which reshapes their natural living conditions.

Lacan's concept of the Name-of-the-Father conveys a similar meaning, because it is held to represent an imposed transcendence of natural provisions with a view of a higher order of mental and social functioning. Although Lacan's notion betrays its grounding in religion, he extended its operation beyond this realm, conceiving it as the guiding principle of every sociocultural organization. Similar to Moses' God, the Name-of-the-Father thereby remained an essentially linguistic principle, not so much due to the fact that it speaks, but rather because Lacan regarded it as the cornerstone of a shared language system. He also pointed out that in most cultures and throughout history the representation of this regulatory father-function is considered to be one of the tasks of real fathers, their relationships with children being less irrefutable than those of real mothers.[12]

The foreclosure of the Name-of-the-Father in psychosis thus means that an individual has been excluded from the possibility of substituting a culturally determined symbolic pact, including injunctions, prohibitions and allowances, for an unblemished, yet chaotic natural condition.[13] In Lacan's view, the psychotic is literally an outlaw, because she has not assimilated the cultural laws of language. As described on p. 12, the effect is not that language is completely eradicated, but that it no longer sets a barrier between the individual and his environment. This foreclosure of the Name-of-the-Father and the ensuing absence of quilting points between the signifier and the signified also entail that the meaning of words no longer shifts, but solidifies to the point where it becomes petrified on the level of the code itself.

This may seem odd when taking into account that the absence of quilting points appears to suggest an endless fluctuation of the signified (the thing-presentation, the culturally imposed meaning) under the signifier (the word-presentation), whereas firmly established quilting points would signal the allocation of a fixed meaning to certain signifiers. Yet, as Lacan saw it, the absence of quilting points precludes semantic ambiguity, because equivocality presupposes that at least two different meanings can be balanced against each other, which in turn requires that at least one meaning has been established.[14] In Freudian terms, the installation of a link between the word-presentation and the thing-presentation implies that the literal meaning of a word can be weighed against the figurative one, whereas the absence of such a link makes this process impossible.

Who or what is responsible for the foreclosure of the Name-of-the-Father is a particularly vexed issue within Lacanian theory. In the final pages of his 1957–58 paper on psychosis Lacan proceeded with the greatest caution when broaching this question. First of all, he repudiated the idea that foreclosure stems from the parent's mutual competition to win and sustain the child's love, whereby the mother would for instance ridicule the father systematically in front of her child. Instead of this parental rivalry to the detriment of one parent (notably the father), Lacan highlighted the place each parent accords to the symbolic position of the Name-of-the-Father in his or her relationship with the child. In this way, he decomposed the classic Oedipal triangle of mother–father–child into two sub-structures, mother–child–Name-of-the-Father and father–child–Name-of-the-Father. Within each of these sub-structures, the parental agencies ought to ensure that the transcendental, symbolic paternal function is acknowledged. This implies that the father and the mother need to let the child know in no uncertain terms that they are subjected to a symbolic order which they cannot alter or control. Both the father and the mother need to acknowledge that they do not epitomize the law, but that the law transcends them and that they themselves are forced to comply with it as much as everybody else. To put it in even more concrete terms, this comes down to the parents telling their children that they are expected to observe certain social rules (for example, the basic 'Freudian rule' of the incest prohibition) and that this expectation also applies to them, despite the fact that they are in a parental position. Such a concession might pose serious difficulties, as Lacan stressed, to those fathers who really have the function of legislators (Lacan 1977h[1957–58]: 218–219).

Needless to say that Lacan's deconstruction of the Freudian Oedipal triangle into two distinct triads does not yet outline the necessary and sufficient conditions for the foreclosure of the Name-of-the-Father and the ensuing emergence of a psychotic structure in the child. Is it sufficient for one of the child's parents to dishonour the paternal function, or should the parents do it in tandem? And if the Name-of-the-Father is debased by both parents, does that automatically induce psychosis in the child or should some auxiliary condition be fulfilled? On occasion, people commenting on Lacan's theory have argued that the mother's refusal to accept the paternal authority is sufficient for psychosis to occur in the child, by which they have reduced Lacan's complex Oedipal schema to its simple triangular roots, and by which they have also realigned it with the post-Freudian view that a child's psychic normality is predicated upon its separation from the pre-Oedipal dyadic relation with the mother, through the intervention of the father and the concurrent 'triangu-lation'.[15] Nowhere does Lacan's work allow us to make these kinds of inferences, yet neither does it suggest a good alternative answer to the problem.

Jacques-Alain Miller (1987) has proposed to complicate Lacan's model even further by taking into account the child's own involvement. Explicitly eschewing a structuralist (social constructionist) conception of Lacanian theory, Miller took his bearings from Lacan's 1946 essay on psychic causality, in which he had asserted that psychosis ultimately rests upon an 'unfathomable decision of being' (Lacan 1966a[1946]:177).[16] According to Miller, 'the formula of foreclosure has paralysed the debate on madness to such an extent that it has become impossible for us to read what is supporting this formula, notably that it is unthinkable without the implication of a subjective position' (Miller 1987:143). When human beings become psychotic, it is not simply because they have been the passive victim of deleterious parental attitudes, but because they themselves have 'decided' to reject the Name-of-the-Father, just as much as neurotics themselves, rather than their parents, have repressed certain traumatic incidents. However, Lacan's statement also underscored that it is impossible to probe into the exact nature of this 'decision'. Although foreclosure cannot be operative without a supporting subject, how, when and where this component has entered, or will enter the play remains a mystery. In its impenetrability, the decision is both untraceable and unforeseeable. Likewise, we are forced to remain silent concerning the question as to whether this decision implies a free choice or has already been shaped by the demands and desires of others, and perhaps also as to whether it is modifiable or not.

PSYCHOTIC TRANSFERENCE

Whilst according a central diagnostic significance to the language disturbances in psychosis, Lacan was eager to emphasize that psychosis is not 'a pure and simple fact of language' (Lacan 1993[1955–56]:61). The foreclosure of the Name-of-the-Father does not only affect the individual's speech, but also influences his sexual identity and relationships with others.

Lacan was of the view that the function of the father – the cornerstone of the symbolic order – overwrites a human being's natural status of 'sexuation', and introduces her into a set of norms dictating what it is to be masculine or feminine and defining what men and women should do if they want to be perceived as belonging to a particular gender (Lacan 1995a[1964]:276). The principle of this symbolic sexual order is the symbolic phallus (Φ), which represents the mark of difference between the signifiers, including those of masculinity and femininity. When the paternal function is foreclosed the phallus does not establish itself within the symbolic order, which induces a peculiar 'blending' of the signifiers (dubbed 'holophrase' by Lacan) and which also blurs the culturally installed differences between masculinity and femininity.[17] In psychosis the symbolic pegs of sexual identity do not hold, through which masculinity and femininity start to melt into one another. Schreber was for instance convinced that his body was being emasculated in view of his final transformation into a woman who, after having been inseminated by the divine agencies, would beget a new human race.[18] In a sense, Schreber's conviction does not exemplify the psychotic collapse of sexual differences as such, because it is already part and parcel of his attempt to introduce a certain order, albeit a delusional one, into his chaotic experiences.[19] However, it does indicate to what extent he did not assume a shared sociocultural system of distinct sexual identities, succumbing to a sexual matrix in which the boundaries between the categories have become very hazy.

With regard to the psychotic's relationships with others, Lacan drew attention to the fact that the exclusion of the Other ushers the individual into strange entanglements with others, which are continuously pervaded by rivalry and competition. The divine agencies invade Schreber's body and mind as much as he invades their own substance, which indicates that his relationship with his tormentors is marked by continuous rivalry. Although Schreber has to comply with the divine bye-laws, the gods bear witness to an incredible stupidity, through which their existence depends as much on him as his existence depends on them. Schreber has a mirror relationship with his world and his own bodily disintegration is reflected in the fragmentation of the divine bodies (Lacan 1993[1955–56]:97–101). It is as if Schreber's persecutors were but the virtual images of himself; figures that would not have existed without him, but whose presence he was unable to plumb and control.

This strictly imaginary relationship with others seriously affects the psychotic's position within the transference, which Freud (1916–17a [1915–17]:431–447) defined as the patient's emotional tie (*Gefühls-bindung*) with the analyst. Unlike Freud, Lacan did not rule out the psychotic's ability to develop a transference relationship with the analyst, yet he distinguished this 'psychotic transference' from the neurotic type, whereby he followed two separate directions. The first one was put into effect during the early 1950s, in the context of his construction of the 'L-schema' as a dynamic model of the analytic process.[20] During this period Lacan distinguished between a symbolic and an imaginary form of transference, the former being the efficacious, beneficial type and the latter merely functioning as an obstacle (Lacan 1988b[1953–54]:109). Symbolic transference presupposes that the patient's speech addresses itself to both the other and the Other, which implies that the way in which somebody approaches the analyst and speaks about himself involves a degree of ignorance (the Other as unknown). At the end of *Seminar I* Lacan even went so far as to say that ignorance is an essential condition for (symbolic) transference to occur:

[I]f the subject commits himself to searching after truth as such, it is because he places himself in the dimension of ignorance – it doesn't matter whether he knows it or not. That is one of the elements making up what analysts call 'readiness to the transference'. There is a readiness to the transference in the patient solely by virtue of his placing himself in the position of acknowledging himself in speech, and searching out his truth to the end, the end which is there in the analyst.

(ibid.:278–279)

The absence of ignorance on the side of the patient also opens the gate to transference, albeit a style of transference that is imaginary, rivalrous and potentially destructive. It is exactly this imaginary type one can expect to find in psychotic people, governed as they are by an exclusion of the Other and a vision of a transparent other. In general, psychotics do not testify to a degree of ignorance about what is happening to them or about what is going on in the world. On the contrary, they act upon a firmly established knowledge, a deep-rooted conviction and a massive certainty about the nature of their suffering. In *Seminar XI*, Lacan argued that in psychotics 'the phenomenon of the *Unglauben*' (unbelief) reigns (Lacan 1977b[1964]:238) because belief (whether positive or negative) always includes an element of doubt, which is completely absent in psychosis.[21] The corollary of this deeply ingrained, solid psychotic knowledge is that the other can only be approached as an alter ego, an imaginary counterpart who supports, sustains and validates the individual's certainty.

The latter point leads to Lacan's second criterion for distinguishing between psychotic and neurotic transference. In *Seminar XI*, he grounded transference in psychoanalysis on the installation of the function of the *sujet supposé savoir*, that is to say of the 'subject supposed to know' or, perhaps better, the 'supposed subject of knowing'.[22] As Lacan put it: 'Whenever this function may be, for the subject, embodied in some individual . . . the transference is established' (ibid.:233). Proceeding from her own ignorance, a neurotic patient would thus come to an analyst in order to interrogate him as a supposed subject of knowing, which signals the start of transference. Psychotic patients, however, have no reason whatsoever to invest the analyst – nor somebody else for that matter – with the function of the supposed subject of knowing, since they already possess (and are possessed by) all there is to know. Whereas neurotics are desperate to find somebody who masters the knowledge they themselves lack, and to put that knowledge to the test, psychotics are adamant that there is nothing more to discover than what they already know. When they address themselves to an analyst, they are not supposing her to be a subject of knowing, but rather someone who will understand and authenticate their experiences. In short, they are trying to find a 'witness for the persecution'.

Apart from the fact that they provide the analyst with a second, fairly reliable diagnostic criterion (alongside the language disturbances), these peculiarities of the psychotic transference cast a nasty chill over the standard analytic techniques of interpretation and transference handling. As Freud realized all too well, the orthodox analytic setting cannot be used with psychotic patients, to which Lacan added that if one takes prepsychotics (people with a psychotic structure but untriggered 'psychotic' phenomena) into analysis, a full-blown psychosis is likely to emerge (Lacan 1993[1955–56]:251). On the one hand, these warnings make it all the more urgent for analysts to diagnose psychotic patients correctly and at the earliest possible stage of the analytic process, whereas on the other hand they also urge them to reconsider their techniques when they venture to work analytically with psychotics.

For Lacan (1977l:12), it was imperative that the analyst does not back away from psychosis, and in the following chapters I shall give some indications of how Lacanian analysts have turned this incentive into a score of technical modifications and recommendations, often relying on minimal rules of thumb suggested by Lacan himself.

NEUROTIC SPEECH

In his 'Rome Discourse' Lacan drew attention to a second clinical paradox in the relations between speech and language. After having categorized as psychotic those people who talk freely and fluently without really speaking, he defined people who also speak beyond the words they consciously use as neurotic. In the first (psychotic) situation, language operates without speech, whilst in the second (neurotic) case speech also functions beyond verbalized language. Whereas psychotics do not manage to speak, however articulate the sentences they produce, neurotics cannot prevent themselves from saying more than what they intend to convey (Lacan 1977e[1953]:69–70). Twenty years later, in his seminar *Encore*, Lacan rephrased this insight as follows: 'I speak without knowing it. I speak with my body and I do so unbeknownst to myself. Thus I always say more than I know' (Lacan 1998a[1972–73]:119).

Here, Lacan aimed less at a reintegration of the communicative value of non-verbal cues in psychoanalysis – he actually vilified clinicians who interpreted the patients' bodily movements as well as their associations (Lacan 1966b[1955]:337) – than at restoring neurotic symptoms, inhibitions and anxieties as meaningful units of analysis. To Lacan, this neurotic paradox, much more than its psychotic counterpart, encompassed 'the privileged domain of psychoanalytic discovery' because Freud would not have developed psychoanalysis if he had not regarded neurotic symptoms (ranging from bodily disorders to slips of the tongue) as being sustained by an unconscious idea (wish, representation) that tries to express itself (Lacan 1977e[1953]:69).

As to the nature of this neurotic economy, Freud had already cleared most of the ground in two seminal essays on the neuropsychoses of defence from the mid-1890s (Freud 1894a; 1896b). In these papers, he had argued that both hysteria and obsessional neurosis originate in an unconscious act of defence against a traumatic experience, whose nature is always sexual.[23] When individuals encounter something that is incompatible with the reigning mass of representations (*Vorstellungsmasse*) in their ego (*Ich*), the latter tries to maintain its integrity by driving the event out of consciousness. Freud believed that this defence (or repression) takes place via a withdrawal of the affect (a quantum of energy) from the event's psychic representation, through which the event itself is transformed into an unconscious memory trace, while its affect is displaced to another representation.

Since repression entails the dismantling and eradication of sexual representations that are impossible to handle, neurotics can only recount their experiences in a lacunary fashion, whereby the gaps can be either exceedingly manifest – some patients say they have no memories at all of what happened to them – or smoothed over by so-called 'screen-memories', which generally serve to make the story coherent. Until the 1910s, Freud was convinced that neurotics had simply 'forgotten' the awkward representations and that one of the analyst's tasks consisted in helping them to recover their lost memories. Yet clinical and theoretical considerations led him to think that instead of suffering from a straight-forward forgetting, patients were animated by a powerful 'not wanting to know' (Freud 1913c:141–142). Therefore he considered it pointless for analysts to imbue their patients with the knowledge they are ostensibly lacking, because this is unlikely to bring about change in the patient's situation – on the contrary, he might immediately erect a protective shield against the analyst's suggestions.[24]

In *Seminar I*, Lacan reformulated this neurotic 'not wanting to know' as the passion of ignorance, a dimension superseding the dualism of knowing and not-knowing (Lacan 1988b[1953–54]:277–278). Simple ignorance does not equal a lack of conscious knowledge and, vice versa, a huge amount of conscious knowledge can perfectly coincide with radical ignorance. As mentioned on pp. 20–21, Lacan maintained that ignorance underpins the patient's capacity for symbolic transference, because it enables him to regard the analyst as a supposed subject of knowing. By contrast, the 'passion of ignorance' is a psychic power which urges patients to prefer the deleterious status quo of their symptomatic condition over the even more painful encounter with that which caused it. The passion of ignorance thus coincides with the unconscious jouissance (enjoyment) the patient derives from his symptom.

In Freud's theory repression not only causes the sexual representation to fall into the unconscious, the original affect also reconnects itself to a relatively innocuous substitute representation. Freud regarded this 'false connection' as the nucleus of the neurotic symptom. Whether a bodily disorder or a compulsive thought process, the neurotic symptom is a compromise between a component of the repressed event (the affect) and an element of the repressive structure (the substitute representation), and thus also an insidious 'return of the repressed'. Via the neurotic symptom, an aspect of the event which had been driven out of consciousness tries to express itself again, although the individual can no longer understand this.

For Lacan, this part of Freud's theory implied that the neurotic symptom conveys a hidden meaning, which the patient can only understand once she has found the laws according to which its constitutive components have been bound up with each other. Put differently, the neurotic symptom means something, but it is impossible to grasp that meaning until the language system governing its combinations has been discovered. Whilst being generally 'silent', neurotic symptoms continue to speak in a language that is unknown to the individual, prompting Lacan to compare them to blazons, enigmas, hieroglyphics, oracles, seals, etc. (Lacan 1977e[1953]:69–70) and to identify them eventually as metaphors (Lacan 1977g[1957]:175). All of these figures include a message, but its exact nature remains a mystery as long as one has not found the proper code to decipher them.[25]

Now it becomes clear how the neurotic's speech differs from the psychotic communication detailed above. Unlike psychotic individuals, neurotics have no privileged access to the true meaning of their words and their general living conditions. They are continuously under the impression that the words they use do not capture exactly what they want to say or, conversely, that these words express much more than they have intended to. Whereas psychotics engage in a stereotypical form of communication which is unmarked by redundancies and ambiguities, neurotics are incessantly aware of the inadequacy of language for conveying their experiences. Sometimes they feel that they simply lack or cannot find the words to say something; at other times they are surprised by the fact that they have said something they did not want to say at all.

Moreover, whilst psychotics are being pervaded by an infallible, full knowledge about themselves and others, neurotics are troubled time and again by the realization that their knowledge is incomplete, inconsistent and incoherent. Eager to find unshakeable evidence, yet struck by its fraudulent character from the moment it is established, neurotics bear witness to a deeply ingrained feeling that nothing is really trustworthy, that they are constantly being deceived by everything and everyone, including themselves. Although they like to think that someone is reliable, or that something is genuine, neurotics realize that their opinion is but a vulnerable belief and that they could easily be duped by appearances. Distrust and suspicion, two affects that are often associated with paranoia, can thus be encountered as readily in neurosis as in psychosis, the difference being that in the latter case they rest upon a firmly rooted conviction, whereas in the former they proceed from profound uncertainty. A psychotic patient will approach someone with due suspicion because he has read the other's intentions, whereas a neurotic will harbour suspicion because she is doubtful about the other, due to the interference of the Other. As Lacan put it in *Seminar III,* the dimension of the unknown, 'the Other of speech . . . is the determining factor in neurosis' (Lacan 1993[1955–56]:168).

This structural difference between neurotic and psychotic people, despite the similarity of their symptoms and affects, often manifests itself during the so-called 'preliminary conversations' (the Lacanian equivalent of Freud's 'trial period') when patients reflect upon the progress they are making. When a neurotic patient voices his concern over the fact that he has not experienced any improvement in his condition since the start of the consultations, he will be poised between the enticing idea that his analyst is probably not very good (indeed, that she may not be a properly trained analyst at all) and the bitter awareness that he himself is after all the one who has chosen her because of her acumen and charisma. A psychotic, on the other hand, will easily reach the conclusion that since she has not made any progress, her analyst must be part of the same conspiracy that is responsible for all her misery. In both instances, the patient fears that the analyst is not what he pretends to be, yet in the former (neurotic) case the suspicion rests upon doubt and uncertainty rather than firm conviction.

Contrary to psychotics, neurotics take account of the Other of speech, which is in turn based on the installation of the 'wall of language' between the speaker and her interlocutors, the presence of quilting points between signifier and signified, and the acknowledgement of the Name-of-the-Father. Neurotics differ from psychotics in so far as they have assimilated the sociocultural rules embedded in language, whose principle is the paternal function.

Throughout his works, Lacan linked this psychic assimilation of the symbolic order to Freud's concept of repression, arguing that the integration of the symbolic system is a necessary and sufficient condition for repression to occur. Drawing on data gathered from Freud's famous case-study of the Wolf Man (1918b[1914]), he stated in *Seminar I*:

> The trauma, in so far as it has a repressing action, intervenes *after the fact, nachträglich*. At this specific moment, something of the subject's becomes detached in the very symbolic world that he is engaged in integrating. From then on, it will no longer be something belonging to the subject. The subject will no longer speak it, will no longer integrate it. Nevertheless, it will remain there, somewhere, spoken, if one can put it this way, by something the subject does not control. [It will be the first nucleus of what one will subsequently call his symptoms.][26]
>
> (Lacan 1988b[1953–54]:191)

Here Lacan tried to explain how events only become painful and fall prey to repression from the moment the subject adopts a symbolic framework of norms and values. What Freud had designated as an incompatibility between two mental representations, Lacan translated as the 'detachment' of signifiers from the symbolic order, as a mere result of its assimilation by the subject. Hence, no event is inherently traumatic; it acquires this epithet 'after the fact', when it becomes meaningful through the intervention of a symbolic system.

Lacan's view entailed that only neurotics, who have integrated the symbolic order and its distinctions between good/right and bad/wrong, separate traumatic from non-traumatic events in a culturally recognizable fashion. A psychotic, who is living in an entirely different world, can put events which a neurotic is likely to experience as shocking in a neutral or even pleasurable context, and the other way round. A psychotic man, for example, can be extremely affected by a score of ostensibly non-intrusive phenomena, whilst remaining unmoved by the fact that he has been repeatedly raped by a group of thugs in the back of a van.[27]

HYSTERIA AND OBSESSIONAL NEUROSIS

Although all neurotics are uniformly under the spell of repression, suffering from something unspoken which none the less continues to speak in a different realm, Lacan maintained Freud's decomposition of the neurotic picture in a hysterical and an obsessional side.[28] From the 1890s till the 1930s, Freud had experimented with a whole gamut of criteria distinguishing hysterics from obsessional neurotics, such as the time and nature of the traumatic sexual experience, constitutional factors, the moment of disease onset, the location of the symptoms, the fixated phase of libidinal development, the type of repression, and the patients' unconscious attitudes towards sexuality. Some of these criteria, notably the nature of the traumatic sexual experience (passive and painful in hysteria versus active and pleasurable in obsessional neurosis), he had come to reject as his theory evolved, whereas others he had suggested without detailing their impact.[29] On various occasions, Freud (1918b [1914]:76; 1926d[1925]:113) had also conceded that every obsessional neurosis seems to encapsulate a hysterical nucleus, out of which it develops along complex, obscure pathways. Unlocking the mystery of obsessional neurosis thus involved the challenge of finding its formula of transformation, something for which Freud never claimed credit.

Lacan dressed his own differentiation of hysteria and obsessional neurosis in his preferred conceptual garments of subject, Other, object, fantasy, desire and jouissance, without betraying his allegiance to Freud. Here, Lacan's Freudian inspiration can be inferred from his unremitting faith in the value of Freud's case-studies of Dora (1905e[1901]), the Rat Man (1909d) and the Wolf Man (1918b[1914]), as well as from his trenchant critique of the purportedly 'deviant', post-Freudian accounts of hysteria and obsessional neurosis, such as the object-relations perspective espoused by Maurice Bouvet during the late 1940s and 1950s (Lacan 1994[1956–57]:26–28; 1998b[1957–58]:387–421).[30] Following Freud (1909d:156), Lacan argued that the analysis of obsessional neurotics is much more demanding than that of hysterical patients, since what the analyst needs is 'not only the plan of a reconstructed labyrinth, or even a batch of plans already drawn up', but also 'the general combinatory that governs their variety . . . [and], even more usefully, accounts for the illusions, or rather shifts of perspective to be found in the labyrinth (Lacan 1977i[1958]:266). In keeping with Freud (1913i:319), Lacan also surmised that hysteria and obsessional neurosis are two neurotic languages, whereby the obsessional idiom is a dialect of the hysterical standard. Towards the end of his career, Lacan even adduced that the psychoanalytic treatment of all neurotics rests upon a 'hysterisation' of the patient, which indicates that he agreed with Freud on the hysterical core within obsessional neurosis (Lacan 1991a[1969–70]:35–36).

Lacan's proposition that every neurotic subject recognizes and is being recognized by the Other (Lacan 1993[1955–56]:168) provides a good starting-point for a summary of his ideas on hysteria and obsessional neurosis.[31] Throughout his seminars, Lacan explored the effects of this neurotic acknowledgement of the Other (the laws of language, the language of laws, the sociocultural rules and regulations), both on the human condition and on the structure of language itself. In a first movement, he aligned the individual's assimilation of the symbolic order with the normal deployment of the Oedipus and castration complexes in Freud's theory, according to which the child relinquishes its primary love-object (the mother) in favour of an identification with the father as the representative of the law (Freud 1924d; Lacan 1994[1956–57]:61, 199–230). Concurrently, Lacan reinterpreted Freud's notion of castration – the boy's observation that his mother lacks a penis and the ensuing fear that his own will be cut off by way of punishment for violating a prohibition – as a symbolic cut resulting from the individual's compliance with the Other.[32] According to Lacan, every society forces human beings to postpone the satisfaction of some of their drives and prohibits the expression of some drives altogether, which implies 'that jouissance [enjoyment] is forbidden to him who speaks as such' (Lacan 1977k [1960]:319). Originally defined by Freud as a perceived punishment for transgressing a symbolic law (the incest prohibition), in Lacan's version castration became part and parcel of leading a law-abiding life. Following this symbolic cut of castration, the neurotic individual experiences both a loss of jouissance, which Lacan designated as $-\varphi$, and an internal lack, which he dubbed S or split subject.[33] The entire operation awakens the neurotic's desire to retrieve what is lost and to annihilate the lack. Desire and jouissance are therefore the two poles of the psychic spectrum within which the neurotic individual has to organize his life (Lacan 1998b[1957–58]:261–317).

In a second movement, Lacan investigated the relationship between the neurotic's lack (the split subject S) and the objects with which she tries to neutralize it, simultaneously satisfying her desire and reinstating the feeling of 'fullness'. This entailed an extrapolation of Freud's suggestion, in the final pages of his 'Three Essays on the Theory of Sexuality' (1905d:222–230), that the objects to which a person turns in adulthood are always but substitutes for a lost primary object which can never be retrieved. From the late 1950s Lacan conceptualized these fascinating, yet inadequate, objects which turn the neurotic individual on because he 'reads' their promise of fulfilment as objects *a*. In *Seminar VI* he described an object *a* as something which 'satisfies no need and is itself already relative, i.e. placed in relation to the subject . . . The object takes the place, I would say, of what the subject is – symbolically – deprived of' (Lacan 1977a[1959]:15). Again in accordance with Freud, Lacan defined an individual's relationship with these purportedly satisfying objects as 'fantasy', for which he constructed the algebraic formula $\$ \lozenge a$ in which $\lozenge$ stands for 'desire of/for' (Lacan 1977k[1960]:313).[34]

To the extent that an individual's partners (parents, peers, lovers, colleagues) have also integrated the Other, they will equally function according to this dynamics of desire and jouissance. Hence, neurotics not only fantasize about what they themselves desire, but also about what other people desire – in their capacity as Other – and about how to transform themselves into desirable, loveable objects for these others. Until his conceptualization of the object *a* during the late 1950s, Lacan contended that a child who wants to satisfy its mother will identify with the imaginary phallus (φ), the object she has ostensibly lost, and vice versa that a mother who uses her child as a new source of enjoyment will approach it as an imaginary phallus (Lacan 1994[1956–57]:71). Later on he argued that human beings can only relate to the Other's objects of desire (the objects *a*), about which they fantasize and with which they try to satisfy the Other. Rather than something with which human beings identify, the objects *a* are a kind of exchange objects which enable them to enter relationships with others, at once attempting to satisfy themselves and their partners. Yet since the objects *a* are but inadequate substitutes for the lost enjoyment, neither of these ambitions to obtain satisfaction will ever be realized. According to Lacan (1998a[1972–73]:126) the formula 'I ask you to refuse what I offer you because that's not it' captured the unconscious truth of any neurotic love-relationship, because the object that is offered by the lover is inefficient for restoring the lost enjoyment of the beloved.

Once the conceptual beacons of Lacan's theoretical itinerary during the 1950s and 1960s have been described, it is relatively easy to explain how he differentiated between hysterics and obsessional neurotics.[35] Hysterical subjects take the Other – whether one of its concrete representatives, or society in general – unconsciously to task for tampering with their enjoyment. They hold the Other responsible for their current misery and swear to take revenge on the Other for all the harm that has been done to them. It is this hysterical accusation of the Other which Freud initially mistook for a genuine account of sexual abuse during an infantile scene of seduction (Masson 1985:212). Subsequently, hysterics attempt to recuperate what they believe to be unjustly in the possession of the Other through arousing the Other's desire, which serves as sufficient proof that the Other has been deprived of something. This hysterical strategy prompted Lacan to propose that 'the hysteric's desire is not the desire for an object, but the desire for a desire, an effort to maintain oneself in front of this point . . . where the desire of the Other is' (Lacan 1998b [1957–58]:407).

To elicit this desire of the Other, hysterics mould themselves into a figure which they think will arouse the Other, something which grips the Other's attention and which provokes interest, fascination, attachment or love. And in transforming themselves into an enticing object for the Other, they try to kill two birds with one stone: whilst inducing the lack of the Other, they also annihilate their own (neurotic) loss of enjoyment. For hysterics unconsciously enjoy their complicated ploys to trigger the Other's desire by incarnating its presumed object.

As to the hysteric's own desire, Lacan stressed on various occasions that it is fundamentally unsatisfied, to the benefit of the desire of the Other (Lacan 1998b[1957–58]:407; 1977i[1958]:261; 1977k[1960]:321).[36] Hysterics give the impression of sacrificing their own interests, of postponing the fulfilment of their own desire, and of putting themselves to extreme inconvenience in favour of the Other. It goes without saying that this self-immolation is only a semblance because it is an inherent part of the hysterical strategy to manipulate the Other. No matter what they display, hysterics do not really want to compensate the desire of the Other, but to sustain it in its very status as lack, deficit, shortcoming. Hysterical subjects are at great pains to keep the Other's desire unsatisfied too, by preventing the Other from enjoying what they have to offer. When the enjoyment of the Other does loom up, hysterics do their utmost best to change their object-status or to disappear altogether. In 1960 Lacan wrote: '[D]esire is maintained [in the Other] only through the lack of satisfaction [the hysteric] produces in it by slipping away from it as object' (Lacan 1977k[1960]:320, translation modified).

In a clinical setting the psychoanalyst can derive this hysterical economy from the way in which patients talk about their professional and/or love relationships. As a matter of fact, there is hardly anything else hysterics talk and complain about. The following example illustrates how hysteria manifests itself on the level of speech. During analysis, a woman describes her continuous efforts to make herself loveable for her environment, whilst complaining about the fact that she only attracts people who want to take advantage of her or who refuse to take her seriously. Every time she manages to secure herself of somebody's love, she feels that her partner uses her merely as an interchangeable commodity or as an instrument designed for the satisfaction of sexual lust, which compels her to escape the relationship, physically and/or mentally. She scorns men for using her vagina merely as a tool for masturbating, but she cannot refrain from offering it to them because it makes her feel important. Whilst priding herself on her ability to lure every partner she wants, she bears witness to an extreme sense of loneliness and despondency. And although she realizes that she is capable of triggering everybody's desire, she basically suffers from the fact that nobody desires her as she wants to be desired, inasmuch as all the people she seduces are still interested in other women, or seem to enjoy her simply as a sex object. In other words, no matter how hard she tries in making people desire her, they never desire her enough, because they either desire other people too, or employ her simply as an object for their own satisfaction.[37] Since she is constantly enmeshed in complicated intrigues, secret affairs and impossible relationships, she wonders about what it really means to be a woman for a man and for other women.[38] To solve this question, she sometimes identifies with other men – assuming that they know women better than women know themselves – or draws other women into friendships that are pervaded by admiration as well as rivalry.

By contrast, obsessional neurotics refuse to accept that the intervention of the Other has in any way affected their enjoyment. Unlike hysterics they do not accuse the Other of stealing something precious from them. Instead they unconsciously strive to minimize the power which the Other exercises by neutralizing the Other's desire. To Lacan, this becomes apparent primarily on the level of language, through the protective formulae with which obsessional neurotics defend themselves against all kinds of imaginary dangers. For example, in *Seminar V* he stated:

> [O]bsession is always verbalised. Freud has no doubts about this. Even when he is faced with a latent obsessional conduct, he bears in mind that it has not revealed its structure until it has taken the shape of a verbal obsession . . . All obsessional formulae have to do with a well articulated destruction . . .
>
> (Lacan 1998b[1957–58]:470)[39]

Besides these formulae, obsessional neurotics espouse a score of other unconscious strategies to neutralize the Other's desire. From time to time they may ensconce in vivid fantasies of oblation, meeting all of the Other's requests following the principle 'Your wish is my command'. By satisfying all of the Other's demands, they believe that the Other will have nothing to desire anymore.[40] Alternatively, they may go to all lengths to obtain the Other's approval before embarking on a particular project, from starting a relationship to choosing a career. The rationale is that if something is done with the Other's explicit permission the desire of the Other can be stilled. Furthermore, obsessional neurotics may harbour sadistic fantasies of torture, destruction and mass extermination, which serve the same purpose of killing the desire of the Other. With regard to these sadistic fantasies, Lacan emphasized in *Seminar V*:

> [W]e cannot content ourselves with articulating them as manifesta-
> tions of a tendency; we ought to see in them an organisation which is
> itself indicative [*signifiante*] of the relationships between the subject
> and the Other as such. It is of the economic role of these fantasies
> as they are articulated that we have to present a formula. In the
> obsessional subject, these fantasies are characterized by the fact that
> they remain on the level of fantasies. Only very exceptionally are
> these fantasies realized and these realizations are always disappointing
> for the subject.
>
> (ibid.:411)

Complicating the picture further, obsessionals may also try to prove to the Other that they possess nothing of value, that they are unworthy of interest, that they lack even the most basic of human qualities, or that they will misuse whatever the Other invests in them. This strategy comes down to letting other people know that they are replenished, thus cancelling out their reasons for seeking fulfilment outside their own realm of functioning.

It goes without saying that none of these unconscious obsessional strategies is completely successful and that obsessionals will encounter the desire of the Other time and again. Whereas hysterics decry the fact that the Other's desire is never enough, obsessionals describe the Other's desire as being always too much. For example, an obsessional patient observes with anger and surprise that his wife is still interested in him, despite his numerous openly confessed extra-marital affairs and despite his carefully directed monstrosities at home. Likewise, another obsessional patient confesses that she has done everything in her power to satisfy her husband and that she has never done anything without negotiating it with him first, yet not succeeding in eradicating her own anxiety in the face of his desires.[41]

Apart from the sheer multiplicity of strategies to neutralize the desire of the Other, obsessional neurotics present a labyrinthine case to the analyst because most of these strategies are outright paradoxical. To preserve their own independence, obsessional neurotics indulge in the most obsequious of behaviours. They can agree with everything the analyst says, simply to maintain their own ideas about what is going on in their lives. Similar to the Wolf Man during his analysis with Freud (1918b[1914]:91), obsessional patients have no problems subjecting themselves to the imposed rule of free association, but they only comply with it to satisfy the analyst and to avoid what really matters to them. Whereas hysterical patients are very uncompromising in their attitude towards the analytic setting – discussing the appointment schedule, breaking the rule of free association by staying quiet, complaining about the lack of attention the analyst is paying to them, in short doing everything to dissatisfy the analyst – obsessional neurotics are generally quite obliging and extraordinarily flexible in making appointments. Hysterical patients often enjoy discussing appointment times, but they hardly miss appointments once they have been made, only to remain silent during the entire session. Conversely, obsessional patients can be extremely reluctant to disagree with a suggested appointment time; they often accept commitments that they know very well they will not meet, or that they know they will only meet in a deceitful way, for instance by acting the part of the good analysand within the analytic play.

Since obsessional neurotics refuse to acknowledge that the Other has curtailed their enjoyment, they cannot bear the manifestations of their own desire because these expressions signal the fact that they have lost something after all. The desire of the obsessional neurotic is not unsatisfied, but impossible (Lacan 1991b[1960–61]:291). Consequently, obsessional neurotics try to avoid everything they associate with the emergence of their desire. For example, one obsessional patient divulges that she only buys the books that do not interest her, because these are the only books she is capable of reading. Sometimes it happens that one of these books does rouse her interest, in which case she has to throw it away or bring it to a second-hand bookstore. Another patient meditates on the exceptional beauty of the girl he secretly covets, but he would not dream of approaching her, much less starting a relationship. During a sexual encounter with a lookalike he was impotent, which has made him think that he is doomed to have relationships with girls whom he does not really desire. As obsessional neurotics set out to kill their own desire as much as the desire of the Other, they obviously worry about what keeps them alive. Therefore the hysterical question 'Am I a man or a woman?' finds its obsessional counterpart in 'Am I dead or alive?'. Whereas the hysterical question highlights the issues of sexual relationships and sexual identity, the obsessional question zooms in on the vicissitudes of existence (Lacan 1966c[1957]:451). To reassure themselves of their existence and to reduce accumulated libidinal tension, obsessional neurotics may engage in all kinds of exploits, from outbursts of senseless violence to relatively innocuous joyriding (Lacan 1998b[1957–58]:417–418). Or they may inflate their behaviours (labouring away night and day) and their personalities (playing ringleader to the crowd), to the point of holding themselves up to utter ridicule (Lacan 1991b[1960–61]:302).

NEUROTIC TRANSFERENCE

From time to time, neurotics fall victim to strange 'diseases' whose origins and features are so mysterious that they feel inclined to discard them as nonsense, were it not for the fact that they are also led to believe some specialist will probably be able to tell them what they are and what they mean. Quite unexpectedly, neurotics might experience extreme anxiety or confusion, states of mind which affect them (and/or their environment) to such an extent that they turn to somebody of whom they expect a solution. The aforementioned 'passion of ignorance' which sustains the neurotic repression is thus paired with a desire to know the truth behind the symptoms (the return of the repressed).

To Lacan (1988b[1953–54]:278–279), this search after the truth of what is unknown, despite the passion of ignorance, is a necessary condition for symbolic transference to occur. If psychotics are only capable of approaching somebody as an alter ego (imaginary transference), neurotics are able to grant someone the authority which they themselves lack and to apply to him with a request for knowledge. The latter aspect signals the installation of a 'supposed subject of knowing' whenever neurotics turn to somebody for help or advice, a supposition which Lacan judged altogether absent in psychotic transference.

This account of neurotic transference can be further elaborated in line with the hysterical and obsessional versions of the neurotic structure. Each of these variants displays a number of singularities of transference, on which analysts can rely for diagnostic purposes and which pose auxiliary challenges to their position during the treatment. In canvassing the properties of hysterical and obsessional transference, Lacan consulted primarily Freud's case-studies of Dora (1905e[1901]) and the Rat Man (1909d), which he explored in two year-long seminars during the early 1950s and to which he returned intermittently until the 1970s.[42]

From a Lacanian point of view, the case-study of the Rat Man contains many instructive passages pertaining to the patient's peculiar investment of Freud with the function of 'supposed subject of knowing'.[43] From the start of the treatment, the Rat Man testified to his profound scepticism and his ambiguous 'emotional tie' with Freud. During the initial contact the young man divulged (ibid.:159) that he had been drawn to him because his own 'efforts of thought' bore a striking resemblance to some of the 'curious verbal associations' Freud had explained in 'The Psychopathology of Everyday Life'. But during the third session the Rat Man defied Freud's expectations of him wanting the analyst to use his expertise to resolve these 'efforts of thought', by pointing out that he merely wanted Freud to give him a certificate endorsing his obsessional behaviours (ibid.:173). On the one hand, the Rat Man presented himself as a model patient, speaking at length about his sexual mischief, producing numerous childhood memories and tentatively pursuing even the most daring of Freud's theoretical constructions. On the other hand, he expressed his doubts about everything Freud told him, identified Freud with the regiment Captain who was so fond of cruelty and spouted 'the grossest and filthiest abuse' upon Freud and his family (ibid.:169, 209). When voicing these terms of abuse, the Rat Man floated around Freud's office, at first because he could not tolerate lying comfortable on the couch whilst offending his analyst, then because he was afraid that Freud was going to hit him (ibid.:209). *Vis-à-vis* Freud the Rat Man behaved in the fashion of a gentleman crook, continuously taking the analyst for a ride within the strictest constraints of courtesy. For the greater part of his analysis, the Rat Man tried to neutralize the subjective aspect of Freud's knowledge by transforming his analyst into an abstract, absolute master who represents knowledge, but whose knowledge is unfortunately a dead loss.

This obsessional attempt to annihilate the subjective component within the 'supposed subject of knowing' can exhibit itself in various other ways. Some obsessional neurotics are not driven to analysts because they expect them to dispel their misfortune; instead of treatment for a particular problem, they seek intellectual adventure, the joy of spontaneous reflection under the watchful eye of a silent, knowledgeable authority. Some patients hope to receive an official confirmation of their (un)suitability for analysis rather than a proper analytic treatment. Some are doubtful about the clinical value of psychoanalysis and the expertise of the analyst, but still hope to be given the opportunity to add some inside clinical experience to what they already know about it. And some claim that psychoanalysis, whilst inadequate for improving the quality of their lives, will enhance their capacity to solve the problems in their environment. In a sense, obsessional neurotics are not waiting for an innovative analytic solution to their questions, because they have already explored all the possible answers themselves. They merely want the analyst to give them permission for carrying out one solution or the other.

Sometimes this obsessional strategy to eradicate the subjective basis of knowledge can resemble the psychotic's eagerness to find an authority who is willing to validate the truth of the delusion. Yet the crucial difference is that obsessionals do acknowledge the other as an (unknown) Other, which betrays itself for example in their unremitting self-assessment in relation to the person they are talking to. After having scorned his analyst the Rat Man wondered: 'How can a gentleman like you, sir . . . let yourself be abused in this way by a low, good-for-nothing fellow like me? You ought to turn me out: that's all I deserve' (ibid.:209). Psychotics do not engage in this type of timorous, irresolute reflection because they are absolutely certain about their own and the other's intentions.

By contrast with the obsessionals' ploys to deny the existence of a subjective body of knowledge, hysterics advocate the incompleteness and relativity of knowledge. In this way, hysterics emphasize what obsessionals endeavour to exclude: the subjective dimension of all knowledge which ratifies its fundamental unsteadiness.[44] This hysterical epistemology first of all affects the way in which hysterics reconstruct and reflect upon their own life-histories. As Freud noticed from his earliest encounters with hysterics, the patients' stories are immensely fragmentary, oblique, incoherent and inconsistent. In the first chapter of his case-study of Dora, Freud attributed this ostensible defectiveness of the hysterical memory to the synergetic action of three interlocking factors (conscious insincerity, unconscious insincerity and genuine amnesia), simultaneously highlighting its clinical usefulness as a criterion for differentiating between hysteria and physical ailments, and the impediment it constitutes to psychoanalytic anamnesis (Freud 1905e[1901]:17). Working from Freud's comments on this 'ambiguity of the hysterical revelation of the past', Lacan interpreted the lacunae in the hysteric's memory as typical manifestations of the unconscious, whose truth can be rediscovered during analytic treatment (Lacan 1977e[1953]:46–50). To Lacan, the 'unconscious is that part of the concrete discourse . . . that is not at the disposal of the subject in re-establishing the continuity of his conscious discourse', and the purpose of psychoanalysis is to indicate to the patient where the truth of these 'censored chapters' lies buried (ibid.:49–50).

The problematic nature of the 'supposed subject of knowing' in obsessional neurosis, and the hysterical promotion of the unconscious (as functional yet inaccessible knowledge) probably emboldened Lacan to argue that the hysterisation of the patient is the subjective condition for the deployment of the analytic discourse. In *Seminar XVII* he put it as follows:

> What the analyst institutes as analytic experience can be said simply – it is the hysterisation of discourse. In other words, it is the structural introduction, under artificial conditions, of the discourse of the hysteric . . .
>
> (Lacan 1991a[1969–70]:35–36)

Hysteria is a precondition for the pursuit of proper analytic treatment because only hysterical transference involves the installation of a 'supposed subject of knowing' in combination with a 'knowledge that is not known' (*un savoir qui ne se sait pas*) (ibid.:32–33). The process of hysterisation itself involves no more no less than the analyst's induction of a question on the side of the analysand. When faced with obsessional neurotics, hysterisation implies that the analyst tries to bring his patients to the point where they admit that the analyst is not merely a necessary burden, a slightly annoying artefact of the analytic disposition, but a figure from whom they can expect a solution to their problems. Such an avowal presupposes the obsessional patients' acknowledgement that they lack conscious control over some key aspects of their lives or, in Lacanese, that some kind of knowledge seems to be at work in them that they themselves know nothing about (a headless knowledge, so to speak).

Analysts might infer from the hysterical supposition of knowledge that it gives them a privileged position in the treatment, to the extent that it enables them to apply their theoretical and clinical expertise to the details of the individual life-history and to initiate their hysterical patients into the true nature of their suffering. However, matters are not that straightforward. By way of example I can refer to Freud's description of what happened in the case of a young girl each time he revealed to her the details of a homosexual experience which she had apparently repressed, and of which the girl's mother had informed him:

> Every time I repeated her mother's story to the girl she reacted with a hysterical attack, and after this she forgot the story once more. There is no doubt that the patient was expressing a violent resistance against the knowledge that was being forced upon her. Finally she simulated feeble-mindedness and a complete loss of memory in order to protect herself against what I had told her.
>
> (Freud 1913c:141–142)

This hysterical patient suffered from a severe lapse of memory and an ardent desire to know the truth, but as soon as Freud told her what had happened she refused to acknowledge it, pretending she had not heard, or developing new symptoms merely to challenge the validity of the analyst's comments.[45]

This process indicates how the hysterical cultivation of the relativity of knowledge not only distorts the patients' memories, but also invalidates the theories with which they are being imbued by those who believe that hysterics are merely seeking to know. By the very nature of their relationship to knowledge, hysterics are keen to find omnipotent sources of learning, but as soon as these master-figures become convinced of the reality of their positions the power of their knowledge is nullified. In yet another discussion of Freud's Dora case, Lacan claimed that the hysteric incarnates the truth of the master, which is that the master is castrated (Lacan 1991a[1969–70]:110).

This dynamics poses a major challenge to the analyst working with (hystericized) neurotic patients, because he must refrain from complying with their incessant demands for knowledge whilst ensuring that this 'refusal to answer' does not eliminate the symbolic transference, i.e. the patient's view of the analyst as a supposed subject of knowing. Another difficulty concerns the hysterical indulgence in so-called 'lateral transferences', whereby patients submerge themselves in a panoply of relationships with alternative 'supposed subjects of knowing' – including friends, family members, and non-analytic professionals – merely to discredit the analyst's interventions. In this situation, the analyst may feel that she has to compete with a score of would-be analysts, since the patient is incessantly comparing her interpretations to those of others.

In the final session of his seminar on Freud's technical papers, Lacan tried to solve these problems by arguing that the analyst's position should emblematize *ignorantia docta*, a 'wise ignorance', in the sense of a recognition of the limits of one's understanding, as described by the German Renaissance philosopher Nicholas Cusanus (Lacan 1988b[1953–54]: 278).[46] At the end of the 1960s, he formalized this analytic *ignorantia docta* in the so-called 'discourse of the analyst', in which knowledge (*savoir*) functions on the place of truth and the 'supposed subject of knowing' is transferred to the side of the patient (Lacan 1991a[1969–70]: 39–42).[47]

WHITHER PERVERSION?

When discerning the three clinical paradoxes between speech and language in his 1953 'Rome Discourse', Lacan did not venture upon an alternative definition of the nosological category of perversion. Instead, he described the third paradox as 'the subject who loses his meaning in the objectifications of discourse', which opened a more metaphysical perspective on the antagonistic relationship between the subject (*sujet*) and the ego (*moi*). Lacan put the 'disguises of perversion' in the neurotic compartment – alongside the 'talking arms of character' and the 'seals of self-punishment' – as 'hermetic elements' which the psychoanalytic exegesis can resolve (Lacan 1977e[1953]:70).

Lacan's hesitation to qualify perversion as a discrete clinical structure permeated much of his work from the 1950s, and is rooted in the theoretical inconsistencies which troubled Freud in his pioneering psychoanalytic explorations of the topic. Using the concept of perversion in its then accepted medico–legal meaning of sexual phenomena precluding genital union and/or the involvement of two consenting adult human beings belonging to the opposite sex, Freud averred in his case-study of Dora and in his 'Three Essays on the Theory of Sexuality' that all psychoneurotics possess forceful, albeit repressed perverse tendencies, and that the sexual constitution of the child, owing to its being ruled by disorganized partial drives, is polymorphously perverse (Freud 1905d:231–232; 1905e [1901]:50). Consequently, the category of perversion was expanded to include children as well as adults, psychoneurotics as well as 'genuine' perverts, and Freud saw himself faced with the question as to what distinguishes true 'positive perversion' (perversion proper) from its false, 'negative' avatars.

After having discarded the nature of the sexual behaviours and the contents of the fantasies, Freud eventually confided in the genuine pervert's fixation on the sexual object and the perverse exclusiveness with regard to the sexual aim, processes which he attributed to an interaction of constitutional and accidental factors (Freud 1905d:162, 235–240). Of course, both fixation and exclusiveness are quantitative rather than qualitative criteria, which probably explains why Freud continued to look for more reliable distinctions between perversion and neurosis.

In 'Fetishism' (1927e), he launched the criterion of disavowal (*Verleugnung*) to explain how a male child develops into a fetishist. When confronted with the reality of sexual difference, the child disavows castration (the mother's lack of a penis) by convincing himself that the mother does possess a penis. As a substitute for the painfully missed penis of the mother, the fetish serves to sustain this psychic reaction of disavowal and produces a split in the child's ego, because it symbolizes both mental triumph and the inherent threat of castration. According to Freud (ibid.: 156–157), this split could also account for the fetishist's ambiguous attitude *vis-à-vis* his objects.

Although a proper qualitative criterion for (fetishistic) perversion, similar to that of repression in neurosis, Freud's mechanism of disavowal proved as indiscriminate as the nature of the sexual behaviours and the contents of the fantasies. For shortly before his death, in 'An Outline of Psycho-Analysis' (1940a[1938]:204), he emphasized the possibility of a disavowal of castration in non-fetishistic subjects, that not only put the specificity of fetishism, but that of the entire category of perversion at risk.

During the early 1950s, Lacan embraced the same definition of perversion as Freud, and embarked on an analogous project of differentiating between the polymorphous perversity of the child, the perverse sexuality of neurotics (and psychotics) and the psychic structure of genuine perverts.[48] In *Seminar I*, he posited that the structure of perversion is characterized by the reduction of the (symbolic) register of intersubjective recognition to an imaginary relationship (Lacan 1988b[1953–54]:221). By this he meant that perverts try to reduce their partners to mere objects, to instruments or idols – short of seeking solace in idealized inanimate objects – whose only function is to satisfy their own desires, with the caveat that the positions within this relationship of submission/dominance can suddenly be reversed so that the original master becomes the slave and vice versa. To the degree that this observation ostensibly enabled Lacan to separate authentic perversion from sexual 'phenomena which one calls perverted' on the 'plane of an exclusively playful execution' (ibid.:215), it did not stand the test of infantile sexuality. For in the same seminar Lacan admitted that '[I]f analytic theory has qualified as polymorphously perverse this or that mode or symptom in the child's behaviour, it is in so far as perversion implies the dimension of imaginary intersubjectivity' (ibid.:217–218).

Lacan returned to this issue in *Seminar IV*, in which he undertook a year-long theoretical analysis of the child's pre-Oedipal, pre-genital object-relations, notably those that were being held to support its status of polymorphous perversity as an imaginary intersubjectivity. Here he defended the innovative idea that the pre-Oedipal relations between a child and its mother are not governed by imaginary intersubjectivity at all, because they are always already inhabited by the symbolic universe in which human beings function. To Lacan the primary mother–child relationship is not a pre-established, symbiotic bond, but an essentially heterogeneous sphere reigned by tension, conflict and misunderstanding on both sides. Criticizing Balint's conception of the primary mother–child interaction as a perfectly tuned, reciprocal exchange, Lacan claimed that mothers do not love (nurture, nurse and nourish) their children simply for the fact that they constitute their precious and vulnerable offspring, but also because the children present them with an additional source of satisfaction.[49] Put differently, a mother loves her child not so much because she is acting upon a natural mother instinct, but because she unconsciously uses the child to cover up her symbolic lack of enjoyment and to obtain supplementary satisfaction in a carefree and selfish way. In Lacan's terminology, there 'is always in the mother, on the side of the child, the requirement of the phallus, which the child more or less symbolizes or realizes' (Lacan 1994[1956–57]:56). As far as the child itself is concerned, Lacan argued that it experiences a psychic crisis when it discovers that in order to secure the love of the mother more is required than simply 'being there', that in order to sustain her love it is not enough to offer oneself. The fact that the child is also 'the phallus, as object of the desire of the mother . . . constitutes an insurmountable barrier for the satisfaction of the desire of the child, which is to be the exclusive object of the desire of the mother' (Lacan 1998b[1957–58]:285–286).

The child can alleviate this conflict in two different ways (Lacan 1994 [1956–57]:81–86). On the one hand, it can try to maintain the satisfaction of its own desire (to be the exclusive object of the mother) by identifying with the phallus (the object of the desire of the mother), whereas on the other hand it can acknowledge the sociocultural exclusion of a fully satisfying relationship with the mother and its concurrent promise of a different, future fulfilment. In the former case the child endeavours to satisfy all of the mother's desires, thus putting its relationship with the mother under the aegis of the imaginary, which entails unselfish inter-dependence and strict reciprocity; in the latter case, the child assimilates the symbolic convention of the prohibited relationship with the mother, accepts its desire to remain fundamentally unsatisfied and engages in a quest for substitute satisfactions. Lacan argued that the former solution leads to fetishism, the 'perversion of perversions' (ibid.:194), whereas the latter introduces the child into the structure of neurosis.[50]

Despite its appeal, this elaborate explanation of perversion proved as unsatisfactory as the previous one (of the reduction of the symbolic to an imaginary intersubjectivity), since it begged the question as to how perverts differ from psychotics, whom Lacan had also located outside the symbolic pact. Neither did Lacan's solution answer the question whether true perverts are any different from the multitude of neurotics and psychotics who display 'perverse' behaviours.[51] Accounting for these neurotic and psychotic 'perverse' behaviours, Lacan often talked about 'paradoxical perverse reactions', perverse 'paroxysms', and *passage à l'acte*, conceding that they too rest upon a shortening of the symbolically regulated distance between the subject and his object of satisfaction, and that ill-advised analysts can easily induce these reductions unknowingly during the course of analytic treatment (ibid.:81).[52]

To resolve the issue of the separation between perversion and psychosis, Lacan returned to Freud's 1919 essay 'A Child is Being Beaten', in order to proclaim that perversion, unlike psychosis, follows the fundamental pattern of the Oedipus complex:

> Perversion is usually considered to be a drive which has not been elaborated by the Oedipal, neurotic mechanism – a pure and simple survival, the persistence of an irreducible partial drive. Freud, on the contrary, in this primordial paper ['A Child is Being Beaten'] and also in many other places, indicates sufficiently that no perverse structuring, no matter how primitive we suppose it to be . . . can be articulated without . . . the process, the organisation, the articulation of the Oedipus complex.
>
> (ibid.:120–121)

One year later, Lacan used almost exactly the same words to describe the Oedipal character of perversion, yet now also broaching the ensuing congruence of perversion and neurosis:

> In order to abandon the notion that perversion is purely and simply the emerging drive, that is to say the contrary of neurosis, one had to wait for the signal of the conductor, that is to say the moment when Freud wrote *Ein Kind wird geschlagen* . . . Perversion does not appear as the pure and simple manifestation of a drive, but it turns out to be related to a dialectical context which is as subtle, as composite, as rich in compromise, as ambiguous as a neurosis.
>
> (Lacan 1998b[1957–58]:230–231)

Later in the same seminar Lacan deployed the structural analogy between perversion and neurosis further by claiming that the neurotic mechanism of repression equally applies to perversion, 'inasmuch as it presents itself also as a symptom and not as the pure and simple manifestation of an unconscious desire' (ibid.:336).[53]

Having postulated this constitutive link between the structures of neurosis and perversion, Lacan's subsequent move was to situate perversion with regard to the neurotic dynamics of jouissance, desire, object a and the fantasy.[54] The groundwork for this new differentiation was done in *Seminar VI*, in which Lacan contended that 'the fantasy [$\mathcal{S} \lozenge a$] marks every human passion with those traits which we call perverse', although 'in the perversion, the accent is on the object a, [whereas] the neurosis can be situated as having its accent on the other term of the fantasy, the $\mathcal{S}$' (1977a[1959]:14, 16). Throughout the remainder of his career, Lacan employed this criterion of the fantasy as a tool to separate neurosis from perversion. In *Seminar XI*, for example, he stated that the structure of perversion is strictly speaking an inverted effect of the fantasy, because it 'is the subject who determines himself as object, in his encounter with the division of subjectivity' (Lacan 1977b[1964]:185).

Unfortunately, it is easier to pinpoint these references than to explain what they mean. The gist of Lacan's argument seems to be contained in a passage from the 1960 text 'The Subversion of the Subject and the Dialectic of Desire in the Freudian Unconscious', in which he wrote:

> Perversion adds [to the privileged place of jouissance] a recuperation of the φ that would scarcely appear as original, if it did not interest the Other as such in a very particular way. Only my formulation of the fantasy enables us to reveal that the subject here makes himself the instrument of the Other's jouissance. It is all the more important . . . to grasp the relevance of this formula in the case of the neurotic, precisely because the neurotic falsifies it.
>
> (Lacan 1977k[1960]:320, translation modified)

If perverts pass through the Oedipus complex, as Lacan had learnt from Freud, then they must experience a loss of enjoyment (-φ) in the same way as neurotics (obsessionals and hysterics) do. Like neurotics they must also set out to retrieve that lost jouissance, a project whose end result would comprise the restoration of subjective fullness. Therefore, the perverse recuperation of the φ scarcely appears as original, because the same mechanism is valid for neurosis. What does distinguish a pervert from a neurotic though, is the former's peculiar involvement of the Other in the subjective process of the recuperation of the lost enjoyment.

I have already explained that in Lacan's idiom hysterical subjects try to come to terms with symbolic castration (the loss of enjoyment) by arousing and sustaining the desire of the Other. In a sense, hysterics derive satisfaction from making themselves desirable, but not enjoyable. When dealing with hysterics one often finds that they are extremely attractive but utterly unpalatable, which is exactly what they intend to achieve. For the hysteric, the enjoyment of the Other is what needs to be avoided at all costs. In a slightly different way, obsessionals try to overcome symbolic castration by neutralizing the desire of the Other. Obsessional neurotics derive satisfaction from an estrangement of/from the Other and perceive complete isolation as the most splendid of life achievements. However palatable obsessional neurotics may be, they do not really want to be desired, let alone enjoyed by others. Hence, despite their divergent strategies *vis-à-vis* the desire of the Other, both hysterics and obsessionals shun the Other's jouissance. The worst thing that can happen to them is to become an object for the enjoyment of the Other.

This is precisely where the perverse structure branches off.[55] In Lacan's view, perverts obtain satisfaction by ensuring the enjoyment of the Other, thereby transforming themselves into an 'instrument of the Other's jouissance'. Deriving satisfaction from conjuring up jouissance in the Other, the pervert's strategy to annihilate the effect of castration involves neither taking things back from the Other (hysteria), nor minimizing the loss (obsessional neurosis), but creating an alternative symbolic order in which jouissance holds pride of place. The pervert transcends the neurotic opposition between jouissance and desire which results from the curtailing impact of the symbolic law, and builds jouissance into the very heart of the Other. In this way, the pervert literally perverts the neurotic law according to which 'jouissance is forbidden to him who speaks as such' (ibid.:319), advocating instead a 'discourse of the right to jouissance' (Lacan 1989a[1962]:60). From an excluded, prohibited privilege in the neurotic's economy, jouissance thus gains ascendancy in the pervert's ideology as a formal universal principle which is applicable to everyone in every situation.[56]

In *Seminar XI* Lacan designated this perverse solution as an inverted effect of the fantasy (Lacan 1977b[1964]:185). Normally, in neurosis, the fantasy contains images of utter bliss in the presence of perfectly adequate, obliging objects. The neurotic fantasy glorifies every imaginable, prohibited sexual activity (and much more), which is why it can be called 'perverse' in line with the aforementioned, classic definition of perversion. By contrast, the fantasy of the pervert is oriented towards pure and unblemished, yet deficient and disconcerted objects that are desperately in need of satisfaction. On the level of the fantasy, the pervert does not desire lascivious and voluptuous studs (or vixens), but ostensibly innocent, sexually deprived angels. The pervert's fantasy is therefore paradoxically less 'perverse' than that of the neurotic, with the proviso that the pervert is keen to corrupt the cherished morality of the fantasized objects.

During the first decade of Lacan's teachings, the original confusion between the polymorphous perversity of the child, the perverse activities of the neurotic and genuine perversion gradually evaporated, giving rise to the delineation of a separate perverse structure. The latter appeared less as a particular type of sexual behaviours, notably all those transcending the adult genital heterosexual standard, but more as a specific relationship between the subject, the object and the symbolic order. None the less, it would also appear that the perverts' construction of an alternative 'law of enjoyment' makes them especially prone to indulge in those sexual behaviours that are culturally prohibited. In other words, Lacan's theory implies that perverse behaviours – defined as above – do not discriminate between neurotics, psychotics and perverts, although perverts are likely to find great comfort in those sexual behaviours that are forbidden by religious, moral or legal standards.[57]

Compared to his numerous reflections on the analytic treatment of neurotics and psychotics, Lacan's suggestions about how to work analytically with structurally perverse patients are extremely limited. Is it possible to diagnose perversion on the basis of the patient's speech and transference? How do perverts relate to knowledge and truth? Are they affected by symptoms and if so, how do they experience them? What, if anything, drives a pervert towards an analyst and would he be approached as a supposed subject of knowing? Can the analyst who is working with a pervert use the same techniques of interpretation and the same procedures for transference handling as those applicable with neurotics? These and other technical questions are largely left in abeyance.

Some authors have insinuated that Lacan's silence concerning the analytic treatment of perverse patients should not bother analysts too much, since perverts hardly ever come to see an analyst, either because they are perfectly happy with their objects and methods of sexual gratification, or because they are afraid that therapy will force them to relinquish parts of their enjoyment (Miller 1996a[1989]:309–310). It has also been advanced that those who do come are seldom interested in a proper analysis; they are rather looking for technical advice on how to carry on with some of their unlawful practices whilst keeping on the 'right side' of the law, which is but a surreptitious demand for extra enjoyment. In the light of these observations, the attention of Lacanian analysts has frequently shifted from the principles governing the analytic treatment of perverts towards the clinical management of so-called 'perverse traits' (fetishistic practices, homosexual object-choice, sadistic fantasies) in neurotic and psychotic patients.[58]

However small the structurally perverse clientele of the analyst may be, it is definitely worth the effort to reopen the issue of how to direct the treatment and, perhaps more significantly, of how to diagnose perversion on the basis of speech and transference. Indeed, one can reasonably assume that some perverts, irrespective of their access to gratifying sexual objects within a self-styled symbolic order, may experience recurrent bouts of anxiety or depression that propel them into psychoanalytic treatment.[59]

Examples of how perverse patients enter analysis, including technical and diagnostic guidelines for the practitioner, have been described in an illuminating fashion by André (1993). Zeroing in on the extraordinary nature of the pervert's speech and transference, this Lacanian analyst contended:

> Perversion is traceable as such within the transference. It manifests itself through a reversal of the relation with the Other and through a radical subversion of the position of the supposed subject of knowing . . . Hearing the pervert speak, it is impossible not to experience an impression of indecency; one always feels a bit violated by the pervert's discourse . . . There is a perverse way of pronouncing the fantasy . . . [Perverts have] a tendency to display their fantasies, often by means of a provocation.
>
> (André 1993:53–54)

This fragment contains all the elements an analyst needs to diagnose a pervert. Unlike neurotics, perverts have no difficulty charting their sexual fantasies and seem to derive enjoyment from embarrassing, shocking or exciting the analyst with their kinky and sleazy details. This is what distinguishes them from the patients on whose stories Freud based his account of the fantasy in 'A Child is Being Beaten', because Freud's patients expressed their masturbatory fantasies with hesitation, uncertainty, resistance, shame and guilt (Freud 1919e:179). In addition, perverts do not consult the analyst as a supposed subject of knowing, but as a supposed subject of enjoying, which means that they assume her to be infatuated with the same things as they themselves are, or desperately seeking the satisfaction which the analytic profession does not allow and which they themselves have on offer. As with everybody else, the pervert prompts the analyst to let go of her restrictive code and to become an ally, or at least to endorse the attractiveness of a life and law of enjoyment. Instead of addressing the analyst as a supposed subject of knowing, perverts present themselves as supposed subjects of knowing. This perverse knowledge concerns the pathways to enjoyment and they will try to convince the analyst, whom they expect to be suffering from an obstinate reluctance to follow these pathways, of their universal value as royal roads to happiness.[60]

Still, these diagnostic indications provide analysts with little guidance as to how they should conduct their clinical vehicle when the passenger happens to be a pervert. In one of his scarce outpourings on the analysis of perverts, and in sharp contrast to the patent complexity of the situation, Lacan maintained that perversion 'is indeed something articulate, inter-pretable, analyzable, and on precisely the same level as neurosis' (Lacan 1977a[1959]:16). Here he reiterated Freud's conviction that 'the positive perversions [perversion proper] are also accessible to psychoanalytic therapy' (Freud 1905d:232). Freud based his assertion on the idea that the fixation and regression to an infantile sexual tendency in the 'positive perversions' must also originate in a repression of mainstream sexual development, consistent with the central psychic mechanism in the neuroses. In Lacan's reading of Freud this meant that perversion is rooted in the Oedipus complex or, in his own terminology, that the perverse individual succumbs to symbolic castration as much as the neurotic does, leading to the installation of divided subjectivity ($), desire, fantasy and (lost) jouissance. Such being the case, Lacan's point seemed to be that neurosis and perversion can indeed be analysed on the same (Oedipal) level.[61]

Nonetheless, the inverted effect of the fantasy in perversion, formalized as $a \diamond \$$, constitutes yet another major challenge for the analyst, because it somehow mirrors the analyst's own position as Lacan conceived it at the end of the 1960s. For the discourse of the analyst which Lacan constructed in *Seminar XVII* (1991a[1969–70]) also has the analyst operating as an object a and the analysand functioning as a divided subject ($, the analytic effect of hysterisation), which implies that there is a remarkable 'structural analogy between the desire of the analyst and the desire of the pervert' (André 1993:17). This formal congruence elicits at least two cardinal questions. First, what prevents the analyst from being an institutionalized pervert? How can we distinguish between the enduring dedication of the analyst and the quintessential commitment of the pervert? And second, assuming that there is a crucial difference between analysts and perverts, how can analysts intervene effectively when their patients represent an image of themselves? How can the non-perverse analyst work with a singularly analytic pervert?

These clinical issues, alongside those emerging from the analysis of neurotics and psychotics, will be elaborated in the following chapters of this book, dealing respectively with the position of the Lacanian analyst within the treatment, the strategies of transference handling and the tactics of analytic interpretation.

NOTES

1 For Freud's views on the unsuitability of psychotic patients for psychoanalysis see also his text 'On Psychotherapy' (1905a[1904]:264) and his 1938 essay 'An Outline of Psycho-Analysis' (1940a[1938]:173).
2 Although Freud did not explicitly mention it, it is reasonable to assume that he also deemed the opposite situation possible, a neurosis concealing itself behind a psychotic picture.
3 The schizophrenic's application of the word to the body prompted Freud to designate this particular use of language as 'organ-speech' (*Organsprache*).
4 In another context, Freud reiterated that hysterical and obsessional symptoms are quite similar to those displayed by patients suffering from dementia praecox, yet again asserting that in the latter group the thing-presentations of objects lie outside the patients' reach, the word-presentations being as far as their libido can stretch (Freud 1916–17a[1915–17]:422).
5 The latter operation reconnects the word-presentation to the body, which seems to be specific for schizophrenia, paranoiac patients reinvesting the word-presentation in a mental, delusional system.
6 In 1946, Lacan had criticized the views of Henri Ey – the founder of the Jacksonian theory of 'organodynamism' in psychiatry – by opposing his own notion of 'psychotic liberty' to Ey's statement that psychosis constitutes a major obstacle to freedom. For a broad survey of Ey's life and works see Garrabé (1997) and Clervoy (1997).
7 'Soul Murder' is the title of an essay August Strindberg submitted to the *Neue Freie Presse* (a Viennese journal) in 1887. See Strindberg (1968 [1887]). For a brief discussion of the cultural history of the notion 'soul murder' see Shengold (1989:17–20).
8 Bruce Fink (1997:93–94) has chosen to translate *point de capiton* as 'button tie', which is perhaps more explicit than 'quilting point' in rendering the technical connotations of Lacan's term, a notion derived from the business of upholstering. Yet contrary to what Fink suggests, the tie does not serve to hold the button in place, but both the button and the tie serve to prevent the stuffing of a chair or mattress from moving. Hence, in Lacan's metaphor the stuff emblematizes the signified (Freud's thing-presentation), the upholstery stands for the signifier (the word-presentation) and the *points de capiton* epitomize the places where the former is connected to the latter, and through which the whole construction becomes solid and usable.
9 To be fair, I should point out that Freud did indicate once that psychosis only occurs when the ego (*Ich*) rejects (*verwirft*) a representation and its affect (Freud 1894a:58), and that at other times he did admit that repression is inadequate to explain the psychotic mechanism (Freud 1915e: 202–203).
10 For 'scotomization', see Laforgue (1926) and Freud (1927e). For alternative

readings of Damourette and Pichon's essay, and a more extensive discussion of foreclosure, see Aparicio (1984), Grigg (1998) and Rabinovitch (1998).

11 Prior to the mid-1950s Lacan wrote Name-of-the-Father without capitals and hyphens, the latter appearing in print for the first time in his 1957–58 text on psychosis (Lacan 1977h[1957–58]). In Lacan's works capitals always indicate that the notion has a symbolic status.

12 To prevent confusion, I should also mention that the Name-of-the-Father does not coincide with the father's name (first name, surname, or both) that is transmitted from generation to generation within patrilineal cultures, as Lacan emphasized in a 1959 discussion with Jean Laplanche (Lacan 1992[1959–60]:65). For a comprehensive mapping of the notion of the Name-of-the-Father in Lacan's works see Porge (1997).

13 In keeping with his accentuation of the linguistic nature of the entire operation, Lacan preferred the term 'metaphor' over 'substitution', which ultimately led to his notorious formula of 'the metaphor of the Name-of-the-Father', or 'paternal metaphor' (Lacan 1977h[1957–58]:200). A detailed commentary of this formula and its vicissitudes falls beyond the scope of this book, but readers will be able to bite off more than they can chew from Fink (1997:79–111), Regnault (1995) and Ragland (1995:182–234).

14 In the formula of the paternal metaphor the installation of ambiguity within the symbolic order, as an effect of the function of the father, is represented by the inscription of the phallus in the Other (Lacan 1977h[1957–58]:200). Lacan interpreted the symbolic phallus as the principle of difference, through which signifiers acquire different meanings depending on the context in which they appear, and through which every signifier can have a 'double meaning' in the sexual sense of the word.

15 For such a reductive reading of Lacan's works, see for instance Grosz (1990:67–74). It goes without saying that the more the mother's mandatory acknowledgement of the paternal authority is emphasized as a necessary condition for the child's psychic integrity, the more feminist authors believe they are entitled to dispose of Lacanian theory as a patriarchal doctrine.

16 All translations from foreign language sources for which no English edition is available are mine, unless otherwise indicated.

17 For holophrase, see Lacan (1988b[1953–54]:225–226; 1977b[1964]: 237–238). For an extensive commentary on this notion see Stevens (1987).

18 See Schreber (1988[1903]:212). For Freud (1911c[1910]:42–44), Schreber's transformation into a woman and his portrayal of Dr Flechsig as a soul-murderer and sexual abuser were all indications of his strong homosexual libido, whereas Lacan (1977h[1957–58]:209–212) interpreted these phenomena as 'transsexual enjoyment' (jouissance). Perhaps neither of these designations is very adequate, considering the fact that Schreber's sexual experiences were completely alien to an established sexual code, from which the terms 'homosexuality' and 'transsexualism' derive their meaning.

19 Rather than the acme of the psychotic illness, the delusional formation should be regarded as an attempt at recovery, as Freud had pointed out in his Schreber study (1911c[1910]:71). Moreover, from a Lacanian viewpoint a human being can have a psychotic structure without displaying any of

the symptoms (hallucinations, delusions, depersonalization, etc.) that are commonly qualified as 'psychotic'. Distinctions should be made between the so-called 'pre-psychotic phase' (before the outbreak), the precipitating constellation (the moment of outbreak) and the 'post-psychotic' labour (the construction of a delusion). During the 1970s, Lacan also coined 'suppletion' as an overarching term for the various outlets (art, writing, psychosomatic illness, etc.) that keep the psychotic symptoms at bay.

20 For a detailed analysis of this model see Chapter 2.

21 The quotation from *Seminar XI* concerns paranoia rather than psychosis in general, but Lacan hardly ever talked about schizophrenia, dementia praecox, manic-depressive psychosis etc. as separate nosological categories. For an interesting Lacanian interpretation of the classical distinction between paranoia and schizophrenia see Miller (1983[1982]).

22 'Supposed subject of knowing' has been suggested by Stuart Schneiderman in his translator's preface to *How Lacan's Ideas are Used in Clinical Practice* (1993[1980]:vii) and renders more adequately what Lacan intended to say with the notion of *sujet supposé savoir*: not that a subject supposes knowledge, but that a 'subject of knowledge' is supposed. See Lacan (1995b[1967]). See also Grigg (1991:104).

23 At the time, Freud also tried to apply this mechanism of defence to paranoia, yet not without distinguishing its peculiar 'projective' quality (Freud 1896b: 184).

24 In Chapter 4, on the tactics of interpretation, I will return to this issue in the context of a discussion of Lacan's comments on a case-study by Ernst Kris.

25 During the 1950s, this portrayal of the neurotic symptom as a 'coded message' induced a conception of analytic interpretation as an exegetic procedure designed to deliver the imprisoned meaning. Later on, Lacan distanced himself from his own view – and from every perspective linking psychoanalysis to hermeneutics – and qualified interpretation as an oracle in its own right (Lacan 1991a[1969–70]:40–41). For a more detailed discussion of this shift in Lacan's works see Chapter 4.

26 The sentence in square brackets is missing from the English translation of *Seminar I*.

27 Of course, the difference between a neurotic and a psychotic is not simply that the latter is capable of becoming anxious, for example, at the sight of a harmless red car, whereas the former is immune to such instances of anxiety. Indeed, a neurotic can also be extremely scared of relatively harmless objects such as red cars, if this just happens to be part of his symptomatic pattern. The difference is rather that for the psychotic 'everything and nothing' can be traumatic, whereas for the neurotic traumatic experiences (signifiers) are always localized. Furthermore, for the neurotic it will be a complete mystery why red cars provoke anxiety (the signifier has been repressed), whereas the psychotic will be fully aware and absolutely certain of the reason why red cars should be avoided at all cost.

28 Although the generic category of neurosis is often held to comprise hysteria, obsessional neurosis and phobia, neither Freud nor Lacan defined phobia as a separate type of neurosis. For example, in his case-study of Little Hans, Freud proffered the thesis that phobias can be filed under anxiety hysteria

and 'should only be regarded as syndromes which may form part of various neuroses' (Freud 1909b:115). Lacan, for his part, saw the individual's installation of a phobic object (or signifier) as the most extreme way of preventing the confrontation with the desire of the Other, an encounter which he deemed inherently frightening in any neurosis, owing to its potential risk of destroying the individual's own desire (Lacan 1991b [1960–61]:305–306). Lacan thus proclaimed that phobic individuals try to sustain their own desire by having recourse to anxiety, which makes phobia the most radical form of neurosis (ibid.:425; 1977k[1960]:321).

29 For hysterical painful passivity versus obsessional pleasurable activity see for example Freud (1896b; 1896c). For Freud's repudiation of this distinction, including the entire 'seduction theory' of psychopathology see Freud (1906a[1905]; 1913i). For a discussion of the differential type of repression in hysteria and obsessional neurosis see Freud (1909d:195–196), and for distinctions pertaining to the moment of onset, constitutional factors, the location of the symptoms and the patients' unconscious attitudes towards sexuality see for example Freud (1926d[1925]).

30 Many of Lacan's ideas on obsessional neurosis during the 1950s originated in his contrasting of the Freudian paradigm to the object-relations theory of Karl Abraham as represented in the works of Bouvet (1967–68).

31 For detailed discussions in English of Lacan's ideas on hysteria and obsessional neurosis see David-Ménard (1989[1983]), Verhaeghe (1997[1987]), Nasio (1997[1990]), Dor (1997[1995]) and Fink (1997:112–164). Fink's chapter is largely based on Soler (1996c[1989]) and includes thought-provoking case-material. For extensive analyses in French of Lacan's views on hysteria see Wajeman (1982), Melman (1984) and Israel (1996[1974]). For French Lacanian studies of obsessional neurosis see Roublef (1994[1964]) and Lachaud (1995). Additional materials can be found in Fondation du Champ freudien (1986) and Actes de l'Ecole de la Cause freudienne (1985), whereas numerous articles dealing with some aspect of Lacan's work on hysteria and obsessional neurosis have been published in the various Lacanian journals and newsletters.

32 Within Lacanian theory, there is no reason why castration should apply to boys and not to girls, which implies that the dissolution of the Oedipus complex does no longer depend on the anatomical difference between the sexes (Freud 1924d; 1925j).

33 The imaginary phallus (φ) as object of symbolic castration first appeared in *Seminar IV* (Lacan 1994[1956–57]), whereas the split subject ($\mathbf{S}$) made its entry in *Seminar V* (Lacan 1998b[1957–58]). Lacan considered the loss of jouissance to be imaginary because human beings can never lay claim to possessing their enjoyment. The Other strips human beings of something they never had, so that the loss is illusory.

34 In 'Three Essays on the Theory of Sexuality', Freud wrote: 'It is in the world of ideas, however, that the choice of an object is accomplished at first; and the sexual life of maturing youth is almost entirely restricted to indulging in phantasies, that is in ideas that are not destined to be carried into effect' (Freud 1905d:226). The formula $\mathbf{S} \diamond a$ appeared for the first time in Lacan's seminar of 1957–58 on *The Formations of the Unconscious*, yet with *a* still defined as the imaginary other (Lacan 1998b[1957–58]:303–317).

35 For more sophisticated discussions of these concepts and their relations
    see, for example, Fink (1995a), Laurent (1995), Soler (1995; 1996c[1989]),
    Evans (1998) and Verhaeghe (1998), as well as the numerous introductions
    to Lacanian theory.

36 'Own desire' is a paradoxical statement within Lacanian theory, because
    Lacan adopted the Kojèvo–Hegelian view that human desire is always
    geared towards and affected by another desire, a view which he condensed
    into the formula 'Man's desire is the desire of/for the Other'. 'Own desire'
    should therefore be read as 'the desire of the Other as it manifests itself in the
    subject'. For Kojève's reading of Hegel's theory of desire (*Begierde*), see
    Kojève (1969[1933–39]:39–40). For Lacan's formula see, for example,
    Lacan (1988b[1953–54]:176–178).

37 This is another reason why the hysteric's desire is fundamentally unsatisfied.

38 The same dynamics applies to male hysterics. As a matter of fact, when
    Lacan introduced the hysteric's question ('Am I a man or a woman?') in
    Seminar III (1993[1955–56]:168–180), he took his bearings from a case of
    traumatic hysteria in a male described by Michael Joseph Eisler. The reader
    who is interested in Eisler's case-study should note that the reference
    provided in the English translation of *Seminar III* is incorrect. For the correct
    reference see Eisler (1921[1920]).

39 For a similar argument pertaining to the Rat Man see Lacan (1991b
    [1960–61]:305).

40 For all their obligingness, obsessionals are as squeamish as hysterics
    when faced with the enjoyment of the Other, which they interpret as
    an indication of the fact that they have been deprived of something.
    Although obsessionals are perfectly happy overwhelming people with gifts,
    they cannot tolerate the idea that someone is taking advantage of their
    goodwill.

41 Again, the dynamics of obsessional neurosis apply to men and women alike,
    despite the predominance of male obsessionals in the psychoanalytic literature.

42 As I have already pointed out in the Introduction to this book, traces of
    Lacan's seminars on Dora and the Rat Man can be found in Lacan
    (1982a[1951]; 1979[1953]).

43 Many authors have discussed Freud's theoretical conception and clinical
    handling of transference in the Rat Man case. For a good survey of opinions
    and a penetrating discussion of Freud's technique on the basis of new
    primary source materials see Mahony (1986).

44 This cultivation of the relativity of knowledge in the hysteric's discourse
    may explain why Lacan eventually linked it to scientific discourse, at least
    in the latter's twentieth century versions hailing fundamental uncertainty
    and the necessary falsification of knowledge (Lacan 1990d[1973]:24). For a
    further exploration of the relationship between the hysteric's discourse and
    the discourse of science see Fink (1995b:133–135, 141–142).

45 One could argue that the girl's amazing reaction is due to the fact that she
    perceived Freud as an associate of her mother, from whom he had obtained
    the information about her homosexual involvements, and therefore not
    merely a defence against analytic knowledge that is being forced upon her.
    Whereas this factor should indeed not be underestimated, the exact source of
    the knowledge professed by the analyst is probably less important than the

act of professing itself, because the neurotic patient will always experience the knowledge of the Other as a disrespectful, alienating imposition, whether it is derived from the analytic transference or from another source.

46 For Cusanus' original (theological) argument, see Cusanus (1985[1449]).

47 The discourse of the analyst will be explained further in Chapter 2.

48 A comprehensive theoretical discussion of Lacan's scattered ideas on perversion is as yet unavailable, neither in English nor in French. None the less, many authors have dealt with aspects of his work and many Lacanian case-studies of a particular type of pervert, or 'perverse trait' in neurosis and psychosis are available. For useful secondary source materials in English see Fink (1997:165–202), Dor (1997[1995]:29–68) and Miller (1996a[1989]). For valuable sources in French see Castanet (1999), Rey-Flaud (1996), André (1993), Granoff and Perrier (1991[1960]), Dor (1987), Fondation du Champ freudien (1990) and Aulagnier-Spairani et al. (1967).

49 Lacan's critique of Balint was focused on a series of papers included in Balint (1952) and represented a rebuttal avant la lettre of Margaret Mahler's theory of infantile development, which postulates a transition from symbiosis to separation (triangulation) and individuation (Mahler 1968; Mahler et al. 1975).

50 In a notoriously difficult passage from Seminar XI Lacan further developed the child's access to the neurotic structure by implying 'the superimposition (recouvrement) of two lacks' (Lacan 1977b[1964]:214). Lacan's argument was that when the child encounters the desire of the Other (its lack), for example by experiencing that its mother is not satisfied by the mere presence of her child, it will try to solve the riddle of the desire of the Other ('So what is it that she wants?') by wondering about the effect of its own disappearance ('What would happen to my mother if I didn't exist anymore, if I were to be abducted, or if I vanished altogether?'). Hence Lacan's statement of a superimposition of two lacks: to the discovery of a lack in, or the desire of the Other the child reacts with the option of its own lack (its physical, bodily absence). Until the late 1950s, Lacan considered fetishism to be the paradigmatic case of perversion (see, for instance, Lacan 1977i[1958]:248), whereas the emphasis shifted towards masochism from the moment he started to theorize the object a during the early 1960s. This shift is especially clear in three unpublished seminars from the late 1960s (Lacan 1966–67; 1967–68; 1968–69).

51 In addition, Lacan racked his brains first over the exact nature of the moment when the child realizes that it is being loved for more than itself, and second over why the child decides in favour of the perverse or the neurotic option. Echoes of these issues can be found throughout Seminar IV (1994[1956–57]) and Seminar V (1998b[1957–58]), and Lacan condensed their insolubility in an oft-quoted sentence from his 1957–58 text on psychosis: 'The whole problem of the perversions consists in conceiving how the child, in his relation to the mother, a relation constituted in analysis not by his vital dependence on her, but by his dependence on her love, that is to say, by the desire for her desire, identifies himself with the imaginary object of this desire in so far as the mother symbolizes it in the phallus' (Lacan 1977h [1957–58]:197–198).

52 To illustrate his thesis, Lacan commented at length on a case-study by

Ruth Lebovici (1956). See Lacan (1994[1956–57]:88–92; 1977i[1958]: 247–248).

53 When comparing this passage to the previous ones, it appears that at the end of the 1950s Lacan was still using drive and desire interchangeably, a conceptual distinction between the two terms not emerging in Lacan's works until 1964. See Lacan (1996a[1964]) and Miller (1996b[1994]).

54 Lacan never elaborated the mechanism of disavowal (*Verleugnung*) as a separate causal hypothesis for perversion, although many commentators on Lacan's works have claimed he did.

55 What is responsible for this Oedipal orientation towards perversion is a question neither Freud nor Lacan have answered, which has not prevented Lacanian scholars from suggesting possible solutions, such as a partial failure of the paternal function (Fink 1997:174). Rather than endorsing this (or another) option I would prefer to revive Lacan's 1946 assertion of an 'unfathomable decision of being' (Lacan 1966a[1946]:177), which could equally apply to psychotics, neurotics and perverts.

56 Lacan elaborated the similarity between the pervert's paradoxical law of jouissance and Kant's categorical imperative in 'Kant with Sade' (1989a [1962]), an extremely dense text from the early 1960s. To facilitate the reading of the first part of this text, I can highly recommend the company of Miller (1996c[1989]).

57 The problem of diagnosing perversion merely on the basis of 'perverse' sexual behaviours was already raised by Otto Rank in his 1922 paper 'Perversion and Neurosis', in which he wrote: 'A first difficulty probably comes from the fact that analysis borrowed these designations for the perversions [exhibitionism, sadism, masochism, homosexuality, etc.] . . . from descriptive psychiatry (Krafft-Ebing) . . . It may then appear that what we, as a matter of habit, are designating collectively as 'perversions' represent in the sense of our metapsychology very varying mechanisms and totally different kinds of libido satisfaction' (Rank 1923[1922]: 272–273).

58 See, for example, Fondation du Champ Freudien (1990). During the early 1970s Lacan went so far as to say that perversion functions as the binding element between the sexes. To the extent that it is impossible to devise a symbolic formula explaining how men and women relate to each other – Lacan's (in)famous 'there is no such thing as a sexual relationship' – perversion (in the fantasy and the dreams of the neurotic) overrules this impossibility. See Lacan (1998a[1972–73]:87; 1990d[1973]: 37–38).

59 As Oscar Wilde put it in one of his unsurpassable aphorisms: 'In this world there are only two tragedies. One is not getting what one wants and the other is getting it. The last is much the worst; the last is a real tragedy!' (Wilde 1990[1893]:417). From a Lacanian perspective the first tragedy could be called neurotic and the second perverse, whereas one could possibly add a third, psychotic tragedy, of not belonging to this world at all.

60 For additional comments on the pervert's adoption of the position of supposed subject of knowing within the treatment see Braunstein and Saal (1990), Aparicio *et al.* (1990), Eidelstein *et al.* (1990) and Miller (1996a [1989]).

61 In 1967 Lacan vehemently refuted the proposition that the pervert's attempts at recuperating enjoyment prevents him from being a subject, arguing that 'the pervert remains a subject throughout the exercise of the question he poses with respect to the jouissance of the Other . . . ' (Lacan 1966–67:session of 31 May 1967).

Chapter 2

What does the analyst want?

FREUD'S ARCHAEOLOGICAL SLEUTHING

In order to explain the general attitude of the psychoanalyst during the treatment, Freud often appealed to highly imaginative metaphors. For example, in his 1914 essay on transference-love (1915a[1914]:170) he defined analysts as warriors who are incessantly waging a threefold battle with their recalcitrant patients, their own oppressive mental forces and their political opponents outside the clinical setting. Years later, in Lecture 34 of the 'New Introductory Lectures on Psycho-Analysis', he argued that analysts are principally in the same position as the medieval woman who is suspected of witchcraft and therefore sentenced to being 'stewed in a cauldron of boiling water' (Freud 1933a[1932]:155), a judgement epitomizing a surreptitious, yet inescapable death penalty.[1]

Freud's most insistent and compelling metaphor of the analyst is definitely that of the archaeologist, a representation which he not only applied to the abstract practitioner in his writings, but which he himself embraced wholeheartedly, from the dawn of his analytic itinerary to his years of forced exile.[2] In his preface to the famous Dora case, Freud's first extensive report of a psychoanalytic treatment, he divulged that he had proceeded like a 'conscientious archaeologist', bringing 'to the light of day after long burial the priceless though mutilated remnants of antiquity' and reassembling the shattered pieces without concealing where 'reconstruction supplements the authentic' (Freud 1905e[1901]:12–13). In his recollections of Freud, the 'Wolf Man' conceded that the Berggasse consultation rooms 'must have been a surprise to any patient, for they in no way reminded one of a doctor's office, but rather of an archaeologist's study', a feature which Freud explained to his patient by stating that 'the psychoanalyst, like the archaeologist in his excavations, must uncover layer after layer of the patient's psyche, before coming to the deepest, most valuable treasures' (Gardiner 1972:139).[3] The metaphor reappeared in 'Civilization and its Discontents' (1930a[1929]:69–72) and in 'Constructions in Analysis' (1937d:259–260), Freud's testament of analytic technique, although he now assured that analysts are in a sense more fortunate than archaeologists, since they have the opportunity to operate on living materials whose structures have not been eroded by the accumulated covers.[4]

In his designation of the analyst, including himself, as an archaeologist, Freud was fascinated by the nineteenth-century German explorer Heinrich Schliemann, who managed to unearth the remains of Troy and a score of Mycenaean treasures with Homer's poetry as his main guide. After the example of Schliemann, Freud aspired to be a tireless digger and proud discoverer, not of the sociocultural heritage of humanity, but of the familial antecedents of the neurotic individual, taking the patient's contrived associations, a series of apparently meaningless words, as his principal lead.[5] Also in the wake of Schliemann, Freud was less concerned with the correct reconstruction of the retrieved fragments than with the historical value of the relics themselves. Historical truth, predicated upon the legitimate connection between a current state of affairs and a historical event, mattered more to Freud than material truth, presupposing a strict congruence between the past and its representation in the present.[6] However elliptic or distorted the patients' accounts and however fantastic their symptoms, Freud maintained that these neurotic phenomena are supported by an unconscious scaffolding, elements which had once been part and parcel of the patients' conscious daily reality.

Consequently, the Freudian clinician was held to gather as many clues as possible from the patients' psychopathology of everyday life, building hypotheses and drawing maps of the original constellation, and penetrating into the submerged psychic architecture in order to reveal the foundations of the symptoms. Whereas the analyst's theoretical framework was profoundly archaeological, his methods were deemed investigative, drawing upon Ovid's formula *Causa latet, vis est notissima* – the cause is hidden but its effect is conspicuous. Yet instead of relying on the most salient features of his patients' clinical condition when venturing this work of reconstruction, Freud put all his trust in apparently meaningless trifles: slips of the tongue, dreams, parapraxes, lapses of memory, etc.

This Freudian analytic procedure of inferring causes from the careful observation of ostensibly insignificant details mirrored the so-called 'method of Zadig', a technique immortalized by Voltaire in a short story from the mid-eighteenth century and subsequently designated by the agnosticist Thomas Huxley as the method of 'retrospective prophecy'.[7] By scrutinizing the trees lining a narrow road and the marks on the ground, Voltaire's Zadig succeeded in describing all the essential characteristics of the horse that had recently passed by, including the length of its tail and the quality of its bit. Yet, apart from Zadig's method, Freud's *modus operandi* was also reminiscent of a widely acclaimed procedure for determining the authorship of works of art which had been developed by the Italian physician Giovanni Morelli during the nineteenth century. Morelli argued that the tiny details of a painting, such as a character's earlobes, reveal more about the identity of the artist than the style of its central depiction. In 'The Moses of Michelangelo' Freud admitted to his long familiarity with Morelli's procedure, and put it on a par with the central research method in psychoanalysis:

> It seems to me that his [Morelli's] method of inquiry is closely related to the technique of psychoanalysis. It, too, is accustomed to divine secret concealed things from despised or unnoticed features, from the rubbish-heap, as it were, of our observations.
>
> (Freud 1914b:222)

To the extent that psychoanalysts, on Freud's account, study their patients' clinical pictures with the Zadig–Morelli method, their mode of operation also resembles that of a host of fictional detectives, the most prominent being Poe's C. Auguste Dupin and Doyle's Sherlock Holmes. To many a reader's delight these characters have been portrayed as expert Zadigs, whose capacities for 'looking awry', coupled with an exceptional acumen, enable them time and again to solve even the most persistent of mysteries. Likewise, and although the metaphor never appeared in his writings, Freud intimated that the analyst is some sort of professional clinical gumshoe, a mental health sleuth whose task consists in dissolving present psychic crises by retrieving their historical causes via the analysis of apparently meaningless details.[8]

Inspired by this contiguity, film directors have often modelled their detectives – from Hitchcock's characters for Ingrid Bergman and Sean Connery in *Spellbound* and *Marnie*, to Peter Falk in the role of the inimitable inspector Columbo – on the image of the Freudian analyst.[9] The setting of the Columbo series is particularly relevant here, because as Slavoj Žižek has noted in *The Plague of Fantasies*:

> [T]he enigma to be resolved is not that of 'whodunit?', but of how the detective will establish the link between the deceptive surface (the

'manifest content' of the crime scene) and the truth about the crime (its 'latent thought') – how he will prove his or her guilt to the culprit.
(Žižek 1997:106)

However, the viewer is not the only person who knows the identity of the murderer in advance for, as Žižek has emphasized, the other distinguishing feature of the Columbo series is that the detective also seems to know the ins and outs of the matter, including the identity of the criminal, from the moment he arrives at the scene (ibid.:107).

In a similar vein, Freud worked from a mysterious yet singularly adequate universal knowledge base, which can deservedly be called 'mythical' since it was anchored in Sophocles' poetic account of the rise and fall of Thebe. Epistemologically, Freud employed an Oedipal template, which allowed him to 'guess' the pivotal elements of his patients' lives even before they had presented them(selves) to him. Which infantile constellation presided over his patients' adult experiences and which relationships determined their mental crises were questions Freud did not need to answer. The only mystery the patients had in store concerned the way in which the historical truth pervaded the intricate cobweb of their present symptoms, a mystery which, for its known Oedipal context, was no less difficult to resolve. Freud's pre-eminent challenge was how to dissolve the patients' smokescreens and confront them with the naked truth of what they had hitherto been hiding from their environment and, of course, from themselves.[10]

Technically, Freud's analytical method of 'retrospective prophecy', or, if one prefers, of 'archaeological sleuthing' followed the same route as that which had led to the formation of the patient's symptoms, albeit in the opposite direction. For the patients this implied that they had to recognize the historical (infantile) causes of their symptoms, after the analyst had succeeded in reconstructing these causes out of the traces they had left behind. As such, Freudian analysis strictly relied on the present perfect tense: events starting in the past were expected to have a lasting, yet unconscious impact on the present and the patients were urged to come to terms with their contemporary condition by acknowledging 'what has been'. This idea corresponds to the classical medical maxim of *Ablata causa, tollitur effectus* (if the cause is taken away, its effect will disappear), and it has contributed enormously to the common designation of Freudian psychoanalysis as a paragon of causal therapy.

Once the (infantile) causes had been liberated from the psychic dungeon to which repression had relegated them, Freud expected these causes to lose their pathogenic effect automatically. In another extensive archaeological metaphor, he underscored that 'in mental life nothing which has once been formed can perish', just like the burial of precious objects under myriad layers of sand contributes to their survival (Freud 1930a[1929]:69–70). But he was keen to add that when these objects are excavated they are so vulnerable that they can rapidly disintegrate into insignificant grains of dust, thus returning to their proper place as objects belonging to a remote past. '[T]he destruction of Pompeii was only beginning now that it had been dug up', he told the Rat Man (Freud 1909d:176). This is precisely what Freud expected to happen with the retrieved historical causes of his patients' symptoms. He anticipated symptomatic effects to disappear spontaneously following the liberation of their historical causes from their secret unconscious shelters. He believed that a patient's assumption of his historical truth (as cause) would have a benign effect on his symptoms, because the patient's acknowledgement would grant these causes a new, conscious and innocuous guise. In the process, the temporal status of psychic events gradually transformed itself from the present perfect into the past tense.[11]

Despite its compelling outlook, Freud noticed that something in the nature of the unconscious itself hindered the full realization of this analytical project. Already in the final paragraphs of 'The Dynamics of Transference' he observed that the patient's unwillingness or inability to subscribe to the rule of free association cannot be attributed entirely to the psychic power of resistance. Freud had to admit that unconscious impulses 'refuse to be remembered' (*wollen nicht erinnert werden*) and are strictly aimed at reproducing themselves (Freud 1912b:107–108). In subsequent texts, he conceptualized this unconscious force alternatively as a not wanting to know (Freud 1913c:141–142), negative therapeutic reactions (Freud 1923b:49) and the compulsion to repeat (Freud 1920g: 18–20), mental derivatives of the death drive which operates beyond the pleasure principle. But naming the force and its engine was not sufficient to eradicate the problem, neither theoretically nor clinically. In Lecture 31 of the 'New Introductory Lectures on Psycho-Analysis', Freud summarized the work of analysis as follows:

> [Impressions] which have been sunk into the id by repression, are virtually immortal; after the passage of decades they behave as though they had just occurred. They can only be recognized as belonging to the past, can only lose their importance . . . when they have been made conscious by the work of analysis, and it is on this that the therapeutic effect of analytic treatment rests to no small extent. Again and again

I have had the impression that we have made too little theoretical use of this fact . . . of the unalterability by time of the repressed.

(Freud 1933a[1932]:73–74)

Returning to this issue in the third chapter of 'Analysis Terminable and Interminable', Freud ultimately concluded that an analysis may have a practical end (when the patient and the analyst stop seeing each other) but not a definitive end, since the treatment procedure is incapable of neutralizing deleterious unconscious impulses for once and for all.

Faced with this theoretical and clinical impasse of the Freudian model, post-Freudian authors have constructed a variety of escape routes. For instance, ego-psychologists have argued that Freud overestimated the clinical impact of the death drive or, conversely, that he underestimated the power of analytic treatment to master its most pervasive outlets, the manifestations of aggression and destruction.[12] From a different angle, psychodynamic therapists have exchanged Freud's paradigm of archaeological sleuthing for an alternative treatment model in which the retrieval of unconscious memories into consciousness is replaced by less demanding, more superficial procedures, such as the creation and maintenance of adequate coping strategies and 'corrective emotional experiences'.[13] In yet another branch of psychoanalysis, object-relations therapists have sustained Freud's general conception of analytic treatment, whilst shifting its focus to the reparation of the patients' early childhood relationships, with the analyst functioning as a 'good enough mother'.[14]

Each of these developments could be canvassed in its historical origins and its clinical–theoretical premises, yet within the scope of this book I will merely focus on Lacan's answer to the apparent deadlock of Freudian psychoanalysis. During the first years of his seminars, Lacan generally espoused Freud's views on the end of analysis – interpreted in terms of its termination, its goal and its results. For example, in the final session of *Seminar I* (1988b[1953–54]:273–287), he argued that the analyst's task consists in encouraging patients to embark on a progressive verbalization of those elements which they have never integrated into their life history, in view of the full realization of their subjective truth. During the late 1950s, this Freudian goal was gradually reformulated as 'the subject's avowal of his desire' in its indebtedness to the desire of the Other (Lacan 1977i[1958]:275; 1991b[1960–61]:234). From the mid-1960s, and especially with *Seminar XI*, Lacan then explored the psychic backdrop of this subjective avowal of desire, which cleared the way for his concep-tualization of 'traversing the fantasy' (Lacan 1977b[1964]:273–274) and 'subjective destitution' (Lacan 1995b[1967]:8) as the most advanced analytic goals, to be reserved for those clinical experiences which have training effects on the analysand. This gradual shift from fullness (the reintegration of one's personal history) to emptiness (the acknowledgement of an irrecuperable loss in the avowal of desire) as the appropriate terminus of analytic treatment correlated with Lacan's ongoing reflection upon the analyst's clinical position and his theoretical re-evaluation of the Freudian unconscious. Eventually, it opened up entirely new perspectives on the clinical politics of the analyst, which he formalized in the so-called 'discourse of the analyst' (Lacan 1991a[1969–70]:31–42).

THE ANALYST AS OTHER SUBJECT

Since Lacan conceived all his contributions to psychoanalytic theory from the early 1950s as recuperations of Freud's legacy, against the reigning discourse of ego-psychology, it does not come as a surprise that his initial attempts to describe the function and position of the analyst were strongly flavoured by his trenchant criticism of mainstream psychoanalysis. In the 'Rome Discourse' he defined the analyst's task primarily in a negative way, choosing his examples of bad practice across the board of psychoanalytic activity. Unscrupulously, Lacan argued that analysts whose aim is to redesign their patients' lives, or to restore their relationships with the outside world, betray their own profession. Scorning the contemporary 'analysis of resistance', he reproached his colleagues for disclosing personal feelings and for presenting themselves as role models (ideal egos) within the 'here and now' of the clinical setting. To Lacan, these analysts were breaking their promise of psychoanalytic treatment because they were simply facilitating introspection, fostering social competence, building intellectual maturity, and nurturing communicative abilities, whilst promoting their own life-style as an image of general psychic health with which the patients were supposed to identify. Lacan believed these therapeutic interventions to be indicative of the analyst's avoidance of the symbolic power of speech and language – the prime source of psychoanalytic effectiveness – in favour of an imaginary level of functioning.[15]

Although Lacan's crusade against the mission statement of American ego-psychology can be seen as an idiosyncratic act of recalcitrance, he was in fact merely rewording one of Freud's admonitions in 'Lines of Advance in Psycho-Analytic Therapy' (1919a[1918]). In this paper Freud criticized the way in which the Swiss school (Jung) and some American psychoanalysts had conceived the analyst's task as similar to that of indomitable educators, godlike creatures who incessantly attempt to mould the uneducated into images of themselves. Against this view, Freud declared:

> We refused most emphatically to turn a patient who puts himself into our hands in search of help into our private property, to decide his fate for him, to force our own ideals upon him, and with the pride of a Creator to form him in our own image and see that it is good . . . In my opinion, this is after all only to use violence, even though it is overlaid with the most honourable motives.
>
> (ibid.:164–165)

As an appropriate alternative Freud suggested the 'rule of abstinence', which consists in the analyst's refusal to gratify the patient's needs and demands so that all substitute satisfactions are avoided and a productive level of suffering is maintained. Freud refused to model the analytic treatment on a mental hospital's policy to look after patients and to make them feel as comfortable as possible inside. He also emphasized that whatever educational effect psychoanalysis may entail, analysts should ensure that their patients do not come to resemble them, but are encouraged in the liberation and realization of their own being.

Lacan's antagonism between the imaginary and the symbolic followed Freud's opposition between non-analytic image building and proper analytic abstinence. It can be summarized as an antagonism between the psychic register of insuperable, yet regulated difference and that of deceptive, yet fascinating resemblance.[16] Apropos of the symbolic, Lacan recognized the paragon of the human symbolic function (the 'original symbolism') in the complex rules of matrimonial alliance, the elaborate laws of kinship and the practices of exchanging gifts that preside over otherwise 'pre-modern', non-industrialized communities (Lacan 1977e [1953]:65–66). Whilst none of these regulations is rooted in a pre-ordained natural order, they structure the natural living conditions in such a way that distinct group members are continuously forced to participate in existing agreements and to negotiate new pacts.[17] By contrast, Lacan located the source of the human imaginary in the so-called 'mirror-stage' (Lacan 1977c[1949]), whereby the child develops its identity (its ego) via an identification with the twin image reflected by the mirror or, in the absence of reflective surfaces, by a similar other.[18] In *Seminar I*, and in reference to Freud, Lacan defined the ego accordingly as an agency that 'is constructed like an onion, one could peel it and discover the successive identifications which have constituted it' (Lacan 1988b[1953–54]:171).[19] Consequently, the human imaginary has nothing to do with the installation and regulation of difference; it is fundamentally geared towards the advancement of similarity and instead of a symbolic truce, it induces jealousy, rivalry, competition and aggression.

At the end of *Seminar II* (1988c[1954–55]:243), Lacan integrated these two discordant dimensions of the symbolic and the imaginary into a comprehensive cartography of psychoanalytic treatment, placing the principles of ego-psychology orthogonally to a clinical practice which he deemed more loyal to Freud's inspiration. This schema of analytic communication (Lacan 1993[1955–56]:14), to which Lacan also referred as the 'Schema L', comprises four terms (S, o, o' and O) and two conflicting relations (imaginary and symbolic-unconscious).[20]

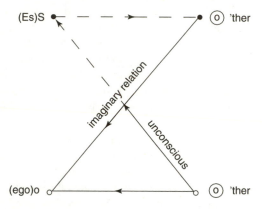

Figure 1 Schema L
Source: J. Lacan, *The Seminar, Book III, The Psychoses*, New York, W. W. Norton, 1993, p. 14.

In this schema the therapeutic alliance between the clinician and the patient in an ego-psychological setting is displayed as an imaginary relation between an ego (o) and another ego (o'). Lacan proclaimed that the majority of contemporary clinicians were viewing the patient as an objectified other whose ego needs 'to gather its strength, to realise itself, to integrate itself' (Lacan 1988c[1954–55]:245). In keeping with his theory of the ego as an imaginary construction, he then argued that the patient's ego 'can only re-encounter and reconstitute itself by way of the fellow being the subject has before him – or behind him' (ibid.:245), which is of course the figure of the analyst. Hence, the patient and the analyst had become allies in an imaginary exchange of egos, leading to the replacement of the patient's former (pathological) identity by the new (healthy) identity of the analyst.[21]

In Lacan's purportedly Freudian alternative, patients had to be approached as subjects with an unconscious, rather than unitary objectified others. In Schema L, the subject (S) is identified with the Freudian Id (*Es*) and the unconscious is emanating from the Other according to a symbolic vector which crosses the imaginary axis. This means that the intervention of the Other (the unknown dimension of the other) is necessary for the revelation of the unconscious. The idea is that if human beings can wonder about the hidden intentions of a fellow being, or if the latter answers their questions in a way which they had never expected, they will also be driven to investigate the (hitherto unconscious) mainspring of their own intentions.[22] Whereas on Lacan's account an ego-psychologist attributed a patient's symptom to a weakness of the ego, or an incomplete self-realization, and remedied this problem by increasing the patient's self-awareness, a truly Freudian analyst defined the symptom as a compromise between unconscious knowledge (the repressed representations) and conscious ignorance. To open up this realm of unconscious knowledge, Lacan posited that the analyst's task is to be somewhere in the place of the Other (Lacan 1993[1955–56]:161).

In various interventions from the early 1950s (1977e[1953]:88; 1988c [1954–55]:246) Lacan specified this task of the analyst as the facilitation of full speech (*parole pleine*) or true speech (*parole vraie*) in the patient. Full speech is opposed to empty speech (*parole vide*), 'where the subject seems to be talking in vain about someone who, even if he were his spitting image, can never become one with the assumption of his desire' (Lacan 1977e[1953]:45). Patients producing empty speech continuously objectify themselves in their words, for example by starting every sentence with 'I think I am a person who . . . ' or by speaking about themselves as objects in the discourse of others, as in 'My best friend says that I am . . . ' Lacan was keen to point out that the identity a patient conjures up in her empty speech can bear a striking resemblance to her actual self-image and the reality perceived by others. Hence, empty speech is not necessarily deceitful speech. Paradoxically, in terms of its correspondence with a factual reality, empty speech might be more 'true' than true speech (Lacan 1966b[1955]:351). For the distinctive characteristic of true speech is not that it represents matters as they really are; its core feature is that it entails a genuine subjective commitment, with a perspective on the future. The truth value of true speech is not related to reality, but to the subject's recognition of the desire which he has hitherto discarded.[23] In Freudian terms, subjective truth should be taken in its historical, rather than its material dimension. In this sense, what 'is at stake in analysis is the advent in the subject of that little reality that this desire sustains in him', whereby the analyst 'guides the subject's discourse towards the realization of his truth' (Lacan 1977e[1953]:68, 93). Patients should finally arrive at the verbalization of what they have kept away from themselves and take responsibility for it, which tallies with Freud's perspective on the goal of analysis as the assumption of one's historical truth.

This facilitation of full speech in the patient is only possible if the analyst is indeed somewhere in the position of the Other. Only in the presence of an unknown Other is the subject able and required to make symbolic commitments, as exemplified in statements such as 'You are my master' or 'You are my husband'.[24] To maintain this position analysts are not allowed to reveal their intentions, much less to present themselves to their patients as familiar others. Analysts are not fellow human beings who fully understand and share their experiences with their therapeutic neighbours.[25] Neither the patient nor the analyst is thus involved in the 'analytic dialogue' as an imaginary object. The analyst is literally the mouthpiece of the patient, to the extent that the analyst is the instrument which enables the patient to make a full statement.[26] In principle this does not imply that analysts ought to remain silent throughout the session on the condition that their interventions are not designed as the staging of an encounter between two egos (Lacan 1988c[1954–55]:245).[27] The analyst's interventions can only have the desired effect of eliciting full speech in the patient if these interventions are themselves paragons of full speech (Lacan 1966b[1955]:359). Again, this does not mean that analysts ought to ensure that their interpretations are demonstrably true, i.e. corresponding with a factual reality, but they must capture the patient's subjective historical truth.[28] Since the process is directed towards the subject of the patient (the acknowledgement of the unconscious drives and desires beyond the ego, which Freud situated in the Id) and analysts themselves function as subjects in the place of the Other (instead of ego-objects for identification), Lacan qualified the entire analytic dialectics as an intersubjective experience.[29]

However, he did not consider it possible for the analytic treatment to deploy itself exclusively on the symbolic axis of the unconscious. From his initial introduction of Schema L, Lacan clarified that no analyst manages to avoid the interference of the imaginary axis. The imaginary interplay between egos is at once an obstacle and a necessary passage in the symbolic progression of psychoanalytic treatment, which is represented in Schema L via the imaginary crossing of the symbolic vector of the unconscious. A close reading of Lacan's argument reveals at least four reasons, two on the side of the analyst and two on the side of the patient, for this unavoidable inflection of the symbolic towards the imaginary.

First, and perhaps most significantly, analysts are not equal to their jobs as subjects in the position of the Other. According to their job description, analysts should be capable of relinquishing their ego, or at least be sufficiently aware of its manifestations to recognize and neutralize them whenever they threaten to intervene – a manœuvre for which their own training analysis should have prepared them. In *Seminar II* Lacan described analysts as 'subjects in whom the ego is absent' (Lacan 1988c [1954–55]:246). In *Seminar III* he argued even more strongly that analysts 'must be dead enough not to be caught up in the imaginary relation' (Lacan 1993[1955–56]:162). And in 'Variations of the Standard Treatment' he asserted that analysts can only be attentive to the full speech of their patients if the mirages of their own narcissism have become transparent (Lacan 1966b[1955]:352). Yet Lacan himself realized that these are theoretical accounts of an ideal situation, since there is 'never a subject without an ego' (Lacan 1988c[1954–55]:246) and since 'the analyst is never fully an analyst, for the simple reason that he is a human being, and that he, too, partakes of the imaginary mechanisms that are obstacles to the passage of speech' (Lacan 1993[1955–56]:162). This difficulty is represented in Schema L on the vector that runs from O to o.

The second reason on the side of the analyst has to do with what Lacan called 'the paradox of the analyst's position' (Lacan 1988b[1953–54]:51). If analysts are supposed to elicit full speech in their patients, they can decide to curb their patients' empty speech by launching interpretations that probe into its hidden aspects. Yet they can hardly do this without relying on their own projections of what is going on in their patients' minds. Hence, when the patients' speech is empty analysts can only intervene effectively by reducing the influence of their own ego to the lowest possible level, that is to say by being 'dead enough', an operation which drives them to silence rather than speech. But when the patients' speech does present an appropriate level of fullness, analysts should keep their interventions at bay in order to avoid disturbing the advancement of this full speech. So, on the one hand analysts cannot really intervene without taking their own ego as measure, whilst on the other hand their full speech is not required! Indeed, if the analysts' task consists in eliciting full speech, it appears that they can only perform it by absenting themselves and remaining silent, every utterance encompassing the danger of a new imaginary alienation. In 'The Freudian Thing', Lacan put it as follows:

> [T]he analyst intervenes concretely in the dialectic of analysis by pretending he is dead, by cadaverizing his position as the Chinese say, either by his silence when he is the Other with a capital O, or by

annulling his own resistance when he is the other with a small o. In either case, and under the respective effects of the symbolic and the imaginary, he makes death present.

(Lacan 1977f[1955]:140)

Third, if analysts too remain subjects endowed with an ego, even after a prolonged analytical training, it is evident that patients undertaking analytical work will not be able to associate freely without objectifying themselves in imaginary identifications with unitary objects. Lacan conceded that even at the end of analysis the subject 'refers to this imaginary unity that is the ego . . . where he knows himself and misrecognizes himself, and which is what he speaks about' (Lacan 1993[1955–56]:161). This ongoing entanglement of the subject with the ego is represented within Schema L in the vector from S to o' (the identifications with the imaginary counterparts on which the ego is based). The emergence of the patient's ego will also reawaken the ego of the analyst, on whose presence it depends during the analytic session. In *Seminar I*, before the actual construction of Schema L, Lacan averred:

> Just when he seems ready to come out with something more authentic, more to the point than he has ever managed to come up with to then, the subject, in some cases, breaks off, and utters a statement, which might be the following – *I am aware all of a sudden of the fact of your presence* . . . the subject himself then feels something like a sharp bend, a sudden turn which causes him to pass from one slope of the discourse to the other, from one aspect of the function of speech to another.
>
> (Lacan 1988b[1953–54]:40)

The experience which Lacan invoked in this passage had already been described by Freud in 'The Dynamics of Transference' (1912b), as an example of how the patient's resistance makes use of the transference, or of how the transference serves resistance. Lacan reinterpreted it as the turn of symbolic transference towards its imaginary avatar, which equals resistance.[30]

Finally, analysts are continuously solicited by their patients to leave their position as an (unknown) Other and to intervene as an ego. In the case of psychotic patients, who are only capable of imaginary transference, the analyst is automatically allocated the place of a transparent, imaginary counterpart.[31] By contrast, neurotic patients are extremely apt at seducing analysts to formulate a judgement, to express an opinion, or to profess a piece of knowledge, which is exactly what the above model (and the mental economy of neurosis) demands them to avoid if they want to be successful. For example, a hysterical patient (or a hystericized patient, for that matter) may engage in lengthy complaints about how he had expected something altogether different from his analyst: answers to his questions, advice on how and what to decide in the usual dilemmas of work and love, concrete recommendations on how to design his future, etc. He may even try to provoke a reaction by stating that he will inevitably be driven to another practitioner if the situation does not change rapidly. Sometimes the challenge is more straightforward, as in the case of a patient who says 'My mother thinks I am a genius and my father is convinced I am a fool. What do you think? Why aren't you saying anything? Since you seem to be unable to make up your mind, you must be a fool yourself.' Depending on the analyst's own narcissism, she will be poised to intervene, in which case the analyst's ego will eclipse her position as a subject. And, of course, if analysts do give their patients concrete advice ('I think you should leave your lover and stay with your husband'), they are bound to discover that the patients will either use it against them, or use it to do exactly the opposite.

Summarizing, it may be said that the main difference between ego-psychology and classical Freudian analysis, as Lacan conceived it during the early 1950s, is not that the former is strengthening the imaginary relationship between ego and (alter) ego, whereas the latter strictly operates within the symbolic framework of subject and Other. The difference is rather that ego-psychologists place their money on ego-building techniques to the detriment of a questioning of the patient's history, whereas Lacan's model aimed to install and explore the symbolic relationship between the subject and the Other, despite the relentless interference of imaginary identifications, both in the patient and the analyst. Not taking the patient's words at face value, much less employing them as building blocks for the construction of a new identity, the analyst's task consisted in bringing the patient to the point where he questions the accepted meaning of words, beliefs and values. In the 'Rome Discourse' Lacan stated that 'the art of the analyst must be to suspend the subject's certainties until their last mirages have been consumed' (Lacan 1977e [1953]:43), so that the subject can make a commitment that is more in accordance with the true nature of her desire.

THE ANALYST AS OBJECT OF DESIRE

Lacan's rekindling of Freud's 'rule of abstinence' as a symbolic, intersubjective relationship between the subject of the analysand and the analyst as Other subject subsisted until the late 1950s. It gave way to an entirely different conception of the analyst's position when Lacan realized that the analyst's functioning as Other subject is not a sufficient guarantee for excluding the occurrence of identifications between analyst and analysand, or for preventing the deterioration of the analytic treatment into a reciprocal working alliance. The following passage from *Seminar V* betrays Lacan's mercurial self-criticism concerning the symbolic relationship between the subject and the Other:

> [T]he distinction between the Other and himself [the subject] is initially the most difficult distinction to make . . . These two modes of ambiguity, these two limits – that which is situated on the imaginary level and the one belonging to the symbolic order, through which desire is founded in the speech of the Other – these two modes of crossing which imply that the subject alienates himself, do not coincide . . . Yet there is always the question as to what happens when these subjects are two of a kind, that is to say, when the subject is supporting itself in the presence of the Other.
>
> (Lacan 1998b[1957–58]:357–358)

Here Lacan acknowledged that a relationship between two subjects, despite one of them being in the position of Other, is as much open to reciprocal solidarity as an imaginary bond between two egos. Although the result may be a symbolic instead of an imaginary identification, it is much the same problem.[32] The issue is illustrated by a common experience of analysts who insist that the patient comply with the rule of free association. The more they demand that the patient comply with the ground rule the more they encounter 'resistance', in the form of a reciprocal demand of the patient that the analyst speak, or a general unwillingness to cooperate.[33] In *Seminar V* Lacan exemplified this by referring to what happens when a mother (as Other subject) demands something of her child (as subject). Before long, the child discovers that its possession of what the Other is asking for equips it with the power to return the question: You want me to give what I have, but I will only give it to you if you are willing to give me what you have first. 'On the level of demand', Lacan stated, 'the subject and the Other are in a situation of reciprocity' (ibid.:359). Seeking to overcome this deadlock, Lacan started to insist on the crucial importance of the Other's desire:

What I would like to draw your attention to, is the function of this desire of the Other, insofar as it makes it possible for the *distinction* between the subject and the Other to establish itself once and for all . . . What needs to be introduced and what is there from the start, latent from the beginning, is that, beyond what the subject demands and what the Other demands from the subject, there is the necessary presence and dimension of what the Other desires.

(ibid.:359, italics added)

In Lacan's theory of the late 1950s, desire originated in the human being's incapability to express its vital, biological needs through the linguistic function of demand. Because human beings grow up in a symbolic world, they are pushed to employ language as a means for conveying their needs to others. A child does not simply act upon its bodily processes when it is hungry, it makes its need clear to an Other by demanding food – whether intentionally and independently, or primarily through the Other's reading of the child's conduct. The same holds for the Other, who does not merely supply the food the child is asking for, but who demands that the child allow itself to be fed (Lacan 1991b[1960–61]:238). Yet when a subject raises its biological need to the level of demand, the need cannot be articulated fully in the signifiers of the subject's language, for language can only inappropriately represent that which is essentially beyond it. Lacan put this discordance between need and demand on a par with Freud's concept of primal repression (Freud 1915d) arguing, in accordance with Freud's idea of the dynamic unconscious, that the repressed inarticulate part of the need will put out a new sprout (*rejeton*), which 'presents itself in man as desire' (Lacan 1977j[1958]:286). Hence, desire is what stems from the leftover need after it has been articulated in the signifiers of a demand.[34]

As if this explanation proved unsatisfactory, Lacan revealed yet another source of desire.[35] Probing further into the nature of human demand, Lacan arrived at the conclusion that a vital need is not the only factor triggering it. Apart from specific objects which can satisfy their primary physiological necessities, people also demand something much more insubstantial, which can be called 'love'. In this case, the object becomes less important than the Other's act of giving it, which the subject perceives as an indication of the Other's affection. When demanding something, a subject is thus not only pressing for the satisfaction of its needs, it is also questioning the love of the Other, even to the extent that the subject will be happy to accept anything as long as it testifies to the Other's loving concern. In this way the subject's demand for what the

Other possesses, an object that is capable of satisfying the subject's needs, is transformed into a demand for what the Other does not possess as an exchangeable object.[36]

Similar to the residue produced by the transformation of a need into a demand, Lacan believed that the transition from the demand for a material object to the demand for love generates a rest. In the demand for love the particularity of the object is annihilated, but the object itself does not disappear.[37] When the demand for an object becomes a demand for love (and, in a sense, demand always already includes this dimension), the object is no longer appreciated for its intrinsic qualities or its use value, but acquires a higher status, incorporating a surplus value.[38] The object in an exchange governed by a demand for love might be something completely useless, indeed it can be 'a piece of shit', but for the partners involved this essentially worthless object will be invaluable as a proof of love. Whereas the demand for love appears to relinquish the objects that feature prominently in the demand for the satisfaction of a need, the former is not a pure negation of the latter, but rather an obliteration (ibid.:287). According to Lacan, the residue of the object, after the annulment of its particularity by the demand for love, constituted the 'absolute condition' for desire:

> [T]his condition indeed brings to a dénouement the aversion which the proof of love has to the satisfaction of a need. Thus desire is neither the appetite for satisfaction, nor the demand for love, but the difference that results from the subtraction of the first from the second, the phenomenon of their splitting (*Spaltung*).
>
> (ibid.:287, translation modified)

The crucial point of this paragraph is that desire, unlike need and demand, never balances towards an object, whether a concrete object of satisfaction or the 'anything and nothing' of love. Contrary to need and demand, desire derives its power from the priceless remainder of an object after it has been accommodated within the symbolic register. In the context of *Seminar V* (1998b[1957–58]), Lacan expressed the same idea when he said that desire is born from the (object of) jouissance that is lost through symbolic castration.[39] Objects functioning in the realms of need and demand have an assuaging, quenching effect, whilst objects in the realm of desire only serve to sustain it. With this conceptualization of desire, as a power beyond need and demand, Lacan revised his original schema of analytic intersubjectivity, newly designating the relationship between patient and analyst as a 'subjective disparity' which revolves around the desire of the analyst.

Lacan's promotion of 'subjective disparity' within analytic treatment coincided with his discussion of transference in *Seminar VIII*. In the opening lesson of this Seminar he explained his decision to introduce the notion of 'subjective disparity' by disclosing his eagerness to find a proper term to describe the opposite of intersubjectivity. Although he himself had advocated intersubjectivity time and again as the only way forward in psychoanalysis, now he could only see the drawbacks of his former prodigy (Lacan 1991b[1960–61]:20–22, 233). As described on p. 70, Lacan had already broached the pitfalls of intersubjectivity in *Seminar V* within the context of a critical discussion on reciprocity. Now, in *Seminar VIII*, he added that transference itself runs counter to intersubjectivity, inasmuch as the position of those involved in a transference relationship is by no means equivalent (ibid.:233).[40] In the 'pseudo-situation' of the analytic treatment – as Lacan described it in *Seminar VIII* – subjective disparity reigns because the patient's demand (for help, advice, happiness, etc.) does not meet a reciprocal demand (for letting oneself be cured) in the analyst. The analyst's policy does not hinge on a demand, but on a specific desire.

The concept of the desire of the analyst appeared for the first time in 'The Direction of the Treatment and the Principles of its Power' (1977i[1958]:252), one of Lacan's most clinically informed writings from the 1950s. Fulminating, yet again, against the deplorable clinical conduct of his contemporaries, Lacan underscored that analysts should be concerned with the direction of the treatment and not with the direction of their patients (ibid.:227). Directing the treatment implied that besides the patient, the analyst too has to pay for what is happening, notably in a triple fashion. First of all, the analyst has to pay the analysand with words taking the form of analytic interpretations.[41] Second, analysts must tolerate their being invested by analysands with all the strengths and weaknesses of the significant others in the analysand's experience. This is what Freud described in 'The Dynamics of Transference' (1912b) as the libidinal cathexis of the analyst by the analysand, through which the analyst is inscribed, *qua* form and contents, within one of the analysand's psychic series. In Lacan's terminology, it meant that an analysand's transference dispossesses the analyst of his identity, and that the analyst's proper handling of the transference entails that he is willing to pay for analysis with his person. Finally, and most significantly, Lacan was also convinced that analysts have to pay with a judgement on the nature of their action, all the more so that to them the precise nature of analytic effectiveness generally remains a mystery too. In 'The Direction of the Treatment' he explained that whereas the first two payments relate to what the analyst says and does, the third corresponds to what the analyst is, i.e. to the analyst's being (Lacan 1977i[1958]:227–228, 250–256).

Loaded with the question as to what an analyst is, Lacan embarked on an investigation of what could possibly lie beyond the technique of psychoanalysis. For what analysts are supposed to say and do in the context of interpretation and transference handling, some technical guidelines can be formulated, yet when it comes to describing what an analyst should be, technical rules are fundamentally inadequate. As I pointed out at the beginning of this chapter, Freud sought solace in a pleiad of imaginative metaphors to answer the question 'What is an analyst?', singling out that of the archaeologist as the most representative trope. Rather than espousing Freud's metaphors, Lacan, for his part, tried to capture their signification within the realm of desire.[42] Not satisfied with the analyst as a clinical archaeologist or a mental health sleuth, Lacan began to explore what really animates these people, adding new and different metaphors to the Freudian list as he went along. In this way, Lacan's concept of the desire of the analyst was born, alongside a profound reflection upon the ethics of psychoanalysis as the necessary counterpart to clinical technique. By situating the most fundamental of analytic policies within the realm of desire and ethics, he at once solved the impasse of reciprocal demands within an intersubjective relationship: the analyst was no longer simply an Other subject but a figure imbued with a specific desire.

But what is this desire of the analyst? Where does it come from and what is it aimed at? If it involves a judgement on the nature of analytic action, what kind of judgement is it? Does the analyst communicate this judgement to the analysand and, if so, how? And how does a concrete analyst experience and sustain this desire during psychoanalytic treatment?

Apropos of the first question, Lacan responded initially, and in his customary mode, by saying what the desire of the analyst should not encompass. Some of these negative definitions followed directly from his previous elaborations. As such, he argued that the desire of the analyst is not a desire to understand the analysand, because the analyst's under-standing will always be illusory and it will inevitably dampen down the production of speech on the side of the patient. In 'The Direction of the Treatment' he wrote: 'To think, it is often better not to understand, and one can gallop through miles of understanding without the least thought being produced' (ibid.:252). The corollary of this first admonition was that the desire of the analyst should neither be a desire to fulfil the analysand's demands – whatever they are and whether implicit or explicit – because responding to these demands can only proceed from an understanding of what they convey (ibid.:254). In light of this ethical principle of non-understanding Lacan later rejuvenated Freud's idea that analysts should suspend their previous knowledge and experience, each time they are confronted with a new case, in order to recognize and reveal its singularity (Freud 1912e:114; 1933a[1932]:173–175). Lacan fully endorsed Freud's opinion, stating that one of the most important matters for psychoanalysis is 'the intentional consolidation in him [the analyst] of his ignorance of each subject who comes to him for analysis, of an ever renewed ignorance that prevents anyone becoming a "case"' (Lacan 1977k[1960]:322).

To the analysand's ignorance, which undergirds both her desire to know the truth about her symptoms and her investment of the analyst with the function of supposed subject of knowing, the analyst is thus held to respond with ignorance too![43] This idea tallies with Lacan's advocacy in *Seminar I* of the analyst's *ignorantia docta* (wise ignorance) as an alternative to the clinical proclamation of knowledge, and follows directly from Freud's observation in 'On Beginning the Treatment' (1913c:141–142) that it is counter-productive to imbue hysterics with the knowledge they consciously lack. However, it is not because the analyst and the analysand proceed from ignorance that their attitude to that ignorance is the same. As Lacan explained in the opening session of *Seminar XX* (1998a[1972–73]:1–2), the analyst's ignorance, his 'I don't want to know anything about it', is perfectly adequate to him, whereas the analysand experiences his ignorance as a burden whose weight can only be reduced by the acquisition of additional knowledge. Moreover, it is not because the analyst refrains from producing knowledge that the analysand will automatically perceive him as stupid, i.e. that he will loose his status as supposed subject of knowing. On the contrary, the analyst hails 'the sublimity of stupidity' (ibid.:13) because he can maintain his position of supposed wisdom more effectively by the enunciation of ostensibly stupid sentences, than by the proclamation of rocket science. This paradox of stupidity (the more one expresses knowledge, the more one is regarded as stupid, and vice versa) and its relation to the maintenance of transference emboldened Lacan on numerous occasions to portray the analyst as a latter-day Socrates or a Western Zen-master.[44]

Even more provocatively, Lacan stated that the desire of the analyst should not be geared towards the advancement of the patient's well-being, let alone the promotion of happiness. Much more than 'The Direction of the Treatment' this theme pervaded Lacan's *Seminar VII, The Ethics of Psychoanalysis*, in which he claimed that analysts who promise their patients a full restoration of their mental, physical and social happiness are simply deluding them with false hopes, despite the fact that happiness may be their patients' one and only demand. To Lacan, the analyst not only does not 'have that Sovereign Good that is asked of him, but he also knows there isn't any' (Lacan 1992[1959–60]:300). Happiness was only one amongst a multitude of values Lacan felt obliged to discard as fraudulent 'analytic ideals' – a proliferous, yet prolific list including also the moral goals of genital sexuality, authenticity, independence and temperateness. This perspective matched Lacan's deep-rooted contempt for the preferential therapeutic goals of psychoanalysis, a view which he deemed fully compatible with that of the founder. For instance, in his 1955 'Variations of the Standard Treatment' he had argued that the analyst is better off without therapeutic ambitions, designating 'health' as a bonus of psychoanalytic treatment:

> Thoroughly warned by Freud to look closely at the effects in his [the analyst's] experience of that whose danger the term *furor sanandi* sufficiently draws the attention to, after all he [the analyst] does not really care to keep up its appearances. If he thus accepts healing as a supplementary benefit of the psychoanalytic treatment, he guards himself against any abuse of the desire to heal . . .
>
> (Lacan 1966b[1955]:324)

In scorning the analyst's 'healing fury' Lacan clearly recalled Freud's assertion in his paper on transference-love (1915a[1914]:171) that a human society needs *furor sanandi* as little as any other type of fanaticism. Applying this principle to his own practice, Freud had actually repeated on various occasions, in private correspondence as well as published writings, that he was not possessed with a desire to heal.[45]

'At every moment', Lacan contended in *Seminar VII*, 'we need to know what our effective relationship is to the desire to do good, to the desire to cure' (Lacan 1992[1959–60]:218). But is there a positive way to define this relationship? After having designated what the desire of the analyst is not, is it possible to name its essential qualities? 'Desire must be taken literally', Lacan proclaimed in 'The Direction of the Treatment' (1977i[1958]:256), which seemed to imply that the desire in question must be contemplated as a restless, objectless yearning, a relentless striving to obtain nothing. So much was at least confirmed in *Seminar VII*, where Lacan compared the analyst's desire to that of Antigone in Sophocles' eponymous play: it concerns a pure desire, a desire for nothing, even a desire for death inasmuch as death is the ultimate non-object (Lacan 1992[1959–60]: 282–283). In Lacan's interpretation, Antigone had succeeded in ridding her desire of all the worldly objects and concerns which foul human desire, in order to follow the course of her desire as a formal ethical duty. Antigone's desire had acceded to the level of a Kantian categorical imperative, with which one complies for no other reason than the naked fact of its imposition.[46] In his ethics of psychoanalysis Lacan accordingly propagated the analysts' mandatory involvement in their practice as categorically desiring beings. The ethical judgement with which analysts have to pay in order to direct their treatment properly concerns the acknowledgement that their action is inhabited by an absolute desire and not, for that matter, by the formulation of demands or the promulgation of moral goals.

Needless to say that an analyst is not born with such a pure desire; his desire is as much governed by 'pathological' objects (in the Kantian sense) and vivid fantasies as that of the majority of people. The analyst's is an 'experienced desire' (ibid.:300–301) which is the result of a fundamental 'mutation in the economy of desire' (Lacan 1991b[1960–61]:220–221) that has occurred during her training analysis. With this 'mutation in the economy of desire', Lacan pointed towards the necessary reduction of the status of the object as a mesmerizing, fascinating otherness in the analysand's fantasy. Since 'being an analyst' also occupies the place of such an object, the upshot was that the candidate who desired to be an analyst was supposed to perform a mutation of that object too, even to the point where it lost all its seductive colours, before he could have access to the pure desire of the analyst. As Lacan conceived it, the desire to be an analyst was as much a hindrance to the emergence of the desire of the analyst as any other 'pathological' desire.[47]

Prima facie, this renewed picture of the analyst seemed to substantiate the popular image of the analyst as somebody who has realized the Stoic ideal of apathy. Stoic wisdom, as exemplified in the works of Epictetus and Seneca, demands *sustine et abstine* (people should endure what they are supposed to do and refrain from doing anything else) whilst simultaneously exonerating people from all blame when they exercise their power or express their desire.[48] Isn't this an accurate representation of the analyst acting upon pure desire? Aren't analysts indeed expected to fulfil their duty without reproaching their patients for indulging in the satisfaction of their unconscious desires? At the end of *Seminar VII* Lacan suggested, albeit implicitly, that the philosophical position of Stoicism cannot be brought in line with the ethics of psychoanalysis. In Stoically tolerating the Other's betrayal of confidence, or the mere whimsicality of the Other's desire, analysts give ground relative to their own desire, in which case they do not act in accordance with the ethical standards of their practice (Lacan 1992[1959–60]:320–321). More fundamentally,

Lacan intimated that analysts who adopt the Stoic ideal of apathy silently associate themselves with the morality of the master/tyrant and, more generally, with the reigning discourse of power.[49] This does not mean that they agree with the Other's limitless enjoyment; they merely believe that once the Other has discovered the meaning of its action, it will automatically repent.

Remarkably, this principle is quite similar to Freud's conviction that recovery will follow spontaneously once the patient's historical truth (the true meaning of the symptoms) has been excavated, according to the paradigm of archaeological sleuthing. Yet Lacan was deeply sceptical about the expected outcome:

> The question is, once it is over, once the return to the meaning of an action has been accomplished, once the deep meaning has been liberated – that is to say, separated out through a catharsis in the sense of decantation – will everything work out right by itself? Or, to be more precise, will there be nothing but goodness?
>
> (ibid.:312)

Whatever their philosophy may dictate, Stoics should not rest assured that their apathy will have a redemptive effect, partly because the Other might just sustain its jouissance, partly because the Other might try to eradicate its repentance by neutralizing the one who instilled it.[50] In refusing to be the guarantees of the jouissance of the Other, in declining to provide their patients with the satisfaction they desperately miss, analysts at once refrain from adopting the position of the pervert, to which the nature of their practice surreptitiously invites them. Put differently, to the extent that analysts neither advocate, nor condone a 'discourse of the right to jouissance', they withstand the looming threat of becoming institutionalized perverts. This is a decisive criterion for differentiating between an analyst and a pervert, whose positions with respect to the fantasy are otherwise remarkably similar.[51]

During the early 1960s, Lacan realized that grounding the desire of the analyst merely in Kant's categorical imperative clears the path for its return as a ruthless, moral tyranny of power. As he demonstrated in 'Kant with Sade' (1989a[1962]), the Sadian universe of radical evil is strictly congruent with the Kantian universe of detached morality.[52] At the end of *Seminar XI*, Lacan reiterated that for Kant 'the moral law . . . is simply desire in its pure state', yet now adding that:

> [it] culminates in the sacrifice, strictly speaking, of everything that is the object of love in one's human tenderness – I would say, not only

in the rejection of the pathological object, but also in its sacrifice and murder. That is why I wrote 'Kant avec Sade'.

(Lacan 1977b[1964]:275–276)

Because the desire of the analyst cannot possibly coincide with an institutionalized, systematic extermination of all goods, Lacan was forced to modify his earlier view on the purity of the analyst's desire. Once the obscene underside of Kant's moral law exposed, he ended his *Seminar XI* with the statement: 'The analyst's desire is not a pure desire. It is a desire to obtain absolute difference' (ibid.:276). Compared to previous definitions, the analyst's desire emerged here not as a desire for nothing, but as a structural, symbolic force which recognizes and sustains the other as Other. Instead of manœuvring the analysands into a situation where they can identify with their analyst, analysts had to manœuvre themselves into a position which enabled their analysands to dis-identify, to discover their desire in its modulation by the desire of the Other, and to avow that desire in its essential nothingness. Lacan believed that this process would only unfold if the analyst puts himself into the position of the support of object *a*, not an object with which the analysands can satisfy their desire, but an object which causes it (ibid.:273).

The difference between Lacan's 1964 conception of the position of the analyst and his earlier view on the topic could not have been more radical. Here the analyst was no longer expected to act as an Other subject in an intersubjective relationship with the analysand, but as an object-cause within a bond marked by subjective disparity. As the support of object *a* within this new bond, the analyst was neither expected to understand the analysand's desire, nor to think about what could possibly be causing it, to the extent that such thinking could only proceed from the illusory constraints of the analyst's own fantasy.[53]

If thinking about the cause of the analysand's desire was not an appropriate solution, then perhaps being this cause was a better one, but how could an analyst ever incarnate an object devoid of substance? Furthermore, being an object *a*, in so far as it is fully achievable, seemed to coincide with a state of jouissance, which one could hardly deem compatible with the desire of the analyst. In a small yet instructive text from the late 1960s, Lacan explained the difficulty of the analyst's position in the following terms:

> The analysand is the one who manages to realize that his 'I think' is an alienation, that is to say who discovers the fantasy as the motor of psychic reality, that of the divided subject. He can only do that by

granting the analyst the function of (*a*), which he [the analyst] would not be capable of being without vanishing immediately. Hence, the analyst ought to know that, far from being the measure of reality, he only clears the ground for the subject's truth by offering himself as support of this disbeing [*désêtre*] . . . Well then, this is where the psychoanalyst finds himself in an untenable position: an alienation conditioned by an 'I am' whose own condition . . . is an 'I am not thinking', reinforced by the addition that . . . he [the analyst] knows it.

(Lacan 1968a[1967]:59)

As one can derive from this paragraph, Lacan's answer to the question as to what analysts should do or be with regard to their supporting of the object *a* highlighted the analysts' disbeing (*désêtre*), their semblance of being object *a*. This position allows them to function as object *a* for the analysand whilst retaining their desire as analysts. Contrary to what he had claimed in 'The Direction of the Treatment', Lacan now stressed that analysts should not act with their being, but with their 'disbeing', and it is easy to see that this guideline did not make the analyst's position more feasible. I will explore the issue further in the final part of this chapter, when discussing Freud's take on psychoanalysis as an impossible profession and Lacan's integration of this impossibility in his formula of the discourse of the analyst.

LACAN'S LOGICAL TIME MACHINE

At this stage, it is necessary to return to the Freudian goals of psychoanalysis and their associated deadlock, in order to show how Lacan reformulated these goals following his own changing perspectives on the position of the analyst.

In the third session of *Seminar XI*, within the context of an inquiry into the ontological status of the unconscious, Lacan revealed what he believed to be a contradiction in Freud's description of the unconscious (Lacan 1977b[1964]:31–32). On the one hand, Freud had stressed on various occasions (Freud 1912b:108; 1915e:187; 1920g:28) that unconscious processes are not structured according to a temporal order (*Zeitlosigkeit*), whereas on the other hand he had noted that repressed unconscious impulses do not change over time (Freud 1920g:28; 1933a[1932]:73–74). To Lacan, Freud's second statement implied that a repressed unconscious impulse, which he dubbed 'desire', does function according to a particular temporal order, notably the order of unvarying duration, which evidently contradicts the first claim on the absence of time in the unconscious. To solve this problem, Lacan proposed a distinction between two kinds of temporal processes: a modality according to which objects are character- ized by duration – a short or prolonged existence over time – and a logical modality, in which the existence of an object can only be established with hindsight, as an inference from the logical succession of two moments (Lacan 1977b[1964]:32).

To illustrate how this modality of logical time functions, Lacan referred to a puzzle he had analysed in an article of 1945 (1988a[1945]). The story runs as follows. A prison governor explains to three prisoners that he wants to set one of them free without taking responsibility for who it shall be. He shows the inmates three white and two black disks, telling them that he will pin one of these five disks between their shoulders, so that each will be able to see the colour of the disk on the back of the two others, but not the colour of his own. He also emphasizes that they are not allowed to mirror themselves nor to engage in conversation, the latter activity running counter to their own interest. The first prisoner who thinks he has figured out the nature of his colour and who can explain how he has arrived at the conclusion will be released.[54]

It goes without saying that the evil governor attaches a white disk to each prisoner's back, thus putting them in the same position.[55] From the moment the exercise starts, each prisoner sees two white disks, which is likely to stir bewilderment, confusion and anxiety. This is what Lacan called 'the instant of the glance' (*l'instant du regard*) (ibid.:206). What happens next is difficult to grasp, yet the prisoner who succeeds in deducing the colour of his disk correctly – 'the moment of concluding' (*le moment de conclure*) in Lacan's terminology – can claim, in retrospect, that the time between these two moments (of seeing and concluding) was taken up by a fruitful 'time for comprehending' (*temps pour comprendre*). Not until the final assertion ('I am black', 'I am white') can the existence of genuine understanding be substantiated and measured in its quality of understanding.[56]

Consequently, the ontological status of what is situated between the instant of the glance and the moment of concluding is highly peculiar. As long as the moment of concluding has not occurred, one cannot be sure that comprehending (the fruitful production of knowledge) exists at all, whereas from the moment a conclusion is reached, comprehending exists no more, relegated as it is to a past experience.

To Lacan, logical time offered a new explanation of how the uncon- scious operates temporally. Disputing Freud's claim that the unconscious is not marked by a temporal order, he argued that it may be impossible to 'measure' the unconscious in terms of duration over time, but that its existence can be substantiated as a logical inference. Like the time for comprehending in the story of the three prisoners, the unconscious thus acquired the peculiar ontological status – although Lacan preferred to call it 'pre-ontological' or 'ontic' – of neither being, nor non-being (Lacan 1977b[1964]:29, 31). Throughout *Seminar XI* he launched a range of terms to capture this status, from the unrealized to the function of limbo (ibid.: 30). In 'Position of the Unconscious', a text contemporary to *Seminar XI*, he even compared the unconscious to a cave where one can never arrive before closing-time and whose gate only opens when somebody knocks from the inside (Lacan 1995a[1964]:267).

With this definition of the unconscious as an elusive, unrealized structure in mind, Lacan returned to the clinical impasse of Freudian analysis. To Freud, remembering reached its limit in the unconscious striving for repetition; a process inherent to the unconscious vehemently opposes the analytic retrieval of repressed impulses and the ensuing reduction of their pathogenic influence. In Lacan's reinterpretation of these dynamics, repetition did no longer constitute an insuperable problem for the progression of psychoanalytic treatment, or a factor whose influence psychoanalysts should try to neutralize. Whereas Freud had argued that repetition symbolizes the inertia of unconscious processes and the imminent failure of the analytic enterprise, Lacan refused to conceptualize repetition as the evil counterpart of remembering. For example, in *Seminar XI* he pointed out:

> Remembering always involves a limit. And, no doubt, it can be obtained more completely by other ways than analysis . . . It is here that we must distinguish the scope of these two directions, remembering and repetition. From the one to the other, there is no more temporal orientation than there is reversibility. It is simply that they are not commutative – to begin by remembering in order to deal with the resistances of repetition is not the same thing as to begin by repetition in order to tackle remembering.
>
> (Lacan 1977b[1964]:40)

In highlighting the non-commutativity of the relationship between remembering and repetition, Lacan claimed that repetition is an essential feature of the unconscious whose power cannot be diminished by encouraging the analysand to remember, although a momentary standstill of the repetitive cycle may induce recollection.[57]

Lacan had already extrapolated Freud's thesis that repetition is inherent to the unconscious, despite being beyond the pleasure principle, in *Seminar II*, in which he had broached the linguistic organization of the unconscious:

> [T]he unconscious is the discourse of the other. This discourse of the other is not the discourse of the abstract other, of the other in the dyad, of my correspondent, nor even of my slave, it is the discourse of the circuit in which I am integrated. I am one of its links. It is the discourse of my father for instance, in so far as my father made mistakes which I am absolutely condemned to reproduce . . . That's what the need for repetition is, as we see it emerge beyond the pleasure principle. It vacillates beyond all the biological mechanisms of equilibration, of harmonisation and of agreement. It is only introduced by the register of language, by the function of the symbol, by the problematic of the question within the human order.
>
> (Lacan 1988c[1954–55]:89–90)

Repetition appears not as an obscure unconscious mechanism which puts human beings continuously under the infernal spell of pain, ultimately driving them towards self-destruction, but as an irreducible aspect of the symbolic embedment of the unconscious. Like the transmission of signals within an electronic circuit, signifiers circulate within the symbolic network of the unconscious, which is what Lacan dubbed 'repetition automatism' (*automatisme de répétition*) (Lacan 1972[1956]:39). The replacement of Freud's 'compulsion' with the new 'automation' signals the self-regulating quality of the process.[58] The pre-eminent clinical implication of this idea is that every analytic attempt at countering repetition unavoidably runs aground on the durability of the unconscious. Since repetition is part and parcel of the symbolically structured unconscious and psychoanalysis cannot lay claim to eradicating the unconscious, the reign of repetition must remain unblemished. This insight prompted Lacan to take issue with the envisaged reintegration of the patient's life history via an induced verbalization of its censored chapters, notably Freud's own view on the goal of psychoanalysis which he himself had embraced during the early 1950s (Lacan 1977e[1953]:46–48).

In *Seminar XI*, Lacan re-examined these dynamics, relativizing his own previous propositions on the signifier as object of repetition. Two central issues were at stake. First, what is the nature of the event that is being repeated? And second, what is responsible for the process of repetition itself? To answer these questions, Lacan mustered the notions of *tuchè* and *automaton* from the second book of Aristotle's *Physics*

(1996:42–48). *Tuchè* literally means 'accident' or 'chance', as in 'something which happens by accident' or 'a chance encounter', yet the term also conveys 'luck' and 'fortune', as in 'I was lucky enough to escape' or 'I was fortunate to have him around'. Each of these meanings points towards uncontrollable circumstances, events which a human being cannot foresee.[59] Lacan redefined *tuchè* in his own nomenclature as an encounter with the real, and designated it as the object of repetition (Lacan 1977b[1964]:69). Whereas Lacan's concept of the real had scarcely outweighed that of common-sense reality during the first ten years of his seminar, he now considered it to be the equivalent of the impossible (ibid.:167). As an encounter with the real, an accident always entails the emergence of the impossible, because the subject never expects the event in question to happen. Since it is impossible to prepare oneself for what happens by accident, Lacan also claimed that encounters with the real are inherently missed and inescapably traumatic (ibid.:55). The event itself can be either pleasurable (*eutuchia*, good fortune) or unpleasurable (*dustuchia*, bad fortune), but this has no bearing whatsoever on its devastating impact. Encounters with the real therefore operate beyond good and bad or, in Freudian terms, beyond the pleasure principle (ibid.:53–54).

Having defined the object of repetition as *tuchè*, an essentially traumatic encounter with the real, Lacan then employed Aristotle's term *automaton* to describe the 'engine' of repetition (ibid.:52). *Automaton* is usually rendered as 'spontaneity' in English translations of Aristotle's *Physics*, a term whose meaning is not too far removed from that of the transliteration 'automatism'. Both 'spontaneous' and 'automatic' indicate that something in the nature of the event itself triggered its occurrence, as in 'spontaneous combustion'. In Lacan's discourse *automaton* coincided with the insistence of the network of signifiers and with Freud's pleasure principle (ibid.:54). This seemingly abstruse connection is fairly easy to understand when taking into account that the transition from 'chance encounter' to 'repetition' involves a transformation of 'contingency' into 'necessity'. Such a transformation can only take place if a de-randomizing operator is capable of reducing the chance element. In other words, for an (unfortunate or lucky) accident to leave an indelible mark, for a trauma to induce ineradicable mental and or physical scars, something must have transformed the missed encounter into unavoidable destiny. Lacan believed that the symbolic order, the network of signifiers functioning in the unconscious, constitutes the powerhouse of this transformation. Without a symbolic structure, however simple or complicated it may be, fate will never catch up with people after they have been the victim of an encounter with the real.[60]

Lacan's analysis of the object and engine of repetition defied Freud's own views on repetition in at least four respects. First, whereas repetition had appeared to Freud as a stubborn resistance to remembering, in Lacan's theory it followed an 'automatic' process based on a real encounter and a symbolic machinery. Second, whilst Freud had situated repetition entirely beyond the pleasure principle, Lacan only assigned the object of repetition to this 'beyond', situating the engine firmly within the boundaries of the pleasure principle. Third, whereas Freud had studied repetition mainly on the level of behavioural acts (as opposed to verbal productions), Lacan conceived repetition as a process strictly belonging to the network of signifiers and thus to the structure of language. In Lacan's account, every repetitive event, whether verbal (digital) or behavioural (analogous), had a symbolic status. Fourth, whilst Freud had remained convinced that the stream of repetition could be embanked, igniting a partial liberation of the pathogenic impulses and their reintegration into the patient's history as past events, Lacan posited that repetition, being an essential function of the symbolic order, cannot be cancelled out.

This does not imply that psychic change is altogether impossible within Lacan's conception of analytic treatment. It simply means that psychic change needs to be situated on an entirely different level. Whereas Freud believed he could dismantle the unconscious machinery of repetition with the lever of remembering, Lacan set out to bring the endless circulation of traumatic events within the machine's memory to a halt by modifying the structure of the machine itself. Indeed, if we accept that the unconscious operates as a pre-ontological, permanently inchoate structure, in accordance with the principle of logical time, and if we also acknowledge that repetition is governed by the network of signifiers, a huge arsenal of new opportunities for psychic change is opened.

Starting with the threefold structure of logical time, the story of the three prisoners makes clear that the moment of concluding, through which the preceding 'time for comprehending' becomes meaningful, is not a moment of certainty. When one of the prisoners finally decides that he is white, the only criterion he can rely on for making that decision is the hesitation, or perhaps the indecisiveness of the two other prisoners, which is of course not a reliable criterion. Hence, on the basis of what he has concocted during the interval, the prisoner cannot be absolutely certain about the truth of his decision. At the moment of concluding, he can only anticipate its truth value. When the director eventually reveals to the prisoner that his disk is white, it will prove to him that he has been correct in assuming that the hesitation of the other prisoners was proof of his being white. In case his disk turns out to be black, it will prove to him that he had erroneously interpreted the hesitation of the others, or that his time for comprehending was not about comprehending at all.

As formations of the unconscious, symptoms are also structured along these lines of logical time. Rather than being controlled by a historical event, the truth of a symptom – including its very status of symptom – is pending, which encouraged Lacan to produce the pun that the reality of the subject is always *en souffrance*, that is to say both 'in a state of suffering' and 'in abeyance' (ibid.:56). Due to the fact that the truth of a symptom depends on something occurring in the future, Lacan exchanged the Freudian 'present perfect tense' for a 'future perfect tense' (*futur antérieur*). The gist of this idea was already contained in a paragraph from his 'Rome Discourse':

> What is realized in my history is not the past definite of what was, since it is no more, or even the present perfect of what has been in what I am, but the future perfect of what I shall have been for what I am in the process of becoming.
>
> (Lacan 1977e[1953]:86, translation modified)

Instead of the classical analytic question 'What has happened to me (during my childhood) that could possibly explain my present misery?', the Lacanian analyst ushers the patient to ask 'What is going to happen to me that will explain both my current situation and my life-history?'. For the analysand, this Lacanian strategy implies that he is freed from the deterministic historical truth and introduced into a new realm of freedom. Whereas in a Freudian setting analysands cannot alter the pathogenic impact of the circumstances they have been subjected to, Lacanian analysands are being given the keys to their own destiny, since the pathogenic impact of an event is dependent upon the future, whose face has evidently not been decided upon. Rather than reducing the impact of traumatic events by liberating them from their historical dungeons and relocating them into a remote, innocuous past, the Lacanian analyst is thus held to liberate history as such by ensuring that its meaning can depend on the future.

A further possibility of change resides in Lacan's assertion that repetition is part and parcel of the network of signifiers. As an organization of innumerable discrete elements, the symbolic order does not represent a closed circuit characterized by stability, inertia and linear causality. Each signifier can contribute to the organization of the symbolic order, a particular series of signifiers can spark off a whole range of subsequent signifiers, one signifier can originate in a variety of previous signifiers, and there is a continuous effect of 'retro-version' (feedback) whereby every signifier is simultaneously the cause and the effect of another signifier (Lacan 1977k[1960]:306). The rise and development of cybernetics during the 1950s inspired Lacan to model this functioning of the symbolic order on the patterns of interaction within natural and artificial systems as described by Norbert Wiener, Ludwig von Bertalanffy and others. The results of cybernetics informed Lacan's *Seminar II* (1988c[1954–55]: 294–308), especially his reading of the itinerary of the letter in Poe's story of 'The Purloined Letter' (1972[1956]), but they continued to support his descriptions of the symbolic order, as well as his graphical representations of unconscious processes.[61]

Because the symbolic order operates according to the principles of an open system, its patterns of repetition are not inherently durable. When durable patterns do occur, it is due to an installed impermeability, an inflexible obduracy, or what could perhaps also be dubbed 'network sclerosis'. Hence, enduring patterns of repetition only come into operation when something (an accident, an encounter with the real) has been sedimented into a sclerotic nucleus. Countering these sclerotic nuclei implies that their force is being weakened to the point where their constitutive parts re-enter a relationship with the other components of the network.

Strange as it may seem, this is exactly what the Lacanian analyst is held to do, at least with neurotics and perverts.[62] Dissolving coagulated centres of signification, undermining the vicious circle of recurrent combinations of signifiers, opening up a space of desire between age-old patterns of demand and complaint, and urging the analysand to avow this desire, the Lacanian analyst operates on the network of signifiers in light of the production of something new. Unlike the Freudian analyst, the Lacanian practitioner does not engage in archaeological sleuthing. Within a Lacanian analytic format, change is not to be expected from plumbing the depths of the psyche – as Freud himself was forced to confess now and again – but only from the reorganization of the symbolic system. To the extent that Freudian analysis can be associated with 'depth psychology', Lacanian practice is therefore extremely 'superficial'.[63]

When faced with psychotic patients, whether in a residential setting or in private practice, Lacanian analysts have also espoused the ethical principle according to which their clinical practice is governed by a desire to obtain absolute difference, and not by the imposition of rules or the promise of happiness. Their strength of purpose reflects a strict adherence to the idea that a treatment can only be called psychoanalysis if its fundamental ethical principle is acknowledged. As far as the analysand's 'avowal of desire' is concerned – the envisaged goal of a Lacanian analytic process – psychotic patients are not regarded as being capable of achieving this aim, owing to the fact that desire is an outcome of the psychic integration of the symbolic order, an effect of the symbolic castration which the psychotic, according to Lacanian theory, has not undergone. Since the three mental structures of psychosis, neurosis and perversion are defined as mutually exclusive categories, trying to neuroticize psychotics by stimulating this symbolic castration is a futile enterprise.

None the less, Lacanian analysts have deployed a plethora of alternative strategies to relieve psychotic suffering, encouraged by Lacan's directive that the analyst must not back away from psychosis (Lacan 1977l:12). In this way, Lacanians have, for example, argued that an analyst working with psychotics should adopt the position of a detached secretary (Lacan 1993[1955–56]:206) or a silent witness who registers the patients' words whilst prompting them to elaborate their visions of the world, in order to accelerate their construction of a solid and stable delusion (Soler 1987). In keeping with Freud's propositions on the stabilizing function of Schreber's delusion (Freud 1911c[1910]:71), these Lacanians believe that the construction of a balanced delusional system has a tranquillizing effect on the patient's mind, facilitating reintegration into society. Relying on Lacan's promotion, in his year-long seminar on Joyce (Lacan 1976–77 [1975–76]), of the term 'suppletion' (*suppléance*) as an umbrella for a variety of phenomena preventing the outbreak of psychosis or stabilizing the psychotic breakdown, Lacanian analysts have also advocated the installation and/or maintenance of suppletions as a possible analytic goal in the treatment of psychotics (Brousse 1988; Liart 1988; Stevens 1988). These suppletions can be imaginary (in the form of identifications leading to the formation of a new ego), symbolic (through writing and fine art) or real (via so-called psychosomatic phenomena). In general they serve as limitations of the psychotic's overwhelming intrusive enjoyment, enabling him to lead a relatively decent social life, whether before the psychosis has become manifest or after the actual outbreak.[64]

In trying to overcome the deadlock of Freudian analysis Lacan thus developed a clinical framework that is less deterministic, for including more radical options of freedom, less historical, for strictly future-orientated, and less restrictive, for also accommodating psychotic patients.[65] Does this make the analyst's task easier, or less impossible than that of the Freudian clinician? Does Lacan's logical time-machine make analysts feel more at home within the constraints of their clinical practice? In order to answer these questions we must return to the concepts Lacan coined during the late 1960s as the theoretical cornerstones of the analyst's position: the desire of the analyst, object *a* and disbeing.

THE IMPOSSIBLE ART OF PSYCHOANALYSIS

Once the purity of the analyst's desire had exploded at the end of *Seminar XI*, Lacan started to investigate the analyst's relation with the object *a* (the cause of the analysand's desire), which the analyst was expected to support in order to elicit (rather than mould or dampen down) the desire of the analysand. What could it possibly mean to be the support of object *a*? Lacan rejected vigorously all the obvious solutions: analysts must try to understand what the cause of the analysand's desire is and convey their understanding, analysts must interpret this cause, analysts must incarnate it. As the only possible alternative, he eventually came up with the idea that the analyst's desire must be to 'disbe' the object *a*, i.e. to be a semblance of the object *a*.

In 1967, Lacan admitted that this is not exactly a tenable position (Lacan 1968a[1967]:59). Yet he recalled that at the end of his career the founder of psychoanalysis had described his invention as an impossible profession too. For in 'Analysis Terminable and Interminable', Freud had written:

> [L]et us pause for a moment to assure the analyst that he has our sincere sympathy in the very exacting demands he has to fulfil in carrying out his activities. It almost looks as if analysis were the third of those 'impossible' professions in which one can be sure beforehand of achieving unsatisfying results. The other two, which have been known much longer, are education and government.
>
> (Freud 1937c:248)

This gloss on the three impossible professions should not be read as a statement in which the notion of impossibility covers a specific psycho-analytic meaning. For impossibility is not a Freudian concept. Moreover, from Freud's reference to the 'impossible professions' in his preface to August Aichhorn's *Wayward Youth* (Freud 1925f), it can be inferred that the entire expression constituted some kind of German commonplace rather than a Freudian invention in its own right. In this preface Freud had conceded: 'From an early period on, I have adopted the joke of the three impossible professions – as there are: educating, healing and governing – and I was also greatly preoccupied with the means of these assignments' (ibid.:273).

A comparison between this mention and the 1937 one reveals that Freud at one stage substituted the analytic profession for the healing profession while keeping the two other professions unaltered. This substitution may be interpreted in at least two different ways. First, one could argue that in 1937 Freud ultimately acknowledged that healing and analysing are the same, that nobody is healed if not subjected to the process of analysis, although both practices are fundamentally impossible. Second, it could be said that Freud finally considered healing to be an altogether possible achievement and therefore out of place within the series of impossible professions, filling the empty space with psychoanalysis. Contrary to the first interpretation, healing is here essentially different from analysing, the former being possible and the latter impossible.

Proceeding from Lacan's conclusion concerning the untenable position of the analyst and his formalization of the analyst's discourse during the late 1960s, I shall argue in favour of yet a third interpretation, saying that healing and analysing are both impossible, but that the impossibility is not the same due to a different position of the agencies. It will appear then that the impossibility of psychoanalysis is highly specific and more related to the position of the analyst than to the analytic process as such.

Impossibility gained momentum in Lacan's works from the mid-1960s onwards. After its initial alignment with the real in *Seminar XI* (1977b [1964]:167) the impossible gradually achieved currency as a central Lacanian concept, defined in *Seminar XX* as 'what does not stop not being written' (Lacan 1998a[1972–73]:59, 94). Although the notion had figured in Freud's 'joke' of the three professions, Lacan did not revive 'impossibility' through the centralization of a marginal Freudian term, as he had done previously with the notion of foreclosure (*Verwerfung*), but by introducing the categories of modal logic into psychoanalytic theory.[66]

One of the seminal texts in which Lacan defined psychoanalytic practice on the basis of an impossibility is the transcript of the opening session of *Seminar XIII, The Object of Psychoanalysis* (1965–66), which was published separately as 'Science and Truth' (1989b[1965]). Here Lacan readdressed the vexed issue with which he had opened and closed his *Seminar XI* in 1964: 'Is psychoanalysis a science?' (Lacan 1977b [1964]:7, 264). In 'Science and Truth', his answer to this question was not only much more elaborate than in *Seminar XI*, it also left little doubt as to the exact position of psychoanalysis *vis-à-vis* science. Whereas in *Seminar XI* Lacan had drawn attention to the 'ambiguity that persists in the question as to what in psychoanalysis is or is not reducible to science' (ibid.:265), in 'Science and Truth' he distinguished sharply between psychoanalysis and science on the basis of their differential relation to the function of truth as cause. Finding support, once again, in the second book of Aristotle's *Physics* (1996:38–42), Lacan argued that science is predicated upon truth as a formal cause, whereas psychoanalysis encompasses truth as a material cause.[67]

In science, Lacan intimated, the nature of a process and its various components is represented in a formal law, such as $E = mc^2$, which is itself the result of extensive empirical research or experimental testing. Scientists use these formulas to explain why certain things happen the way they do, which tallies with Aristotle's description of a formal cause:

> A second way in which the word [cause] is used is for the form or pattern (i.e. the formula for what a thing is, both specifically and generically, and the terms which play a part in the formula). For example, the ratio 2:1, and number in general, cause the octave.
>
> (Aristotle 1996:39)

Lacan proclaimed that in science truth functions as a formal cause because truth is the quality assigned to properly developed scientific laws (Lacan 1989b[1965]:22). Scientific formulas stemming from controlled observations or carefully conducted experiments are believed to be true (generally or under specific circumstances), and their truth value indicates the extent to which they can be used to explain certain events. Put differently, the extent to which a formula explains (causes) a certain phenomenon provides an indication of the formula's truth.

In psychoanalysis, however, truth functions as a material cause and the materiality is conditioned by the signifier (ibid.:22–23). To understand Lacan's point, one should note that for Aristotle the material cause was an answer to the question 'What is this thing made of?' rather than 'Why and how has this thing come about?'. In claiming that psychoanalytic truth functions as a material cause by means of the signifier, Lacan thus argued that in psychoanalysis the truth of an event (say, a symptom) is always embedded in the symbolic order; it is made of signifiers, so to speak. As he had already tried to demonstrate via the rhetorical figure of a prosopopea ('I, truth, will speak') to a bemused audience of Viennese psychoanalysts in 1955 (Lacan 1977f[1955]:121–123), Lacan contended that psycho-analysts could only proceed from the idea that the truth is something which speaks internally and not, as scientists claim, something 'out there' which is silent and simply waiting to be laid down in formal knowledge.[68] Yet assuming that the truth speaks implies that it is impossible to develop a knowledge which represents this truth fully and adequately, for knowledge also takes root in language and there is no language through which the truth does not speak.[69]

Hence the first and foremost impossibility in psychoanalysis: it is impossible to cover truth by relying on knowledge, whether the knowledge is that incorporated and acted on by the analyst or that produced by the analysand. In yet another piece of bravado, Lacan summarized his thesis as follows in the opening paragraph of *Television*:

> I always speak the truth. Not the whole truth, because there's no way, to say it all. Saying it all is literally impossible: words fail. Yet it's through this very impossibility that the truth holds onto the real.
>
> (Lacan 1990d[1973]:3)

Due to this epistemological impossibility, psychoanalysis is more akin to art than science. Freud would have been quite reluctant to accept such a designation, because in his view psychoanalysis had to be based on truthfulness and the eradication of semblance and deceit – art only generating illusions.[70] Lacan however had favoured a conception of 'psychoanalysis as art' from the very start of his teachings. For instance, in the 1953 lecture 'The Neurotic's Individual Myth', he prepared his audience of philosophers for his new interpretation of the Rat Man by broaching the contentious issue as to whether psychoanalysis is a science. His answer could not have been more categorical:

> It is often said that psychoanalysis is not, strictly speaking, a science, which seems to imply by contrast that it is quite simply an art. That is erroneous if one takes it to mean that psychoanalysis is only a technique, an operational method, an aggregate to formulas. But it is not erroneous if you use this word *art* in the sense in which it was used in the Middle Ages to speak of the liberal arts – that series going from astronomy to dialectic by way of arithmetic, geometry, music, and grammar.
>
> (Lacan 1979[1953]:406)

Lacan claimed that the medieval 'liberal arts' distinguish themselves from the sciences due to their 'fundamental relation to human proportion', a relation which is 'implied pre-eminently in the use of speech' (ibid.:406). His ensuing assertion on the singular status of psychoanalysis as a fundamental art clearly foreshadowed his formulation on psychoanalytic truth as a material cause in 'Science and Truth':

> It is in this respect that analytic experience is not definitively objectifiable. It always implies within itself the emergence of a truth

that cannot be said, since what constitutes truth is speech, and then you would have in some way to say speech itself which is exactly what cannot be said in its function as speech.

(ibid.:406)

With the concept of the impossible established, Lacan returned to Freud's three impossible professions, in order to situate them with regard to his theory of the four discourses. In 1970 Lacan was interviewed on the topic of his theoretical contributions to psychoanalysis by the academic Robert Georgin, whom he described contemptuously as 'a funny Belgian who has asked me some questions' (Lacan 1991a[1969–70]:213).[71] Part of the interview was first broadcasted by the French-speaking official Belgian radio station and afterwards also by the official French station. 'Radiophonie' (1970), the text of Lacan's carefully prepared answers, constitutes one of his most important later works.[72] Lacan's answer to Georgin's seventh question, which was never on the air, is of particular significance here. The question ran as follows:

Governing, educating and psychoanalysing are three untenable challenges. None the less, it is necessary for the psychoanalyst to commit himself to this perpetual dispute of every discourse, especially his own. The psychoanalyst clings to a knowledge – the analytic knowledge – which he disputes by definition. How do you solve – or not – this contradiction? Status of the impossible? The impossible, is it the real?

(ibid.:96)

Endorsing the equivalence of the impossible and the real, Lacan emphasized that it is rather premature to state that the three Freudian challenges are impossible and therefore real. Instead of defining the practices of government, education and psychoanalysis as equally and indistinctively impossible, Lacan posited that they each comprise a specific impossibility, based on a specific impotence, as illustrated in his formulas of the four discourses.[73]

To substantiate these differing impossibilities, he pointed out that the discourse of the analyst transforms the impossibility of the discourse of the master into impotence (*impuissance*), and its impotence into impossibility. This transformation becomes clear when comparing the formulas of the discourse of the master and the discourse of the analyst, which Lacan introduced in the first session of *Seminar XVII* (1991a [1969–70]:9–27).

$$
\frac{S_1}{\text{\$}} \; \rightarrow \; \frac{S_2}{//\;\; a} \qquad\qquad \frac{a}{S_2} \; \rightarrow \; \frac{\text{\$}}{//\;\; S_1}
$$

The master's discourse   The analyst's discourse

In Lacan's formulas of discourse, impossibility always directs the relationship between the two upper terms (represented by an arrow), whereas impotence is characteristic for the relationship between the two lower terms (represented by a double slash). As such, it can be verified that the impossibility between S_1 and S_2 in the master's discourse becomes an impotence in the analyst's discourse, whereas the impotence between a and \$ becomes an impossibility. In this way, the discourse of the master reveals itself as the opposite of the discourse of the analyst, or, in other words, governing is the reverse of psychoanalysing.[74]

But how are impossibility and impotence to be interpreted here? What does it mean for the impossibility of the master's discourse to be transformed in impotence in the analyst's discourse, and vice versa? In 'Radiophonie' Lacan divulged that in the master's discourse, the impossibility signifies the failure of the agency (S_1) to command knowledge (S_2). Whether a socially identified ruler or the psychic mastery of each and every individual, no matter how hard a master (S_1) tries to govern and control knowledge (S_2), the latter will always partially escape. The reason for this lack of control is to be found in the impotence which characterizes the relationship between the two lower terms of the formula. Governing produces a result (the object a), but this result is powerless in relation to the truth of the whole process. The truth of the master's discourse is that knowledge is partly unconscious and that this unconscious part does not comprise a subject (\$). Unconscious knowledge is not known by a particular agency; the only thing that can be said about this knowledge is that it works and that it knows itself. Unconscious knowledge is strictly self-contained and organizes the life of human beings without they themselves knowing it. At the level of unconscious knowledge there is a lack of agency, which is just another way of saying that in the realm of unconscious knowledge the subject is barred (\$). The product of the master's discourse is not capable of reducing this lack, for this product, which Lacan calls object a, is but a substitute stop-gap – not at all adequate for annihilating the lack (\$) and for producing some kind of jouissance. Therefore it is impossible to command knowledge. Whatever the result of governing, the lack remains, due to the barrier of jouissance on the level of impotence.

In the analyst's discourse, the impossibility between S_1 and S_2 of the master's discourse becomes itself an impotence. This implies that the discourse is based on the powerlessness of a signifier (S_1) to control an existing frame of knowledge. The master signifier (S_1) is unable to organize the body of signifiers (S_2) for once and for all, and to reveal the definitive signification of knowledge. In terms of what I have explained above (see p. 87) within the context of the analyst's task to dissolve coagulated centres of signification in light of the analysand's avowal of desire, the impotence of the analyst's discourse rests upon the unavoidable production of new master signifiers, new loci of control whose power does not extend beyond the reorganization of the symbolic order. This specific impotence of the analyst's discourse is responsible for a specific impossibility, which I wish to designate here as the impossibility to analyse what is merely a lack. If the process of analysis were to enable the analysand to make sense of all (conscious and unconscious) knowledge, the analysand would become the material agent of his condition and 'complete analysis' would be possible. But as it happens, the patient remains a barred subject and the only thing that can ever follow is her acceptance of this position. Rather than effects of signification, the analyst's discourse has effects of non-sense, in so far as meaning is always fleeting, elusive.[75] This seems to me the reason why Lacan said in *Seminar XXII* that 'The effect of meaning required of the analytic discourse is not imaginary. It is neither symbolic. It has to be real.' (Lacan 1975c[1974–75]:4/96).

The critical importance of Lacan's point of view cannot be overrated, especially when compared to what many psychoanalysts have done and some continue to do. Instead of acknowledging the barrier their discourse imposes on the process of 'sense-making', they radically eliminate it. Many analysts indeed only try to make sense of other people's lives and of a whole range of sociocultural phenomena. The analyst's job allegedly consists in making sense where all others have failed; if nobody is capable of making sense of what happens, there is still the analyst who can. Here, the analyst is convinced that the master signifiers of his discourse do control knowledge and he is obviously enjoying it. Alongside the aforementioned situation (see p. 78) of analysts advocating a discourse of the right to jouissance, this could be a second instance of a surreptitious lapse of the analyst's discourse into the realm of perversion.

When the analyst's discourse is supported by the enjoyment of making sense it cannot possibly be analytic anymore, because in Lacan's representation of the analyst's discourse, the barrier between S_1 and S_2 is insuperable. The whole Lacanian dynamics of the analyst's discourse can thus be reduced to a single formula, which could serve as a rewording of the 'paradox of the position of the analyst': one cannot enjoy being an analyst and continue to be one.

The corollary of this paradox should not come as a surprise anymore. After excluding the jouissance of the analyst, Lacan re-emphasized the desire of the analyst. In relation to the formula of the analyst's discourse this desire comprises two aspects. First, it is a desire to put knowledge in the place of truth. Indeed, in the analyst's discourse knowledge (S_2) is situated in the lower left-hand corner, which Lacan defined as the place of truth (Lacan 1991a[1969–70]:106). On first sight, this could be seen as contradicting the impossibility between knowledge and truth. Yet Lacan argued that knowledge functioning on the place of truth has nothing to do with knowledge being used as unquestionable truth. When analysts are expected to use their knowledge as a manifestation of truth, they should let their knowledge speak within everything they say, whilst realizing that its base does not contain all the answers to the analysand's problems. This point is similar to what I have discussed above (see p. 75) apropos of the analyst's ignorance and the paradox of stupidity.[76] Second, the desire of the analyst is evidently related to 'disbeing', to making oneself appear as the cause of the desire of the analysand, even to making the analysand believe that the analyst is the cause of her desire. This entails a second impossibility, although it is essentially the same as the one described above (see p. 95) as 'the impossibility to analyse what is merely a lack'. It is impossible for the analyst to cause the desire of the other through being the object a, because the object a is not something a human being can identify with, and in so far as the analyst would try to confront the analysand directly with the cause of his desire the analysand is likely to experience anxiety.[77] Hence, the desire of the analysand can only be invoked if it is sustained by an object which the analysand assigns to the analyst, but of which the analyst knows nothing about. In *Seminar XVII*, Lacan described the ensuing impossibility in the following terms: 'what is at stake in the position of the analyst [is] this seduction of truth he presents, insofar as he would know something about what he principally represents. Do I emphasize enough the relief of the impossibility of his position?' (ibid.:205). So, if the enjoyment of the analyst is excluded, it appears that the desire of the analyst harbours a double impossibility: an impossibility between truth and knowledge and an impossibility to cause the desire of the analysand. The counterpart of the above formula on the enjoyment of the analyst could therefore read: one cannot adopt the desire of the analyst and also analyse.

In Lacanian theory, psychoanalysis is not simply an art; it is a real art. This implies that it is an impossible art, but also that it is unrealized.

Psychoanalytic organizations tend to transform the practice of psycho-analysis into a respectful profession, but in this way, the ontological impossibilities of psychoanalysis are remodelled into the various necessities of science: knowledge has to be true, the position of the researcher-agent has to be well defined, results have to be validated, intentions have to be clarified, the whole process has to be (quality) controlled.

Lacan's itinerary contains an implicit argument against the professionalization of psychoanalysis, if professionalization means that those who practice psychoanalysis can become authorized clinicians when they are able to prove that the effects they produce are valuable to their analysands and to society in general.[78] However, Lacan also constructed an argument substantiating psychoanalysis as an impossible profession, not reading Freud's joke as a demand to overcome a deplorable social condition, but as an accurate assessment of a complicated practice which must be maintained as such.[79]

But if psychoanalysis is a real art and as such twice as impossible, and if it should remain that way, what can stop us from abolishing it altogether? If there is only psychoanalytic impossibility and an argument in favour of its necessity is not psychoanalytic, where does psychoanalysis derive its *raison d'être* from? To these questions, there is only one possible answer: because of contingency, or what Lacan dubbed 'what stops not being written' (Lacan 1998a[1972–73]:94). As Freud himself advocated in his metaphor of archaeological sleuthing, psychoanalysis is geared towards making discoveries, towards the creation of wonder and surprise at the revelation of the unexpected, in short towards the crystallization of new signifiers that reduce the painful necessity of repetition and are therefore able to change the analysand's life. In this sense, the Lacanian practice of psychoanalysis is a genuine labour of love – not a love which turns the contingency of an encounter into the necessity of a relationship, but a love which cherishes both the marvel and the uncertainty of the first accidental meeting (ibid.:145). Since Lacan conceived his practice as radically Freudian, the inspiration for this idea had evidently come from the founder. 'Essentially, one might say, the cure is effected by love', Freud had written to Jung in December 1906 (McGuire 1974:12–13), repeating his phrase to a group of followers in January 1907 as 'Our cures are cures of love' (Nunberg and Federn 1962:101).

In a sense, what Freud defined as love in these passages concerned the analysand's transference more than the analyst's clinical intentions. This evidently stirs the question as to how analysts, inasmuch as their practice is inhabited by love, should deal with the transference-love on the side of their patients. Freud formulated a tentative, quite unsatisfactory answer in his 'Observations on Transference-Love' (1915a[1914]), whereas Lacan explored the issue in his year-long *Seminar VIII* on transference (Lacan 1991b[1960–61]). It is to these clinical vicissitudes of transference that I will direct my attention in the following chapter.

NOTES

1 As I have illustrated in Chapter 1, Freud used this metaphor specifically to invoke the clinical deadlock of psychoanalytic diagnosis.
2 For Freud's earliest archaeological references, see his extended allegory of his new therapeutic method in 'The Aetiology of Hysteria' (1896c) and his comparison of this procedure to 'the technique of excavating a buried city' in *Studies on Hysteria* (Freud and Breuer 1895d:139).
3 For a fascinating tour around Freud's personal collection of antiquities, including an indispensable essay by Freud-biographer Peter Gay, see Gamwell and Wells (1989). For an even more arresting picture of Freud-the-collector, see Marinelli (1998), a catalogue comprising scholarly essays on various aspects of Freud's fascination with ancient objects.
4 For more detailed discussions of Freud's references to archaeology, see for example Cassirer Bernfeld (1952), Weiß and Weiß (1989), Kuspit (1989), Reinhard (1996) and Stockreiter (1998).
5 For Freud's ongoing commitment to Schliemann's accomplishments, see for example his letters to Wilhelm Fließ of 28 May and 21 December 1899 in Masson (1985).
6 For the distinction between historical and material truth, see Freud (1937d:265–269; 1939a[1937–39]:127–131). For a critical reading of Freud's categories, see Spence (1982).
7 I have borrowed these and the following references from a small piece by Michael Shepherd (1985) on Sigmund Freud and Sherlock Holmes, which is as entertaining as it is perceptive.
8 For critical readings of the 'Sherlock Holmes paradigm' in Freudian psychoanalysis, see Ginzburg (1980), Brooks (1992[1984]), Marcus (1984:247–248), Shepherd (1985), Spence (1987) and Van het Reve (1994[1987]).
9 In the realm of literature, Nicholas Meyer has staged Sherlock Holmes and Sigmund Freud as team workers in his acclaimed novel *The Seven-per-cent Solution* (1974), which formed the basis for Herbert Ross's eponymous 1979 feature film.
10 To illustrate this procedure, it suffices to invoke Freud's remark, on the occasion of Little Hans's first visit to the Berggasse, that long before the child had been born, he (Freud) already knew that one day a Little Hans would come who would be so infatuated with his mother that he must therefore be afraid of his father (Freud 1909b:42). Needless to say that Freud's knowledge was less infallible than that of Inspector Columbo, particularly in terms of its clinical effectiveness – a fact he witnessed to his

own discredit when Dora broke off her analysis after he had tried to convince her that her true, unacknowledged desire was to marry Mr K (Freud 1905e[1901]:108–109).

11 In a similar vein, when Columbo's criminals finally admit to having committed the murder and are being carried away to prison they are paradoxically freed from all the horrendous worries which clouded their post-crime existence – from the painful compulsion to cover up their tracks to the even more unbearable task of having to deal with a persecutory inspector.

12 For a brief summary of views see Boothby (1991:1–10). For a major survey of post-Freudian interpretations of the death drive, excluding the early repudiations by Hartmann, Kris and Loewenstein, see Weatherill (1998).

13 As exemplified, for instance, in the works of Mardi J. Horowitz, Anthony Ryle, and Lester Luborsky. See Horowitz (1998), Ryle and Brockman (1992), Luborsky (1984).

14 This perspective has of course gained momentum through the works of Melanie Klein and Donald W. Winnicott.

15 On similar objectives within contemporary American psychoanalysis see Muller (1996:128–133).

16 Lacan's differentiation of the symbolic and the imaginary does not coincide with the distinction between language and images, for the imaginary order cannot operate without language and the symbolic register also incorporates the dimension of the image. It is impossible to discuss all the aspects of these two cardinal Lacanian orders and their interaction within the space of this book. Any of the numerous introductions to Lacanian theory will offer the reader substantial explanations of the symbolic and the imaginary. See, in particular, Benvenuto and Kennedy (1986), Lee (1990), Bowie (1991) and Julien (1994[1981]).

17 Anthropological data abound in the second part of the 'Rome Discourse', most of which Lacan derived from the works of Lévi-Strauss (1969[1949]) and Mauss (1988[1925]).

18 Even more than the dialectics of the imaginary and the symbolic, the various components of the Lacanian mirror-stage have been unpacked in the numerous primers of Lacanian theory. I myself have endeavoured to paint a new, concise picture of its central stakes in Nobus (1998), but the most detailed exposition of the concept can be found in Jalley (1998).

19 In 'The Ego and the Id' (1923b:29–30), Freud speculated that the ego emerges out of consecutive identifications with objects whose libidinal cathexis by the Id had been relinquished.

20 Apart from 'analytic communication', Schema L also represents the four interconnected pillars over which a human being's psychic apparatus is stretched. See Lacan (1977h[1957–58]:194).

21 Lacan recognized this practice in Kleinian object-relations therapy, in the 'two body psychology' of Michael Balint, and in the radical ego-psychology of Hartmann, Kris and Loewenstein. He illustrated its potential dangers with numerous examples from psychoanalytic literature, the full references of which can be found in the bibliographies of the English editions of *Seminar I*, *Seminar II* and *Seminar III*. In Chapter 4, I will come back to one particular case by Ernst Kris, which will serve as an illustration of Lacan's theory of interpretation.

22 During the second half of the 1950s, Lacan started to conceive the Other
    not merely as the unknown other, but also as 'the place of speech' (Lacan
    1994[1956–57]:80) and 'the locus from which the question of his [the
    patient's] existence may be presented to him' (Lacan 1977h[1957–58]:194),
    in short as the compass of the unconscious.

23 The theme of the 'recognition of desire' is of course derived from Kojève's
    seminars on Hegel's *Phenomenology of Spirit* (Kojève 1969[1933–39]),
    which Lacan attended during the 1930s and which had a lasting influence on
    his theorization of desire.

24 In these paradigms of full speech, which Lacan invoked in many of his texts
    from the early 1950s, both the form of address ('You are . . . ') and the
    nature of the attribution (master, husband) are important. First, in giving a
    place to the Other by structuring the message as an address, the speaker
    is simultaneously positioned as a subject: in saying what you are (a master)
    I myself am being defined (as servant). Second, in qualifying the Other
    as master or husband, the Other is acknowledged in its symbolic status, for
    'master' and 'husband' only have meaning within a symbolic system of
    interactions.

25 Understanding the patient is a clinical evil against which Lacan continued to
    warn his audience. See, for example, Lacan (1988c[1954–55]:87; 1993
    [1955–56]:6–7; 1991b[1960–61]:234). Yet the principle was less innovative
    than generally accepted, since it had already been advocated by Theodor
    Reik in the final chapter of his much acclaimed *Listening with the Third Ear*
    (1948:503–514), a book Lacan knew well.

26 In 'Variations of the Standard Treatment', Lacan wrote that 'The
    unconscious indeed closes itself inasmuch as the analyst no longer "carries
    the word", because he already knows or thinks he knows what it has to say'
    (1966b[1955]:359).

27 For the same reason, i.e. because it stages an encounter between two egos,
    Lacan (1988b[1953–54]:40) also refuted Freud's advice in 'The Dynamics
    of Transference' (1912b:101), ironically the most concrete recommendation
    he formulated throughout his technical papers, that whenever a patient's
    speech comes to a halt during the session the analyst can revive it by saying
    that she must be governed by an idea which is directly related to the person
    of the analyst.

28 In the 'Rome Discourse' Lacan illustrated this point in reference to Freud's
    case-study of the Rat Man (1909d), in which he continuously hammered
    on the importance of the castrating father, although this motive only
    played a secondary role in the entire case. Whereas Freud's intervention
    may have been factually wrong, Lacan highlighted its effect on the Rat
    Man's subjective truth owing to its representation of the patient's uncon-
    scious desire (Lacan 1977e[1953]:88–89). I will come back to this issue in
    Chapter 4.

29 The notion of intersubjectivity was omnipresent in Lacan's works from the
    early 1950s and often fell apart in an imaginary and a symbolic type. Only the
    symbolic type counts as intersubjectivity proper, because the imaginary
    intersubjectivity, which Lacan utilized to qualify perversion (see Chapter 1)
    is more of an 'interobjectivity'. The notion itself partly stems from Lacan's
    adoption of the Hegelian dialectics of master and slave, in which the

intersubjective recognition of desire is crucial, and partly reflects his critical analysis of Sartre's existentialist philosophy, whose influence on contemporary debates was considerable. For a concise discussion of Lacan's Hegelianism, see Žižek (1996). For Lacan and Sartre, see Macey (1988: 103–107). For a general discussion of Lacan's notion of intersubjectivity within a wider philosophical context, see Frie (1997).

30 For the distinction between symbolic and imaginary transference see Chapter 1. I will return to the relationship between these two 'slopes' of the transference in Chapter 3.

31 See the section on psychotic transference in Chapter 1. Lacan went so far as to suggest that ego-psychologists, in their promotion of a solid ego within an imaginary relationship, artificially created a human being whose 'strong personality' is not all that different from that of a psychotic (Lacan (1977e [1953]:68–69, 109, footnote 52).

32 In 'Kant with Sade', a notoriously difficult text from the early 1960s, Lacan defined reciprocity as 'a reversible relation because it establishes itself upon a simple line uniting two subjects who, from their "reciprocal" position, hold this relation to be equivalent' (1989a[1962]:58–59), which again indicates that he did not deem reciprocity to be the exclusive privilege of imaginary relations between egos.

33 From this perspective one can see why Lacan at one point observed that 'the only real resistance in analysis is the resistance of the analyst' (1988c[1954–55]:324; 1977i[1958]:235). Indeed, a patient's intransigence can be regarded as mirroring the intransigence of the analyst.

34 For an interesting elaboration of Lacan's term *rejeton* and its Freudian roots see Guyomard (1998:79–85).

35 From 1964, Lacan redefined the desire coming from the first source as drive and reserved desire proper for the second source only. Until that moment in his teaching Lacan did not distinguish systematically between drive and desire. See Lacan (1996a[1964]) and Miller (1996b[1994]).

36 Because the demand for love annuls the particularity of the object, Lacan designated this demand as unconditional (*inconditionné*), and because love is embedded in a symbolic gesture of giving, irrespective of the object of the gift, he called it an act of giving what one does not have (Lacan 1977j[1958]:286–287).

37 In 'The Signification of the Phallus' Lacan wrote that 'demand annuls (*aufhebt*) the particularity of everything that can be granted by transmuting it into a proof of love' (1977j[1958]:286), expressly including the Hegelian term *Aufhebung*, which means removal as well as elevation, to indicate that the object itself does not disappear in the operation.

38 At the end of the 1960s Lacan accordingly designated the object *a*, cause of desire, as surplus jouissance (*plus-de-jouir*) in reference to Marx's notion of surplus value (Lacan 1968–69:session of 13 November 1968; 1991a[1969–70]:19).

39 See my discussion of this point in Chapter 1.

40 I will return to the issue of transference and its relation to intersubjectivity in Chapter 3.

41 I will explore this issue further in Chapter 4.

42 In Lacanian theory, a metaphor is defined as the substitution of one signifier

for another, and it always contributes to the emergence of new signification. See Lacan (1977g[1957]:164).

43 See also Lacan's 1967 'Proposition', in which he claimed: 'It is clear that of the supposed knowledge he [the analyst] knows nothing . . . Let us note this fact so as to reduce the strangeness of the insistence with which Freud advises us to begin each new case as if we had acquired nothing from his initial decipherings' (1995b[1967]:6).

44 On Socrates as the model analyst see for example Lacan (1977e[1953]: 80–81; 1977k[1960]:323; 1992[1959–60]:199–213). On the analyst as a Zen-master, see Lacan (1988b[1953–54]:1; 1977e[1953]:100–101).

45 See, for example, Freud (1912e:115; 1933a[1932]:152). In a letter to Jung dated 25 January 1909 he had openly conceded: 'I often appease my conscious mind by saying to myself: Just give up wanting to cure; learn and make money, those are the most plausible conscious aims' (McGuire 1974:202–203). For an extensive discussion of Freud's views on the goals of psychoanalysis and his own implication see Cottet (1996[1982]).

46 For an interesting critical assessment of Lacan's reading of *Antigone*, see Guyomard (1992). For astute explorations of Lacan's theory of 'pure desire' in relation to Kant's *Critique of Practical Reason* (1996[1788]) see Baas (1992), Julien (1995), Zupančič (1995, 1998).

47 For a more detailed discussion of the relation between Lacan's conception of analytic training and the position of the analyst within the treatment see Libbrecht (1998). In order to enable his self-created school, the *Ecole freudienne de Paris*, to verify that such a mutation in the economy of desire had indeed taken place amongst analytic candidates, Lacan later invented the contentious procedure of the pass, which I will discuss in the final chapter of this book.

48 In 'Kant with Sade', Lacan illustrated the 'artifice of the Stoics' by introducing it into the Sadian universe: 'Imagine a revival of Epictetus in Sadian experience: "See, you broke it," he says, pointing to his leg' (1989a[1962]:60).

49 Seneca was of course Emperor Nero's senior tutor.

50 Nero asked Seneca to commit suicide, which in the best Stoic tradition he also did.

51 See the end of Chapter 1.

52 For illuminating discussions of Lacan's text, see Miller (1996c[1989]) and Žižek (1999).

53 This is a point to which Lacan devoted most of his *Seminar XIV, The Logic of the Fantasy* (1966–67), which also comprised a renewed exploration of Descartes' *cogito ergo sum*. For a meticulous analysis of Lacan's works from this period see Sipos (1994). For concise discussions in English of these parts of Lacan's teaching see Fink (1990) and Dolar (1998).

54 For an excellent discussion of Lacan's paper and the various implications of this logical puzzle see Fink (1996b).

55 Of course, this is the only thing the governor can do if he does not want to decide for himself who shall be released. For each of the two other possibilities (two blacks and one white, one black and two whites) would imply his putting one prisoner (the white one) at an advantage over the two others (in the first case) or his putting one prisoner (the black one) at a

disadvantage over the two others (in the second case), which his resolve to let the prisoners decide for themselves does not allow. So by merely saying to the prisoners that he does not want to take the decision himself, he is implicitly informing them of the nature of their colours.

56 I do not wish to claim that my reading of Lacan's 'sophism' in this paragraph is the only valid interpretation of the story. Throughout his works, Lacan himself produced various alternative readings, often depending on the context in which he referred to the dynamics of logical time. I will return to the story of the three prisoners in Chapter 4, in order to show how Lacan used it to argue in favour of his controversial technique of variable-length sessions.

57 In this passage, non-commutativity equals non-reciprocity, which means that there is no reversible relation between remembering and repetition. During the 1950s Lacan also introduced a distinction between biological memory, symbolic remembering (recollection) and imaginary reminiscence (Lacan 1977g[1957]:167).

58 Lacan engaged in a lengthy exposition of the principles of repetition governing the unconscious symbolic chain in the three postfaces to his 'Seminar on "The Purloined Letter"' (1972[1956]). These appendices have hitherto not been translated into English, but good critical analyses of their contents can be found in Muller and Richardson (1988:55–98) and Fink (1995a:153–172; 1996a). Lacan's entire demonstration also served as an exemplification of his formula that the unconscious is structured like a language (Lacan 1993[1955–56]:165–167).

59 Aristotelian scholars generally prefer to translate *tuchè* as 'fortune' or 'chance' instead of 'luck'. See, for example, Sorabji (1980), Judson (1991) and Sachs (1995).

60 For a more detailed reading of Lacan's re-definition of *tuchè* and *automaton*, and his relationship to the Aristotelian opera in general, see Cathelineau (1998).

61 In placing his commentary of Poe's 'The Purloined Letter', featuring the amazing C. Auguste Dupin, at the head of his *Ecrits*, Lacan could be seen as even more eager than Freud to align the analyst and the detective. Yet the story served more complex purposes than that of an allegory of psychoanalytic treatment, and Lacan's portrayal of the analyst as a latter-day Dupin was largely limited to his detached involvement with the circulating letter. Poe's story is also radically different from the bulk of the subsequent whodunits, because in 'The Purloined Letter' the truth is not hidden. It is readily accessible to everybody, but unfortunately nobody (apart from Dupin of course) wants to see it.

62 Emboldened by Lacan's 1959 statement that perverts are analysable on the same level as neurotics (Lacan 1977a[1959]:16), I have decided not to restrict these guidelines to the treatment of neurotics. However, this does not imply that the management of the transference is similar too. I will return to this issue in Chapter 3.

63 For Lacan's critique on the portrayal of psychoanalysis as a 'depth psychology' see, for example, Lacan (1977i[1958]:240; 1977k[1960]:294; 1989b[1965]:7; 1991a[1969–70]:61).

64 A full exposition of the (often contradictory) contemporary Lacanian

perspectives on the analytic treatment of psychotic patients falls beyond the scope of this book. The reader who wants to know more about the subject will find solace in Actes de l'Ecole de la Cause freudienne (1987), Fondation du Champ freudien (1988), Apollon *et al.* (1990) and Fink (1997:101–111).

65 In a controversial 1972 interview for Belgian television, Lacan was asked about his views on freedom, to which he responded that he had never talked about it. Needless to say that this statement needs to be taken with a pinch of salt, for the notion figures prominently in the final part of the 'Rome Discourse' (1977e[1953]:77–107) and pervades many of Lacan's works from the 1950s and 1960s. As a matter of fact, it was not the first time Lacan disclaimed interest in a particular topic despite his having discussed it in great detail from the start of his teachings. For example, in the final session of *Seminar XVIII, On a Discourse that Would Not be of Semblance* (1970–71:session of 16 June 1971) he stated that he had never broached the concept of the superego.

66 When Lacan first introduced the impossible as a concept in *Seminar XI*, he immediately linked it to the possible, its counterpart in modal logic, yet warning his audience that 'the impossible is not necessarily the contrary of the possible' (Lacan 1977b[1964]:167). After this first categorization, he continued to use the operators of modal logic in order to structure a great many of his insights: alienation and separation, the sexual relationship, making sense, speaking truth, etc.

67 In his *Physics*, Aristotle discerned four types of causes: the material cause, the formal cause, the final cause and the efficient cause. Apart from the latter, none of these types would still be regarded as causes, neither within contemporary epistemology nor within our common sense understanding of causality. When reading Aristotle's *Physics* and Lacan's references to it in 'Science and Truth' one should therefore take into account that the Aristotelian causes differ significantly from the causes in our general scientific conception of the world. Lacan allocated Aristotle's efficient and final causes to magic and religion respectively, thus arriving at a fourfold tabulation of the realms of human activity, which somehow resembled Freud's picture of the 'three powers [religion, art and philosophy] which may dispute the basic position of science', in 'The Question of a *Weltanschauung*', his 35th lecture of the 'New Introductory Lectures on Psychoanalysis' (1933a[1932]:158–182).

68 Lacan implicitly disputed Freud's view that psychoanalysis can and should adopt the scientific *Weltanschauung*. Unlike Freud, who believed that psychoanalysis ought to promote science and that the domain of science would be incomplete without it, Lacan was convinced that science should never function as an ideal for psychoanalysis. Quite to the contrary, he claimed that psychoanalysis should function as an ideal for science, because psychoanalysis is the only discipline acknowledging the fundamental gap between knowledge and truth. For a highly interesting discussion of this point, see Milner (1995).

69 This idea was already present in 'The Subversion of the Subject and the Dialectic of Desire', in which Lacan had written that 'no metalanguage can be spoken, or, more aphoristically, that there is no Other of the Other' (1977k[1960]:311). In the first ten pages of this text Lacan had raised the

same issues as in 'Science and Truth', yet approaching them from a Hegelian rather than an Aristotelian angle. For more extensive commentaries on Lacan's changing views on the relation between psychoanalysis and science see Baas and Zaloszyc (1988), Laurent (1994), Fink (1995a:138–146; 1995b) and Porge and Soulez (1996).

70 See, for example, Freud's comments on the creation of illusions within art in 'The Question of a *Weltanschauung*' (1933a[1932]:161) and his discussion of truthfulness (*Wahrhaftigkeit*) as an ethical value of psychoanalytic practice in 'Observations on Transference-Love' (1915a[1914]:164).

71 During the 1970s Georgin himself wrote two books on Lacan. See Georgin (1973, 1977).

72 Of this text only a small fragment is available in English. See Lacan (1985[1970]).

73 I cannot offer a thorough explanation of Lacan's four discourses (of the master, the hysteric, the analyst and the university) within the space of this book. Useful introductory studies in English are Bracher *et al.* (1994), Quackelbeen (1994), Verhaeghe (1995) and Fink (1998).

74 Hence the title of Lacan's *Seminar XVII: L'envers de la psychanalyse* (The Other Side of Psychoanalysis) (1991a[1969–70]).

75 I will develop the antagonism between meaning and signification further in Chapter 4.

76 The principle of knowledge functioning on the place of truth also formed the basis for the (revised) theory of interpretation Lacan developed during the 1970s. See Lacan (1991a[1969–70]:39–40). I will return to this point in Chapter 4.

77 This, at least, was Lacan's central thesis in his *Seminar X, Anxiety* (1962–63).

78 The topic of the authorization of psychoanalytic practice will be addressed in the final chapter of this book.

79 As a matter of fact, when Freud reminded his readership of the impossible profession of psychoanalysis, he suggested nothing to counter this particular status. For Freud it was rather a sharp observation, perfectly rendering the essence of psychoanalytic practice.

Chapter 3

Strategies of transference

THE MANY FACES OF TRANSFERENCE

In a small, seemingly futile passage on the termination of analysis in 'On Beginning the Treatment', Freud confessed that since the start of his psychoanalytic career he had noticed a remarkable change in his patients' attitudes towards the progression of their analysis:

> In the early years of my psychoanalytic practice I used to have the greatest difficulty in prevailing on my patients to continue their analysis. This difficulty has long since been shifted, and I now have to take the greatest pains to induce them to give up.
>
> (Freud 1913c:130)

Freud did not clarify the mainspring of this problem, but numerous examples can be adduced to demonstrate that the entire issue was dominated by the vicissitudes of transference.

For instance, shortly before publishing 'On Beginning the Treatment', Freud had informed Sándor Ferenczi about his ticklish experience with Elma Pálos, whom he had agreed to treat for a short period of about three months, until Easter 1912:

> With Elma things continue to go gloomily. She has brought out several quite surprisingly intelligent insights, but she doesn't want to get into the experience with you and doesn't seem to want to finish with me; i.e., because of the transference she wishes to extend her stay past Easter, which I don't want to do. So I am cooling off noticeably again.
>
> (Brabant *et al.* 1993:362)

This was neither Freud's first encounter with a patient reluctant to leave, nor was it the first time he attributed the phenomenon to the power of transference. In April 1900, at a moment when he was still groping his way as to the nature and function of the transference, Freud had already told Wilhelm Flieβ about its effect on the duration of his analysis of a certain Mr E:

> I am beginning to understand that the apparent endlessness of the treatment is something that occurs regularly and is connected with the transference . . . The asymptotic conclusion of the treatment basically makes no difference to me, but is yet one more disappointment to outsiders . . . Since he had to suffer through all my technical and theoretical errors, I actually think that a future case could be solved in half the time.
>
> (Masson 1985:409)

Freud did not have to wait long to test the value of his assertion, for some six months later an eighteen-year-old hysterical girl suffering from a welter of psychic and somatic symptoms was referred to him by her father (ibid.:427). Compared to Mr E's treatment, which lasted for more than a year, Freud's analysis of Dora (Freud 1905e[1901]) took a mere three months. This could be seen as an even better result than that which Freud had anticipated in his letter to Flieβ, were it not for the fact that the girl herself decided to break off her analysis before reaching a satisfactory solution of her problems.[1] Again Freud felt that he had made a technical and theoretical error, and again he regarded his patient's behaviour as the corollary of her 'transferences' [sic], clinical phenomena encompassing 'new editions or facsimiles of the impulses and phantasies which are aroused and made conscious during the progress of analysis' whereby the patient replaces 'some earlier person by the person of the physician' (ibid.:116). On the one hand Freud conceded that he must have been blinded by Dora's diligence, not seeing that her identification of him with the dreaded Mr K fuelled her desire to take revenge. On the other hand he ventured the hypothesis that his technical mistake must have been rooted in a failure to direct Dora's attention to her unconscious homosexual love for Mrs K.[2] Whatever the nature of Freud's mistake, Dora's transference did not catalyse an interminable analytic process, but prompted her to finish the treatment prematurely.

Years later, Freud applied what he had learnt from the Dora case in his treatment of another eighteen-year-old girl (Freud 1920a). Like Dora, this girl had expressed a desire to kill herself. Much like Dora's, her parents had become so upset with her demeanour that they decided to seek Freud's help. And in keeping with Dora's erotic interest, albeit more overtly, this girl's homosexual orientation underpinned many of her symptoms. When the girl produced a series of dreams in which she featured as a happily married mother, Freud declared that she merely wanted to deceive him, in line with her long-established habit of betraying her father. Having acknowledged the girl's hostility towards her father and her concurrent unconscious animosity towards himself as a father representative, Freud subsequently ended the treatment on his own initiative, insisting that the girl continue her analysis with a female analyst. By pinpointing the deceitfulness of his patient's productions and by effectively dropping his patient before she had the opportunity to leave her analyst, Freud was eager to avoid a retake of the Dora case. Yet once again the transference – in this case an unconscious negative attitude towards the father – proved decisive in light of the continuation of the analytic process.

A first conclusion to be drawn from Freud's remarks on transference is that its manifestation can lead to the analysis becoming either unpursuable or interminable. Owing to this strong connection between transference and the duration of psychoanalytic treatment, Lacan proclaimed in *Seminar I* that 'one can say that the transference is the very concept of analysis, because it is the time of analysis' (Lacan 1988b [1953–54]:286).[3]

Here the question emerges whether the analyst's 'management' of the transference or something in the nature of transference itself decides over the continuation of the analytic process. Freud's comments on his technical mistakes in the Dora case strongly support the former option, whereas his position in the treatment of the young homosexual woman seems to endorse the latter. The same ambiguity pervades Freud's theoretical discussions of transference in his papers on technique and the introductory lectures on psychoanalysis. For example, in 'The Dynamics of Transference' he noted: 'Where the capacity for transference has become essentially limited to a negative one, as is the case with paranoiacs, there ceases to be any possibility of influence or cure' (Freud 1912b:107). A different account, implicitly underscoring the analyst's power over the transference, appeared in the paper on transference-love: 'No doctor who experiences this [the patient's falling in love] for the first time will find it easy to retain his grasp on the analytic situation and to keep clear of the *illusion* that the treatment is really at an end' (Freud 1915a[1914]:162, italics added).

It seems that for Freud the clue to the entire question lay in the differential faces of the transference. The mild positive, conscious face of transference is beneficial for the continuation of analysis, whereas its resistance face, epitomized by the analysand's unconscious negative, hostile or intensely erotic feelings towards the analyst, is a recipe for disaster, unless the analyst manages to explain their infantile origin to the analysand (Freud 1916–17a[1915–17]:444; 1940a[1938]:174–177). Because he regarded the analysand's feelings in the (hostile or erotic) transference as a blueprint of a repressed unconscious pattern (Freud 1910a[1909]:50–51), Freud defined the analyst's task accordingly as overcoming the aspect of repetition controlling the transference and opening the psychic avenues of remembering (Freud 1926e:226–228).[4]

In his re-reading of Freud's technical papers during the early 1950s, Lacan progressively exchanged the two constitutive axes (positive, negative vs. conscious, unconscious) of Freud's taxonomy of transference for a structural classification embedded in his own distinction between the imaginary and the symbolic (Lacan 1988b[1953–54]:284). In emphasizing the imaginary and symbolic dimensions of transference Lacan at once endeavoured to solve the Freudian riddle why transference is simultaneously the engine of psychoanalytic treatment and the strongest weapon of resistance (ibid.:284). To Lacan this clinical puzzle could not be brought to a satisfactory conclusion by merely relying on the faces of transference; it required entering into the dialectics of the imaginary and the symbolic. Consequently, whereas Freud had predicated the continuation of analysis on the analyst's ability to handle the inherently detrimental faces of transference by exposing their roots in a repressed, infantile conflict, Lacan emphasized that the analyst's duty consisted in guaranteeing that the transference does not disintegrate into an imaginary relationship of jealousy, rivalry and competition. At the same time Lacan did not discard the qualities of love and hate within the transference. On the contrary, he argued that love and hate are the two central constituents of both symbolic and imaginary transference, with the caveat that they cannot operate without an additional, generally neglected factor of ignorance (ibid.:271).

Apart from the question as to how transference influences the continuation of analysis (with respect to its differential form or in keeping with the analyst's handling of it), Freud was also intrigued by the origin of transference. Is it a phenomenon elicited by the conditions of psychoanalytic treatment or something proceeding from a natural disposition in neurotic people? If it is triggered by psychoanalysis itself, should it be attributed to the person of the analyst or to the singularity of the analytic procedures? And if it can be explained through the analytic procedures, which of its components are most significant?

Freud broached these questions in many of his writings without formulating consistent answers.[5] In the Dora case he championed the view that transference is 'an inevitable necessity', not created by psychoanalysis but merely brought to light as part of the analytic revelation of the patient's unconscious tendencies (Freud 1905e[1901]:116–117). He rehearsed this view in 'The Dynamics of Transference', at once challenging the idea that transference is an exclusively psychoanalytic phenomenon (Freud 1912b:101). Yet soon after, in his essay on transference love, Freud balanced towards the other alternative: 'He [the analyst] must recognize that the patient's falling in love is induced by the analytic situation and is not to be attributed to the charms of his own person' (Freud 1915a[1914]: 160–161). But the explanation Freud had given in the Dora case resurfaced in his 'Introductory Lectures on Psycho-Analysis': '[W]e must . . . recognize that we are dealing with a phenomenon which is intimately bound up with the nature of the illness itself . . . [W]e do not believe that the situation in the treatment could justify the development of such feelings', although 'the opportunity offered by the analytic treatment' enables the patient to transfer these feelings onto the analyst (Freud 1916–17a[1915–17]:442).

Compared to Freud's, Lacan's take on the source of transference was at the same time less ambiguous and more radical. Reassessing Freud's conduct in the Dora case, Lacan averred that transference – here to be understood in its pernicious, imaginary side – 'always has the same direction, of indicating the moments of error and orientation of the analyst' (Lacan 1982a[1951]:72, translation modified). Subsequently, he also held the analyst to play a crucial part in the emergence of the symbolic transference, not simply by allowing the analysand to mistake him for somebody else, nor by introducing the rule of free association, but by embodying the function of supposed subject of knowing. Repudiating the idea that transference is the spontaneous outcome of a presumed neurotic disposition, Lacan thus argued that it is evoked by the analytic setting, notably by the analyst's own implication.[6]

Since the analyst is *de facto* implied in the transference, whatever its form and structure, Lacan went on to state that countertransference is not an analytic evil, but a necessary counterpart of the analysand's trans-ference (Lacan 1991b[1960–61]:233). On Lacan's account, the notion of countertransference ought not be employed as an umbrella for the analyst's technical failures, but as a concept conveying the unavoidable implication of the analyst in the analysand's transference.[7] Instead of assigning the transference to the quirks of the neurotic condition or to the artificiality of the analytic setting, Lacan defended the analyst's responsibility within the entire process, eventually summarizing his point provocatively in the formula that there is only one transference in psychoanalysis, namely that of the analyst (Lacan 1973–74:session of 19 March 1974).

The analyst's essential share in the analysand's transference also emboldened Lacan during the early 1960s to reject Freud's frequent alignment of transference and repetition.[8] Although he himself had supported this equivalence during the 1950s, Lacan gradually realized that seeing transference as a pure repetition of an ancient, repressed infantile conflict, i.e. as something completely alien to the analyst's position, not only reduced the analyst's responsibility for the direction of the treatment, but also restricted her capacity for manipulating the transference (Lacan 1962–63:session of 9 January 1963). As I will demonstrate in the succeeding sections of this chapter, this inevitable implication of the analyst in the analysand's transference was not the only factor motivating Lacan's separation of transference and repetition, but it was definitely the most clinically informed one.

Thus far I have presented two series of questions emanating from Freud's scattered glosses on transference: 'How does transference affect the continuation (the time) of psychoanalytic treatment?', and 'Where does transference stem from?'. A third, even more contentious issue can be added to this list, that hinges on the differentiation of transference and suggestion. If the analysand's mild positive transference constitutes a guarantee for psychoanalytic success (at least in Freud's conception of the treatment), how can the effects of psychoanalysis be distinguished from those obtained by suggestion within traditional forms of hypnosis and other healing practices? And if analysts are supposed to take advantage of the analysand's mild positive transference, curbing all its complementary forms of expression, in order to obtain the desired results, to what extent do they act upon a position of power and what prevents them from abusing the power relegated to them?

In 'The Dynamics of Transference' Freud did not eschew the proposition that 'the results of psychoanalysis rest upon suggestion', if suggestion means that one person is being influenced by another (Freud 1912b:106). Developing this point further in his 'Introductory Lectures on Psycho-Analysis', he impressed on his audience that a patient's 'tendency to transference' (*Übertragungsneigung*) is synonymous with Bernheim's notion of suggestibility if only its realm of action is extended to include negative feelings, and provided one is prepared to acknowledge the libidinal engine of this suggestibility (Freud 1916–17a[1915–17]:446).[9] Faced with the objection that this inextricable link between transference and suggestion undermines the originality of the psychoanalytic edifice and might contribute to its deterioration, Freud subsequently nuanced his opinion, drawing attention to a dual gulf separating direct hypnotic and psychoanalytic suggestion. First of all he claimed that contrary to hypnotic procedures, the analytic *modus operandi* is not geared towards covering up the patient's problems with additional layers of mental strength, even less towards the prohibition of symptoms. Instead it seeks to rid the analysands of their symptoms by exposing their underlying conflicts (ibid.:450–451).[10] Second, and more importantly, Freud stressed that whatever remains of the suggestive influence of the analyst's interventions is bound to perish under the weight of analysis itself: 'In every other kind of suggestive treatment the transference is carefully preserved and left untouched; in analysis it is itself subjected to treatment and is dissected in all the shapes in which it appears' (ibid.:453).

Not convinced by Freud's arguments, Lacan remained adamant that transference and suggestion ought to be kept separate if the analyst is to steer away from a surreptitious abuse of power.[11] In his *Seminar V* he pointed out that analysts have an ever-looming suggestive influence over their patients by virtue of their transference, which is being abused whenever they take advantage of it, whether to satisfy their patients' demands, to force an interpretation, or to present themselves as reliable, competent analysts with whom it is worth identifying (Lacan 1998b [1957–58]:427–428). Of course, the upshot of Lacan's idea was that psychoanalytic interventions which do not encompass an element of suggestion are extremely difficult to define, especially when taking into account that the analysts' mere presence could be regarded as a suggestive fulfilment of the analysands' demand that they be there. Lacan tried to escape this clinical impasse for each of the three levels in his schema of the direction of the treatment: the politics of the analyst, the strategies of transference and the tactics of interpretation (Lacan 1977i[1958]).[12]

First, as I have explained in the previous chapter, he intimated that the analyst's position must be characterized both by the death of the ego and the disbeing of the object *a*. Second, with respect to the contents of an interpretation, Lacan replaced the analyst's mandatory full speech with the essential ambiguity and nonsensicality of his expressions.[13] Finally, on the level of transference, he exposed the widespread analytic practice of interpreting the transference, whereby its infantile sources are revealed to the analysand, as a vicious circle:

[T]his interpretation, if he [the analyst] gives it, will be received as coming from the person that the transference imputes him to be. Will he [the analyst] agree to benefit from this error concerning his person?

Analytic morals do not contradict this, on condition that the analyst interprets this effect, otherwise the analysis will amount to little more than a crude suggestion. An incontestable option, except that the analyst's words will still be heard as coming from the Other of the transference, the subject's way out of the transference thus being postponed *ad infinitum*.

(ibid.:231, translation modified)

Transcending the inappropriate, inherently suggestive *interpretation of* the transference, Lacan ensuingly deployed the principles of a genuine *analysis of* and *interpretation within* the transference, predicated on its calculated manipulation by the analyst in light of the downfall of the supposed subject of knowing (Lacan 1967–68:session of 10 January 1968).

The above three issues, which cover the relationship between transference and the continuation of the treatment, the origin of transference, and the relation between transference and suggestion, arise from three clinical problems in Freud's *œuvre* and represent three central concerns within Lacan's theory of transference. Although continuously in touch with the letter of Freud's writings, Lacan sought to advance the founder's theory of transference by reformulating these problems and introducing new concepts. In the following sections of this chapter I will detail these reformulations and new concepts, mapping the evolution of Lacan's own views between the early 1950s and the late 1960s, when his exploration of transference reached its zenith.[14] In this way, I hope to show that Lacan's theory of transference is neither 'characterized by obscurity and linguistic play', nor 'leaves one uncertain as to his actual technical approach' (Esman 1990:12).

FROM PSYCHOLOGY TO INTERSUBJECTIVITY

Lacan's first extensive protocol on the topic of transference, his 1951 'Intervention on Transference', took off from yet another trenchant critique of mainstream psychoanalysis. Now the unfortunate bugbear was called Daniel Lagache, an analyst who unlike many of Lacan's future adversaries was more drawn to the scientific ideals of academic psychology than the therapeutic ambitions of ego-psychology.[15]

Echoing a criticism by Maurice Bénassy on the encyclopaedic position paper on transference Lagache had prepared for a 1951 conference, Lacan developed a vehement rebuttal of Lagache's explanation of the repetitive nature of transference via the so-called Zeigarnik effect.[16] According to this effect, originally described in 1927 by Bela Zeigarnik, an associate of the cognitive learning theorist Kurt Lewin, incomplete tasks are more likely to stay in people's minds than properly resolved ones.[17] Taking his lead from a book by Maslow and Mittelmann (1951[1941]:66), Lagache had claimed that it is easy to put Zeigarnik's incomplete tasks on a par with the unresolved infantile conflicts and the thwarted wishes in the mental life of neurotics, which could elucidate the spring of Freud's unconscious repetition compulsion and its ruling over the analysand's transference.[18]

In his reply, Lacan followed Bénassy's argument that instead of repetition and transference being determined by the Zeigarnik effect, matters might very well be the other way round, the Zeigarnik effect depending on the nature of the transference between the experimenter and the participants. Whereas Bénassy had illustrated his point in reference to the conditions of psychometric testing, Lacan applied it directly to the psychoanalytic setting, saying that 'it proceeds entirely in this relationship of subject to subject, which means that it preserves a dimension which is irreducible to all psychology considered as the objectification of certain properties of the individual' (Lacan 1982a[1951]:62). All individual reactions, Lacan posited, are governed by the primacy of an intersubjective relationship, which implies that transference can only be explained through the dialectical process between the analysand and the analyst.[19]

So how does the analyst play a part in the emergence of the analysand's transference? Three years before his 'Intervention on Transference', in 'Aggressivity in Psychoanalysis', Lacan had implicitly espoused Freud's recommendation that the analyst 'should be opaque to his patients and, like a mirror, should show them nothing but what is shown to him' (Freud 1912e:118). Lacan emphasized that the analyst's attitude of general impassibility is exactly what facilitates the beneficial reactivation of unconscious 'archaic imagos' in the analysand (Lacan 1977d[1948]: 13–15). He even embraced Melanie Klein's theory of the paranoiac's projection of bad internal objects onto the outside world, in order to argue that the opaque psychoanalyst induces a state of controlled paranoia in the analysand (ibid.:15). Whilst Lacan's account of transference in this early paper did not attain the high level of sophistication characteristic of his later work, its central message that the analyst's controlled inertia within the treatment determines the analysand's transference would resound for years to come.[20] Furthermore, Lacan maintained that when the analysand's transference turns into an unmanageable aggressive tension, the analyst is as much responsible for these deleterious developments as for the initial emergence of transference. These negative reactions only occur when an analyst exchanges his 'pure mirror of an unruffled surface' (ibid.:15) for admonitions curtailing the analysand's wishes or interventions saturated with good advice (presumably with the best of philanthropic intentions).

In his 'Intervention on Transference', Lacan took advantage of Freud's trouble with Dora to illustrate how the girl's negative transference had indeed taken shape in accordance with Freud's own clinical conduct, confirming the assertion that transference follows a dialectics of intersubjectivity:

> [T]he case of Dora, because of what it stands for in the experience of transference when this experience was still new . . . [was] the first case in which Freud recognised that the analyst played his part . . . I will be attempting *to define in terms of pure dialectics the transference*, which we call negative on the part of the subject as being the operation of the analyst who interprets it.
>
> (Lacan 1982a[1951]:64–65)

Restructuring Freud's entire case around a series of dialectical reversals and subsequent developments of subjective truth, Lacan ascribed Dora's negative transference, which triggered her departure, to Freud's failure to implement one crucial reversal. Freud had refrained from showing to Dora that she was not interested in Mrs K because the woman was her closest rival, but because she incarnated the mystery of femininity.[21] Put differently, Lacan could only see one reason behind Freud's downfall: the father of psychoanalysis had been so fixated on the love he believed Mr K must have inspired in the young girl that he could not understand her love for Mrs K. At the time, Lacan designated Freud's fixation as countertransference, 'the sum total of the prejudices, passions and difficulties of the analyst, or even of his insufficient information, at any given moment of the dialectical process' (ibid.:71).[22] He concluded accordingly that 'transference does not arise from any mysterious property of affectivity', but always reflects the analyst's own position (ibid.:71).

Having situated transference firmly within psychoanalytic inter-subjectivity, Lacan probed deeper into the phenomenology of transference with the goal of formulating a more fundamental set of alternatives than the classic Freudian opposition between an advantageous, mild positive transference and its infelicitous (erotic or aggressive) counterpart. The upshot was a clear theoretical distinction between imaginary and symbolic transference, each incorporating all possible shades of the entire affective spectrum.

In *Seminar I* Lacan tabulated symbolic transference as the efficacious side of the coin, identifying it quite simply with the act of full speech: 'Each time a man speaks to another in an authentic and full manner, there is, in the true sense, transference, symbolic transference – something takes place which changes the nature of the two beings present' (Lacan 1988b[1953–54]:109). On this symbolic plane, transference operates as the motor of analysis and it can take either the form of love or hate, and quite possibly a mixture of both.[23] To corroborate the idea that transference is inextricably linked with the symbolic structure of language, he referred to Freud's description of 'the fact of transference' in the final chapter of *The Interpretation of Dreams*, where he had associated it with the transmission of energy from an unconscious representation to a preconscious day's residue (Freud 1900a:562–563).[24] Here, Lacan stipulated, Freud had explained how transference takes place when a forbidden unconscious discourse takes hold of a more accessible, preconscious discourse in order to express itself (Lacan 1988b[1953–54]:247).

What Lacan dubbed 'imaginary transference' coincides with the type of transference Freud had encountered as an obstacle to the treatment, with the proviso that Lacan put its dialectical rather than its affective qualities centre stage. Analysands who are under the spell of an imaginary transference only approach their analyst as an alter ego, an other who presents a mirror image of themselves. The love analysands experience on this plane is strictly narcissistic. Not tolerating the other's difference, they only bring into relief those features which the other has in common with themselves. Likewise, imaginary hate is not oriented towards breaking a mutually agreed contract, but towards continuous rivalry, competition and jealousy. Lacan contemplated the analysand's projection of archaic infantile images onto the analyst as a standard example of this imaginary transference. And for all its prevalence within ego-psychology, he considered it detrimental to the continuation of psychoanalysis:

> To bring into play the illusory projection of any one of the subject's fundamental relations with the analytic partner, or again the object relation, the relation between transference and counter-transference, all this, remaining as it does within a two body psychology, is inadequate.
>
> (ibid.:261)[25]

This claim is of course quite remarkable in light of Lacan's previous assessment of the transference in 'Aggressivity in Psychoanalysis'. For what had originally appeared as the essence of transference, namely the reactualization of archaic imagos, now emerged as its evil underside – a clinical avenue to be avoided rather than cleared.

The second nuance Lacan added to his initial picture of transference relates to the power of analytic intersubjectivity for eliciting the analysand's reactions. To the extent that transference operates according to the criteria of full and empty speech, it is difficult to see how analysts, simply by virtue of their acting as dark mirrors, would actually evoke these responses. Lacan was forced to conclude from his own restructuring of the transference phenomenon that 'the dimension of transference exists from the start, implicitly, well before analysis begins, before this concubinage, which analysis is, triggers it' (ibid.:271). This perspective was of course in keeping with Freud's explanation of transference in the Dora case – an inevitable necessity brought to light by the circumstances of psychoanalytic treatment (Freud 1905e[1901]:116–117) – but it also revived the spectre of the neurotic's predisposition and the spontaneous appearance of transference. Therefore Lacan hastened to specify that if there is a 'readiness to the transference' in the patient 'it is solely by virtue of his placing himself in the position of acknowledging himself in speech, and searching out his truth to the end, the end which is there, in the analyst' (Lacan 1988b[1953–54]:277–278).[26] Although not diminished, the analyst's responsibility was consequently restricted to the emergence of the analysand's transference along one of the axes of the symbolic–imaginary divide.[27]

FROM REPETITION TO ENACTMENT

In 1954–55 Lacan devoted a substantial part of his *Seminar II* to a theoretical analysis of Freud's concept of the compulsion to repeat (*Wiederholungszwang*). As he explained on at least two occasions during this *Seminar* (1988c[1954–55]:118, 123), this was a logical step to take after having dissected the phenomenology of transference, taking account of the amalgamation of transference and repetition in Freud's works.[28] It was also an occasion for Lacan to address a Freudian dilemma Lagache had rehashed in his numerous contributions to the topic of transference: does transference conform to the repetition of a need, or to a need for repetition? (Lagache 1952:94–95; 1953[1951]:4–5; 1993[1954]:137). In presenting this dilemma, Lagache had opposed Freud's description of transference as the repetition of an unfulfilled need for love (Freud 1912b:100), following the pleasure principle, to his subsequent account of transference as a derivative of the compulsion to repeat, and thus of what functions *beyond* the pleasure principle (Freud 1920g:20–21). Hence, the apparently futile question raised by Lagache opened up onto a cardinal issue: does transference operate in keeping with the pleasure principle, or does it work against it?[29]

Lacan's trajectory in *Seminar II* sparked a new interpretation of 'Beyond the Pleasure Principle' (Freud 1920g), in which Freud had conceptualized the repetition compulsion as an infernal cycle compelling people to re-experience unpleasurable events time and again. By analogy with the notion of resistance, Lacan dubbed the repetition compulsion an *in*sistence, linking its compulsive nature to the continuous return of the signifiers within the symbolic order. Again minimizing the explanatory value of the Zeigarnik effect, he attributed the repetition compulsion to the incessant intrusion of the symbolic machinery which governs all human life forms, similar to the ongoing exchange of messages within an isolated, closed circuit (Lacan 1988c[1954–55]:87–90). Hence, if transference follows the repetition compulsion and the latter equals the insistence of the signifiers within the symbolic order, then transference must be characterized by that same symbolic insistence and not, for that matter, by the power of *re*sistance. This conclusion urged Lacan to decide in favour of the analysand's transference as an unconscious, symbolic need for repetition functioning beyond the pleasure principle, and it bolstered his critique of clinicians advocating the analysis of the transference as a resistance.[30] This is not to say that Lacan completely rejected the resistance side of transference, but he considered it an unproductive, deceitful departure from its bona fide repetition side – a deterioration for whose emergence the analyst is as much responsible as for that of the symbolic insistence.

Armed with this new distinction between transference insistence (symbolic repetition) and transference resistance (imaginary projection), Lacan returned to the case-studies of Dora and the young homosexual woman, putting Freud's technical errors into a different light. Following a juxtaposition of the two cases in *Seminar IV*, he argued that whereas in the Dora case Freud had radically ignored the imaginary element of deceit within Dora's transference, in the case of the young homosexual woman he had made exactly the opposite mistake, concentrating exclusively on the deceitfulness of her dream (to be a happily married woman) without acknowledging its truthful symbolic articulation (Lacan 1994[1956–57]: 135–136). In his treatment of Dora Freud was led astray by his unshakeable belief that his patient was unconsciously, yet honestly reliving her love for Mr K in her relationship with her analyst, whilst in his analysis of the young homosexual girl he was mistaken in excluding the possibility that her dream of a happily married life transpired a deeply felt, though unconscious wish.

At the end of the 1950s, with *Seminar VII* (1992[1959–60]), a radical shift of perspective took place. Although the entire seminar was intended as a revaluation of the aims and objectives of psychoanalytic treatment, Lacan entered into a digression concerning the relation between the pleasure and reality principles in Freud's *œuvre* to redefine the status of the signifier. Contrary to what he had proffered in previous seminars, he now located the signifier, or what Freud had called *Vorstellung* (representation), firmly within the realm of the pleasure principle (ibid.: 134). Relying on Freud's 'Project for a Scientific Psychology' (1950a[1895]), Lacan intimated that the pleasure principle, the primary unconscious process regulating the distribution of libidinal energy between representations, cannot operate without these representations. Rather than being an agency functioning beyond the pleasure principle, the signifier thus became part and parcel of the primary process.

This new conception of the signifier evidently challenged the connection between transference and repetition. Initially, Lacan had correlated transference with the repetition compulsion and the latter with the insistence of the signifier beyond the pleasure principle. Now, with the new alliance between the signifier and the pleasure principle, transference could no longer be associated with the repetition compulsion, unless the symbolic mechanism of transference itself was entirely revised. In addition, the proposed congruence of transference, the signifier and the pleasure principle seemed to topple Lacan's original take on Lagache's polarization (need for repetition vs. repetition of need) into the opposite direction, transference appearing quite conspicuously as the repetition of a need.

Avoiding this inconsistency in *Seminar VII*, Lacan devoted his next seminar entirely to the topic of transference, which incited him to ponder the two sides of Lagache's opposition again and to offer the following provisional solution:

> [I]t seems impossible to me to eliminate from the phenomenon of transference the fact that it manifests itself in relation to somebody spoken to. This is a constitutive fact. It constitutes a frontier and it simultaneously indicates to us that we should not drown the phenomenon of transference in the general possibility of repetition constituted by the existence of the unconscious. In analysis, there are of course repetitions linked to the constancy of the signifying chain

in the subject. These repetitions need to be distinguished strictly from what we call transference, even when in some cases they may have homologous effects.

(Lacan 1991b[1960–61]:208)

It would be erroneous to infer from this passage that Lacan took issue with his own previous equivalence of transference and the need for repetition, now realigning the occurrence of transference with the repetition of a need. As a matter of fact, he was making a rudimentary case for the radical separation of transference and repetition on the basis of an evaluation of the inherently creative dimension in the transference phenomenon. On the one hand, Freud's definition of transference as the analysand's reproduction in acts of a repressed historical event within the presence of the analytic situation (Freud 1914g:150) encouraged Lacan to loosen the knot between transference and the compulsion to repeat. The element of acting and the incessant implication of the present within the transference prompted him to approach transference as something more than the emergence of the compulsion to repeat. On the other hand, he questioned the view of transference as the repetition of an ancient unfulfilled need from the vantage point that the analysand never simply succumbs to this need, but always recreates it within the novel context of the analytic experience (Lacan 1991b[1960–61]:206–207).

The vexed issue of the relationship between transference and repetition was reopened in 1962–63, when Lacan spent a whole year investigating the topic of anxiety. Broaching yet again the conjunction of transference and the compulsion to repeat, he underscored that transference cannot be reduced to the reproduction of an anterior, unresolved conflict. If the analysand's transference is marked by love, this affect is always already related to an object in the present, which Lacan (1991b[1960–61]: 179–195) illustrated with Socrates' interpretation of Alcibiades' love in Plato's *Symposium* (Plato 1951).[31] Concurrently, he insisted that the reduction of transference to repetition obfuscates the importance of the analyst's own part in the entire affair. For if the transference always integrates an object in the present, analysts cannot escape their being made into the object of their analysands' transference, through which they not only elicit but also crucially shape their patients' reactions. Downplaying the repetitive component of transference and upgrading the analyst's creative part in it, Lacan also replaced his previous definition of countertransference as the sum of the analyst's prejudices, insufficient information, passions and difficulties, by the analyst's essential implication in the analysand's transference, whose cautious management must proceed from the purified desire of the analyst (Lacan 1991b[1960–61]: 221; 1962–63:session of 27 February 1963).[32]

Lacan's most distinguished view on the nature of transference appeared in *Seminar XI* (1977b[1964]), in which he designated transference and repetition as two distinct fundamental concepts of psychoanalysis.[33] Disregarding his own previous assertions and criticizing Freud for presenting a confused account, Lacan proclaimed that repetition has nothing in common with transference (ibid.:33, 69). Whereas repetition occurs when a missed, traumatic encounter (beyond the pleasure principle) is integrated within the network of signifiers (following the pleasure principle), transference 'is the enactment of the reality of the unconscious' (ibid.:146, 149).[34] Gradually disclosing the meaning of this new, highly aphoristic description of transference, Lacan specified that the reality of the unconscious is always sexual and that this unconscious sexual reality underpins all the analysand's demands within the transference. For example, if an analysand demands that the analyst say something because she has the impression that the latter does not seem to be interested in her associations, this demand represents an avatar of the analysand's unconscious sexual reality, notably that she derives excitement from awakening people's interest and that she cannot tolerate the idea that somebody might not be attracted to her. If the analyst remains mute, the analysand is bound to interpret his silence as an indication of the analyst's lack of interest or, more commonly, as evidence of his lack of professionalism, and she is likely to employ this interpretation as an explanation for her own lack of analytic progress. More specifically, she will attribute the fact that the analyst is not giving her enough (nice interpretations, kind words, love) to his being a bad practitioner, and she will try to change his habits by intermittently threatening him with her imminent departure. Conversely, when an analysand requests that the analyst remain silent so that he can devote himself fully to the exploration of his thoughts, this demand too harbours an unconscious sexual reality, inasmuch as the analysand might enjoy destroying whatever interest people may show in him so that he can devote himself quietly to the narcissistic enjoyment of his own isolated condition.

Substantiating earlier statements on the analyst's responsibility, Lacan added that this enactment of the sexual reality of the unconscious should not be understood as a mere effect of the analysand's psychic structure:

> The transference is a phenomenon in which subject and psycho-analyst are both included. To divide it in terms of transference and

countertransference – however bold, however confident what is said on this theme may be – is never more than a way of avoiding the essence of the matter.

(ibid.:231)

Apropos of the aforementioned examples, this means that the analysand in the first case will not regard the analyst as a passive figure who lacks all interest and commitment, expressly formulating the demand that he start working and acting as a proper analyst, if the latter did not cultivate an attitude of prolonged silence. *Mutatis mutandis*, the analysand in the second case will not vilify the analyst for intervening, impressing on him the idea that good analysts are supposed to listen and not talk, if the analyst himself did not engage regularly in asking questions and launching interpretations. The analyst's conduct in these two cases is crucial for the emergence of the analysand's transference as the enactment of the sexual reality of the unconscious and it simultaneously gives form to it.

Needless to say that the analyst's conduct in these matters reflects a particular desire and rests upon an appreciation of the psychic structure of the analysand before and during analytic sessions. In the first case, the analyst's sustained silence will normally proceed from a diagnosis of the analysand as a hysteric, whereas in the second case the analyst's nagging interventions will be based on a diagnosis of obsessional neurosis. Since hysteria revolves around an ardent desire to elicit the desire of the Other, the analyst's silence encompasses a refusal to enter the hysterical dynamics and is well suited to trigger the hysteric's fantasy within the transference. In 'Subversion of the Subject and the Dialectics of Desire' Lacan wrote:

> [A] calculated vacillation of the analyst's 'neutrality' may be more valuable for a hysteric than any amount of interpretation, despite the frenzy which may result from it. That is to say, so that this frenzy does not entail a rupture and the sequel convinces the subject that the desire of the analyst was by no means involved.
>
> (Lacan 1977k[1960]:321–322, translation modified)

Vice versa, since obsessional neurosis hinges on a desire to neutralize the desire of the Other, the analyst's interventions confront the analysand with a living presence by which the analyst guards himself against the tentacles of the obsessional apparatus and conjures up the obsessional fantasy.[35] In these two cases, the analyst's attitude is complementary, yet in each case it is based on what Lacan called the desire of the analyst, i.e. a desire that analysands reach the point where they avow their own desire.

LOVE OF KNOWLEDGE AND THE *AGALMA*

The intersubjective relationship between the analysand and the analyst, and the analyst's ineluctable involvement in the analysand's transference indicate that Lacan's original outlook of transference singled out the analytic situation as a constructive dialogue on the symbolic plane of full speech or, better still, as an interaction between two subjective desires. Many of Lacan's glosses on transference from the 1950s could be mustered to corroborate this picture and many of Lacan's attacks on the techniques of transference handling within ego-psychology could be read as implicit arguments for the revival of psychoanalytic treatment as a symbolic interaction between two subjects.[36]

Lacan's post-1960 contributions cleared the way for a completely different view. To see how radically his ideas on transference changed over the course of a decade, it suffices to contrast a statement from his 1957 'The Agency of the Letter' (1977g[1957]) with a passage from his 'Proposition of 9 October 1967 on the Psychoanalyst of the School' (1995b[1967]). Referring again to Freud's explanation of transference in *The Interpretation of Dreams* (1900a), Lacan reported in the former text that 'transference . . . gave its name to the mainspring of the intersubjective link between analyst and analysand' (Lacan 1977g[1957]:170). Ten years later he shattered any remaining faith in the value of this name, stating with undisguised disdain:

> I am astounded that no-one has ever thought of objecting to me, given certain of the terms of my doctrine, that the transference alone is an objection to intersubjectivity. I even regret it, seeing that nothing is more true: it refutes it, it is its stumbling block.
>
> (Lacan 1995b[1967]:4)

Prepared in the course of his *Seminar V* (1998b[1957–58]:357–358) and advanced more emphatically in 'The Direction of the Treatment' (1977i [1958]:229–230) and the 'Remark on the Report by Daniel Lagache' (1966e[1960]:655–656), Lacan's self-criticism of intersubjectivity had reached a first peak in *Seminar VIII, On Transference* (1991b[1960–61]), which initiated a less homogeneous, more conflict-ridden version of the analytic relationship.[37]

Seminar VIII was strewn with references to the insuperable inequity which the transference instates between the analysand and the analyst. Sometimes Lacan designated this inequity as a 'subjective disparity' (Lacan 1991b[1960–61]:11, 233), at other times he qualified it as a fundamental discordance or dissymmetry (ibid.:53, 68). As I have pointed out in the previous chapter (pp. 72–73), Lacan's self-criticism had grown out of the observation that intersubjectivity does not exclude the perils of a reciprocal, imaginary 'therapeutic alliance' between the analysand and the analyst.[38] In *Seminar VIII* he argued that intersubjectivity is an altogether erroneous description of what takes place within the analytic setting, quite simply because this setting is governed by transference, which is in turn pervaded by love. To demonstrate that transference runs counter to intersubjectivity Lacan thus rejuvenated his Freudian equivalence of transference and love, initially adumbrated in *Seminar I* (1988b[1953–54]:90), now showing that love entails everything but a harmonious interaction between two complementary subjects. The conflict-ridden undertow of the psychoanalytic process also emboldened him to criticize mainstream descriptions of the treatment as an analytic 'situation', a term which he preferred to replace by 'pseudo-situation' because 'the position of the two subjects present is by no means equivalent' (Lacan 1991b[1960–61]:11, 233).[39]

Taking his lead from the *Symposium* (Plato 1951), which he presented as the minutes of a series of psychoanalytic sessions (Lacan 1991b [1960–61]:38), Lacan identified the analysand with the lover, the analyst with the beloved, and the resulting strategies of transference with the dynamics of love. What characterizes the lover is an immanent feeling of lack.[40] Although the lover is hardly aware of this lack, much less of its exact nature, he none the less believes that the loved object possesses the means to neutralize it, thus restoring a sense of completeness.[41] To Lacan, the fact that the lover lacks knowledge about the existence and the status of this lack was sufficient proof to claim that the lack is unconscious.[42] When the beloved recognizes the other's love, the beloved reckons that she must have something which provokes the other's interest, yet she does not have a clue as to what it is (ibid.:52–53). Hence both the lover and the beloved are in a position of partial ignorance, but their ignorance is not the same. The lover does not know much about the immanent lack, but does know the beloved can annihilate it; the beloved does not know what he has, yet does know the lover wants it. The lover's ignorance is more related to an absence (what the lover misses), whereas the beloved's ignorance is more associated with a presence (what the beloved owns).

Relying on Ancient Greek mythology, Lacan stated that love reaches its highest degree of expression when the beloved becomes a lover in turn and starts returning the lover's love. When this occurs the positions within the relationship are no longer distributed according to who lacks (the lover) and who possesses something (the beloved), since each partner wants something from the other and also has something to offer. Lacan designated the moment when the beloved becomes a lover as 'the metaphor of love', and in accordance with his own definition of metaphor he drew attention to its potential for revealing a new signification, notably the genuine, true signification of love (ibid.:49–64).[43]

For all its ostensible rosiness, the portrait of love Lacan painted in *Seminar VIII* was of course predicated upon a tragic misunderstanding between the partners. What the lover discovers in the beloved is no more no less than the object of the lover's own fantasy, and has nothing to do with what the beloved really has to offer. Conversely, what the beloved believes she possesses as an object for the lover, without knowing for sure what it is, equally relates to the beloved's fantasy and has no bearing whatsoever on what the lover really lacks. Each of the partners mistakes fantasy for reality, adding error to error when entering the metaphor of love.

Applying this picture to the analytic 'pseudo-situation', Lacan compared the analysand to a lover because analysands generally expect their analysts to possess the key to their difficulties – inhibitions, symptoms and anxieties which they cannot understand, let alone solve. In *Seminar VIII* Lacan described this key, as seen through the eyes of the analysand, in two different ways. In the opening stages of the *Seminar*, he cut the analyst's key from the substance of knowledge:

> The psychoanalyst is a human being one comes to see in order to find the knowledge [*science*] of what is most intimate to oneself – this is the state of mind in which one usually approaches him – and thus of what we must assume to be initially most alien to him. None-the-less, this is what we encounter at the start of psychoanalysis; this knowledge [*science*] is what he is supposed to have.
>
> (ibid.:81–82)

Lacan's observation that analysands commonly regard their analysts as experts of the human psyche whose specialized knowledge will dissolve the symptoms ultimately crystallized into his concept of the 'supposed subject of knowing', which continued to undergird his ideas on transference until the end of his career.[44]

Yet as his work progressed he underscored that this function of the 'supposed subject of knowing', the constitutive element of the transference, does not imply that the analysand automatically perceives the analyst as somebody who knows (Lacan 1977b[1964]:233; 1967–68: session of 22 November 1967; 1971–72:session of 2 December 1971). In his 'Proposition of 9 October 1967 on the Psychoanalyst of the School' he even went so far as to state:

> We shall have to see what qualifies the psychoanalyst to respond to this situation [of the supposed subject of knowing] which one can see does not envelop his person. Not only is the supposed subject of knowing not real in effect, but it is in no way necessary that the subject who is active in the conjuncture, the psychoanalysand (the only one who speaks initially), impose it upon him. Not only is it not necessary, it is not usually true: which is demonstrated in the initial stages of the discourse by a way of assuring oneself that the suit does not fit the psychoanalyst – an assurance against the fear that he will put, if I may say so, his creases in it too soon.
>
> (Lacan 1995b[1967]:5, translation modified)

Without devaluing the importance of the supposed subject of knowing for the transference, Lacan relativized its impact as a truthful and honest expectation with which most analysands approach their analysts, considering the spurious relationship they have with knowledge professed by somebody else. As I have explained in Chapter 1, it is not because people do not know what is wrong with them, and, following their wish to know the truth, urge professionals to tell them what they know, that they will be willing to accept the professionals' knowledge. An analysand's investment of her analyst with the supposed subject of knowing is always relative: on the one hand she wants her analyst to be wildly knowledgeable, whereas on the other she already knows in advance that from the moment he will start professing his knowledge, it will prove fatally flawed. Or, if the analysand has been sufficiently hystericized, he will simultaneously expect his analyst to be knowledgeable, to convey this knowledge, to admit it is inadequate, to seek more knowledge, to allow him to find knowledge elsewhere, etc.[45]

None the less Lacan remained convinced that the supposed subject of knowing constitutes 'the pivot on which everything to do with the transference is hinged' (ibid.:5). Even when analysands refuse to accept their analysts as paragons of absolute knowledge, the supposed subject of knowing (and transference) will continue to operate if only the analysands believe that one day they will become masters in their own house. In this sense Lacan's supposed subject of knowing conveys nothing more than the analysand's opinion that all knowledge can be endowed with a subject, i.e. that there is no such thing as a knowledge which has to remain funda-mentally subject-less. In more psychological terms, the supposed subject of knowing refers to the individual's belief that it is possible to attain the climax of full self-realization, a status characterized by the definitive cancellation of all nonsense, the complete understanding of oneself and the discovery of the true signification of life.[46] The supposed subject of knowing is evidently at odds with the divided subject ($) of the unconscious, because it glorifies the transparency of all knowledge and aims for the restoration of a psychic economy without loss. The supposed subject of knowing 'is the postulate of which it is the case that it abolishes the unconscious' (Lacan 1968c[1967]:46).

In his 1967 'Proposition', Lacan formalized the installation of the supposed subject of knowing in a new algorithm of transference (Lacan 1995b[1967]:5):

$$\frac{S \longrightarrow S^a}{s(S^1, S^2, \ldots S^n)}$$

The sequence under the bar represents the analysand's assumption of an agency controlling the signification of all knowledge (the undivided subject of the unconscious, the thinker behind the unconscious thoughts), whereby s stands for (undivided, present) subject and $(S^1, S^2, \ldots S^n)$ for the unconscious thoughts (the symbolic network of signifiers). The S above the bar is the so-called 'transference-signifier' (*signifiant du transfert*) which, in its relation to any old signifier (S^a), makes the supposition possible. The link between S and S^a is the connection between two signifiers without which the supposed subject of knowing would remain without signification for the analysand.[47] Indeed the assumption that all knowledge can be subjectified only becomes significant for the analysand because he has 'transferred' one of the signifiers (ideas, representations) in his psyche to a particular signifier belonging to another subject, the analyst for that matter.[48]

In *Seminar XX* Lacan translated this craving for complete knowledge within the transference in the terminology of love, proclaiming that 'love is the desire to be One', and that love proceeds from the belief 'we are but One' (Lacan 1998a[1972–73]:6, 47).[49] Love (and transference) equals believing that the other is not an Other affected by an irreducible lack, but the incarnation of the perfect One, and it cherishes the hope that this One will spill over onto one-self. Since the entrapment of love is part and parcel of the neurotic's psychic economy, it is by no means restricted to the psychoanalytic setting, which again explains why transference can easily exist outside the walls of the psychoanalytic cabinet.

If the unconscious is a knowledge without a knowing agency (a headless body so to speak) and the supposed subject of knowing correlates with the complete mastery over knowledge, it is clear why Lacan contended in *Seminar XI* (1977b[1964]:130–133) that transference involves a closure of the unconscious. In its striving for unity love favours the redemption of the absent subject of the unconscious or, to use Lacan's terms in *Encore*, it aims at being, to be understood here as self-fulfilment (Lacan 1998a[1972–73]:40). Once again this point repeated a feature Freud had noted in his paper on transference-love and which he had attributed to the influence of resistance:

> At a first glance it certainly does not look as if the patient's falling in love in the transference could result in any advantage to the treatment. No matter how amenable she has been up till then, she suddenly loses all understanding of the treatment and all interest in it, and will not speak or hear about anything but her love, which she demands to have returned. She gives up her symptoms or pays no attention to them; indeed, she declares that she is well.
>
> (Freud 1915a[1914]:162)

Alienated to the transference-signifier, analysands deceive themselves and their analysts when supposing the subject of knowing, not only in their sudden extirpation of the debilitating effects of the symptoms, but also in the special demands they put upon their analysts. In the former case the analyst runs the risk of losing his patient because she declares herself healthy and cannot think of any good reason to continue the treatment. In the latter case, a patient may consider breaking off the treatment because he feels that the analyst is not paying enough attention to him, does not give enough of her time, tends to run shorter sessions with him than with other analysands, does not appreciate the (financial) effort he has put into the whole enterprise, in short does not love him enough. Of course, the analyst needs to ensure that the analysis does not come to a halt because the analysand's transference makes him feel 'cured by magic' or 'just treated like everybody else'. To solve this clinical problem, Lacan advised that the analyst overturn the dead weight of the analysand's demands within the transference with the lever of desire, a recommendation to which I will return in the following section of this chapter.

As mentioned earlier, the analysand's perception of the analyst as a character equipped with knowledge of his most intimate experiences is not the only factor Lacan distinguished in *Seminar VIII* to explain the eruption of love. After having cut the analyst's key to the analysand's problems, as seen through the latter's own eyes, from the material of knowledge, Lacan used the sparring match between Socrates and Alcibiades at the end of the *Symposium* to delineate the function of the *agalma* within the transference (Lacan 1991b[1960–61]:163–195). *Agalma* is the term Alcibiades used to grasp the hidden, yet fascinating object he believed to be enclosed in the depths of Socrates' hideous body. A mysterious gem whose preciousness he had savoured as a young man during a privileged moment of revelation, the *agalma* had sparked Alcibiades' infatuation with Socrates and served to justify his eulogy of Socrates' attractiveness.

In *Seminar VIII* Lacan surmised that the part played by the *agalma* in the emergence of transference must be at least as important as that of the supposed knowledge, yet his subsequent invocations of the topic were rather disappointing. Apart from a small, yet valuable gloss in his 'Proposition of 9 October 1967 on the Psychoanalyst of the School' (1995b [1967]:7), references were often limited to simple mentions of the term. It is tempting to argue that Lacan gradually replaced the *agalma* with his own concept of the object *a*, so that each passage on the function of the object *a* in the transference would contain an implicit reference to the *agalma*. I wish to challenge this idea, not so much because it is difficult to entertain on the basis of Lacan's own works, but mainly because the equation of the *agalma* and the object *a* makes it extremely difficult to comprehend some of Lacan's later statements on the position of the analyst in the treatment.[50] For example, when Lacan argued in *Encore* that analysts are 'in the best position to do what should rightfully be done, namely to investigate the status of the truth as knowledge', when they put the object *a* in the place of semblance, does this mean that the analyst is supposed to sustain the analysand's love in order to realize the analytic goals? For if *agalma* (as the mysterious object triggering love) equals the object *a* and the analyst is held to occupy the position of object *a* in the analytic discourse, how can the transference ever be analysed?

The conflation of the *agalma* and the object *a* also gives rise to a confusion of love and desire in Lacan's work, since the object *a* is traditionally defined as the object cause of desire. Lacan himself to some degree contributed to this confusion by using love and desire as interchangeable terms in *Seminar VIII*, and by elucidating the metaphor of love in his two subsequent Seminars as a substitution of the desiring (*le désirant*) for the desirable (*le désiré*).[51] However, from the mid-1960s he charted love and desire as two separate experiences on whose distinction the entire progress of psychoanalytic treatment depends. The promotion of desire as the analyst's lever to overturn the analysand's love in *Seminar XI*

(1977b[1964]:235) can exemplify this. Hence the *agalma* of love does not equal the object *a* of desire, because like the supposed subject of knowing the *agalma* relates to the analysand's perception of the Other as a perfect being, containing the precious jewels of happiness and salvation, whereas the object *a* is strictly situated within the dimension of semblance. Whereas the *agalma* represents the ideal stone of wisdom, the object *a* is but a partial, replaceable commodity.[52]

KNOWLEDGE OF LOVE AND THE OBJECT *a*

Thus far I have only examined the role of the analysand as a lover within the transference. But what about the position of the analyst as a loved object? Elaborating Socrates' response to Alcibiades' declaration of love in the *Symposium*, Lacan stressed in *Seminar VIII* (1991b[1960–61]:185) that the analyst ought to avoid entering the metaphor of love. Like Socrates the analyst is approached as a loved object, invested with the supposed subject of knowing and the *agalma*, yet she is not meant to return the analysand's love if the psychoanalytic process is to continue. Needless to say that this guideline is but a reformulation of Freud's warning in 'Observations on Transference-Love' (1915a[1914]:165–166) that the analyst who considers entering a love relationship with the analysand is inevitably drawn into something else than psychoanalysis.

Even more important than the analyst's avoidance of the metaphor of love is her refusal to identify with the supposed subject of knowing. When handling the transference the analyst should again follow Socrates' example inasmuch as he incessantly impressed on his acolytes that he knew nothing at all, his only objective in life being the ongoing evaluation of what they themselves purportedly knew. When Lacan claimed that analysts are supposed subjects of knowing in the transference, it is therefore crucial to understand that this may be representative of how analysands perceive their analysts, but not of how analysts should present themselves *vis-à-vis* their patients. On numerous occasions Lacan declared that analysts should refrain from incarnating the supposed subject of knowing. As such, he warned in *Seminar IX*: 'We need to learn how to rid ourselves of this supposed subject of knowing at every moment. We can never have recourse to it; that is excluded' (Lacan 1961–62:session of 22 November 1961). Six years later, in *Seminar XIV*, he contended that analysts ought to know that they are not subjects endowed with knowledge, and that one of the analyst's main tasks consists in the rectification of the effects of the analysand's supposition (Lacan 1966–67:session of 21 June 1967).

Taking this precept one step further, one could say that the analyst's identification with the supposed subject of knowing is as much a recipe for the termination of psychoanalytic treatment as engaging in the metaphor of love, with the caveat that in this case the relation between the analyst and the analysand will be governed by objectification, suggestion and the therapeutic abuse of power rather than the mutual sharing of losses and gains. Not offering themselves as reservoirs of knowledge and not satisfying the analysand's demands – a venture in which they engage automatically when they identify with the supposed subject of knowing – analysts are expected to bring about a psychic transformation from demand to desire in the analysand (Lacan 1998b[1957–58]:430; 1977i[1958]:269). In *Seminar XI* Lacan put it as follows:

> In so far as the analyst is supposed to know [according to the analysand], he is also supposed [according to the ethics of psycho-analysis] to set out in search of unconscious desire. This is why I say . . . that desire is the axis, the pivot, the handle, the hammer, by which is applied the force-element to the inertia that lies behind what is formulated at first, in the discourse of the patient, as demand, namely the transference.
>
> (Lacan 1977b[1964]:235, translation modified)[53]

At the end of *Seminar XI* he reconstructed this mandatory analytic transition from demand to desire – the only way out of the clinical impasse of transference – in the so-called 'schema of the interior eight' (ibid.: 271):

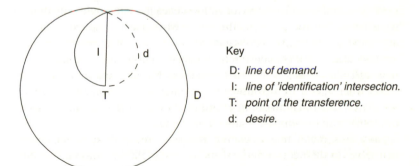

Key

D: *line of demand.*
I: *line of 'identification' intersection.*
T: *point of the transference.*
d: *desire.*

Figure 2 The interior eight
Source: J. Lacan, *The Four Fundamental Concepts of Psychoanalysis,* Harmondsworth, Penguin, 1994, p. 271.

In this figure the outer line symbolizes the demands (D) verbalized by the analysand during the initial stages of the analytic process. Through these demands the analysand inevitably arrives at a point of transference (T), notably when he bears witness to a belief in the supposed subject of knowing. If this moment does not prompt the analysand to withdraw from the treatment, it constitutes a nodal point where the trajectory of demand bifurcates, continuing either via the line of identification or via desire.

On the one hand analysts can take advantage of their analysands' transference to present themselves as ego ideals, proving to their patients that they honestly care about them (thus fulfilling their demands), cultivating a mutual working alliance, and facilitating processes of social and behavioural modelling. This is the approach Lacan situated on the intersecting line of identification, and which he had designated earlier as the hallmark of suggestion and the analytic abuse of power (Lacan 1998b[1957–58]:423–438; 1977i[1958]:270).[54] When analysts opt for this strategy of transference handling, analysands identify with their analysts and enter an endless cycle of identical demands.[55] On the other hand, however, the analyst can also halt before the pathway of identification and direct the analysand towards the realm of desire (d), which Lacan depicted as an interrupted line piercing the plane of demand at the point of trans-ference, thus circumventing the line of identification before rejoining that of demand.[56] To open this sequence, the analyst should neither satisfy nor frustrate the analysand's demands (Lacan 1977i[1958]:255), but use them as launch pads for eliciting a series of questions in the analysand: 'What do you (analyst) want (from me)?', 'What do others want (from me)?', 'What is it that I want (others to want from me)?', and 'How is what I want influenced by what others want (from me)?'. Again the analyst is not supposed to answer these questions, because that would only imply his renewed identification with the supposed subject of knowing. Rather he is expected to enable analysands to voice their own answers, which normally leads to the (re)construction of their fantasies and, eventually, to their realization that it is impossible to know for once and for all what it is they want since they are human beings endowed with an unconscious. For analysts the linchpin of this entire procedure is their constant refusal to identify with the supposed subject of knowing.

Does this mean that Lacanian analysts are entitled to ensconce themselves in their comfortable seats without bothering too much about the acquisition of psychoanalytic knowledge? Not at all. In his 'Proposition of 9 October 1967 on the Psychoanalyst of the School', Lacan proclaimed: 'It is clear that of the supposed knowledge he [the analyst] knows nothing . . . This in no way authorises the psychoanalyst to be satisfied in the knowledge that he knows nothing, for what is at issue is what he has to come to know' (Lacan 1995b[1967]:6). And in a contemporaneous intervention on the relation between psychoanalysis and reality he declared: 'Psychoanalysts are the wiseacres of a knowledge about which they cannot converse with each other. This is something else than the mystagogy of non-knowledge' (Lacan 1968a[1967]:59). But what is this functional knowledge analysts are asked to acquire and which is seemingly powerful enough to guarantee their ignoring what they know? During the early 1950s Lacan believed it was sufficient for analysts to know that their knowledge is but a symptom of their ignorance, and that the success of their interventions crucially depends on their ability to ignore what they know (Lacan 1966b[1955]:349, 358). Yet from *Seminar VIII* he underscored that analysts succeed in 'knowing that they have to ignore what they know' only if they know something about love (Lacan 1991b [1960–61]:135). In other words, knowing something about transference is a prerequisite for suspending the knowledge one has accumulated from training sessions, books and previous experience.

Once again Lacan referred to Socrates who, in spite of his incessant confession of ignorance, did admit that he knew something about love. Of course, when Socrates transmitted his knowledge about love he did not speak in his own name, but through the mouth of a mysterious woman named Diotima. Lacan interpreted this singularity of the Socratic discourse as a move necessitated by the antagonism between Socrates' dialectical method of inquiry and the epistemological status of the knowledge in question. To Lacan knowledge of love escaped Socrates' dialectical method, forcing him to rely on what he had learnt from the common-sense opinions of Diotima (ibid.:142–148). Socrates' knowledge of love did not belong to the established realm of *episteme*, a series of hard and fast scientific facts, but merely to the ethereal sphere of *doxa*, the shared ideas of popular wisdom.

Analysts need to possess knowledge of love to be capable of ignoring what they know and to ensure the maintenance of analytic standards, but the knowledge of love itself constitutes a limit. This is the problem Lacan set out to investigate in *Seminar XX* (1998a[1972–73]), not so much with the brief of enhancing our understanding of love, but more with the aim of clarifying the rationale behind this limit of love and knowledge. From the start of the seminar he informed his audience: '[W]hat I say of love is assuredly that one cannot speak about it . . . I spoke of the love letter, of the declaration of love – not the same thing as the word of love' (ibid.:12). Operating beyond the signifier, Lacan defined love as a sign, and more specifically as a sign that one changes reason or discourse. Unlike the signifier, love is unequivocal to the extent that it can always be taken as indicating a transition from one discourse to another (ibid.:16). However, love is at once the most awkward sign to recognize: neither the jouissance of the Other, the sexual characters appearing on the surface of the partner's body, nor the receipt of love letters, nor the awareness that the Other knows you so well that he can predict your whereabouts offer reliable criteria for ascertaining the Other's love.[57] Lacan's entire *Seminar XX* hovered around an amazing paradox: love always constitutes a sign, but nothing ever constitutes a sign of love. When love takes over, it inevitably alters the course of human action, yet testimonies of love are impossible to confirm by established facts. A woman might be convinced of her own love and the ravages it provokes, without ever being able to prove her love to her partner and without ever being successful in ratifying his own love for her. The crucial implication for the analyst is that she must never take ostensible signs of love (transference) in the analysand at face value, whilst acknowledging that love dramatically changes the analytic picture. In addition, analysts ought to realize that knowing everything about love is an illusion, and that what knowledge they have must be subject to continuous revision.

Not complying with the metaphor of love and ignoring what he knows on the basis of a (necessarily limited) knowledge of love, the analyst's task also consists in dismantling the ideals which the analysand has conferred onto him. Whilst supporting the functions of the supposed subject of knowing and the *agalma* in order to elicit the analysand's fantasy, the analyst needs to ensure that the transference can be analysed. Indeed, for all his scepticism about the so-called 'liquidation' of the transference – one of the pillars of mainstream French psychoanalysis during the 1950s – Lacan never disputed the analyst's duty of bringing about the fall (*chute*) or the reduction (*réduction*) of the analysand's transference (Lacan 1967–68:session of 10 January 1968).[58] Inducing the fall of the supposed subject of knowing means that the analyst ought to lay bare its illusory character after having exploited (but not identified with) its value for the construction of the analysand's fantasy. An elimination of the deceptive aspect of the transference is the only meaning Lacan was willing to grant to the practice of transference-liquidation (Lacan 1977b[1964]: 267). As such, the Lacanian clinic does not dislodge the transference, the analyst cannot prevent the unconscious from being re-enacted or closing up, yet the analytic process does contribute to dissolving the dissimulation which the supposed subject of knowing sustains.

In Lacan's conception of the treatment, working towards the destabilization of deceit equalled progressing towards the realization of truth. By contrast with the established schools of psychoanalysis he did not flaunt the essential replacement of (the analysand's) transference with (the analyst's) reality, even less the slow maturation of the transference to the level of genital object-relations, defending instead the gradual substitution of truth for knowledge.[59] Saying that the analyst should act in the name of truth (Lacan 1966–67:session of 21 June 1967) or that his feigning the position of supposed subject of knowing is the only access to truth (Lacan 1967–68:session of 22 November 1967) seemed even more conceited and presumptuous than proposing a transformation of the 'hysterical misery into common unhappiness' (Freud and Breuer 1895d:305) or staging a confrontation between the analysands' pleasurable fantasies and the standard requirements of reality. Although supported by Freud's professed love of truth (*Wahrhaftigkeit, Wahrheitsliebe*) (1915a[1914]:164; 1937c: 248), Lacan was vilified for his uncompromising espousal of veracity as the ultimate goal of psychoanalysis, the more so after launching statements such as 'I, the truth, am speaking' (Lacan 1977f[1955]:120–123; 1989b[1965]:15) and 'I always speak the truth' (Lacan 1990d[1973]:3). But against the expectations Lacan's notion of truth did not signal the perfect match between reason and reality, the scientific 'correspondence criterion' of truth embedded in the medieval adage of *adaequatio rei et intellectus* (an intellect that is in line with the thing).[60] Neither did it advance the traditional psychoanalytic goal of the analysand's discovery of a repressed unconscious representation, and its reintegration into a conscious series of thoughts. The Lacanian truth emblematized no more no less than the very absence of definitive truths within human existence, owing to the fact that not all knowledge can be subjectified, that the enjoyment of fullness is forever excluded, that the symbolic law of castration compels (neurotic) subjects to desire until the end of their days.

In 'Subversion of the Subject and the Dialectic of Desire' Lacan decanted this truth (of an irreducible absence or lack) into the aphorism 'There is no Other of the Other', and its algebraical equivalent $S(\emptyset)$, carefully delineating its implications for analytic practice:

> The lack referred to here is indeed that which I have already formulated: that there is no Other of the Other. But is this mark made by the Unbeliever of the truth really the last word that is worth giving in reply to the question, 'What does the Other want of me?', when we, the analysts, are its mouthpiece? Surely not, and precisely because there is nothing doctrinal about our office. We are answerable to no ultimate truth; we are neither for nor against any particular religion.
>
> (Lacan 1977k[1960]:316)

The impossibility to unearth the final truth about oneself should not embolden the analyst to answer the analysand's question – once the fantasy has been constructed – of 'What does the Other want from me?' with stock expressions such as 'You will never know' or 'This is impossible to find out'. For these statements are as much tributary to a definitive truth as their vexed counterparts ('This is what the Other wants', 'I possess the solution to your problem'). Pontificating that it is impossible to know for once and for all what the Other wants becomes a definitive truth in its own right, which contradicts the principle that there is no such thing as a final truth. It is therefore sufficient for analysands to relativize their own time-honoured answers to what the Other wants from them, that is to say to question the trust they had put in their fantasies. Analysts should not (and cannot) prevent analysands from formulating new answers and creating new fantasies, their only hope being that the distrust they have developed towards the old ones affects their attitudes towards the new versions. In his 1967 'Proposition' Lacan described this process, which coincides with the end of the transference relation, as a subjective destitution (*destitution subjective*), issuing it as the analysand's entry ticket to the analytic profession (Lacan 1995b[1967]:8).

Lacan was adamant that the fall of the supposed subject of knowing and its concurrent effect of subjective destitution on the side of the analysand cannot be realized through an array of transference-interpretations, that is to say interpretations whose object is the nature of transference itself. As he had explained in *Seminar V* (1998b[1957–58]:428) and 'The Direction of the Treatment' (1977i[1958]:231), the analyst cannot construct a 'neutral' platform outside the analysand's transference from which to operate on this transference. If the analysand accepts the analyst's interpretation of the transference, this acceptance needs to be interpreted in its own right because the analysand is bound to hear the interpretation as coming from the supposed subject of knowing and thus from within the transference. Giving meta-interpretations after the transference has been interpreted does not make a difference, since these meta-interpretations would also require interpretation, *ad infinitum*. As Lacan put it in his 1969 summary of *Seminar XV*: 'There is no transference of the transference' (Lacan 1984[1969]:25).

Lacan's solution to this deadlock lay in the deployment of a tactics of interpretation which points towards the analysand's desire rather than the demands (for love) within the transference. The analyst makes clear that she knows nothing about the analysand, that whatever knowledge the analysand has assembled is futile, and that additional knowledge (whether practical know-how or deep wisdom) is not what the analysand can expect from the experience. On the contrary, if knowledge is at all involved at the end of the psychoanalytic process it will appear as an acknowledgement of the limit of the imperative to 'Know Thyself!' (Lacan 1967–68:session of 13 March 1968). This tactics of interpretation evidently challenges the meaning of analytic interpretation as such, because the analyst neither explains the analysand's symptoms, nor makes sense of what the analysand says, nor translates the analysand's actions into new significant units, etc. Vacillating between silence, the punctuation of the analysand's discourse and the formulation of oracular sentences, the analyst cultivates the atopia of the Socratic position (Lacan 1991b [1960–61]:126–127). I will discuss the underlying principles of these Lacanian tactics of interpretation at length in the following chapter of this book.

From the mid-1960s Lacan associated the fall of the supposed subject of knowing with the analyst's functioning as an object *a*, his disbeing (*désêtre*) the analysand's cause of desire. For example, in *Seminar XV* he stated:

> The end of analysis consists in the fall of the supposed subject of knowing and its reduction to the accession of this object *a*, the cause of the division of the subject, which replaces it. The only thing the analyst, who fantasmatically plays the game with the analysand as regards the supposed subject of knowing, supports at the end of analysis is this rest of the known thing which is called the object *a*.
> (Lacan 1967–68:session of 10 January 1967)

To understand the meaning of this proposition it suffices to look back at what Lacan concluded at the end of *Seminar VIII*:

> What Socrates knows, and what the analyst at least has to see, is that on the level of the small *a* [the object *a*], the issue is completely different from that of the access to an ideal. Love can only grasp the field of being. And the analyst can only think that any object can fulfil it. This is where we analysts are brought to balance, on this limit where the question is raised of the value of any object that enters the field of desire.
> (Lacan 1991b[1960–61]:459–460)

Disbeing the object *a* involves encouraging analysands to realize that the supposed subject of knowing and the *agalma*, whose brilliance once reassured them in their love, are but replaceable objects *a*, semblances of being whose power does not outmatch that of other potential objects and whose promise of enjoyment is doomed to remain inadequate.[61] The result of this operation, which the analyst effectuates by reducing himself to nothing but a gaze or a voice (Lacan 1995b[1967]:10; 1967–68:session of 7 February 1968), is that the analysand can undertake a 'crossing' (*traversée*) (Lacan 1977b[1964]:273) or succeeds in dropping out (*déçoir*) (Lacan 1995b[1967]:8) of his fantasy.[62] Again, this result corre-lates with a moment of subjective destitution which, as mentioned on p. 136, Lacan promoted as the precondition for entering the practice of psychoanalysis.

As I have indicated at the end of the previous chapter, during the early 1970s Lacan opened yet another new perspective on the goal of psycho-analytic treatment, combining Freud's idea that psychoanalysis operates via the pathways of love (McGuire 1974:12–13) and his own assertion that love is always a sign of changing discourses (Lacan 1998a[1972–73]: 16). The theoretical framework for this new perspective can be derived from a juxtaposition of two of Lacan's numerous aphorisms in *Seminar XX* and *Television*, statements produced in 1973 with an interval of a mere six months. In the final pages of *Seminar XX* Lacan posited:

> I incarnated contingency in the expression 'stops not being written.' For here there is nothing but encounter . . . The displacement of the negation from the 'stops not being written' to the 'doesn't stop being written', in other words, from contingency to necessity – there lies the point of suspension to which all love is attached. All love, subsisting only on the basis of the 'stops not being written', tends to make the negation shift to the 'doesn't stop being written' . . . Such is the substitute that . . . constitutes the destiny as well as the drama of love.
> (ibid.:145)

This fragment loses much of its mysterious character if one exchanges the notion of love for that of transference. For then it becomes clear that Lacan hinted at the inauspicious transference situation Freud had held responsible, in the letter to Fließ from April 1900 quoted on p. 107, for 'the apparent endlessness' and the 'asymptotic conclusion of the treat-ment' (Masson 1985:409): an accidental encounter (contingency) which develops into an indispensable compulsive relationship (necessity).

The tenor of Lacan's words at the end of *Seminar XX* chimed with his oration on love in *Television*, although the latter concerned itself more explicitly with the analyst's coordination of its labours. After having expounded that the analytic discourse promises to introduce something

new within the field of love (Lacan 1990d[1973]:28), an arena marked by
the impasse (closure) of the unconscious, he contended that this novelty

> requires only that somewhere the sexual relation stops not being
> written, that contingency be established (what it comes down to),
> so as to make headway on that which will later be completed by
> demonstrating such a relation to be impossible, that is by instituting
> it in the real.
>
> (ibid.:39, translation modified)

This sentence contains first of all an argument to bring the necessity of the
analysand's transference back to its underlying contingency. Chosen in an
unexpected, yet fortunate encounter and gradually transformed into a
standard feature of the analysand's life, the analyst tries to re-establish her
original position as an accidental, replaceable find. This restoration of
contingency is a prerequisite for the analysand's discovery that everything
will fall short of the 'perfect match' or, to use Lacan's words in the second
part of the above sentence, that the sexual relation is impossible.

If the analyst moves from contingency to necessity and back, then
the same could be said of the entire analytic process. Lacan's words
in *Television* could indeed be read as also comprising an argument for
calibrating psychoanalytic practice around surprise, revelation, sudden
discovery, etc. Conceiving psychoanalytic treatment as a discipline
of contingencies could also solve the question as to how the discourse
of the analyst can subsist if it is predicated upon love and if love is the
sign of changing discourses. As I have mentioned before (see p. 134),
Lacan stipulated at the beginning of *Seminar XX* that the sign of love
strikes whenever a subject is moving from one discourse to another. But
if psychoanalysis is indeed effected by love, how is it possible to
institutionalize a discourse that is no more no less than the transition from
one discourse to another? One answer could be that the entire period
between the analysand's entry into and departure from analysis represents
a transition from one discourse, say a deeply ingrained life-style, to
another. A second answer could be that the transition from one discourse
to another takes place every time an analysand has a session with the
analyst.

Each of these answers is valid only if one forgets that analysands do
not immediately change their ways when entering psychoanalysis,
neither during individual nor over consecutive sessions. Despite the rule
of free association, analysands commonly fall back on their usual, current
discourse. Some analysands even believe that the day they will be able to

engage in free association will also constitute the end of their analysis. My answer to the above problem is that the transition from one discourse to another takes place at irregular moments, both during the course of psychoanalytic treatment and outside a psychoanalytic setting. The only difference between the emergence of these transitions is that within the treatment they are consciously provoked by the analyst, whereas outside they occur more or less haphazardly. When Lacan stated in *Television* that conceiving something new requires contingency (what stops not being written), this applies directly to how the analytic discourse affects the analysand who is subjugated to the necessities of other discourses: not the regular pattern of analytic sessions, but the unexpected appearance of a new signifier governs the process of change.

Since the destiny and drama of love hinges on a shift from contingency to necessity, as Lacan put it in *Seminar XX*, the ultimate psychoanalytic effect can only involve a reduction of the established necessity of the analytic effects themselves to the status of simple contingency. This process requires an analysis of the analytic experience, in which the analysand can come to realize that it was no more than an accident on his particular journey through life. The ultimate analytic effect thus coincides with the termination of psychoanalysis, after which the analysand will hopefully understand, at least if the treatment was Lacanian, not the true signification but the nonsensicality of the entire experience, not the necessity but the impossibility of finding definitive answers to the questions of life.

BEYOND THE TRANSFERENCE PRINCIPLE

At the end of this chapter I feel obliged to say something about the strategies of transference in psychotic and perverse patients, and their proper management within the constraints of Lacanian psychoanalysis. For the majority of the aforementioned conceptions apply to neurotic (obsessional or hysterical) patients and cannot be extrapolated without modification to other clinical structures. As I have already pointed out in the two previous chapters, extensive theoretical discussion and concrete technical advice on these matters must not be expected from the study of Lacan's works, the apparent standstill of his genius being even more conspicuous in the playground of perversion than in the arena of psychosis.

Scrutiny of Lacan's *Seminar III, The Psychoses* (1993[1955–56]) and its corollary, the *écrit* 'On a Question Preliminary to Any Possible Treatment of Psychosis' (1977h[1957–58]), suffices to observe his reluctance in classifying the psychotic's peculiar interactions with others as transference. After having claimed in his 'Rome Discourse' (1977e[1953]:68) that the psychotic's freedom of speech, prevaricating recognition, poses an obstacle to transference, Lacan described in *Seminar III* how Schreber's paranoid relations with all the masculine characters in his surroundings can be regarded as transference, simultaneously indicating that the notion 'is undoubtedly not to be taken in quite the sense that we usually mean' (Lacan 1993[1955–56]:31). Returning to the structure of Schreber's delusions at the end of the seminar, he added that the disturbed relationships with others within the delusional system are clearly connected to a transference mechanism (ibid.:310), which does not imply that the persecutory relationships constitute a transference in themselves.[63]

Without resolving the issue Lacan simply referred to Schreber's 'delusional "transferences"' [*sic*] in his seminal text on psychosis (Lacan 1977h[1957–58]:190), dismissing the bulk of the psychoanalytic literature on transference and psychosis as an instance of the swiftness with which 'psychoanalysts claim to be able to cure psychosis in all cases where a psychosis is not involved' (ibid.:192).[64] At the very end of his text, Lacan revealed that his preliminary question to any possible treatment of psychosis introduced 'the conception to be formed of the handling, in this treatment, of the transference', yet he refused to enter that area of research because his aim had been to 'return to' and not to go 'beyond Freud' (ibid.:221). Lacan addressed the issue of psychosis on a regular basis in later years, without gathering up the loose threads of his previous explorations.

The most oft-quoted and perhaps the only valuable statement on psychosis and transference within Lacan's later work is his 1966 introduction to the French translation of Schreber's memoirs (Lacan 1996b[1966]).[65] On a theoretical level Lacan instated a new opposition between the subject that is represented by a signifier for another signifier, i.e. the already conceptualized divided subject (S) of the unconscious, and the subject of jouissance purportedly underpinning the structure of paranoia (ibid.:2).[66] From a practical viewpoint he impelled psychoanalysts working with psychotics to adapt themselves to a clinical constellation which puts them 'in the position of object of a sort of mortifying erotomania', similar to the place Schreber assigned to Flechsig in his delusional constructions (ibid.:4). The upshot of this constellation would be that the psychoanalyst is not invested with a transference signifier supporting the supposed subject of knowing, but with an imaginary 'persona' subjugated to the unsavoury intentions of an infatuated stalker.

These scant indications conjure up the picture I outlined in the first chapter of this book, of the psychotic patient whose lack of ignorance excludes the supposed subject of knowing and prefigures a destructive, competitive, imaginary bond. On the question of how to deal with this type of transference, Lacanian psychoanalysts have formulated a plethora of clinical guidelines, often based on what they have learnt from their private experience with single case-studies. The following series of ideas is a summary of what I consider to be the most important technical features. The series does not pretend to be exhaustive, and clinicians are encouraged to approach these ideas as recommendations and not as established principles or hard-and-fast rules, in keeping with Freud's warning in the opening paragraphs of 'On Beginning the Treatment' (1913c:123).

It is first of all believed that analysts run the risk of invigorating the 'mortifying erotomania' when helping to disclose the signification of the psychotic's experiences. Like Schreber, who suffered immensely from the realization that 'All nonsense cancels itself out' (Schreber 1988 [1903]:151–152), psychotics are engulfed by the significance of their condition, and do not benefit from people who question or solidify this significance. More radically than in the case of neurotics, the analyst ought to abstain from being a mind-reader or seer, because this position consolidates the psychotic's mental state and seriously jeopardizes the analytic setting (Alquier *et al.* 1992:171). By contrast, analysts are held to offer an address (Broca 1984:50), a stable place at which the psychotic patient can call, and which they occupy in the function of secretaries or witnesses of the psychotic's experiences (Soler 1987).

Additionally Lacanian psychoanalysts have reached an agreement on the importance of the clinician's calculated restrictiveness with regard to the psychotic's intrusive jouissance. Because symbolic castration does not operate in psychotic patients, jouissance has not been severed from the Other (Miller 1993:11), which compels psychotics to an existence as mere objects for the whimsical jouissance of the Other. To counter this painful situation, Lacanian analysts have attempted to regulate the Other's overwhelming jouissance by imposing a set of symbolic rules, through which certain aspects of the psychotic's jouissance, such as the recourse to self-mutilation, are being prohibited, and others are being enforced. In curtailing the psychotic's jouissance analysts epitomize a semblance of castration, which is meant to be conducive to the creation of an artificial space of desire and a socially adapted lifestyle. The semblance of castration can be implemented via the analyst's radical 'No!' as a response to particular expressions of the psychotic's jouissance (Silvestre 1984:56), or it can be effectuated more surreptitiously through the analyst's demand that patients engage in new social bonds and make themselves accessible to new encounters (Broca 1985, 1988). As regards the encouragement of specific outlets for the psychotic's jouissance, Lacanians have valued the analyst's role as a clinical Maecenas for the artistic projects in which patients may indulge (Soler 1987:31). Whether painting, writing or any other type of creative activity, these forms of expression contribute to the fixation of the psychotic's jouissance, which in turn increases the chances for developing social competence.

Finally, on the vicissitudes of the transference in cases of perversion, even Lacan's followers have maintained their silence. Relying on Lacan's 1959 statement that perversion 'is indeed something articulate, inter-pretable, analyzable . . . on precisely the same level as neurosis' (Lacan 1977a[1959]:16) and André's argument that perverts approach their analysts as supposed subjects of enjoying, presenting themselves as supposed subjects of knowing (André 1984:18; 1993:56), I intimated at the end of Chapter 1 that analysts will have the utmost difficulty in treating perverse patients, because they somehow display an image of themselves.

Analysing the perverse patient on the same level as a neurotic would imply that the analyst endeavours to twist the pervert's fantasy in such a way that it becomes reinvested with desire at the expense of jouissance. This seems only feasible if analysts explicitly refuse the attributed position of supposed subject of enjoying by avoiding any complicity with the pervert's strategies and (re)emphasizing their own desire to know, notably about what the pervert so ardently pretends to know about jouissance. Challenging the pervert's knowledge, exposing its inadequacies, incoher-ence and inconsistencies, may then lead to the pervert's acknowledgement that some knowledge does escape subjective mastery, and the renewed installation of the supposed subject of knowing. Whereas the supposed subject of knowing needs to fall at the end of the neurotic's analysis, the installation of this function may thus constitute the terminus of the pervert's analytic itinerary. In both cases the cure is indeed 'effected by love' (McGuire 1974:12–13) and therefore situated 'on precisely the same level' (Lacan 1977a[1959]:16), but whilst in the neurotic compartment love needs to travel from necessity to contingency, in the perverse arrangement it needs to emerge as a necessity. In other words, the analysis of a pervert may be regarded as finished if he manages to comply with the necessities of love.

NOTES

1 The literature on Freud's Dora case is too expansive to mention in full. Most source materials have been covered extensively in Decker (1991), which still counts as the definitive historical survey of Dora's life history, and in Mahony (1996), which presents a comprehensive re-evaluation of the case-study with special reference to its textuality. Alongside these monographs, an excellent selection of critical essays is available in Bernheimer and Kahane (1985). For an original, phenomenologically inspired assessment of Freud's technique in the Dora case see Thompson (1994:93–132).

2 Some confusion is possible as regards the date of Freud's second explanation of his technical error, which he relegated to a long footnote at the end of the case-study. In some editions of Freud's works, including the 1954 French translation by Marie Bonaparte and Rudolph Loewenstein (Freud 1954), the footnote is preceded by an indication that it concerns an addition of 1923, but this is confirmed neither by the German text of Freud's *Gesammelte Werke* nor by the *Standard Edition*. When researching his 'Intervention on Transference' Lacan based himself on the aforementioned French translation, which explains his observation that 'the second reason only strikes him [Freud] as the most crucial in 1923' (Lacan 1982a[1951]: 69).

3 For a more sophisticated reading of Lacan's statement, see Soler (1996b).

4 On the antagonism between repetition and remembering in Freud's works see Chapter 2.

5 It would be erroneous to think that Freud's indecisiveness has long since been eradicated and that contemporary psychoanalysts agree on how transference comes about. Looking at a fairly up-to-date reader such as Esman (1990) suffices to discover that the relative influences of the analyst's person and the neurotic disposition on the emergence of the analysand's transference are still being debated.

6 In *Seminar XI* Lacan underscored that his view does not imply that transference can only occur within the analytic setting – a restrictive position which had for example been advanced by Ida Macalpine in her seminal critique of the multifarious theories of transference (Macalpine 1950). Lacan's point was that 'Whenever this function [of the supposed subject of knowing] may be ... embodied in some individual, whether or not an analyst, the transference ... is established' (Lacan 1977b[1964]:233).

7 It is well known that countertransference occupies a very marginal place in Freud's *œuvre*. After having coined the term in a 1909 letter to Jung (McGuire 1974:231), Freud used it publicly one year later in his paper 'The Future Prospects of Psychoanalytic Therapy' (1910d), after which he mentioned it only once, in his essay on transference-love (1915a[1914]: 160). None the less, countertransference gained prominence as a central technical concept during the 1950s, following heated discussions on the organization and control of analytic training. In some psychoanalytic schools, especially those taking their bearings from the works of Klein and Winnicott, countertransference was gradually stripped of its pejorative connotations, clinicians arguing in favour of its use as a supplementary therapeutic tool to understand the patient, with the proviso that the original

Freudian meaning of countertransference had been narrowed down to the analyst's reactions to the patient's transference. For a wide selection of articles on countertransference, with a brief historical survey of the stakes, see Wolstein (1988). For critical summaries of the divergent theoretical views on the topic see Orr (1954) and Jacobs (1999). For detailed elaborations on the therapeutic use of countertransference, including its erotic components, see Gorkin (1987), Alexandris and Vaslamatzis (1993) and Mann (1997, 1999).

8 The convergence of transference and repetition appeared for the first time in 'Remembering, Repeating and Working-Through': '[T]he transference is itself only a piece of repetition, and . . . the repetition is a transference of the forgotten past . . . ' (Freud 1914g:151). As can be inferred from Freud (1920g:20; 1923c[1922]:118; 1937d:258; 1940a[1938]:175), he never changed his mind in this matter.

9 The sexual (libidinal) origin of suggestibility would become one of the main foci of attention in Freud's 'Group Psychology and the Analysis of the Ego' (1921c).

10 For similar arguments, see Freud (1905a[1904]:260; 1926e:190–191, 225).

11 Neither have Freud's arguments persuaded a lobby of anti-psychoanalytic critics, the most prominent being Mikkel Borch-Jacobsen and Adolf Grünbaum. Unlike Lacan, these authors have not developed supplementary criteria for distinguishing transference and suggestion. Instead they have argued that psychoanalysts cannot prove that their results are due to the validity of their procedures (and the theory on which they rest) and not, for instance, to the impact of hypnotic suggestion or the so-called placebo effect. See Borch-Jacobsen (1992; 1996), Grünbaum (1984; 1993).

12 Although the reference is absent from Lacan's paper, he clearly derived inspiration from Carl Von Clausewitz's widely acclaimed treatise *On War* (1976[1832]) to construct this hierarchy of the politics of the analyst's position, the strategies of transference and the tactics of interpretation. The hierarchy (from tactics to politics) presents descending degrees of freedom for the analyst, in combination with ascending degrees of influence allocated to the intervention. Hence, analysts are most free in selecting their interpretations because the latter have the lowest impact on the direction of the treatment.

13 The issue will be discussed at length in the following chapter of this book.

14 The most wide-ranging discussion of transference within Lacanian theory and practice can be found in Association de la Fondation du Champ freudien (1992), a dense volume of conference proceedings which is not very reader friendly. Additional papers, concentrating primarily on the clinical vicissitudes of transference, are included in Actes de l'Ecole de la Cause freudienne (1984), whereas extensive theoretical surveys are available in Safouan (1988) and Le Gaufey (1998). In English, the literature dealing with Lacan's views on transference is extremely limited. Good introductory reading is offered by Rodríguez and Rodríguez (1989), Grigg (1991) and Gueguen (1995).

15 For a brief exposition of Lagache's professional career see Roudinesco and Plon (1997:606–608). For an excellent evaluation of Lagache's influence on French academic psychology during the second half of the twentieth century see Ohayon (1999).

16 Bénassy was the colleague Lacan designated in his 'Intervention on Transference' with the initial B. (1982a[1951]:62). For Lagache's position paper on transference see Lagache (1952).

17 For Zeigarnik's original paper see Zeigarnik (1927).

18 Lagache's idea, though founded on a psychological effect, was later endorsed by Leo Stone in two influential essays from the 1960s on the nature and development of transference. See Stone (1961; 1967).

19 This was Lacan's first explicit rebuttal of the popular psychoanalytic conception of transference as the spontaneous outcome of a neurotic disposition. This conception can of course be traced back to Freud, but his pupils were much more convinced of its value as a hard-and-fast rule. Transference was, for example, defined as an immanent psychical mechanism in pivotal contributions on the topic by Ferenczi (1980[1909]), Abraham (1979[1908]) and Anna Freud (1966[1936]).

20 For additional references to the analyst as a 'dark mirror', see Lacan (1966a[1946]:188; 1988c[1954–55]:246; 1998b[1957–58]:435).

21 The two dialectical reversals Freud did manage to implement, in Lacan's re-reading of the case, entail first, Dora's acknowledgement of her own part in the circumstances she had been subjected to and, second, her admission that she was jealous of her father's affair because Mrs K attracted her interest.

22 For similar definitions of countertransference in Lacan's works see Lacan (1988b[1953–54]:23; 1998b[1957–58]:390).

23 In *Seminar I* Lacan pointed out that transference *is* love, thereby radicalizing Freud's stance in 'Observations on Transference-Love' (1915a[1914]:168). Although he entertained this thesis until the end of his career, it did not exclude transference being coloured by hate, for love and hate were conceived as communicating vessels. Lacan's coinage of the neologism *hainamoration* (hateloving) in *Seminar XX* (1998a[1972–73]:98) illustrates this.

24 Lacan often claimed that this is the first occurrence of the notion of transference in the Freudian corpus, but Freud had already used the term in the more widespread sense of a patient transferring unconscious wishes onto the analyst in his contributions to *Studies on Hysteria* (Freud and Breuer 1895d:302).

25 The term 'two body psychology' was introduced into psychoanalytic theory by Rickman at the end of the 1940s to represent 'the less simple neurology of Conditioned Reflexes, and in the clinical field . . . the derivations of two-person relationship, e.g. of mother and child' (Rickman 1957[1951]:208). During the early 1950s Balint adopted Rickman's expression, defining psychoanalytic treatment as a Two-Body Situation (Balint 1952:221–222).

26 'Readiness for transference' is an expression culled from Herman Nunberg (1951).

27 As I have explained in the first chapter of this book, Lacan believed that psychotics are only capable of imaginary transference owing to their lack of ignorance, that is to say their absent recognition of the Other. Yet here too it can be argued that the analyst is responsible for the crystallization of this exclusively imaginary transference within the treatment, and thus for the appearance of a central diagnostic criterion for psychosis. In other words,

transference is not an objective diagnostic sign which transcends the analyst and which she can evaluate from a distance in a strictly detached fashion, but something which thoroughly implies her own position. The consequences of this view, which I cannot canvas comprehensively within this book, are enormous because it entails that those analysts who do not succeed in placing themselves outside the position of an alter ego are bound to trigger an imaginary transference (narcissistic love, jealousy, competition and aggression) in their neurotic analysands, that they can then (mis)take for an underlying psychosis or, perhaps more commonly, a borderline personality disorder.

28 Lacan originally intended to organize his *Seminar II* around a commentary of Freud's case-study of Schreber (Freud 1911c[1910]), yet the more he delved into Freud's papers on technique the more he discovered that the notion of the ego posed so many problems to the theoretical advancement of his own work that a deferral of the proposed topic imposed itself. Hence the renewed focus on the ego in *Seminar II*. See Lacan (1988b[1953–54]:272).

29 Because of the issue's crucial theoretical importance Lacan praised Lagache now and again (1977i[1958]:241; 1998b[1957–58]:207; 1962–63:session of 9 January 1963) for drawing attention to this opposition between the repetition of a need and the need for repetition. In a close reading of the third paragraph of Lacan's 'The Direction of the Treatment', Skriabine has interpreted Lacan's praise of Lagache as 'full of irony' (Skriabine 1993:28), yet in my opinion there are at least two good reasons for taking Lacan's remarks at face value: first, Lagache's opposition is rooted in Freud's explanations of transference; second, the ensuing question as to how transference relates to repetition and the pleasure principle was one of Lacan's own key preoccupations till the early 1960s.

30 For many years, Lacan rallied against the idea that the analysis of the patient's resistance constitutes the primordial task of psychoanalytic treatment – a popular post-Freudian practice whose source can be traced back to many of Freud's own technical writings – as a mere exercise of power which circumvents the true objectives of psychoanalysis. To Lacan, the main problem was that post-Freudian authors, and ego-psychologists in particular, had wrongly regarded resistance as a function of the ego instead of a feature of the analysand's speech, thus confusing resistance with the ego's mechanisms of defence. Analyzing the patient's resistance came down to breaking the ego's defences, through which the analyst turned into an aggressor who was incessantly involved in a type of psychic warfare with the patient, along the imaginary axis of inter*objec*tivity. An additional problem, still according to Lacan, was that post-Freudian analysts completely failed to acknowledge their own part in the analysand's resistance, attributing it to an inherent characteristic of the ego rather than the dialectics of the clinical process. For trenchant criticisms of the analysis of resistance in Lacan's early works see Lacan (1977e[1953]:42, 46–47; 1988c[1954–55]: 325; 1966b[1955]:333; 1977f[1955]:130; 1977i[1958]:235). For Lacan's assertion that resistance only manifests itself on the level of the analysands' speech (their associations), an idea which he had borrowed from Freud and Breuer (1895d:288–292) and Freud (1912b:103), see Lacan (1988b [1953–54]:39, 89, 107, 284).

31   I will return to Lacan's reading of Plato's *Symposium* in subsequent sections of this chapter.

32   For Lacan's notion of the desire of the analyst see Chapter 2.

33   The two other fundamental concepts were the unconscious and the drive. On Lacan's distinction between transference and repetition in *Seminar XI* see also Silvestre (1993[1984]).

34   Lacan returned to this statement in *Seminar XV* (1967–68:session of 15 November 1967). For Lacan's notion of repetition and its grounding in Aristotle's concepts of *tuchè* and *automaton* see Chapter 2.

35   For the difference between hysteria and obsessional neurosis see Chapter 1.

36   See, for instance, Lacan (1966d[1956]:461; 1966c[1957]:454).

37   To the best of my knowledge, Lacan's last documented use, in a non-contemptuous fashion, of the term intersubjectivity can be found in his 1960 'Remark on the Report by Daniel Lagache' (1966e[1960]:655–656). In this text Lacan criticized Lagache's use of intersubjectivity as a relation between two subjects, and advocated an alternative 'intersubjectivity' between the subject and the signifier.

38   The term 'therapeutic alliance' was introduced by Zetzel (1956) in reference to a previous paper by Bibring (1937). Over the years it was replaced with the still popular notion of 'working alliance', which was first advocated by Greenson (1965).

39   Of course 'analytic situation' was not a post-Freudian invention. One can find the expression *die analytische Situation* in Freud (1915a[1914]:161; 1916–17a[1915–17]:441). For additional criticisms of the term 'situation' in Lacan's works see Lacan (1977i[1958]:229–230).

40   This is no more than a reformulation and summary of Freud's idea (1921c:111–116) that being in love coincides with a limitation of narcissism, traits of humility and self-injury, and an emptying out of libido from the ego, but it also draws on the Platonic tradition of personal 'Eros-love', as opposed to divine 'Agape-love'. For a meticulous analysis of the philosophical debates on love since the era of Plato and Aristotle see Soble (1990).

41   Miller (1994[1992]) has characterized this relationship between the lover and the beloved as an antagonism between castration (on the side of the lover) and the phallus (on the side of the beloved).

42   From the early 1960s, Lacan indeed defined the unconscious as a knowledge without a subject, a series of thoughts without a thinker, a machine without an operator, a discourse from which the subject has been barred, etc. In *Seminar XX* he put it even more radically when stating that knowledge is in the Other, although the Other knows nothing (Lacan 1998a[1972–73]: 97–98). As a knowledge to which a human being has no conscious access, this unconscious leaves behind traces in a variety of formations: dreams, slips of the tongue, symptoms.

43   For Lacan's definition of metaphor as the substitution of one signifier for another signifier, see Lacan (1977g[1957]:164; 1991c[1961]).

44   'Supposed subject of knowing' (*sujet supposé savoir*) appeared for the first time as a concept in the first session of Lacan's *Seminar IX, Identification* (1961–62:session of 15 November 1961). During the early 1960s Lacan's original distinction between symbolic transference (featuring full speech) and imaginary transference (equalling empty speech) disappeared, the

'supposed subject of knowing' becoming the flag of a new unitary conception of transference. Explaining the rationale for this theoretical shift would require a more detailed exposition of Lacan's changing views on the nature of speech. Suffice it to say that his equation of symbolic transference and full speech posed serious problems to the analysis of the transference, since full speech was considered a necessary ingredient of analytic effectiveness. As Miller (1984b:35) has noted, the novelty of Lacan's concept of the 'supposed subject of knowing' was that it severed the traditional link between transference and affects, and resituated the relationship between analysand and analyst within the realm of knowledge.

45 The reader will understand by now that this description is only true for neurotics, and hysterics in particular, since neither psychotics nor perverts consider the analyst as a supposed subject of knowing.

46 In *Seminar XI*, Lacan identified the supposed subject of knowing accordingly with the God of Descartes, the ultimate guarantee that the true signification of all knowledge cannot be missed (Lacan 1977b[1964]: 224–225). Later on he extrapolated the supposed subject of knowing to the God of the philosophers in general (Lacan 1968b[1967]:39; 1968–69: session of 30 April 1969).

47 Lacan's idea that the supposed subject of knowing results from a connection between signifiers emanated from his definition of the signifier as 'what represents a subject for another signifier'. It is noteworthy to observe here that until the early 1960s (during his intersubjective period, one could say) Lacan argued that a subject does not emerge without another subject. In his *Seminar VI*, for instance, he did not hesitate to impress on his audience that 'there can be no other subject than a subject for a subject' (Lacan 1958–59:session of 20 May 1959). Lacan's perspective shifted dramatically after his trenchant criticism of intersubjectivity in *Seminar VIII* (1991b [1960–61]) and culminated in the above definition of the signifier in *Seminar IX* (1961–62:session of 6 December 1961). From that moment onwards, Lacan kept emphasizing that the subject does not exist without the Other, that is to say that the symbolic order is a necessary precondition for the emergence of the subject. In the 1967 'Proposition' he returned to this point, writing 'that no subject can be supposed by another subject' (1995b[1967]:4). For a reading of Lacan's algorithm of transference as an extrapolation of the Saussurian distinction between the signifier and the signified see Miller (1995b[1994]).

48 For additional readings of Lacan's algorithm see Safouan (1988:226–227), Rodríguez and Rodríguez (1989:168–170) and Le Gaufey (1998:68–72). For an interesting discussion of the relationship between the installation of the transference-signifier and the precipitation of the symptom see Miller (1984a).

49 In these fragments 'One' refers to the philosophical and theological notions of unity, harmony and perfection, and not to the mathematical '1' of what constitutes the beginning of a series. It is important to bear this difference in mind when studying Lacan's comments on the One, for he continuously opposed the imaginary One of unity to the symbolic 1 of difference without always specifying the register in which he was operating.

50 It should be noted that Lacan himself linked the *agalma* to the object *a* in *Seminar VIII* (1991b[1960–61]:177).

51 Of course one could argue that Lacan's alignment of love and desire in
    Seminar VIII was merely an artefact of his sustained commentary of Plato's
    Symposium, in which the subject of the dialogue shifts surreptitiously from
    love to desire when Socrates makes his first intervention. For Lacan's
    explanation of the metaphor of love with the terms of desire see Lacan
    (1961–62:session of 21 February 1962; 1962–63:session of 16 January
    1963).

52 Lacan's argument in *Seminar XX* that love is geared towards the object *a* as
    a semblance of being (1998a[1972–73]:92–95) seems to contradict my
    interpretation here, yet Lacan's point is about the essential misunderstanding
    in love: lovers believe that they have encountered the Other's true being in
    the *agalma*, without realizing that the only thing that has been revealed to
    them is a semblance of that being, namely an object *a* functioning within the
    constraints of their own fantasies.

53 I have decided to adopt a slightly modified version of Sheridan's translation
    because he gives a very awkward rendering of the French original, that does
    not really make sense.

54 The line of identification 'intersects' because the inner circle is located in
    a different plane. An easy way to visualize the three-dimensional aspect
    of Lacan's schema is to situate the large circle within the horizontal plane
    (the plane of the paper) and the small circle within the vertical plane. In a
    sense Lacan had already adumbrated the constant risk of the analyst's falling
    into the trap of suggestion in his pioneering 'Rome Discourse', notably in a
    paragraph which he later connected with the supposed subject of knowing.
    Addressing the analysand's expectations of psychoanalysis, Lacan wrote
    in 1953 that they rest on an illusion 'by which the subject [the analysand]
    believes that his truth is already given in us [analysts] and that we know it in
    advance; and it is moreover as a result of this that he [the analysand] is wide
    open to our objectifying intervention' (Lacan 1977e[1953]:94). Similar to
    any common experience of love, transference makes analysands extremely
    vulnerable and it is enticing for analysts to exploit this weakness in order to
    impose their own views. Hence Lacan's admonition that analysts should
    steer away from the conviction that they possess the knowledge the
    analysand is craving for, or that they have reached the pinnacle of self-
    knowledge to such an extent that the analysand can model himself on them.

55 Satisfying somebody's demands does not contribute to their disappearance.
    On the contrary, the more one fulfils the other's demands, the more the other
    believes he is entitled to demand more. With Lacan's idea that every demand
    is essentially a demand for love (1977j[1958]:286–287) the vicious cycle of
    demand becomes even more apparent: the more one assures the other of
    one's love by saying 'I love you', the more the other feels inclined to ask 'Do
    you (still) love me?'.

56 Schema L, which I discussed in Chapter 2 has a similar interrupted line
    'beyond' the imaginary vector of reciprocity and identification. And indeed,
    although Lacan's ideas on transference during the 1960s were by no means
    a blueprint of those deployed during the early 1950s, analytic progress was
    already conceived at the time as withstanding the seductions of identification
    and travelling towards the unconscious well of desire.

57 This (non-exhaustive) summation of deceitful signs of love cannot be found

as such in Lacan's *Seminar XX*, but has been distilled from propositions scattered throughout the seminar. On page 6 of the official translation of the book Fink has rendered *caractères sexuels* as 'sexual characteristics', yet Tony Chadwick has pointed out that this translation fails to convey the meaning of 'characters' and the act of reading implicit in the French *caractères* (Chadwick 1999). I have therefore chosen to refer to 'the sexual characters of the body' in my list of inadequate signs.

58 The concept of *liquidation* has entered French psychoanalysis as a translation of what Freud called the '*Aufhebung*' (in inverted commas), *Lösung* or *Auflösung* of the transference. In the *Standard Edition* Freud's terms have been rendered as 'removal' (1912b:105), 'resolution' (1912e: 118; 1916–17a[1915–17]:455) and 'dissolution' (1913c:143) respectively. Most Anglo-American authors have employed 'resolution', although 'dissolution' has also made an occasional entry into the literature. For 'liquidation' see Lagache (1952:112–113). For Lacan's critique of the idea see Lacan (1977b[1964]:267; 1995b[1967]:10). For readings of Lacan's critique see Cassin *et al.* (1992) and Baton *et al.* (1992).

59 Lacan's most disrespectful critique of the resolution of the transference within ego-psychological (Annafreudian), object-relations (Kleinian) and Hungarian (Ferenczian, Balintian) frameworks can be found in 'The Direction of the Treatment' (1977i[1958]:242–247).

60 Lacan debunked the adage on numerous occasions, yet the most 'accessible' criticisms can be found in Lacan (1977f[1955]:131; 1990d[1973]:20).

61 In *Seminar XI* Lacan also described this process as a transition from alienation to separation (1977b[1964]:213, 257). Explaining the relative impact on the transference of alienation and separation, Lacan's two constitutive causes of the divided subject, would require a great deal of abstract theoretical work. In brief, Lacan's idea was that the analysand moves from a psychic alienation to the (transference) signifier (the first stage of transference) to a separation from that signifier (the second stage) in confrontation with the object *a*. For detailed discussions of alienation and separation in relation to transference and the end of the treatment see Fink (1990; 1995a:49–68), Verhaeghe (1998) and Nobus (forthcoming).

62 The reader should note that in the passage from *Seminar XI traverser* has been translated as 'traversing'.

63 In the English translation of this fragment, Lacan's *une perturbation de la relation à l'autre* has been rendered as 'a disturbance of the object relation'. Although Lacan does refer to object relations (*relations d'objet*) in the following sentences, this contentious theoretical term should have been avoided in the passage on delusion.

64 In making this point Lacan found inspiration in Macalpine and Hunter's preface to their English translation of Schreber's memoirs (Macalpine and Hunter 1988[1955]), one of the few psychoanalytic contributions to psychosis he commended in his text.

65 I deliberately disregard Lacan's interrupted 1963–64 seminar on 'The Names-of-the-Father' (*Les Noms-du-Père*) (1990b[1963]) as a potential continuation and revision of his earlier work on psychosis, because Lacan only delivered his introductory speech. Having been barred from the lectern by the International Psychoanalytic Association (see Chapter 5 of this book),

he refused stubbornly to take up the subject of The Names-of-the-Father ever again (Lacan 1989b[1965]:28, note 44; 1968b[1967]:39; 1991a [1969–70]:125).

66 Eleven years later, in the discussion following Lacan's opening of the 'Clinical Section' in Paris, Jacques-Alain Miller could barely disguise his surprise when Lacan reaffirmed that in 'paranoia the signifier represents a subject for another signifier'. 'It would have to be shown', Miller said, to which Lacan replied: 'It would definitely have to be shown, it's true, but I won't show it tonight' (Lacan 1977l:12).

Chapter 4

Tactics of interpretation

DREAMS OF INTERPRETATION

On at least two separate occasions Freud underlined that handling the transference requires more skill and expertise from the analyst than making interpretations. In the case-study of Dora, originally intended as a supplement to *The Interpretation of Dreams* (1900a), he posited: 'It is easy to learn how to interpret dreams, to extract from the patient's associations his unconscious thoughts and memories, and to practise similar explanatory arts: for these the patient himself will always provide the text' (Freud 1905e[1901]:116). More than a decade later, in 'Observations on Transference-Love', Freud reiterated this point, warning inexperienced analysts that the technical difficulties of interpretation are insignificant compared to those emerging from the management of transference (Freud 1915a[1914]:159).

Despite Freud's trust in the swiftness of the interpretive action in psychoanalysis, few if any analytic principles have sparked more controversy than the practice of interpretation. Whereas Freud has hardly been taken to task for his views on diagnosis, the analyst's position within the treatment, the (traditionally vexed) issues of time and money, and the clinical problems of transference, his ideas on interpretation have been challenged from every possible angle since the day he first conceived them. Already during his lifetime many researchers disputed the intricate connections between associations and the unconscious wishes Freud had disclosed in *The Interpretation of Dreams* (1900a) and *The Psychopathology of Everyday Life* (1901b), sometimes taking issue with the procedure in general, but more often concentrating on just one example of Freudian analytic deduction.[1] In line with the standardization of research methods in the social sciences, Freud's method of interpretation was ensuingly discarded as unscientific, either for its lack of testability, reliability and validity, or (in a Popperian fashion) for its complete defiance of systematic refutation.[2] Nowadays *The Interpretation of Dreams* (1900a) remains a popular springboard for laying bare the rickety foundations of the psychoanalytic edifice, the devious intentions of its architect, or the fallacious beliefs underpinning the clinical applications of psychoanalytic theory.[3] To the extent that *The Interpretation of Dreams* remains a staple of recommended reading lists, it is rarely as the manifesto of a new clinical discipline, but frequently as a contrived gothic novel (Young 1999).

It is important to note here that many critics who repudiate Freud's method of interpretation do not for that matter invalidate his thesis that dreams, slips of the tongue and, by extension, all cultural products are intelligible and explainable, i.e. that they can reveal something about a human being's state of mind. What they question is the nature of the meaning to be ascribed to these phenomena (a repressed unconscious sexual wish on Freud's account) and the *modus operandi* through which this meaning is being generated (drawing inferences from free associations). These two aspects are evidently interrelated, since Freud only arrived at the conclusion that all dreams are wish-fulfilments after having interpreted his patients' dreams on the basis of the thoughts 'revealed' by their associations, the distorted fragments of unconscious wishes within the manifest dream content itself, and actions performed within and outside the psychoanalytic setting (Freud 1937d:258). In addition, his key insight that dreams epitomize the royal road to the unconscious was entirely predicated upon an 'art of interpretation' which privileged the patient's 'stream of consciousness' over the contents of the dream as such.

The disputed nexus of psychoanalytic interpretation thus concerns Freud's idiosyncratic approach to the materials with which he was presented. Refusing the fixed keys hailed by popular dreambooks (the so-called decoding or *Chiffrier* method) and nuancing the value of symbolic interpretations (reading dream symbols as expressions of cultural inheritance), Freud (1900a:96–98) tapped from the source of a person's loosely produced ideas to unearth the latent dream thoughts. Although advanced as convenient, user-friendly and less demanding than transference handling, this procedure soon attracted the odium of arbitrariness. For if the analyst is to 'guess' the meaning of a dream through a series of individual thoughts, it is awkward to formulate concrete rules of interpretation, and strictly impossible to develop criteria against which the value of an interpretation can be judged empirically and independently. For all its practicality, the corollary of Freud's method is that it can be identified with the promotion of 'anything goes', a methodological freedom open to every imaginable source of bias on the part of the interpreter.

To some degree Freud himself nourished these criticisms by steering away obstinately, throughout his work, from any suggestion of rules of thumb for making interpretations. To many a novice's surprise *The Interpretation of Dreams* does not contain a single precept that is readily applicable within a clinical setting.[4] And to many a student's despair Freud's papers on technique do not comprise any hard-and-fast rules that can be integrated directly into a psychoanalytic action plan.[5] For a number of years, Freud did entertain the project of publishing a general methodology of psychoanalysis, yet he abandoned the idea in favour of a general code of conduct and a set of indicative recommendations for good practice in brief articles, so as to safeguard the variability of clinical situations and the plasticity of individual experiences (Freud 1913c:123).

The founder's reluctance in formulating clinical algorithms did not prevent his followers from specifying the parameters of psychoanalytic interpretation. However, these elaborations did not silence the detractors, because most post-Freudian research on the nature of interpretation was conducted on a descriptive level, the procedure's mainspring and rationale being pushed into the background. As such, the post-Freudian literature on interpretation was chiefly concerned with the classification of various types of interpretations, how they differ from other analytic acts and how they affect the progress of the treatment. Exemplary in this respect is Strachey's hugely influential paper on 'The Nature of the Therapeutic Action of Psycho-Analysis' (1934) in which he launched the concept of 'mutative interpretation' and distinguished between deep and surface, transference and extra-transference, premature and timely interpretations.[6] Driven by a similar urge to capture the true nature of psychoanalytic interpretation, and strengthened by Freud's own disjunction between interpretations and constructions (Freud 1937d), post-Freudian authors subsequently defined the notion in opposition to confrontation (Devereux 1951), reassurance (Schmideberg 1935), interposition (Colby 1951:69), intervention (Loewenstein 1951), clarification (Bibring 1954) and explanation (Paul 1963), yet instead of delineating the proper meaning of interpretation, they inadvertently fostered a complete semantic evacuation of the concept.

To this massive proliferation of terms in the works of his contemporaries Lacan reacted with a stroke of Occam's razor, retracing the footsteps of the first psychoanalyst when circumscribing the place of interpretation in psychoanalytic treatment (Lacan 1977i[1958]:232–240). Just as much as Freud, he avoided every demarcation of the rules of interpretation, motivating his decision negatively by drawing attention to the potential deterioration of specific instructions into a sterile clinical formalism (Lacan 1977e[1953]:31, 98), and positively by emphasizing the radical freedom of the interpretive act:

> As an interpreter of what is presented to me in words or deeds, I [the analyst] am my own oracle and articulate it as I please, sole master of my ship after God, and of course far from being able to measure the whole effect of my words, but well aware of the fact and striving to guard against it, in other words always free in the timing, frequency and choice of my interventions, to the point that it seems that the rule has been arranged entirely so as not to impede in any way my own freedom of movement . . .
>
> (Lacan 1977i[1958]:228)

An oracular statement in its own right, Lacan's declaration prefigured the elevation of all interpretive guidelines to the status of heuristics that do not impinge upon the analyst's liberty. In addition, the professed freedom of choice stimulated an argument minimizing the therapeutic risks of potentially inaccurate or inexact interpretations. Also, the interpretive creativity attributed to the analyst invited new reflections upon the purpose of the analysts' interventions, and most significantly it begged the question as to how the suggestive power of their clinical acts could be neutralized.

Lacan addressed these challenges throughout his works, designating the meaning of interpretation in terms of punctuation, temporality, misunderstanding and equivocation, and situating its purpose in relation to meaning, desire, truth and nonsensicality. Comparable to his conceptual substitution of the supposed subject of knowing for the emotional bond in the sphere of transference, Lacan exchanged the traditional characterizations of interpretation as an epistemic, or empathic response for a framework in which interpretations function as enigmatic enunciations whose power does not depend on the analyst's knowledge. In other words, whereas Lacan moved the realm of transference from emotion to knowledge, he shifted interpretation from knowledge to the conundrum. Lacan already broached the coordinates of this transition in his 1953 'Rome Discourse', but he did not elaborate its governing principles until the early 1970s.

In the following sections of this chapter I will discuss Lacan's ideas on the nature and purpose of psychoanalytic interpretations as they developed from the 1950s to the 1970s, demonstrating how he redefined and transcended the boundaries of Freud's works, and how his views can be applied to concrete clinical realities. Once again the reader must bear in mind that most of the presented materials only relate to the psycho-analytic treatment of neurotic (hysterical or obsessional) analysands. How the analyst should make interpretations, if at all, in the case of perverse and psychotic patients is a question neither Lacan's *œuvre* nor that of his pupils answers.[7]

THE MEANING OF INTERPRETATION

In the first sentence of the preface to his 'Rome Discourse' Lacan wrote that the 'surrounding circumstances' of his text 'had some effect on it' (Lacan 1977e[1953]:30). He ensuingly revealed how the French psychoanalytic community had recently split following the creation of a training institute, the official party line preventing him and his followers from speaking at a formal gathering of francophone psychoanalysts in Rome.[8] According to Lacan the dissension had occurred when certain members of the French group had tried to impose a series of rigid training rules, yet a Bulletin of the International Psychoanalytic Association (IPA) makes clear that in reality the debate hinged on the incompatibility between Lacan's habit of conducting sessions of variable length and the existing professional standards (Eissler 1954:267–290). Lacan's unruly behaviour constituted a thorn in the side of many an IPA council member, the more so that he had apparently promised to abide by the deontological code without effectively doing so (ibid.:276).

In his 'Rome Discourse' Lacan minimized the historical contro-versy surrounding his idiosyncratic technique in favour of a sustained theoretical defence of its application, yet the vehemence with which he endorsed the variable-length session, against the formalism advocated by the establishment, indicates the issue's crucial importance within contemporary psychoanalytic circles. Lacan's principal argument in support of variable-length sessions was that the analyst's manipulation of time functions as an interpretive intervention in so far as it punctuates the analysand's speech. In the first chapter of the 'Rome Discourse' he put it as follows:

> It is therefore, a beneficent punctuation, one which confers its meaning on the subject's discourse. This is why the adjournment of a session – which according to present-day technique is simply a chronometric break and, as such, a matter of indifference to the thread of the discourse – plays the part of a metric beat which has the full

value of an actual intervention by the analyst for hastening the concluding moments.

(Lacan 1977e[1953]:44)

Further in the text he added that analysands inevitably experience the analyst's suspension of the session as a punctuation of their discourse (ibid.:98). So if interpreting equals punctuating the analysand's speech, suspending the session will have effects similar to those induced by more traditional forms of interpretation. In Lacan's view, professional regulations about analytic time-keeping, such as 'Every session lasts 50 minutes', were just arbitrary rules imposed by anonymous authoritarian bodies on both the analyst and the analysand, depriving the analyst of the possibility to use the interpretive power of time in a responsible and calculated fashion to the benefit of the analytic treatment. Complying with a preset working-time is worse than manipulating it, because in the former case it is impossible to control the effects of the session's interruption on the analysand's condition (ibid.:99). Partly because Lacan transformed an agreed professional standard into a flexible technical tool, partly because his innovation was perceived as stretching the limits of the analyst's power over the patient, high representatives of the IPA considered his practice unacceptable, and refused to give way on this point when Lacan's group applied for a new official recognition during the early 1960s.[9]

Precision is not a liberating factor and conjecture does not pre-empt rigour, Lacan argued (ibid.: 74, 98). No matter how rebellious to any type of formalism, he believed that the analysts' temporal interventions could be presented in rigorous and unambiguous terms. For the development of this new clinical formalization, Lacan took his lead from his own theory of logical time, in which he had distinguished between the 'instant of the glance', the 'time for comprehending', and the 'moment of concluding', on the basis of an analysis of the sophism of the three prisoners (Lacan 1988a[1945]).[10] Because each prisoner's freedom is dependent upon the reduction of the time for comprehending, after the instant of the glance, Lacan averred that the analyst's suspension of the session should always be geared towards the precipitation of the moment of concluding and thus towards the reduction of the time for comprehending (Lacan 1977e[1953]:48).[11] This is why, in the above citation, he described the value of an analytic intervention as hastening the concluding moments. With their interpretations analysts need to ensure that the amount of time analysands spend on understanding, brooding and plotting is reduced to a minimum. These mental activities are considered counter-productive because just as in the story of the three prisoners they bar the roads to freedom.[12] To put Lacan's principle in more psychological terms: through her interpretations, including the suspension of the session, the analyst has to facilitate and accelerate decision-making processes in the analysand; he has to urge the analysand to make decisions about his life in line with his desire, despite the fact that he does not master all the knowledge necessary to be sure that these decisions are right.[13]

In Lacan's conception of the treatment, compressing the time for comprehending facilitates the moment of concluding because it stimulates 'the meditation of the subject [the analysand] towards deciding the meaning [*sens*] to attach to the original event' (ibid.:48).[14] A necessary mediating factor between the analyst's interventions and the analysand's conclusions, the crystallization of meaning is the first corollary of an appropriate analytic interpretation.[15] Lacan accordingly underlined that psychoanalysis is 'an action whose effects are entirely dependent on meaning' (ibid.:33). Yet, against all odds, he also intimated that this dependency of the analytic effects on meaning does not imply that analysts are expected to reveal the meaning of their analysands' symptoms through their interpretations. The content of the analyst's interpretations is not tailored to the meaning of what the analysand is suffering from. When interpreting the analyst is not supposed to tell the patient what his symptoms mean. During the 1950s, Lacan stressed on numerous occasions that symptoms are legible and need to be deciphered (Lacan 1977f [1955]:127, 133; 1977g[1957]:159–160; 1977h[1957–58]:184, 194), but this process of exegesis (Lacan 1977e[1953]:70) should not be read as an activity whereby the analyst discovers or guesses the meaning of the analysand's symptoms and offers the results of his quest to the patient.[16] After all, were that to be a requirement it would be difficult to see how the analyst's suspension of the session could function as an interpretation, since these scansions contain not a single meaningful detail about the patient's symptoms and life history.

The motive behind this precept revives the contentious relationship between transference and suggestion I have discussed in the previous chapter of this book. Despite his insistence on the importance of the analyst's exegesis of the patient's formations of the unconscious Lacan believed that detailing their meaning has an objectifying and alienating effect on the analysand. If analysts were to disclose the meaning of the analysands' symptoms in their interpretations, they would convey knowledge about the origin of these symptoms to their patients, implicitly telling them that as analysts they are capable of understanding the problems at hand. Long before the introduction of the supposed subject of knowing, Lacan criticized this interpretive style for its suggestive impact.

In *Seminar I*, for instance, he underscored that interpretation, despite its being predicated upon the action of speech, should not count as an intellectual activity (Lacan 1988b[1953–54]:274). He vilified Anna Freud's proposition to use interpretation as a means of educating the ego for its hidden intellectualist tendencies, which can only be detrimental to the advancement of the treatment (ibid.:65–67).[17] In 'Variations of the Standard Treatment' he put it even more bluntly:

> This knowledge [of the analyst] has without doubt much increased . . . but one must not pretend to have distanced oneself from an intellectualist analysis in this way, unless one acknowledges that the communication of this knowledge to the subject [the analysand] only functions as a suggestion to which the criterion of truth is alien.
>
> (Lacan 1966b[1955]:337)

After his conceptualization of the supposed subject of knowing, Lacan repeated his admonition in the phrase that the analyst is never to identify with this supposed subject of knowing (Lacan 1961–62: session of 22 November 1961; 1966–67: session of 21 June 1967).[18]

In a similar vein, Lacan disqualified all analytic attempts at understanding the analysand's problems. 'To interpret and to imagine one understands are not at all the same things. It is precisely the opposite' (Lacan 1988b[1953–54]:73). Two years later, in *Seminar III*, he stated: 'It's always at the point where they [students] have understood, where they have rushed in to fill the case in with understanding, that they have missed the interpretation that it's appropriate to make or not to make' (Lacan 1993[1955–56]:22). An even more provocative assertion appeared in *Seminar IV*, in the context of a discussion of Freud's case of Little Hans (Freud 1909b):

> This observation [of Little Hans] unfolds entirely within the register of misunderstanding. I will add that this is the case with all types of creative interpretation between two subjects. This is the way one has to expect interpretation to develop, it is the least abnormal of all, and it is precisely in the gap of this misunderstanding that something else will develop, that will have its fecundity.
>
> (Lacan 1994[1956–57]:341)

Additional comments on the inherent dangers of understanding abound in Lacan's seminars from the 1960s and 1970s, and one of the reasons why he eventually decided to dissolve his own school was that he believed his pupils to be too convinced that they understood the meaning of his words.[19] As his work progressed, Lacan argued that apart from nurturing suggestion and proceeding from the analyst's own fantasies and prejudices, understanding is a response to the analysand's demands (to be understood), whereas these demands need to be maintained (supported, propped up) and questioned in their signifying structure (Lacan 1991b[1960–61]: 234–235; 1977i[1958]:255).

But how are analysts supposed to interpret then if they ought to avoid offering meaning, producing knowledge and conveying understanding? What is left of the classic definition of interpretation as an act of translation or explanation that facilitates insight into a certain matter through the revelation of meaning?[20] Although he retained the notion of meaning to represent the proper effect of analytic interpretations, Lacan rejected all the standard approaches to interpretation and presented an alternative based on Hindu linguistic philosophy and Zen Buddhism. Through these two oriental traditions he discovered 'resonance' as a new feature of speech. Due to this characteristic, speakers can say something without effectively saying it on the level of the statement; they can induce ideas in the mind of the listener which are the opposite of those included in the text of the transferred message. This is how Lacan explained 'resonance' as an appropriate interpretive tool in his 'Rome Discourse':

> There is . . . no doubt that the analyst can play on the power of the symbol by evoking it in a carefully calculated fashion in the semantic resonances of his remarks. This is surely the way for a return to the use of symbolic effects in a renewed technique of interpretation in analysis. In this regard we could take note of what the Hindu tradition teaches about *dhvani*, in the sense that this tradition stresses the property of speech by which it communicates what it does not actually say.
>
> (Lacan 1977e[1953]:82)

According to Pandey's *Indian Aesthetics*, a volume from which Lacan distilled most of his information on Hindu linguistics, *dhvani* is the power of words to invoke something else than what they literally say. Pandey's example, which Lacan dutifully copied, runs as follows (Pandey 1950: 219–220; Lacan 1977e[1953]:82).[21] A young courting couple agrees to meet in a secluded garden on the bank of a river. Waiting for her boyfriend, the girl notices how a religious man she knows is approaching their hide-out. For obvious reasons she wants the man to disappear as quickly as possible, yet she does not want to tell him off explicitly. Having decided to drive him away without showing her true intentions, she says: 'O religious minded man! you can now roam freely over this place. For the dog, of whom you were so afraid, has been killed today by the proud lion, who, as you know very well, lives in the impervious thicket on the bank of Godavari' (Pandey 1950:220). If the man, after hearing the girl's words, decides to run off as fast as he can, it is, Pandey argues, 'because of the negative meaning understood by him in a positive statement' (ibid.:220). In Lacan's reading of this passage, the man flees because he hears something the girl's words do not actually say. She says 'You can now roam freely', but he hears 'I need to get out of this place as soon as possible'.

At the end of his 'Rome Discourse' (1977e[1953]:106–107) Lacan adduced another, slightly different example of the resonances of speech from the teachings of the *Brhadaranyaka Upanisad*, which he had borrowed from T. S. Eliot's *The Waste Land* (1974[1922]).[22] When the threefold offspring of Praja-pati had completed their training in sacred knowledge with their father, they wanted him to say something. To the gods (*deva*) Praja-pati responded with the syllable 'Da' and when asked whether they had understood the gods said: 'Yes, we have understood. You said to us "control yourselves" (*damyata*)'. Upon which Praja-pati said: 'Yes, you have understood'. To the men (*manusya*), Praja-pati replied with the same syllable 'Da' and they too said they had understood: 'You said to us "give" (*datta*). Praja-pati replied: 'Yes, you have understood'. Finally, Praja-pati told the demons (*asurah*) 'Da' and they said: 'We have understood. You said to us "be compassionate" (*dayadhvam*)'. Praja-pati said: 'Yes, you have understood' (Radhakrishnan 1953: 289–291).

Like the previous example, this story shows how the addressees understand something the speaker has not actually said. In addition it demonstrates how each of the three groups attach a different meaning to the same signifier, in a way that is presumably concomitant with their different status as gods, men and demons. However, in this example it is unclear what the speaker wants his listeners to understand. Whilst the girl on the river bank evidently wanted the religious man to disappear, Praja-pati's intention remains a mystery. Or rather it seems that whatever the meaning his children attribute to his words, he is happy to go along with it.[23]

Neither in his 'Rome Discourse' nor in any other spoken or written intervention did Lacan detail the implications of this passage from the *Upanisads* for psychoanalytic practice. None the less, it appears to me that Praja-pati's response is more indicative of Lacan's take on the analytic employment of the resonances of speech during the early 1950s than the parable of the girl and the religious man. In Pandey's illustration of *dhvani* the girl knows perfectly well which meaning she wants to imbue the religious man with, and unless he is stupid he will not hesitate to run. The girl is betting on the proverb that a nod is as good as a wink to a blind horse, and if it had turned out that the man needed more than a word to be wise, it is likely that she would have had recourse to a less subtle tactic for making him leave. The meaning she wants him to acknowledge is unambiguous, despite the fact that her words cover this meaning with the veils of courtesy and modesty. Put differently, she does not want to impose herself, but her words are nevertheless extremely suggestive.

In Praja-pati's words, the resonances are much more obscure, and he does not seem to expect his listeners to read his 'Da' in a particular way. One could argue that his eternal wisdom allows him to know that the three categories of his offspring will hear his 'Da' exactly as he wants them to hear it. But we do not know whether this is indeed the case. Perhaps he was sure about the effects of his words, perhaps he had no intentions whatsoever, perhaps he just wanted his children to gain understanding, regardless of its nature and consequences. In this respect, Praja-pati's intervention is much less suggestive than the girl's response to the religious man. On the one hand Praja-pati satisfies his children's demand to tell them something, but when he starts to talk he does not really say anything. The meaning of what he says is fleeting; it remains 'in abeyance' until it is pinned down by his listeners. This procedure tallies with the Zen technique Lacan evoked in the opening paragraphs of *Seminar I*:

> The master breaks the silence with anything – with a sarcastic remark, with a kick-start. That is how a buddhist master conducts his search for meaning, according to the technique of *zen*. It behoves the students to find out for themselves the answer to their own questions.
>
> (Lacan 1988b[1953–54]:1)

Although analytic treatment is by no means a relationship between master and student, the fact that the Zen-master believes that the students possess all the knowledge necessary to answer their questions relieves him of the task to produce that knowledge in a suggestive, objectifying fashion, bringing his interventions very close to those Lacan described as analytic interpretations. In sum, the meaning of interpretation, as Lacan conceived it during the early 1950s, is that it sets meaning in motion on the side of the analysand whilst being in itself a meaningless intervention.

The consequence of this approach is that interpreting, as an activity by which meaning is accorded to a certain event, takes place in the analysand rather than the analyst.[24] As Freud put it at the end of 'On Beginning the Treatment', the analyst 'supplies the amounts of energies' and 'shows him [the patient] the paths along which he should direct those energies' (Freud 1913c:143), but that is as far as the analyst's interventions go. In Lacan's outlook of the 1950s the analyst supplies a signifier, which is by its very nature meaningless, and facilitates the analysand's (re)integration of that signifier into an already existing series of signifiers (a circuit of knowledge). Consequently, a new meaning will arise, which should encourage the liberating 'moment of concluding'.

In setting out the coordinates of this new interpretive style, Lacan also attacked the positions of his contemporaries. Despite its prominence within mainstream psychoanalysis, he repudiated the analyst's interpretation of the patient's ego-resistance, because he was convinced that it transformed the analytic process into an imaginary struggle between two parties striving for recognition (Lacan 1988b[1953–54]:51).[25] For the same reason he rejected the analyst's interpretation from ego to ego in the here-and-now of the clinical setting. Taking his lead from a paper by Margaret Little on countertransference (Little 1951) in which she reported the instance of an analyst interpreting the analysand's present state of mind (a mixture of anxiety, confusion and depression) by referring it back to the analyst's own current interests ('You think that I, your analyst, am jealous of you'), Lacan argued that the 'analyst here believes himself authorised to offer . . . an interpretation from ego to ego, or from equal to equal . . . whose foundation and mechanism cannot in any way be distinguished from that of projection' (Lacan 1988b[1953–54]:32).[26]

Because they merely reflect the analyst's presumptuous use of 'inside knowledge', Lacan opposed even more vehemently all types of interpretations that circumvent the analysand's discourse. With biting sarcasm he declared in 'Variations of the Standard Treatment' how it had become 'standard' practice amongst analysts to seek out the analysand's truth by interpreting her gait, his grooming, her position on the couch, his borborygmi, her way of shaking hands, etc. (Lacan 1966b[1955]:337). As long as these behaviours operate beyond language, as long as analysands do not give them a place within their discourse, the meaning ascribed to them (resistance or compliance, denial or acceptance) simply mirrors the analyst's symptomatic use of his alleged clinical expertise. Finally, Lacan also desacralized the popular idea of moving from 'surface' to 'deep' interpretations (Fenichel 1941[1938–39]:44–46). In his opinion, the analysand's speech is a multilayered surface showing traces of recent as well as foregone conflicts on each level. Lacan did not believe one had to remove the dust of everyday life in order to discover the repressed treasures. He did not think the surface to be superficial, nor depth to be hidden beneath the surface. This is why, in *Seminar I*, he advised his audience to take up the study of geology: 'My dear fellows, you wouldn't believe what you owe to geology. If it weren't for geology, how could one end up thinking that one could move, on the same level, from a recent to a much more ancient layer?' (Lacan 1988b[1953–54]:74).[27]

Lacan's wrath was as much unleashed by the analysts' interpretive tactics as by the inappropriateness of their interpretations. For instance, in his discussion of Little's example, he admitted that the analyst's interpretation 'hadn't failed to have some effect, since he [the analysand] had instantly recovered his spirits' (ibid.:31). The analysand had accepted the analyst's intervention, it had effectuated a radical change in his condition and the analysis had continued for another year. Yet to Lacan the clinical impact of the interpretation did not prove that it was correct or, better, that it was a precise evaluation of the source of the analysand's problems. Little herself conceded in her article that the interpretation may have been accurate in terms of the analyst's feelings towards the patient, but that it did not capture the essence of the patient's grief, his acceptance of it having been fostered by his identification with the analyst (Little 1951:32).

Having observed that inappropriate interventions can have amazing clinical effects, Lacan re-read an influential study by Glover on 'The Therapeutic Effect of Inexact Interpretation' (1931) in order to ascertain the status of true, correct interpretations.[28] The most important conclusion he drew from Glover's article is that an interpretation can be analytically correct without conveying the factual reality of an analysand's condition, and vice versa. In Little's example, the analyst's interpretation was incorrect in spite of the fact that it may very well have been an adequate representation of a present state of affairs. Conversely, Lacan assessed Freud's interpretations in the case of the Rat Man as factually inexact, yet nevertheless correct with regard to the mental condition of his patient and the overall progress of the treatment (Lacan 1977e[1953]:88; 1977i[1958]: 237).[29] To decide whether an interpretation is correct one should not judge its correspondence with a factual reality. Nor can the correctness of an interpretation be inferred from its immediate benefits for the analysand, whether the disappearance of the symptoms, a general change of attitude, or the emergence of new plans for the future. Hence, the truth value of an interpretation depends neither on its relationship with reality, nor on its healing power, even less on the analysand's acceptance or refusal.

Volunteering to formulate a different criterion for assessing the truth (correctness) of an analytic interpretation, and relying on Freud's exposition of the topic in 'Constructions in Analysis' (1937d), Lacan stated in *Seminar I*: 'I consider the proof of the correctness of an interpretation to lie in the confirmatory material the subject supplies. And even that needs to be put more subtly' (Lacan 1988b[1953–54]:31). In 'The Direction of the Treatment' he subsequently confirmed the validity of his own interpretation when writing that 'it is not the conviction with which it is received that matters, since the conviction will be found rather in the material that will emerge as a result of the interpretation' (Lacan 1977i[1958]:234). A more 'subtle' picture did not emerge until 1966, in *Seminar XIV* on *The Logic of the Fantasy* (1966–67). Here Lacan argued that if an interpretation's only effect is the analysand's production of more material it still falls under the rubric of suggestion. For interpretations to be correct, he claimed, they need to have an effect of truth (Lacan 1966–67: session of 14 December 1966; 1970–71:session of 13 January 1971).

THE INTERPRETATION OF MEANING

From the mid-1950s Lacan started questioning the nature of meaning as an effect of psychoanalytic interpretation. Locating the point of departure for any type of analytic interpretation in *The Interpretation of Dreams* (1900a) he insisted that Freud's discovery of the meaning of a dream always entails the revelation of the dream(er)'s unconscious wish (Lacan 1998b[1957–58]:319–320). Therefore, the interpretation of dreams and, by extension, of any formation of the unconscious, is focused on the emergence of the repressed desire sustaining it.[30]

Because Freud had explained dreams, parapraxes and neurotic symptoms as fulfilments of a repressed wish, Lacan contended that the formations of the unconscious simultaneously conceal and satisfy a particular desire, which can only be uncovered via a calculated use of interpretations (ibid.:326). In other words, the meaning of a symptom correlates with its underlying desire and this motive only becomes apparent when the symptom has been properly interpreted. If interpretation can be conceived as a process whereby meaning is accorded to a certain phenomenon, the interpretation of meaning, the meaning to be allocated to meaning, is that it coincides with the expression of a desire. This is why Lacan, in his *Seminar VI* on *Desire and its Interpretation*, portrayed the analyst as somebody who assists analysands in giving birth to their desire (Lacan 1958–59:session of 1 July 1959). This is also why he replied to the philosophical question as to the meaning of meaning (what does meaning mean?) with the statement 'meaning escapes' (Lacan 1975d[1973]:11).[31]

Like desire, meaning is constantly shifting, and despite the fact that language always carries meaning, it is incapable of fixating it. Inasmuch as the analysand's demands are embedded in language, their desire will always be articulated in these demands (desire will speak through the verbalizations), but the demands will never fully articulate their desire. 'Although it always shows through demand . . . desire is nonetheless beyond it' (Lacan 1977i[1958]:269). Desire (meaning) is always articulated, but never fully articulatable (Lacan 1998b[1957–58]:329–330). Or, as Lacan put it in 1973: meaning is always fleeting from the cask of language (Lacan 1975d[1973]:11).

As his work progressed Lacan separated the effect of meaning (*sens*) from the emergence of signification (*signification*). In 'The Agency of the Letter' he hinted at this conceptual difference when stating that 'the value of the image [in Egyptian hieroglyphics, for instance] as signifier has nothing whatever to do with its signification' (1977g[1957]:159). Whereas the signification of a certain image may be 'vulture', its meaning may be the letter 'A'. Meaning is what results from the translation of one text into another, whereas signification, in its dependence upon common-sense understanding, does not require any form of transcription. Convergent on the production of meaning (desire), and not on signification, interpretation (deciphering) can therefore also be compared to a process of translation.[32] Moreover, once a message has been deciphered, once its meaning has been revealed, one can still fail to understand it. Meaning does not necessarily give rise to signification, although signification annihilates meaning. The Biblical story of Daniel's interpretation of the writing on the wall serves as a good example of this.[33] Daniel translated God's Aramaic words 'Mene, Mene, Tekel, Upharsin' as 'Numbered, Numbered, Weighed, Broken' but it did not make the Babylonians any wiser. After Daniel had revealed to King Belshazzar what the words represented, the Babylonians were still puzzled about their significance.[34] Hence, the revelation of the meaning of a coded message does not eradicate the question as to what it refers to, or why it has been produced in the first place. The acknowledgement of a desire does not solve the mystery surrounding its origin and object. But finding the signification of a message does imply that the meaning of that message disappears, to the extent that it can no longer be interpreted in a variety of ways.

In relation to clinical practice Lacan was adamant that 'interpretation is on the side of meaning and goes against signification' (Lacan 1973 [1972]:37). The analyst needs to ensure that the analysand's messages (dreams, symptoms, demands, etc.) are deciphered in such a way that the elusiveness of meaning (the ethereal character of desire) is maintained.

Whereas meaning keeps desire open, signification kills it because there is nothing left to desire anymore.

This idea was already present in Lacan's works from the early 1950s, when he pondered the value of 'naming' desire as a psychoanalytic action. In *Seminar I* he was quite appreciative of Strachey's idea (1934) that the analyst's interventions should be confined to naming the pervasive yet inexpressible aspects of the analysand's discourse (Lacan 1988b [1953–54]:188). Yet one year later, in a discussion of *The Interpretation of Dreams*, he claimed that 'behind what is named, there is the unnameable' and that everything 'revealed as nameable is always on the level of the dream-work', 'a symbolisation, with all its laws, which are those of signification' (Lacan 1988c[1954–55]:211). In other words, naming is part and parcel of the psychic process that transforms a latent, unconscious wish into a manifest dream-content: the dream-work proceeds from the repressed (the unnameable) to the expressible (the nameable).[35] Since the interpretation of dreams follows the opposite route, from manifest to latent, it is precisely the naming, the formulation of the wish that should be unravelled. Challenging his audience, Lacan accordingly averred: '[W]hat we are looking for in the interpretation of the dream, [is] this x, which in the end is desire for nothing. I defy you to bring me a single passage from the *Traumdeutung* which concludes – this is what the subject desires' (ibid.:211). None the less, Lacan continued to use the naming of desire as an interpretive act, yet changing the connotation of naming from 'defining' and 'designating' (Lacan 1998b[1957–58]:329) to 'creating', 'recognising' 'restoring' and 'bringing into existence' (Lacan 1988c [1954–55]:228–229; 1958–59: session of 26 November 1958).

To illustrate how his procedure differed from the prevalent tactics of interpretation within ego-psychology Lacan intermittently referred to a case-example adduced by Ernst Kris in an influential paper on interpretation (Kris 1951). The case concerned an academic in his thirties who had come to see Kris because he experienced great difficulty in publishing the results of his researches, thus reducing his chances for promotion, due to the belief that he was always copying other people's ideas.[36] One day the patient reported that just before he was about to embark on a new project for publication he had discovered a book in the library containing a blueprint of the thesis he was on the verge of publishing. When Kris compared the text in the library with his patient's views he concluded that, despite some similarities, his analysand had projected his fantasy of plagiarism onto the book. Kris told the man that he was not plagiarizing, that his anxiety was completely unjustified, and that it originated in an infantile wish for a successful father. Kris waited for the patient's response and after a lengthy silence the young man said:

> Every noon, when I leave here, before luncheon, and before returning to my office, I walk through X street [a street well known for its small but attractive restaurants] and I look at the menus in the windows. In one of the restaurants I usually find my preferred dish – fresh brains.
>
> (ibid.:23)

Kris did not elaborate on this peculiar testimony, but for Lacan it signalled the analysand's recourse to an acting-out as a result of Kris' spurious interpretation. His verification of the analysand's fear incited him to interpret the problem as having no basis in reality: 'You may think that you are copying somebody's ideas, but I can assure you that this is not the case!' In Lacan's reading, this interpretation could be termed correct as regards the factual reality of the analysand's situation, but it simultaneously suffocated the analysand's desire to plagiarize. When resorting to the consumption of fresh brains, the analysand tried to preserve his desire, against his analyst's demand that he exchange it for an acceptance of the facts.[37] By eating fresh brains the analysand addressed himself with his desire to the analyst after the latter had neutralized it by his interpretation.[38] Although Kris' intervention was geared towards the analysand's desire (his wish), it was at once an attempt to efface it in favour of the young man's adaptation to the reality of his situation. As an alternative to Kris' interpretation ('Rest assured, you do not steal') Lacan proposed in 'The Direction of the Treatment' an intervention whereby the analysand would come to avow his desire to steal whilst acknowledging that the object of this desire is 'nothing' (Lacan 1977i[1958]:239). Rather than an acting-out, this restoration of the analysand's desire around the object 'nothing' would have triggered a further analytical exploration of its dialectical relationship with the desire of the Other, and its continuous transitions (metonymical) from one inadequate object to another.

Although it demonstrates on the one hand how the analyst smothers the analysand's desire with 'true' interpretations and on the other how a proper psychoanalytic intervention should operate, Lacan's critique of Kris' case-example is also potentially misleading, as it may foster the view that the analyst ought to tell the analysand what he believes he desires or, even more radically, that he desires nothing.[39] Because such an inference contradicts Lacan's ideas that the analysand is the chief interpreter, that the analyst should not name the patient's desire, and that naming means restoring rather than defining, it should be avoided. But how should the

analyst facilitate the emergence of the analysand's desire and its interpretations? In 'The Direction of the Treatment' Lacan formulated the
following abstruse guideline:

> In order to decipher the diachrony of unconscious repetitions, inter-
> pretation must introduce into the synchrony of the signifiers that
> compose it something that suddenly makes translation possible . . .
>
> (ibid.:233)

What Lacan called 'the diachrony of unconscious repetitions' in this
passage is nothing else than the mechanism controlling the changing
manifestations of a symptom over a certain period of time. For instance,
the academic described by Kris had regularly pinched sweets and books
during his adolescence, so that his current symptom of plagiarism was just
another avatar of an insistent unconscious core. Interpretation does not
entail finding and offering the signification of the analysand's history of
symptoms, as in Kris' explanation that all his symptoms were rooted in a
wish to incorporate his father's penis (Kris 1951:23), but discovering the
representations (signifiers) that preside over each of the symptoms ('the
synchrony of the signifiers') and translating these representations in such
a way that the analysand's desire becomes apparent. In the former case
the symptoms are regarded as representations whose signification should
be revealed, whereas in the latter the symptoms function as significations
in themselves, as products of a pathological interpretation whose principles
should be clarified. Unlike the traditional methods of interpretation, which
proceed from representation to signification, Lacan advocated an approach
proceeding from signification to representation and to desire.

More specifically, Lacan contended that the translation of the synchro-
nous signifiers will only occur if interpretation introduces something into
that synchrony.[40] It is not enough for the analysand to realize which set
of representations has governed each of his symptoms since the onset
of his illness. These representations need to be translated into a desire
(their meaning), and the analyst can only ensure that the translation will
not follow the same paths as those that have led to the appearance of the
symptoms if she intervenes in such a way that the set is being reorganized.
The process can be compared to the precipitation of a substance in a
saturated solution as a result of the addition of a reacting agent. The
analyst's interpretation serves as a reacting agent which facilitates the
precipitation of the analysand's desire out of the saturated solution of
her unconscious repetitions. Analytic interpretation is what separates
desire from a recurrent series of alienating symptomatic demands, which

prompted Lacan to designate its essential status as a cut (*coupure*) (Lacan 1958–59:session of 1 July 1959; 1970:70). When and how often this cut should be performed, and whether it should be effectuated via a temporal or linguistic punctuation or via the introduction of a signifier, is for the analyst to decide.[41] As Lacan pointed out in 'The Direction of the Treatment', the analyst is free in the timing, frequency and choice of his interpretations (Lacan 1977i[1958]:228).[42]

Being free in the timing also implies that the analyst does not have to postpone his interpretations until the analysand has developed a sufficiently strong transference. Against Freud's recommendation in 'On Beginning the Treatment' that not 'until an effective transference has been established in the patient, a proper *rapport*', should the analyst disclose 'to him the hidden meaning of the ideas that occur to him' (Freud 1913c: 139), Lacan underscored that such an adjournment of interpretations will automatically reduce their impact, because once the transference has been established the analysand will hear every interpretation as coming from the person he has identified the analyst with (Lacan 1977i[1958]:231).[43] Supporting Freud's early intervention in his case-study of the Rat Man (Freud 1909d), Lacan maintained that before the transference has been well established, the analyst should bring about a rectification of the subject's relations with the real, even if this triggers an aggravation of the symptoms (Lacan 1977i[1958]:237). In Lacan's opinion Freud's shocking interpretation of the Rat Man's compulsive fear as the derivative of an unconscious wish to harm his father need not be dismissed as an indoctrination, but applauded as an ingenious mapping of the Rat Man's subjective position. 'Rectification of the subject's relations with the real' does not entail forcing the analysand to face the reality of his condition, but it entails enabling him to acknowledge the motive supporting the place he adopts in his speech. If Freud had put himself on the side of reality, he would have told the Rat Man: 'Despite the fact that you think you are a criminal, I can tell you that you have never committed a serious criminal offence'. Yet putting himself on the side of the subject's relations with the real, he said: 'If you think you are a criminal, you'd better start recognizing the nature of the unconscious crimes you have committed'.

ORACLES AND THE PRECIPITATION OF TRUTH

Thus far I have explained how Lacan moved from a delimitation of the meaning of interpretation as a meaningless intervention stimulating the analysand's own interpretation in view of the crystallization of meaning, towards an interpretation of meaning as the desire encapsulated in the analysand's formations of the unconscious. In this account, desire and the symptom are situated on opposite sides of the interpretive spectrum. At the end of 'The Agency of the Letter in the Unconscious', Lacan described the antagonism between desire and the symptom as follows:

> [I]f the symptom is a metaphor, it is not a metaphor to say so, any more than to say that man's desire *is* a metonymy. For the symptom *is* a metaphor whether one likes it or not, as desire *is* a metonymy, however funny people may find the idea.
>
> (Lacan 1977g[1957]:175)

Lacan dubbed the symptom a metaphor because it is the substitution of one signifier (representation) for another signifier, inducing signification. The symptom functions as a replacement for a repressed wish that cannot express itself directly and, just as much as the manifest dream content, it appears as a creative psychic phenomenon whose nature can be described. Desire is called a metonymy because it coincides with the displacement from one signifier to another signifier, devoid of signification.[44] Desire shifts continuously from one object to another, so that it is impossible to capture and define its nature.[45]

If the symptom is metaphor and desire is metonymy, does that imply that interpretation, to the degree that it has to bring desire into existence, should be metonymy too? If so, how can an analytic interpretation, whether verbal or non-verbal, acquire this status of metonymy? Isn't an interpretation always to some extent a metaphor, that is to say a signifier which replaces an already existent one in the discourse of the analysand, and which subsequently has creative, therapeutic effects? But if interpretation is metaphor, how does it differ from a symptom, or how can the analyst prevent herself from feeding the analysand's symptoms? In *Seminar VIII* Lacan formulated the problem in the following terms:

> [T]he margin of incomprehension is that of desire. It is insofar as this is not recognized that an analysis terminates prematurely and, in a word, is missed. Of course, the pitfall is that when interpreting you give the subject something on which speech is feeding itself . . . Hence, each time you introduce – and you are probably obliged to do so – the metaphor, you stay in the same lane as that which gives consistency to the symptom. It is unquestionably a simplified

symptom, but it is nonetheless a symptom, at least with regard to the desire one is to set free.

(Lacan 1991b[1960–61]:246)

Without explicitly devaluating the metaphorical dimension of an interpretation, Lacan ensuingly dissected the questions of how an interpretation can follow the metonymical axis, and how such a metonymical interpretation may affect the formations of the unconscious.

Reviving the idea that analytic interpretations have to be metonymical, i.e. favouring 'the connection of a signifier to a signifier', Lacan clarified in *Seminar XI* that this does not warrant the conclusion that interpretation is 'open to all meanings', nor that it 'is in itself nonsense' (Lacan 1977b [1964]:250). But if interpretation is not open to all meanings, how can the analyst avoid impressing a new set of meanings onto the analysand? How can he avoid falling into the trap of suggestion again? It took Lacan another five years to fabricate a satisfactory solution to this problem, and his answer uncannily reflected one of his earliest remarks on the nature of interpretations, a small passage in 'Aggressivity in Psychoanalysis' in which he had stated that the analyst's interventions must take an oracular form (Lacan 1977d[1948]:13).

To justify his portrayal of interpretations as oracles, Lacan referred to conceptions of meaning within the pre-Socratic tradition. More specifically, he resuscitated a fragment from Heraclitus in which the philosopher had described the words of the Delphic oracle as follows: 'The Lord whose oracle is in Delphi neither speaks out nor conceals, but gives a sign' (Kirk and Raven 1957:211). Oracular words do not reveal and they do not hide, they simply signify (Lacan 1998a[1972–73]:114; 1975d[1973]:16). In another context Lacan wrote that interpretations are not modal judgements, propositions assigning a predicate to a subject, but apophantic statements, that is to say declarations pointing in a certain direction (Lacan 1973 [1972]:30).[46]

To Lacan the peculiar rethorical quality of the oracle showed how knowledge can function on the place of truth, and how the analyst can make use of this in his discourse (Lacan 1991a[1969–70]:39).[47] Once again, it is important to note here that 'knowledge operating on the place of truth', 'truth as knowledge' (*vérité comme savoir*) does not mean that the knowledge is true. It means that whatever knowledge a statement carries, this knowledge is only half-said (*mi-dire*) (ibid.:40). The knowledge appears between the lines, so that whoever receives the message will simultaneously know and not know. Although the receiver observes that there is some knowledge in the message, it does not make her any wiser.

In *Seminar XVII* Lacan advanced two kinds of interventions that comply with this rule of 'truth as knowledge': the enigma and the citation (ibid.:39–40). An enigma is an enunciation whereby the exact nature of the statement remains unclear. When confronted with an enigma, like Oedipus with the riddle of the Sphinx, one knows where the expression is coming from, but one does not know what it conveys. Conversely, a citation is an expression whereby one can remain unsure about its correct attribution or, to use Lacan's terms: it is a statement whose enunciation is problematic (ibid.:40). The enigma and the citation constitute the two axes of analytic interpretation, because they enable the analyst to tailor his interventions to the metonymy of desire. Enigmas and citations are not open to all meanings, and they are not in themselves nonsensical, yet the meaning flees from their appearance, either because the true relevance of the statement is unclear (in the enigma) or because the true identity of the 'author' can be doubted (in the citation), and this opens up the space of the analysand's desire.[48]

As regards the application of these interpretive techniques in a clinical setting, the analyst is of course not supposed to produce enigmas at wish, let alone to quote her preferred authors without acknowledging, giving the analysand the task to find out the origin of the citations. Lacan's point was that the analyst should cull the enigmas and citations from the texture of the analysand's discourse and return them to her in an interpretation (ibid.:40). For example, if an analysand, during free association, launches a formula such as 'a dutiful man keeps the church in the middle', the analyst may distil that formula from the analysand's discourse and return it to him as an enigma. Within the analysand's discourse the formula can have a fixed signification, and the analysand may very well enjoy that signification, yet in returning the formula to him the analyst invites the analysand to reflect upon it and to reinvestigate what it actually conveys.[49] In other words, the formula acquires the status of an enigma from the moment the analyst returns it, and the anticipated effect is that the analysand will explore its impact on his life.[50]

Alternatively, the analyst may extract and return a sentence from the analysand's discourse in order to invite reflection upon its origin. It happens regularly during analysis that analysands talk about themselves through the mouth of others. For instance, if an analysand says 'I am really too shy', this statement does not necessarily represent the analysand's own belief; it might very well be a judgement passed by his mother when he was little and with which he has identified. Here, citation means that the analyst literally takes up the analysand's words and returns them to him, stimulating reflection upon their provenance. The same effect would probably result from direct questions such as 'Who said that?' or 'Where do these words come from?', yet when using a citation the analyst does not imbue the analysand with the idea that he is possessed with a desire to know, and he simultaneously keeps the meaning of the intervention afloat, so that the analysand who hears his own words coming back to him from the analyst can still ask himself the question 'Why is he doing this?', 'What does he have in mind?', 'What does he want . . . ?'.

If Lacan's earliest accounts of psychoanalytic interpretation, as a process directed at the emergence of meaning, could still be considered an enlightened version of hermeneutics, the theory of interpretation he developed from the mid-1960s was radically anti-hermeneuticist.[51] Whereas Lacan had been keen to associate himself with Paul Ricoeur during the late 1950s and early 1960s, he violently rejected Ricoeur's interpretation of Freud after the publication of his massive treatise on Freud and philosophy in 1965 (Ricoeur 1970[1965]).[52] To ascertain the vigour of Lacan's theoretical move, it suffices to compare the opening lesson of *Seminar XI* with some of his later statements on hermeneutics. Whereas in *Seminar XI* he had conceded that 'we analysts are interested in this hermeneutics' and that there is 'at least, a corridor of communication between psychoanalysis and the religious register' (Lacan 1977b[1964]: 7–8) he later dismissed hermeneutics as 'a vague, soft and fraudulent field of research' (Lacan 1965–66:session of 23 March 1966) and a mere 'academic obscenity' (Lacan 1968b[1967]:37).

Sustaining his contention that interpretation serves the emergence of desire, Lacan at once pointed out that interpretation 'is directed not so much at the meaning as at the reduction of the signifiers to their nonsensicality' (Lacan 1977b[1964]:192, translation modified).[53] Here, discovering desire as the meaning of the dream is equated with the retrieval of something nonsensical, such as the formula for trimethylamine, on which Freud's entire dream of Irma's injection converges (Freud 1900a:116–117). This nonsensicality results from the reintegration of a meaningful, yet alienating primary signifier (S_1), say the self-description with which an analysand has identified over the years ('I am a doubter'), within the chain of signifiers (S_2, the binary signifier, the symbolic network), so that the pathogenic meaning of the primary signifier falls into nothingness. The process also entails the re-emergence of the absent (split) subject of the unconscious ($\cancel{S}$) and the analysand's acknowledgement, against the transference principle, that some knowledge will continue to escape.[54] Analytic treatment proceeds from alienation (to a primary signifier) to separation (from this primary signifier), whereby the analyst's interpretation helps the analysand in setting free 'the aphanisic effect of the binary signifier', that is to say the contribution of the signifying chain to the disappearance of deeply ingrained significations and the (re)creation of desire (Lacan 1977b[1964]:219).[55]

Eventually Lacan designated this function of interpretation as a movement towards the precipitation of truth (1966–67:session of 14 December 1966; 1970–71:session of 13 January 1971). As I have explained in the previous chapter, truth must not be understood here as a correspondence between knowledge and reality. In Lacan's theory of the late 1960s truth has nothing to do with objectivity, validation, factual knowledge, etc. Against all traditional philosophical and epistemological conceptions of truth, Lacan's notion flags the absence of definitive truths, the irreducible status of the unconscious as a knowledge without a knowing agency, the insuperable effect of symbolic castration, and the perennial dynamics between desire and its objects – psychic powers for which one can never be fully prepared.

One of Lacan's most arresting descriptions of the nature of psychoanalysis and its effects, with which I want to conclude this chapter, appeared in a 1967 essay on the relation between psychoanalysis and reality:

> [Psychoanalysis is not] the mystical assumption of a meaning beyond reality, of some universal being that manifests itself there in figures . . . Surely, the one who would take psychoanalysis for that kind of way would choose the wrong door. To the extent that it may lend itself to the control of an 'internal experience', it will be at the cost of changing its status . . . In a word, it excludes the worlds which open up onto a mutation of consciousness, an ascesis of knowledge, an effusion of communication. Neither on the side of nature, its splendour or evil, nor on the side of destiny, psychoanalysis does not make interpretation into a hermeneutics, a knowledge in no way illuminating or transformative. No finger would be able to indicate itself there as that of a being, divine or not. No signature of the things, nor providence of events. This is well underlined in its technique, due to the fact that it imposes no orientation of the soul, no opening up of intelligence, no purification as a prelude to communication. On the contrary, it plays on non-preparation . . . What is expected from the session is exactly what one refuses to expect, out of fear of putting too much one's finger on it: surprise, Reik has underlined.
>
> (Lacan 1968a[1967]:52–53)

NOTES

1 See for example Wells (1913–14), Tannenbaum (1917) and Wohlgemuth (1923).

2 For a comprehensive survey of the rebuttals see Macmillan (1997). One of the most vehement attacks on Freud's analyses of slips of the tongue in *The Psychopathology of Everyday Life* was undertaken by Timpanaro in *The Freudian Slip* (1976[1974]), a book which resuscitated many a dormant Freud critic in feminist and Left-wing circles during the 1970s and 1980s.

3 See for example Kitcher (1992) and Welsh (1994).

4 This remarkable absence of concrete instructions for the potential dream-reader in *The Interpretation of Dreams* prompted Alexander Grinstein, some eighty years after the publication of Freud's text, to release a volume entitled *Freud's Rules of Dream Interpretation* (1983).

5 One of the few exceptions to this (absence of) rule is Freud's assertion, in 'The Dynamics of Transference' (1912b:101), that whenever patients fall silent analysts are entitled to ask which thoughts they have had in relation to their analysts. As I have pointed out in Chapter 2, Lacan waived this technical principle because he believed it contributed to the installation of an unproductive imaginary relationship between the analyst and the analysand (Lacan 1988b[1953–54]:40).

6 Although Strachey paid less attention to the difference between deep and surface interpretations than to his other categories, the distinction gained momentum during the 1940s and 1950s by virtue of Fenichel's seminal monographs on psychoanalytic technique (1941[1938–39]; 1945).

7 This absence of theorization is borne out by a recent volume of Lacanian texts on interpretation prepared for an International Encounter of the Freudian Field (Association Mondiale de Psychanalyse 1996). For additional elaborations of Lacan's views on interpretation by distinguished Lacanians see Miller (1984b; 1995a[1994]; 1995b[1994]; 1996d), Soler (1996d), Fink (1997) and Burgoyne (1997).

8 I will discuss the historical context of Lacan's 'Rome Discourse' more extensively in the next chapter of this book.

9 The circumstances of Lacan's definitive excommunication will also be elucidated in Chapter 5.

10 See my discussion of Lacan's logical time machine in Chapter 2.

11 In Sheridan's translation of the 'Rome Discourse', the second and third stages of Lacan's logical time appear as 'time for understanding' and 'moment of concluding'.

12 Indeed, the only thing on which a prisoner can base his conclusion that he is white, after he has observed the two white disks on the back of his fellow inmates, is their hesitation. But because each prisoner is in the same position, no prisoner has any time to lose. The prisoner who obtains freedom is the one who is able to decide more rapidly than the others which colour he has, despite the fact that the criterion of hesitation is unreliable. The prisoner who decides that he is white can only anticipate the certainty of his decision since the others may have been hesitating simply because they are stupid and not because they are bemused by his own whiteness. None the less, if the prisoner waits until he reaches certainty, the only certainty he will have is

that he will stay imprisoned because the others are likely to have made up their own minds by then.

13 In the 'Rome Discourse' (1977e[1953]:48) and in *Seminar I* (1988b [1953–54]:285) Lacan also justified his idea by referring to Freud's remark in his case-study of the Wolf Man (1918b[1914]:45) that an interpretation is correct if it annuls the time interval between the re-emergence of a traumatic experience during the patient's childhood and the patient's conscious representation of that experience during analysis.

14 In some English translations of Lacan's works, the French term *sens* has been rendered as 'sense' whereas 'meaning' has been reserved for *signification*. I have decided to use 'meaning' for *sens*, and 'signification' for *signification*, thus following Sheridan's and Forrester's options, because Lacan himself employed *sens* as a translation of 'meaning' (Lacan 1975d [1973]:11). For a brief survey of the different renderings of *sens* and *signification* in the various English translations see the translator's note in Lacan (1988b[1953–54]:viii).

15 Of course, Lacan merely paraphrased Freud's opinion in *The Interpretation of Dreams*: '"[I]nterpreting" a dream implies assigning a "meaning" [*Sinn*] to it – that is, replacing it by something which fits into the chain of our mental acts as a link having a validity and importance equal to the rest' (Freud 1900a:96). In the last chapter of his book, Freud divulged that the processes governing dream formation do not differ significantly from those active in the formation of hysterical symptoms (ibid.:605–608). The method of dream interpretation could therefore function as a paradigm for the clinical interpretation of symptoms.

16 That all formations of the unconscious are legible is a thesis Lacan derived from Freud's typification of the manifest dream content as a pictographic script, a rebus, and even Holy Writ (Lacan 1988c[1954–55]:124; Freud 1900a:277–278, 514).

17 Lacan's critique was addressed at the procedures Anna Freud had advocated in *The Ego and the Mechanisms of Defense* (1966[1936]).

18 See Chapter 3.

19 Lacan's final seminar in Paris, on 10 June 1980, was entitled *Le malentendu* (Misunderstanding) (1981a). At the very end of his presentation he disclosed that the title of that year's seminar had been *Dissolution*.

20 For an instructive survey of the meanings that have been attributed to interpretation in medicine, psychology, psychoanalysis and psychotherapy see Jackson (1999:325–341).

21 According to Miller (1995b[1994]:15–16) Lacan may also have drawn inspiration from two articles by René Daumal entitled 'The Powers of Speech in Hindu Poetics' (1972a[1938]) and 'Approaching the Hindu Art of Poetry' (1972b[1940]) in which he had translated *dhvani* as resonance.

22 Nowhere in his 'Rome Discourse' did Lacan refer to *The Waste Land* but he had already used the poem's epigraph (from Petronius's *Satyricon*) at the head of the text's third chapter, on interpretation (1977e[1953]:77), and he had also quoted from *The Hollow Men* in the previous chapter (ibid.:71).

23 For a more in-depth exploration of the two stories and their significance within Lacan's 'Rome Discourse' see Khiara (1996).

24 'The interpreter is the analysand', Lacan declared in . . . *ou pire* (Lacan

1971–72:session of 21 June 1972). It is worthwhile mentioning here that in 1914 Freud added a footnote to *The Interpretation of Dreams* in which he indicated that his technique of interpretation differed from that of the Ancients in one crucial respect: psychoanalysis requires dreamers to do the interpretive work themselves (Freud 1900a:98).

25 See also Chapter 3, note 30.

26 In the French edition of Lacan's *Seminar I*, Little's paper has been wrongly attributed to Annie Reich, who had also published an essay on counter-transference in the same issue of *The International Journal of Psycho-Analysis* (Reich 1951). The case Little described in her paper concerns a patient who, shortly after the death of his mother, agrees to present his views on the radio concerning a topic of which he knows it also interests his analyst. The day after the broadcast he comes to the analytic session in a state of anxiety and confusion, and the analyst interprets his analysand's condition as fear induced by the expectation that the analyst will envy his success. Years after her paper was published, Little (1990:31–38) revealed that the example was taken from her own training analysis with Ella Freeman Sharpe. She herself was the patient in the article, the radio broadcast was in reality a paper she had to present to the British Psycho-Analytical Society, as part of her membership application, one week after her father's funeral. She had written the paper on counter-transference in 1949, two years after finishing her training analysis, which had taken seven years, and before embarking on a second analysis with Winnicott to relieve herself of the psychotic trends which the first analysis had left unresolved.

27 For additional criticisms on the reduction of psychoanalysis to depth-psychology see the references mentioned in note 62 of Chapter 2.

28 For Lacan's discussions of Glover's ideas on interpretation see Lacan (1977e[1953]:87; 1977i[1958]:223; 1998b[1957–58]:458–459; 1966–67: session of 21 June 1967).

29 Freud told the Rat Man that his hostile feelings towards his father and his indecisiveness in his relationship with his girlfriend must have been instilled by his father's objection to his son getting married to a poor girl. Lacan noted in 'The Direction of the Treatment' that this interpretation is 'contradicted by the reality it presumes' (Lacan 1977i[1958]:237), yet he did not specify which reality Freud's intervention was actually contradicting. A close reading of Freud's published case study (Freud 1909d) in combination with the complete text of Freud's case notes (Freud 1974[1907–8]; 1987 [1907–8]) reveals that Freud's interpretation could have been factually wrong in at least two respects: first, when the couple considered marriage the Rat Man's father had already passed away; second, there was definitely some form of opposition to the marriage, but rather on the part of the mother. When Lacan delivered his 'Rome Discourse' he could not have been aware of Freud's case notes, since they were not released until 1955 (Freud 1955a[1907–8]). Moreover, the latter edition only contained a partial transcription of Freud's notes, so that Lacan only had access to an incomplete supplement when writing 'The Direction of the Treatment'. As I have mentioned in previous chapters, in 1952–53, the year before he started his public lectures at Sainte-Anne, Lacan conducted a seminar on the Rat Man at his house, the results of which were summarized in 'The Neurotic's Individual Myth' (1979[1953]).

30 *Désir* (desire) is Lacan's translation of Freud's *Wunsch* (wish). In 'The Direction of the Treatment' (1977i[1958]:256–257) he agreed that the French term *désir* is stronger than the German *Wunsch* and the English 'wish', without compromising on the point that *désir* is the proper way of rendering in French what Freud was trying to describe with *Wunsch*. Since *désir* had already been used as a translation of Hegel's notion *Begierde*, Lacan may also have tried to bridge the gap between the Hegelian and the Freudian corpus, a thesis which could be further substantiated with his article 'The Subversion of the Subject and the Dialectic of Desire in the Freudian Unconscious' (1977k[1960]).

31 When broaching the issue of the meaning of meaning (*le sens du sens*) Lacan always resisted the positivist approach defended by Ogden and Richards in their influential study from the early 1920s (Ogden and Richards 1923).

32 Of course, the comparison of interpretation with translation had initially been suggested by Freud (1900a:277–278; 1913c:140).

33 Lacan referred to the story on three occasions, in *Seminar II* (1988c[1954–55]: 158), *Seminar XIV* (1966–67:session of 23 November 1966), and in 'The bungled action of the supposed subject of knowing' (1968b[1967]:38), without elaborating on it.

34 The story could also be used as a parable for what takes place within psychoanalytic treatment. Yet in the light of the above remarks on the analysand as an interpreter, one should not fall into the trap of picturing Daniel as the analyst. He is more in the position of the analysand, the analyst being the mysterious creature who produces enigmatic words.

35 The dream-work thus also involves a type of translation, and the manifest dream-content could be considered an interpretation of the latent dream thoughts. In 'The Unconscious' (1915e:193) Freud argued that becoming conscious of an unconscious idea does not merely encompass an act of perception, but probably also a process of translation (*Übersetzung*). To Lacan, this implied that 'the unconscious . . . has already in its formations – dreams, slips of the tongue or pen, witticisms or symptoms – proceeded by interpretation' (Lacan 1977b[1964]:130). In his 1931 paper Glover had also explained symptoms as incorrect interpretations of sources of anxiety (Glover 1931:400), something which Lacan noted with surprise in 'The Direction of the Treatment' (1977i[1958]:233), presumably because he was not expecting an author who did not rely on the linguistic structure of the unconscious to make such claims. For a further comment on dreams as interpretations see Lacan (1968–69:session of 26 February 1969).

36 Kris divulged that the man had already been through an analysis with a woman and that this previous treatment had improved his potency and reduced his social inhibitions, which had in turn induced a general change of lifestyle. He also revealed that the details of the man's first treatment had been reported by Schmideberg in a paper from the mid-1930s (Schmideberg 1934).

37 For Lacan's comments on the various issues raised by Kris' paper see Lacan (1977e[1953]:83; 1988b[1953–54]:59; 1993[1955–56]:79–81; 1966f[1954]: 393–399; 1977i[1958]:238–240; 1958–59:session of 1 July 1959; 1966–67: session of 8 March 1967).

38 From a Lacanian point of view, an 'acting-out' is always the expression of a

thwarted desire. It functions as a substitute for a speech act and is primarily addressed at the person who has failed to recognize or attempted to kill one's desire. Lacan's most extensive theoretical discussion of the differences between a symptom, an acting-out, and a 'passage to the act' (*passage-à-l'acte*) can be found in Lacan's *Seminar X, Anxiety* (1962–63).

39 A similar difficulty governs Lacan's reading, in *Seminar VIII*, of Socrates' reply to Alcibiades at the end of the *Symposium* (Plato 1951). Socrates responded to Alcibiades' eulogy by saying that he had only spoken in such high terms to destroy Socrates' relationship with Agathon, Alcibiades' true beloved. In Lacan's view Socrates had pointed, in a truly psychoanalytic fashion, towards the secret spring of Alcibiades' desire (Lacan 1991b [1960–61]: 164, 179, 189, 210–212) which had earned him the title of precursor of psychoanalysis (Lacan 1977k[1960]:323). In so far as Socrates' intervention was directed at Alcibiades' desire it can indeed be called psychoanalytic, but to the degree that it named Alcibiades' desire (to destroy Socrates' relationship) and its object (Agathon) it defied the principles of Lacanian psychoanalytic interpretation. In *Seminar IX* Lacan repeated his 'diagnosis' of Socrates as a psychoanalytic interpreter *avant la lettre* (Lacan 1961–62:session of 21 February 1962), but later he labelled Socrates a hysteric (Lacan 1975d[1973]:16; 1975c:6).

40 Whereas in 'The Direction of the Treatment' Lacan wrote that interpretation must 'introduce' something, he later preferred to call it an 'addition' (Lacan 1962–63:session of 21 November 1962), a 'supplement' (Lacan 1971–72:session of 4 May 1972), or a *falsum*, in the sense of something that is being dropped off the mark (Lacan 1991a[1969–70]:157; 1970:80; 1973[1972]:15). The ambiguity of the Latin verb *fallere* (dropping, deceiving) prompted Lacan to decree the inherent falsity of analytic interpretations (1970:80). Lacan's conception of interpretation was radically opposed to that championed by Devereux, who argued that the analyst's interpretation must never add anything to the analysand's materials (Devereux 1951). It is also worth mentioning here that whenever Lacan discussed the effect of an interpretation on the analysand's mental representations (her knowledge), he stressed that the translation occurs 'suddenly', 'unexpectedly', 'in a flash of light', etc. The element of surprise is a quintessential part of the interpretive act, explaining why Lacan often expressed his admiration (1977b[1964]:25; 1968a[1967]:52) for Reik's (1935) emphasis on discovery and surprise in psychoanalytic treatment.

41 Miller (1996d:12) has drawn attention to the difference between interpretation as cut and interpretation as punctuation in Lacan's work, but in my opinion this distinction is not crucial.

42 In Lacan's theory, interpretations are called 'premature' not when they are given too soon, but when they convey a ready-made understanding. See, for example, Lacan (1991b[1960–61]:246).

43 In *Seminar XI* Lacan added that it is futile, and even paradoxical, to await the establishment of the transference before giving interpretations, since transference is a closure of the unconscious (Lacan 1977b[1964]:130–131, 253). See also my discussion of interpretation within the transference in Chapter 3.

44 In light of the aforementioned distinction between meaning and signification

it is crucially important not to confuse Lacan's considerations on the effects of signification in metaphor and metonymy with an evaluation of their effects of meaning. In other words, when Lacan argues that metaphors have an effect of signification, he does not suggest that they generate meaning, on the contrary.

45 When addressing the desire of the analyst in the penultimate session of *Seminar XI*, Lacan indicated that one can circumscribe but never name a desire (Lacan 1977b[1964]:254).

46 The notion *apophansis* (declarative discourse) originates in Aristotle's treatise *On Interpretation* (*Peri Hermeneias*) (Aristotle 1963).

47 For the discourse of the analyst see Chapter 2.

48 Lacan had already foreshadowed this idea in his discussion of the dream of Irma's injection and the writing on the wall in *Seminar II*, in which he said: 'Like my oracle, the formula [trimethylamine] gives no reply whatsoever to anything. But the very manner in which it is spelt out, its enigmatic, hermetic nature, is in fact the answer to the question of the meaning of the dream. One can model it closely on the Islamic formula – *There is no other God but God*. There is no other word, no other solution to your problem, than the word' (Lacan 1988c[1954–55]:158).

49 Towards the end of his career Lacan sometimes stated that the analyst's interpretations are directed at the relationship between speech and jouissance (Lacan 1971–72:session of 4 November 1971; 1978[1973]:69). This may seem odd considering the antagonism between language (the Other) and jouissance Lacan defended during the 1950s and 1960s. Yet from the early 1970s onwards he pointed out that speech is not completely devoid of jouissance, in so far as the knowledge embedded in speech can function as a means for obtaining (phallic) jouissance (Lacan 1991a[1969–70]:43–59). Hence, the analyst's interpretations are aimed at the analysand's jouissance to the extent that they seek to dismantle the (self-)knowledge which he has acquired and cultivated over the years, and with which he adorns himself in his speech.

50 Although convinced that psychoanalytic theory can produce a calculus of interpretations, Lacan also believed that the effects of interpretations cannot be calculated. The analyst can structure her interpretations on the basis of certain heuristics, yet she cannot foresee which effects her interpretations will have on the analysand. See Lacan (1975d[1973]:16; 1973–74:session of 20 November 1973).

51 Some psychoanalysts within the International Psychoanalytic Association did embrace hermeneutics as a valuable philosophical framework for their interpretive actions. For a recent critical discussion of hermeneutic psychoanalysis see Saks (1999).

52 Apart from theoretical considerations, Lacan's repudiation of Ricoeur's approach may have been sparked by more personal matters too. See the sections on Lacan's encounters with Ricoeur in Roudinesco (1990[1986]) and Reagan (1996).

53 Sheridan has translated Lacan's phrase '*réduire les signifiants dans leur non-sens*' as 'reducing the non-meaning of the signifiers'. However, this procedure would have exactly the same effect as increasing the meaning of

the signifiers, whilst Lacan wanted to oppose the increase of meaning to something else.

54 See my discussion of transference as a closure of the unconscious in Chapter 3.

55 In *Seminar XI*, Lacan used the Greek term *aphanisis*, which he had borrowed from a paper by Ernest Jones on female sexuality (Jones 1950[1927]), as a synonym for the fading and disappearance of the alienated individual and the re-emergence of the split subject. The passage from *Seminar XI* on the liberation of the aphanisic effect of the binary signifier, to which I have referred, has also been mistranslated by Sheridan. As a matter of fact, Sheridan's translation says exactly the opposite of what Lacan is arguing for. It reads that the subject has to free himself of (get rid of) the aphanisic effect of the binary signifier, whereas Lacan suggests that this effect has to be set free, has to be released from the psychic chains in which it has been kept.

Chapter 5

Authorizing analysis

SIGNS OF THE TIMES

Since Freud's development of psychoanalysis in the latter years of the nineteenth century, its practice has never sparked more vehement discussions as during the present day and age. In various European countries, the fundamentals of psychoanalytic practice are being reconsidered in the slipstream of the creation of the European Association for Psychotherapy (EAP) and of the trend-setting legal regulations of the psychotherapeutic profession in Austria and Italy. Many psychoanalytic associations in Europe have seized upon these first steps towards a social policy for psychotherapists in order to re-address the historically vexed issues of the psychoanalyst's rights and duties, of the contents and the organization of an adequate psychoanalytic training programme, of the criteria for recognizing new analysts, and of the procedures for controlling each individual psychoanalyst's performance.

Whatever the answers to these questions may be, they strongly affect the institutional politics of the psychoanalytic associations and also influence the social authorization of the theory and practice of psychoanalysis. The Lacanian *Ecole de la Cause Freudienne* (ECF) recently transformed itself from an 'ECF–1' into an 'ECF–2' (Wachsberger 1992; Miller 1992; Klotz 1993), whose major difference is the implementation of the 'second proposition of the pass', as suggested by Lacan in a 1974 letter to three Italian psychoanalysts (Lacan 1982b[1974]). This 'second proposition' implies that the procedure of the pass, in which an analysand testifies to his experience of analysis without it necessarily being finished, is not only used to recognize new analysts, but also to recruit new members of the school, as an alternative to more common criteria such as the candidate's number of analytic sessions, his degrees, a set of written papers, the general contribution to the psychoanalytic community and so on. The acceptance of this entry procedure by the members of the ECF was a direct outcome of their reaction against Serge Leclaire's proposal to establish an 'analytical order' – by analogy with the 'medical order' – in which the practice of psychoanalysis would be regulated by a specific set of rules designed by the analysts themselves, on a European level (Miller 1990; Leclaire 1990). It represents a refusal to marry psychoanalysis with some sort of unifying state ordinance, through which somebody would be qualified to practice psychoanalysis following her compliance with a pre-established, public promulgation of analytic capacity.

Another effect of the European policy making for psychotherapists is that psychoanalytic associations have newly reflected on the theoretical and epistemological underpinnings of their own discipline. Questions regarding the relationship between psychoanalysis and psychotherapy, and the position of psychoanalysis *vis-à-vis* science have been reconsidered and rephrased. As far as the relationship between psychoanalysis and psychotherapy is concerned, some analysts have argued that there is no fundamental difference between them, since psychotherapy is an essential part of psychoanalysis and both are dealing with the same objects and mechanisms. These analysts have welcomed the recent steps towards policy making for psychotherapists, they have underscored the necessity for psychoanalysts to accept the professional framework of psychotherapy in order to preserve their own socioeconomic future, and they have envisaged the unification of all mental health disciplines in the inter-disciplinary environment of a world association for psychotherapy. Otto Kernberg, one of the chieftains of American psychoanalysis, offers a good example of this position:

> I believe that training in psychoanalytic psychotherapies as well as in standard psychoanalysis strengthens rather than weakens the identity of the psychoanalyst. In the absence of such training, the analyst is poorly equipped to treat patients for whom psychoanalysis is not indicated, as evidenced by the number of stalemates with which many a practice has been strewn. Psychoanalytic psychotherapy used to be perceived as second-rate treatment; the analyst's self-esteem was diminished if he practised this treatment rather than psychoanalysis. An integrated conception of a broad spectrum of treatments grounded in psychoanalytic theory would, in my view, sharpen the method as well as strengthen the identity of the psychoanalyst.
>
> (Kernberg 1993:58)

There was a time when psychoanalysts did not treat patients for whom psychoanalysis was not indicated and when the indications for psychoanalysis were very limited (Freud 1905a[1904]). Now it seems that psychoanalysts also have to treat patients who do not require standard psychoanalysis – whatever that may be – but something else.[1] Furthermore, there was a time when the psychoanalytic associations provided the analysts in need of identity with basic social and professional credentials and sometimes, if this need was a trifle out of proportion, with psychoanalysis. Now we seem to have reached a time when the identity of the analyst has suffered so much damage that only a universal, integrated and state-controlled body of professional psychotherapists, who of course all take their bearings from psychoanalysis, is capable of restoring the analyst's social position. The purpose of this new psychotherapeutic *Weltanschauung* for psychoanalysts is not merely to revitalize the worn-out psychoanalytic image and to rectify the deteriorating clinical and social relevance of psychoanalysis, but also to adjust the profession to changing socioeconomic realities. In other words, the implicit purpose of many a contemporary psychoanalyst's ambition to belong to the psychotherapeutic professions has perhaps less to do with raising identity and more with raising dough.

Of course, it has been observed that the demand for psychoanalysis has changed since the time of Freud. During the first decades of this century, people from all over the world travelled to Vienna, Berlin or Budapest to be analysed. Before and after World War II, European analysts who had fled to the United States enjoyed a huge clientele and were anything but concerned with their social status.[2] In those halcyon days, psychoanalysis was new, controversial, rapidly expanding and very much alive and kicking. In this *fin de siècle*, the situation is radically different. The dissemination of psychoanalysis continues for sure, but rather as a theoretical body of ideas with cultural relevance, than as a method of clinical treatment for specific disorders. Many people are ignorant about psychoanalysis as an available form of treatment, although few people have never heard of Freud. Those who are aware of the practice of psychoanalysis would rather prefer cognitive-behavioural or family therapy, possibly due to the influence of negative media coverage, but definitely owing to general considerations of time and money. So indeed the demand has changed – short-term, financially attractive and time-saving psychotherapy instead of long-term, expensive and time-consuming psychoanalysis.

Confronted with this situation, the analyst can choose between at least two alternatives. Either he can repudiate the current situation and try to alter the existing demand by reformulating the offer of psychoanalytic treatment, or he can accept the status quo and tailor psychoanalysis to the new requirements. The latter *aggiornamento* of psychoanalysis through an adjustment of its objectives, the enlargement of its scope and its overall adaptation to changing social realities is exactly what a strong psychoanalytic force is currently aiming at, not only within the IPA tradition, but also within object-relations, Kleinian and even within some Lacanian groupings. Surely this alternative seems easier to realize than the other one – trying to comply with a demand is probably easier than trying to transform the demand itself – and it will presumably pay off more quickly to the analyst when she tries to change her practice instead of the public demand. Hence, the metamorphosis of psychoanalytic treatment in a sense corresponds to the same socioeconomic dynamics as the contemporary evaporation of the demand for psychoanalysis.

A similar process governs the way in which modern psychoanalysts deal with the issue of the relationship between psychoanalysis and science. The basic questions psychoanalysts have to address here are not new; they have merely been revived and expanded as a consequence of the disastrous effects of Recovered Memory Therapy (RMT), which in the eyes of some has produced monsters rather than healthy human beings (Ofshe and Watters 1994). The basic assumption of RMT is that patients – in most cases women suffering from Multiple Personality Disorder (MPD) – have repressed a memory of infantile sexual abuse, which therefore needs to be recovered during psychotherapy. However, instead of healing MPD patients and making them into socially adapted, responsible individuals, RMT has often produced false memory syndromes of parental rape and satanic ritual abuse, revictimizing the former victims of repressed child abuse as well as their families and the legal system in general. Due to the central importance of repression in RMT, critics have used the RMT fad as an excellent opportunity to reopen the issue of the scientific value of psychoanalysis, thereby neglecting the fact that RM therapists themselves have vituperated Freud for refusing to believe his patients' accounts. Roughly, the critics have contended that it is impossible to validate clinically and empirically the key psychoanalytic concept of repression, that the psychoanalytic method of treatment does not allow the analyst to postulate causal relationships between current clinical symptoms and former life events, and that it is impossible to prove that the effects produced during psychoanalysis actually stem from psychoanalytic technique and not, for instance, from suggestion.

These being the main epistemological criticisms levelled against psychoanalysis, it is immediately clear that they outweigh the concrete application of some basic principles in a clinical setting, and question its scientific foundations. Moreover, the fact that these criticisms are corroborated and substantiated by highly respected philosophers of science, such as Adolf Grünbaum, makes it all the more urgent for psychoanalysts to formulate some kind of answer (Grünbaum 1984; 1993).

Again, two different positions can be delineated. One way to deal with these criticisms is to admit that the epistemological status of psychoanalysis is flawed and to focus on the transformation of psychoanalysis into a hard-nosed scientific discipline. In this respect, it is probably not a coincidence that psychoanalysts are currently trying to find the missing link between psychoanalytic theory and the so-called neurosciences (Solms 1998, 1997, 1995; Solms and Saling 1986). This interest has little or nothing to do with some constitutional curiosity of the psychoanalyst for what goes on in the world of rocket science. Its aim is to integrate neuroscientific methods and concepts into the realm of psychoanalysis, to prove that psychoanalysis and neuroscience have the mind as a common object of study and to establish a unity between soft-core psychoanalytic ideas and hard-core neuroscientific principles. In short, the transformation of psychoanalysis into a respected scientific discipline is expected to run along the lines of a psychoanalytic incorporation of the most recent developments in science.

From an alternative point of view, one could assert that the epistemology of psychoanalysis is not flawed, yet fundamentally different from the scientific one. From this vantage point the criticisms of psychoanalysis described above (see p. 187) merely originate in a misapprehension of the fact that psychoanalysis deals with subjective unconscious processes that are pervaded by a singular, para-consistent logic. As such, statements concerning the impossibility to validate psychoanalytic concepts could be regarded as true, albeit completely irrelevant, in so far as their proponents fail to appreciate the entire psychoanalytic enterprise. As a matter of fact, these statements assume that the quest for validation should be of paramount importance in psychoanalysis, whereas psychoanalysis has indicated and accepted the impossibility of validation as a theoretical cornerstone.

The latter idea is Lacanian rather than Freudian, since Freud was quite convinced that psychoanalysis could espouse the correspondence criterion of truth, producing a kind of knowledge that tallies with reality (Freud 1915c). From a Lacanian perspective, correspondence between knowledge and truth is strictly impossible, and thus the issue of validation becomes obsolete. Psychoanalysis should not apply at the office for empirical validation, but continue to criticize this scientific tradition for its promotion of the illusion that a correspondence between theories and realities is viable.

Whereas in the first case, science is accepted as an ideal for psychoanalysis and psychoanalysts proceed with amendments to their theoretical tenets, in the second case psychoanalysis could function as an ideal for science, due to its acknowledgement of a fundamental gap between knowledge and truth (Milner 1995). In the short term the first position, which, for example, includes the integration of psychoanalysis and neuroscience, will probably prove the most successful one for guaranteeing the psychoanalyst's social status, because it favours interdisciplinarity and promotes the psychoanalyst as somebody who is willing to negotiate and compromise. Whether it will also contribute to the future of psychoanalysis as an original method of treatment and research remains to be seen, since integration usually takes place at the expense of singularity. In the long run it could simply secure Freud's invention a place among the history of ideas.

On numerous occasions, Lacan has discussed the same issues as those emerging within the current European debate on the theory and practice of psychoanalysis. However, the nature of his uncompromising contributions is often overshadowed by the grandeur of their effects: schisms within the French psychoanalytic community, Lacan's excommunication from the IPA, schisms within the Lacanian community itself, Lacan's dissolution of his own school, and so on. In the final chapter of this book I wish to focus on what lies behind some of the major institutional dissensions produced by Lacan, particularly on that which led to the establishment of the *Société Française de Psychanalyse* (SFP) in 1953 and the one prompting him to create his own school, the *Ecole Freudienne de Paris* (EFP) in 1964. In this way I hope to make clear that Lacan's views on the training and authorization of the analyst, and on the organization of a psychoanalytic association are still highly relevant for modern debates on the status of psychotherapy.

A RENEGADE PLEA FOR SINGULARITY

In 1972, Lacan at one stage reflected on his expulsion from the French psychoanalytic establishment and the start of his public seminar some twenty years earlier:

> I wish to emphasise a historical event that is a key point in my itinerary, insofar as it has any importance. By virtue of this conspiracy

against which Freud directed his article on *Laienanalyse*, and which
occurred shortly after the war, I had already lost my game before even
having started it.

(Lacan 1971–72:session of 1 June 1972)

From this statement it could be inferred that there was a direct connection
between the problem of lay-analysis and the start of Lacan's public
teachings in the autumn of 1953. However, this assessment of the situation, formulated by Lacan in 1972, differs from what he had written
immediately after the events, in the preface to his 'Rome Discourse'
(1977e[1953]). There he had attributed his problems with the French
psychoanalytic society to the latter's authoritarian regulation of analytic
training, that he contemptuously likened to the procedure for issuing a
driver's licence (ibid.:33). Moreover, from the viewpoint of the French
psychoanalytic establishment itself, it has always been stressed that the
major dissensions surrounding French psychoanalysis in the beginning of
the 1950s had to do with the implementation of psychoanalytic technique
and, more particularly, with Lacan's practice of sessions of variable
length (Eissler 1954:272). Hence, depending on the perspective and the
amount of hindsight, one or the other aspect within a complex network
of interlocking forces – the problem of lay-analysis, the organization of
an analytic training programme and the standards of analytic technique –
has been highlighted, which makes it worthwhile delving into the historical
sources in order to clarify some points.

Founded in 1926, the first French psychoanalytic society was called
the *Société Psychanalytique de Paris* (SPP). Originally, it had nine
members, among them Princess Marie Bonaparte, Rudolph Loewenstein
– who would become Lacan's analyst – and Edouard Pichon, from whom
Lacan borrowed the notion of foreclosure (Mordier 1981; Roudinesco
1982:343–411; Scheidhauer 1985). Lacan joined the SPP in 1934 and
presented his first paper as a member of the society at the fourteenth IPA
congress of Marienbad in 1936, where his talk on the mirror-stage
was prematurely interrupted by Ernest Jones (Lacan 1977c[1949]; 1966a
[1946]:184–185). During World War II, the SPP suspended its activities,
not resuming its regular meetings until the end of 1946. From 1947, Sacha
Nacht acted as the chairperson of the society, while Lacan's influence
in its organization grew steadily. In September 1949 Lacan presented an
extensive document to his fellow members, in which he meticulously
stipulated, *inter alia*, the necessary qualifications of people applying
for psychoanalytic training, the contents of a psychoanalytic training
programme and the procedures for the recognition of a trainee as a new

analyst of the society (Lacan 1976a[1949]). Since a detailed discussion of all the aspects of this document falls beyond the scope of this chapter, I will restrict myself to the points relating to the issues at stake here.[3]

As regards the relation between psychoanalysis and medicine, Lacan's statement was quite ambiguous. On the one hand, he contended that 'psychoanalysis is essentially a medical technique' and that 'medical qualifications . . . are the most recommendable ones for psychoanalytic training' (ibid.:33). On the other hand, he pointed out that 'no degree of technical competence will be prohibited for non-medical psycho-analysts', although none of the lay analysts was, still according to Lacan, to 'undertake the treatment of any patient without this patient being referred by a medically trained psychoanalyst' (ibid.:34). As to the organization of the analytic training programme, Lacan championed the creation of a coordinating committee whose members were partly re-elected after a regular interval of two years, thus decentralizing power and involving more members of the society in the implementation of selection, teaching and homologation procedures. Lacan's final article emphasized the necessity for a psychoanalytic society to guarantee the transmission of a pure, orthodox analytic technique, defining this technique not as a set of rules for the direction of the treatment, but as a practice 'which respects the entire register of the personality, without eluding any of its antinomies' (ibid.:35).

Lacan's project did not elicit any major disagreements, but then its tone was of course quite moderate and it did not comprise any ideas that were not already accepted by most members of the society. It was not until the end of 1952 that a crisis in the SPP occurred. During the summer of that year, Sacha Nacht, who was still the president of the SPP, had formulated two proposals, one regarding the policy of a future 'Institute for Psychoanalysis' and one regarding the names of those in charge of this Institute. Both proposals were endorsed by the SPP. In November 1952, Nacht also devised a provisional programme of seminars for the coming year and, more importantly, the articles of the Institute. These articles were interpreted by some lay members of the SPP, including Marie Bonaparte, as clearly aiming at the restriction of psychoanalysis to medical doctors, whereas the letter of Nacht's articles was rather ambiguous on that point. Nevertheless, owing to the opposition, Nacht resigned from his official functions and Lacan was elected the new provisional president of the Institute.

In January 1953, Lacan proposed his own articles for the Institute, which differed from Nacht's in at least two respects (Lacan 1976b[1953]). First, whereas Nacht had put his project under an epigraph taken from a neurobiological treatise on psychopathology (Mourgue and Von Monakow 1928), which proclaimed that human neurobiology is the most fundamental discipline from which all other sciences emanate, Lacan chose to begin his project with an excerpt from Freud's text on lay analysis, in which Freud had listed all the subjects to be included in the programme of an imaginary analytical faculty (Freud 1926e).[4] In this way, Lacan endeavoured to maintain the originality of psychoanalysis, with due respect to its founder, without relinquishing the importance of other disciplines for the psychoanalytic enterprise. Although psychoanalysis was not to be reduced to psychology or medicine, these disciplines were still to be included in a psychoanalytic training programme. The following excerpt makes this clear:

This is why psychoanalysis cannot be reduced to neurobiology, nor to medicine, pedagogy, psychology, sociology, the science of institutions, ethnology, mythology, the science of communication, nor to linguistics . . . To all of these, psychoanalysis has given a decisive turn and from all of these it has to get its information. This is why the Institute, far from locking up psychoanalysis in doctrinal isolation, shall consider itself the designated host of every confrontation with these related disciplines.

(Lacan 1976b[1953]:56)

The second difference between Lacan's and Nacht's articles concerned the distribution of power within the Institute. Lacan vigorously opposed an Institute in which all the power is centralized in one person or in one committee, and whose primary aim is not to train and assure the transmission of psychoanalysis, but to dominate people and to dismantle opposing forces as much and as quickly as possible – in short to produce a large number of strictly conforming individuals. This is less obvious from the contents of Lacan's articles, than from a letter he sent to Loewenstein in the summer of 1953, in which he explained the circumstances surrounding the conflict. Concerning Nacht, Lacan wrote to his analyst:

[W]hen, thanks to his [Nacht's] efforts, the Institute was physically ready in November, it was shattering for me to hear from his own mouth with what cynicism he planned to make a purely political use of it: 'giving loads of courses', for example to those whose action he planned to neutralize . . . Nacht achieved point by point what had been his intention . . . : ensuring, through a massive entry of the directorial committee (including the administrative secretary!) into the Educational Committee, a permanent majority in the ordinary and the extraordinary functioning of that Committee: that is, having the subjects examined at every stage by a commission of four members only, the director of the Institute being the sole permanent element having, to be sure, a preponderant voice, which, given the fact that it is his secretary who designates the three others, assures him, you can understand this, I think, of a rather handsome probability that he will never be countered, etc.

(Lacan 1990a[1953]:56–60)

Despite Lacan's election as provisional president of the Institute, Nacht's articles were passed, probably under the influence of Marie Bonaparte, who unexpectedly changed caps and started to support Nacht instead of Lacan. According to Lacan himself, Bonaparte's sudden displacement of loyalties was the upshot of his having forgotten to mention 'the Princess or her honorary functions' in his articles of the Institute (ibid.:60). However, from the reports of the business meeting at the eighteenth congress of the IPA, held in London in July 1953, it appears that for Bonaparte the problem had to do with a 'divergence of technique', and notably with 'the fact that one of these members [Lacan of course] . . . promised to change his technique, but did not keep his promise' (Eissler 1954:272). Removed from his office in the Institute, Lacan was elected as the new president of the SPP in January 1953, but only for five months, for in June of that year, Michel Cénac, with whom Lacan had written a paper on psychoanalysis and criminology some three years earlier, stood up to ask for Lacan's expulsion (Lacan 1996c[1950]). The Socratic charges included inciting the students against their masters and violating the rules of the society. Lacan finally stepped down as president of the SPP and shortly thereafter, Daniel Lagache, Françoise Dolto and Juliette Favez-Boutonnier resigned as members of the SPP, joining forces to create the SFP, which Lacan joined immediately. In September 1953, the SFP held a kind of shadow congress alongside the official SPP congress in Rome, where Lacan delivered his 'Rome Discourse'. Two months later he gave the opening lesson of his first public seminar on *Freud's Papers on Technique* in the Hôpital Sainte-Anne (Lacan 1988b[1953–54]).

Looking back at these tumultuous events, it seems that the various reasons mentioned by Lacan and others to explain the 1953 schism in the French psychoanalytic community are all valuable, but that only one thing motivated the creation of the SFP and the beginnings of Lacan's teachings.

The rulers of the SPP considered Lacan a renegade who was not willing to subject himself to the agreed standards of psychoanalysis, and who was suspected of trying to exhort people to undermine the established structures of power. Lacan did not resign because he could not agree with Nacht's proposition on the acceptability of lay analysis, nor because he could not compromise with the other members on the organization of the association and the Institute, but because he was somehow forced to resign due to his lack of conformism. In the aftermath, he turned the Socratic accusations into a virtue, promoting it in his life-style, his writings and teachings, as well as in his conception of psychoanalysis in general. His criticisms directed at the representatives of ego-psychology during the 1950s have often been misunderstood as a critique addressed at the IPA, but it was certainly aimed more at its promotion of formalism than at its organizational principles. If it had been focused on the organization itself, Lacan would presumably never have supported the SFP's own demand for IPA affiliation at the end of the 1950s.[5]

Apart from Lacan's relentless refusal of conformism, two other aspects of his position within the French psychoanalytical debate of the 1950s stand out. First, there is his explicit striving to safeguard and develop the originality of Freud's discovery: no concessions as to the subsumption of psychoanalysis under whatever related discipline, which was precisely what Nacht aimed at when he chose the fragment by Von Monakow and Mourgue as an epigraph for his articles, and which was also the purpose of the ego-psychologists in the 1940s and the 1950s, who attempted to transform psychoanalysis into a new type of behavioural engineering. Instead of trying to affiliate psychoanalysis with other disciplines, Lacan stressed the importance of a return to Freud, the necessity of which presented itself in 1953 more than ever before, in view of the dissemination of ego-psychology in the United States and the eclectic ideas proclaimed by the leaders of the French psychoanalytic society.[6] Once again, Lacan's intentions to counter these processes were clearly stated in the preface to his 'Rome Discourse':

> In any case I consider it to be an urgent task to disengage from concepts that are being deadened by routine use the meaning that they regain both from a re-examination of their history and from a reflection on their subjective foundations.
>
> (Lacan 1977e[1953]:33)

Perhaps this incitement should be revived in this day and age, when transference is being reduced to a working alliance, when the unconscious has penetrated the realm of common sense to such an extent that consciousness is being promoted as a revolutionary object of study, and when the drive is increasingly being explained by intersynaptic processes within the neural network of the brain. Indeed, the question is whether contemporary psychoanalysis does not require a fundamental reconsideration of its singularity, at a time when its major proponents are willing to seek affiliation with the rapidly expanding domain of professionalized psychotherapy and established science. Perhaps psychoanalysis itself is again in need of psychoanalysis, that is to say of a reflection upon its history and future through the verbalization of its present symptoms.

A second aspect of Lacan's position in the 1950s, next to his striving to safeguard the originality of Freud's discovery, concerns his rejection of a hierarchically structured psychoanalytic society, in which a sovereign body of self-nominated members not only sets out the theoretical lines, but also decides over the selection, training and promotion of candidates. Whereas the first aspect of the return to Freud was immediately put into practice by Lacan and continued to characterize his approach for at least a decade, this second aspect proved far more difficult to realize. Lacan unquestionably tried to regenerate psychoanalytic theory and practice by resituating its basic concepts within their original context and by injecting them with ideas taken from anthropology, philosophy and linguistics, but whether he succeeded in creating the ideal psychoanalytic society, an institution in which power is decentralized and in which the juniors just as much as the seniors have the power of decisions, is a much more contentious issue. The more Lacan's influence grew and the more his institutional initiatives expanded, the more he was regarded as an autocrat, tolerating only those who were absolutely loyal to his cause and who did nothing else but parrot his ideas and sell his name. At the end of the 1950s, some of Lacan's acolytes within the SFP were willing to 'assassinate' their master in return for an official IPA recognition, an act reminiscent of Freud's myth of the murder of the primal father, which led to the second major schism in the history of psychoanalysis in France.

AN OUTLAW PLEA AGAINST POWER

In July 1959, some six years after its creation, the SFP asked the IPA for affiliation (Hesnard 1959). During the twenty-first International Congress in Copenhagen, the president of the IPA, William H. Gillespie, reported that the Central Executive did not have enough information about the activities of the SFP to be capable of endorsing the request. Therefore he suggested the installation of an *ad hoc* committee, whose purpose was to investigate the activities of the SFP on the spot and to report back the conclusions of its inquiry to the Central Executive, which would then decide whether or not the SFP could be affiliated (King 1960). This recommendation was passed and Gillespie appointed a committee comprising Paula Heimann, Ilse Helmann, Pieter Jan Van der Leeuw and Pierre Turquet.

Two years later, during the twenty-second International Congress in Edinburgh, Gillespie declared that the committee had done a sterling job and that the Central Executive had decided to grant the SFP the status of Study Group, controlled by an IPA committee, which had to watch over the training procedures within the Group (Zetzel 1962:366–367). The SFP accepted the IPA's decision and its recommendations, only to discover afterwards that the IPA had included an additional point to its list of requirements, demanding the progressive exclusion of Lacan and Dolto. The SFP expressed its dissatisfaction with the added point, but continued to accept the IPA's decision, thinking that the situation would probably change in years to come (Favez-Boutonnier 1977[1961]). However, instead of removing the disputed requirement, the IPA committee strengthened it. At the twenty-third International Congress in Stockholm, following a report by Turquet in which the problem of the SFP was characterized as the 'Lacan-problem', the Central Executive decided to retain the SFP as a Study Group, simultaneously indicating that the SFP would lose this status if it did not exclude Lacan as a training analyst before the end of 1963 (Rapport Turquet 1977[1963]). On the night of 19 November 1963, a majority of SFP members approved a motion to exclude Lacan as a training analyst. The next day, Lacan gave the first and final lesson of his seminar 'The Names-of-the-Father', ending with the statement:

> I am not here in a plea for myself. I should, however, say, that – having, for two years, entirely confided to others the execution, within a group, of a policy, in order to leave to what I had to tell you its space and its purity – I have never, at any moment, given any pretext for believing that there was not, for me, any difference between yes and no.
>
> (Lacan 1990b[1963]:95)

Before long, Lacan resumed his seminar on *The Fundamentals of*

Psychoanalysis, weaving the opening lesson around the most basic of questions: 'What is psychoanalysis?', 'What grounds psychoanalysis as a praxis?', 'Is psychoanalysis a science?', 'What is the analyst's desire?' (Lacan 1977b[1964]:1–13). While the seminar regained its verve, the conflicts within the SFP escalated, leading to the creation of two new societies, the Association Psychanalytique de France (APF), comprising among others Daniel Lagache, Jean Laplanche, Jean-Bertrand Pontalis and Didier Anzieu, and the Ecole Française de Psychanalyse (EFP), founded by Lacan, and comprising among others Serge Leclaire, Françoise Dolto and Jean Clavreul.[7]

Shortly before Lacan read the founding act of the EFP in June 1964 (Lacan 1990c[1964]), Clavreul presented an extensive report to those who had chosen to resign from the SFP, in which he defined the originality of the group, explained the consequences of its position, addressed the problematic issue of analytic training and proposed a less hierarchical structure for the analytic society (Clavreul 1977[1964]). Regarding the originality of the group, Clavreul was both clear and decisive. According to him, being a Lacanian did not imply having been analysed by Lacan, nor having approved of everything he said, but having agreed on certain theoretical points, among others that being respected because of keeping up good social relations and submitting oneself to international standards is but an imaginary construction that covers the fundamental law of the symbolic, to which every subject is in debt (ibid.:138–148). In relation to analytic training, Clavreul opposed the traditional distinction between an ordinary analysis and a training (or didactical) analysis, saying that there is no difference between subjects demanding an analysis because of some psychic problem and those demanding an analysis because they want to become an analyst. In other words, if somebody consults an analyst with a demand for analysis simply because she wants to become an analyst, this demand can be treated as a symptom. Sometimes it might even turn out that this demand is a very nasty symptom indeed, and that it has nothing to do with the desire of the analyst as such. In addition, concerning the hierarchy within the analytic society, Clavreul advocated the sole distinction between full members (*membres titulaires*) and associate members (*membres adhérents*), the second group comprising all practising analysts, and the first group representing those that are also considered able to train new candidates.

Some of these ideas were laid down in principles within Lacan's own 'Founding Act' of the *Ecole Freudienne de Paris* (EFP), or were implemented by the EFP during the 1960s and 1970s. The EFP set out with a different aim from that of becoming an IPA society. In the second paragraph of his 'Founding Act', Lacan explained the basic objective of the organization as follows:

> That title [at that stage the *Ecole Française de Psychanalyse*], in my understanding, represents the organism in which a labor is to be accomplished – a labor which, in the field opened up by Freud, restores the cutting edge of his truth – a labor which returns the original praxis he instituted under the name of psychoanalysis to the duty incumbent upon it in our world – a labor which, through assiduous criticism, denounces the deviations and compromises that blunt its progress while degrading its use. This working objective is inseparable from a training to be dispensed within that movement of reconquest.
>
> (Lacan 1990c[1964]:97)

These lines obviously read as a political statement, for Lacan asked the members of the EFP to reconquer the Freudian field and to denounce all movements hampering its principal lines of force.

Of course, the question is how this Freudian field should be defined, where it begins and where it ends, and where one has to start with its reconquest. Rather than a worldwide colonization of the unconscious according to the rules of some form of Western analytical imperialism, Lacan's invocation represented a continuous striving for the purity of the analytical discourse. His statement implied neither a submission to the official standards of analytic practice, nor an integration of psychoanalysis within the framework of already established, socially recognized professions.

With regard to training, Lacan confirmed that there is only one type of analysis and that in some cases analysis may prove to have 'training effects'. In other words, a psychoanalyst is born through a process of psychoanalysis, although no process of psychoanalysis whatsoever can predetermine the advent of an analyst. The stunning consequence of this principle is that a selection of candidates is not required anymore. Everyone is entitled to choose his analyst without any restrictions as far as the analyst or the subject are concerned, in view of the future recognition of the subject as analyst. Every analysand's analysis can have training effects, thus preparing the analysand for the function of analyst.

Three years after his creation of the EFP, in his 'Proposition of 9 October 1967 on the Psychoanalyst of the School', Lacan specified this point by launching two controversial principles. The first principle was that 'the psychoanalyst derives his authorisation only from himself' (Lacan

1995b[1967]:1; 1982b[1974]:7). For Lacan this idea did not require any further elaboration, but for the psychoanalytic establishment it proved once again that the EFP was built on very weak foundations. For many an IPA representative, Lacan's principle implied that anybody in the EFP could call himself an analyst and that the School did not care about the maintenance of professional clinical standards. Of course, this is not what Lacan meant. When stating that the psychoanalyst derives his authorization only from himself, he underscored that the analyst's own experience of analysis (and not a theoretical training programme or a fixed number of analytical sessions with a training analyst) is the only valid criterion for judging someone's analytic capacity. Lacan's assertion did not entail that every analysand should be allowed to authorize herself as an analyst whenever she feels like it, but that the nature of the analysand's own analytic experience, regardless of its frequency, duration and the name of the analyst, is the single decisive factor for her qualifying as an analyst.[8]

In Lacan's view, this principle did not prevent the School from guaranteeing that an analyst functioning within its boundaries had been authorized on the basis of an analytic experience with training effects. The guarantee could proceed along two lines, depending on whether the analysand had asked for it or not. When the School observes that somebody has proved himself as an analyst, it may decide to give him the grade of A.M.E. (Analyst Member of the School). When somebody wants to be recognized as an analyst on her own initiative, she is entitled to the grade of A.E. (Analyst of the School), provided she has successfully completed the procedure of the pass (Lacan 1995b[1967]:1).

The procedure of the pass was the second principle Lacan introduced in 1967, and it proved even more controversial than the previous one. The pass requires an analysand who wants recognition as an 'Analyst of the School' to talk about her experience during analysis to three other analysands, who in turn advise a jury of what they have heard, after which the jury decides whether the analysand is to be recognized as an Analyst of the School or not. The procedure implies that there is no direct contact between the candidate and the decision-making organ. The candidate does not have to prove to his seniors that he would be a valuable analyst. The candidate does not have to pass some kind of exam; he simply has to testify to an experience in front of three people who are his equals. In addition, the jury does not judge any kind of knowledge presented by the candidate, but a knowledge spoken by people who have nothing to gain or to lose in the entire procedure. The members of the jury and the three analysands are chosen at random from a list of analysts and analysands respectively.

This procedure of the pass broke with all the traditional regulations concerning the admission of a candidate to the status of analyst and differs radically from what is still common within the IPA and other, non-Lacanian organizations, where recognitions are based on the amount of training sessions with an allocated training analyst and all kinds of professional and social credentials. Nevertheless, despite its democratic intentions, the pass did not work as it was intended to, and many conflicts arose over the decisions of the jury and over the impact of Lacan himself. Few discussions within the EFP and, after its dissolution, within the *Ecole de la Cause Freudienne* (ECF) have been so intensive and violent as those regarding the design and the implementation of the pass.[9] Whether the pass is indeed the best procedure for qualifying an analyst, or for authorizing somebody to practice psychoanalysis, is difficult to determine. In any case, it reduces the power that is traditionally held by the veterans of a society; it does not exclude anybody from the process of becoming an analyst and it opens an enormous field of potential expertise among the young, whose desires and responsibilities are the only true bet. Unfortunately, within the current European context, the profession-alization of psychotherapy brings about new formalisms, which could be denounced as 'compromises blunting the progress of analysis'. These will certainly affect the future of psychoanalysis, if only because many analysts, even Lacanian ones, are more than willing to exchange what they have achieved for a large-scale social recognition and a batch of new loyalties.

Finally, on the subject of the concrete organization of the analytic society, Lacan proposed yet another innovation, which would prove even more controversial and even more impossible than the procedure of the pass. In the 'Founding Act' he stated:

> For the execution of the work, we shall adopt the principle of an elaboration sustained in a small group. Each of them (we have a name for designating the groups) will be composed of at least three individuals, five at most, four being the proper measure. PLUS ONE charged with selection, discussion, and the outcome to be accorded the efforts of each. After a certain period of functioning, the elements of a group will be invited to shift to a different group. The task of directing will not constitute a form of leadership whose service rendered might be capitalized into access to a higher rank, and no one will be inclined to regard himself demoted for entering at a rank of base-level work.
>
> (Lacan 1990c[1964]:97)

The small group Lacan introduced here is the 'cartel', which was supposed to function as the organizational cornerstone of the school. Within the cartel there were to be no hierarchical differences between the members, whatever their qualifications, their titles, or their position within the school. As a member of a cartel, the director of the school functioned on the same level as the other members, despite their having been perhaps only just admitted as members of the school. Membership of the cartels was not limited to those who were authorized analysts of the school, but applied to all the members of the school, including not only analysts and analysands, but also people who were not directly involved in the practice of psychoanalysis. Inasmuch as the function of the 'plus one' of the cartel could be seen as leading, controlling, or coordinating, it was the members of the cartel themselves who selected the 'plus one', who could therefore never be reproached for having elected himself as a leader.

However, organizing a society around another discourse than the one of power seemed extremely difficult, perhaps less because individual members continued to promote themselves as leaders, than because members carried on installing their own masters, while disputing those that had already been appointed by others. Perhaps this is the fundamental drama of an analytic society that tries to organize itself according to the principles of the discourse of the analyst. Where members are not supposed to exert power, but rather to cause the desire of the Other, the effect is that the other is hystericized and in turn installs the other as a master, whether he likes it or not. The major difficulty, if not the impossibility of the discourse of the analyst has less to do with taking up the position of the analyst as such, than with preventing the analysand from attributing the position of the master to the analyst. Therefore, it remains to be seen whether an analytic society can function beyond the discourse of power and whether it is able to structure itself according to the principles directing the very practice that constitutes the rationale behind its existence.

NOTES

1   Miller (1998) has equally argued in favour of a cancellation of the so-called contra-indications for psychoanalysis, not by broadening psychoanalytic treatment to psychoanalytic psychotherapy but by separating the psycho-analytic process from the psychoanalyst. Miller's point was that whatever the contra-indications for psychoanalysis may be, there are no contra-indications for an encounter with a psychoanalyst.

2   And those who were *persona non grata* in the official institutions, such as Theodor Reik, were keen enough to create their own organization and to start all over again.

3 For a more detailed discussion of its contents see Vanier (1990).

4 Lacan subsequently decided to use the same lines by Mourgue and Von Monakow as an ironic epigraph for his 'Rome Discourse', sarcastically revealing their pure meaning in a long footnote (Lacan 1977e[1953]:30, 110–111, footnote 84).

5 In a recently published conversation with R. Horacio Etchegoyen, Jacques-Alain Miller did not hesitate to confirm that during the 1950s Lacan indeed aspired to become an IPA member again, but he at once expressed his doubts about Lacan's desire in these matters (Etchegoyen and Miller 1996:48–49).

6 Let us not forget that Marie Bonaparte had already tried to merge biology and psychoanalysis during the 1930s. See Bonaparte (1938[1936]; 1952).

7 Soon after its creation, the EFP changed its name from *Ecole Française de Psychanalyse* to *Ecole Freudienne de Paris*, in this way highlighting its theoretical orientation at the expense of its national identity (Lacan 1990c[1964]:103).

8 For a more thorough discussion of this principle and its implications for analytic training, see Safouan (1983), Liart (1985) and Le Gaufey (1998).

9 The procedure of the pass that was adopted by the EFP in 1969 differed significantly from that suggested by Lacan in 1967. See Lacan (1986[1967]; 1977m[1973]) and Miller (1977). Detailing the complicated vicissitudes of the pass within the EFP and (from 1981) the ECF is not appropriate within the context of this chapter. For a succinct historical survey of the stakes until the mid-1980s, see Attié (1985). Discussions of how the procedure has been implemented can be found in almost every issue of *La cause freudienne*, the official journal of the ECF.

Conclusion

It has often been heard, and it is likely to resound for many years to come, that Lacan's theory of psychoanalysis is but an impenetrable amalgamation of self-indulgent nonsense, which has little or no bearing on the everyday clinical reality of human suffering. This judgement has not only been passed by researchers belonging to the so-called natural sciences, as part of an attempt to debunk everything smelling of Theory, (Post)structuralism and Postmodernism, it has also been formulated by representatives of the social and human sciences, in their concern to safeguard these disciplines against the ever-looming threats of philosophy and metaphysics.

The fact that Lacan's work has penetrated the Anglo-American world primarily via the arts and humanities, spearheaded by authorities within English Literature and, more recently, Gender and Cultural Studies, has only augmented this prevailing outlook of Lacan as an indefatigable promulgator of oblique ideas lacking coherence, consistency and, most importantly, empirical validation. Although the efforts of Anglo-American scholars in securing a respected place for Lacan within contemporary academia are extremely laudable, the newly created environment for Lacanian studies, paired with the general crisis of clinical psychoanalysis in anglophone countries, has by no means facilitated Lacan's rehabilitation as a psychoanalyst concerned with the pivotal aspects of clinical work.

In view of Lacan's lifelong commitment to the grassroots of psycho-analytic treatment and the dissemination of its structuring principles, one is also forced to conclude that however prestigious Lacan's current position within the arts and humanities may be, he is mainly respected for the wrong reasons. Of course, Lacan had a soft spot for philosophy, linguistics, anthropology, history and the arts, but only to the extent that he believed these disciplines could provide him with the necessary conceptual tools to make sense of what happens between the four walls of the psychoanalytic consultation room. Just as Freud had relied, albeit often implicitly, on the achievements of psychophysics, the philosophy of Schopenhauer and the techniques of archaeology, Lacan imported a diversity of ideas into his work to elucidate the nature of a unique clinical event. Even when deciding to embark on the manipulation of complicated topological figures such as the Borromean knot, during the last decade of his career, he impressed on his audience that his only purpose was to account for the mainspring of psychoanalytic practice. Hence, contemporary studies of Lacanian theory display an extraordinary reversal of perspective: whereas Lacan continuously employed ideas within the arts and humanities to develop his Freudian paradigm of psychoanalysis, the latter is now being used to broaden conceptions within the arts and humanities.

My main intention in this book was to restore the concrete clinical impact of Lacan's propositions, to demonstrate how they are deeply embedded in Freud's body of works, and to illustrate their significance for the entire realm of 'modern psychotherapy'. Therefore I have organized each chapter around an issue which is not specific to Lacanian psychoanalysis, but which spans the whole tradition of psychodynamic psychotherapy. In order to appreciate the value of Lacan's work for this tradition, it is of the utmost importance to ascertain that Lacan started from the exceedingly simple observation that psychoanalytic treatment is predicated upon the power of speech. Because psychoanalysis is a 'talking cure', as Anna O. so perceptively put it, any account of its *modus operandi* has to proceed from an evaluation of this symbolic framework. During the early 1950s Lacan accordingly argued that the neglect of 'the function and field of speech and language in psychoanalysis' by post-Freudians, in favour of an enlightened behaviourism, necessitated a renewed reflection upon the symbolic foundations of Freudian psychoanalysis. As a result he undertook a profound exploration of what it means for people to say everything that comes to mind, of the distinct modalities of speech that can emerge, of how speech is addressed to somebody else, of how human beings are affected by their subservience to language, etc. Similar questions governed his dissection of the analyst, although evidently more tailored towards the (symbolic) position he is being granted and held to adopt, the ethics of psychoanalytic treatment, the analyst's employment of knowledge, etc. In this book I have concentrated more on the various psychic structures (psychosis, neurosis, perversion), the analyst's position within the treatment, and the strategies for transference handling, than on the tactics of interpretation and the organization of psychoanalytic training. This tallies with Lacan's conviction that working according to distinct ethical principles, and handling the analysand's transference in line with an appreciation of the psychic structures and one's own stance with regard to knowledge are more important for the maintenance of psychoanalytic treatment than all the other features of the clinical process.

Alongside the assessment of a human being's relationship with speech and language, Lacan also paid attention to what falls beyond the symbolic framework. Apart from what is actually being said during a psychoanalytic encounter, he plumbed those inchoate experiences which continuously pervade language without ever fully expressing themselves, those experiences which are exiled to the sanctuaries of perennial silence, the spectacles of an acting out, or the gripping intensity of a desperate scream. Contrary to what has been advanced from time to time, his theory was therefore not just a redemptive reinvention of psychoanalysis as a clinical practice of the signifier, to the detriment of the affect. Of course, those parts of Lacan's theory 'beyond the language principle' are more difficult to grasp, if only owing to the central paradox governing every endeavour to put into language what falls essentially beyond it.

I am aware that many readers of this book might judge my intention to redress Lacan as a clinician futile, taking account of the book's lack of detailed clinical material and its circumvention of specific technical guidelines for the prospective Lacanian psychoanalyst. However, the clinical importance of Lacan's theory does not lie within a series of rules for the practitioner, but within a fundamental heuristics for the direction of the treatment. Freud himself was reluctant to provide concrete rules of thumb, let alone a general methodology of psychoanalysis, in light of the plasticity of psychic processes and the endless variety of clinical situations. In fact, the danger of reducing any clinical theory of psychoanalysis to a set of technical guidelines is dual: first, the necessary formalization of the treatment edges towards a sterile formalism which leaves no room for improvization and creativity; second, instead of promoting the relativity of the psychoanalyst's knowledge, the technical manual can reinforce unshakeable beliefs in the value of a particular intervention. In order to avoid these risks, every self-respecting psychoanalyst who indulges into the formulation of concrete clinical advice will ultimately have to admit that clinical realities are far more complex and challenging, and that novices ought not take the recommendations at face value. Such disclaimers, when put at the end of a book, are likely to elicit anxiety in the reader, if not frustration at having to go through the rules only to learn afterwards that psychoanalytic treatment is still something else.

In the previous chapters, I have decided to follow a different route, explaining clinical principles of Lacanian psychoanalysis whose value transcends the particularity of the single case. However abstract these principles may still be, their rigour implies that clinicians can rely on them to organize their practice and to conduct a Lacanian treatment to its end, provided they have taken the responsibility for their own training first. Applying these principles to a concrete case is not an easy task and can stir bewilderment in newborn and wool-died analysts alike. Here the anxiety will not be induced by the pressure of an imposed strait-jacket which does not seem to fit, but by the confrontation with the extraordinary diversity of human misery. But if the main challenge for psychoanalysts is knowing how to deal with what is unbearable in their analysands, this is simultaneously the mainspring of their anxiety and their creativity, something for which no book can prepare.

Chronology

1901	*13 April* birth of Jacques-Marie Emile Lacan in Paris, the first child of Alfred Lacan (1873–1960) and Emilie Baudry (1876–1948), a middle-class Roman-Catholic family.
1902	Birth of Raymond, Lacan's brother.
1903	*25 December* birth of Magdeleine-Marie, Lacan's sister.
1904	Death of Raymond Lacan.
1906	*16 November* birth of Marie-Louise Blondin, Lacan's first wife.
1907	Lacan enters the Collège Stanislas, where he completes both his primary and his secondary education (1907–1919).
1908	*1 November* birth of Sylvia Maklès, Lacan's second wife. *25 December* birth of Marc-Marie, Lacan's brother.
1919	*Autumn* Lacan decides to embark on a medical career and enters the Paris Medical Faculty.
1920	Lacan meets André Breton (1896–1966) and becomes interested in the surrealist movement.
1921	Lacan discharged from military service due to thinness. *December* Lacan attends the first public reading of *Ulysses* by James Joyce (1882–1941) at Shakespeare and Co in Paris.
1926	*4 November* creation of the *Société Psychanalytique de Paris* (SPP), the first association of French psychoanalysts. Lacan conducts his first case-presentation, at the *Société Neurologique* in Paris. He publishes his first paper, co-authored with Th. Alajouanine and P. Delafontaine, in the *Revue neurologique*, based on the case presentation of 4 November.
1927–28	Clinical training at the Clinique des Maladies Mentales et de l'Encéphale, directed by Henri Claude (1869–1945), which is connected to L'Hôpital Sainte-Anne in Paris. Lacan meets Henri Ey (1900–1977).

1928	Engagement with Marie-Thérèse Bergerot, to whom Lacan will dedicate his doctoral thesis. Marriage of Georges Bataille (1897–1962) and Sylvia Maklès.
1928–29	Clinical training at L'Infirmerie Spéciale de la Préfecture de Police, under the supervision of Gaëtan Gatian de Clérambault (1872–1934).
1929	Lacan's brother enters the Benedictine Order and moves to the abbey of Hautecombe in the French Alps, adopting the new name of Marc-François on 8 September 1931, when he takes his monastic vows.
1929–31	Clinical training at L'Hôpital Henri Rousselle, also connected to Sainte-Anne Hospital in Paris.
1930	Meets Salvador Dalí (1904–1989).
	First non-collaborative paper in *Annales médico-psychologiques*.
	10 June birth of Laurence Bataille, daughter of Georges Bataille and Sylvia Maklès.
	August–September work placement at the Burghölzli clinic in Zürich.
1931	*18 June* Lacan examines Marguerite Pantaine-Anzieu (1892–1981), who is admitted to Sainte-Anne hospital after an attempt to assassinate the actress Huguette Duflos. Lacan's investigation of the case constitutes the central part of his doctoral thesis ('Le Cas Aimée').
1932	Lacan translates Freud's paper 'Some Neurotic Mechanisms in Jealousy, Paranoia and Homosexuality' (1922b[1921]).
	June Lacan starts his analysis with Rudolph Loewenstein (1898–1976).
	November Lacan obtains his doctor's title with a thesis on paranoia. His dissertation is published by Le François and Lacan sends a copy to Freud, who acknowledges receipt by postcard.
1933	Lacan falls in love with Marie-Louise Blondin, the sister of his friend Sylvain Blondin (1901–1975).
	October Lacan starts attending the seminar on Hegel's *Phenomenology of Spirit* by Alexandre Kojève (1902–1968) at the Ecole Pratique des Hautes Etudes, where he meets Georges Bataille and Raymond Queneau (1903–1976).
1934	Lacan sees his first private patient.
	Georges Bataille and Sylvia Maklès separate.
	29 January Lacan marries Marie-Louise Blondin.

November   Lacan becomes a candidate member (*membre adhérent*) of the SPP.

1936   *3 August*   Lacan attends the 14th Congress of the IPA at Marienbad (Máriánské Lázně, Czech Republic), where he presents 'Le stade du miroir'.

1937   *8 January*   birth of Caroline Marie Image Lacan, first child of Lacan and Marie-Louise Blondin.

1938   Writes a long text on the family for the *Encyclopédie française* commissioned by Henri Wallon (1879–1962) and Lucien Febvre (1878–1956).

Lacan starts a relationship with Sylvia Maklès-Bataille.

5 June   on his way to London, Sigmund Freud stops in Paris, where Marie Bonaparte organizes a party in his honour. Lacan does not attend.

December   Lacan finishes his analysis with Loewenstein and becomes a full member (*membre titulaire*) of the SPP.

1939   *27 August*   birth of Thibaut Lacan, second child of Lacan and Marie-Louise Blondin.

23 September   death of Sigmund Freud in London.

1940   *June*   installation of the Vichy regime. The SPP suspends all its activities.

26 November   birth of Sibylle Lacan, third child of Lacan and Marie-Louise Blondin.

1941   *Spring*   Lacan moves to 5, rue de Lille in Paris, where he will continue to see patients until his death.

3 July   birth of Judith Bataille, daughter of Lacan and Sylvia Maklès-Bataille.

15 December   Lacan and Marie-Louise Blondin are officially divorced.

1944   *Spring*   Lacan meets Jean-Paul Sartre (1905–1980), Pablo Picasso (1881–1973) and Maurice Merleau-Ponty (1908–1961). He becomes Picasso's personal physician.

14 February   birth of Jacques-Alain Miller, Lacan's future son-in-law.

1945   *September*   Lacan travels to England, where he studies the practice of British psychiatry during the war.

1946   The SPP resumes its activities.

9 August   divorce of Sylvia Maklès and Georges Bataille.

1948   Lacan becomes a member of the Teaching Committee (Commission de l'Enseignement) of the SPP.

21 November   Death of Lacan's mother.

1949	Lacan meets Claude Lévi-Strauss.

17 July Lacan attends the 16th Congress of the IPA in Zürich, where he presents another paper on the mirror-stage.

1951   Lacan introduces sessions of variable length in his practice; this worries the other members of the SPP. During the following years he regularly explains his position without managing to convince his colleagues. Meanwhile, he gives a seminar on Freud's Dora-case at his house, and acquires a splendid summer-house at Guitrancourt, some 50 miles to the west of Paris.

2 May 'Some Reflections on the Ego', lecture at the British Psychoanalytic Society.

1951–52   Seminar on Freud's case of the Wolf Man.

1952   *Summer* Sacha Nacht (1901–1977), president of the SPP, presents his views on the organization of a new training institute (Institut de Psychanalyse).

December Nacht resigns as director of the Institute, and Lacan is elected new director *ad interim*.

1952–53   Seminar on Freud's case of the Rat Man.

1953   *20 January* Lacan is elected president of the SPP, and Nacht regains control of the Institute.

16 June Lacan resigns as president of the SPP. Creation of the *Société Française de Psychanalyse* (SFP) by Daniel Lagache (1903–1972), Françoise Dolto (1908–1988) and Juliette Favez-Boutonnier (1903–1994); Lacan joins soon after.

July the members of the SFP are informed that they do not belong to the IPA anymore.

8 July Lacan gives the opening lecture at the SFP on the symbolic, the imaginary and the real.

17 July marriage of Lacan and Sylvia Maklès.

26 September Lacan delivers his 'Rome Discourse', 'The Function and Field of Speech and Language in Psychoanalysis'.

18 November Lacan starts his first public seminar at Sainte-Anne Hospital with a series of lectures on Freud's papers on technique. The public seminars will be held until June 1980. Simultaneously, Lacan conducts weekly clinical presentations at Sainte-Anne Hospital.

1954   Lacan visits Carl Gustav Jung (1875–1961) at his home in Küssnacht (Switzerland).

1955   *Easter* Lacan visits Martin Heidegger (1889–1976) in Freiburg (Germany).

July the IPA rejects the SFP's request for affiliation.

August–September Lacan entertains Heidegger and his wife at his summer-house.

1956   *Winter* first issue of the journal *La Psychanalyse*, containing Lacan's 'Rome Discourse' and his translation of Heidegger's 'Logos' (1951).

1959   *July* the SFP renews its request for affiliation to the IPA. Nomination of a committee of enquiry.

1960   *15 October* Death of Lacan's father.

1961   *August* the SFP is accepted as an IPA Study Group on the condition that Lacan and Dolto are progressively removed from their training positions.

1963   *August* the IPA stipulates that the SFP will lose its status if Lacan continues to be involved in training matters.

19 November a majority of SFP members decides to accept the IPA recommendation.

20 November first and final session of Lacan's seminar on 'The Names-of-the-Father'.

1964   After extensive legal proceedings, Judith adopts the name of her father.

January Lacan starts a seminar on the foundations of psychoanalysis at the Ecole Normale Supérieure (Rue d'Ulm, Paris), where he lectures under the auspices of the Ecole Pratique des Hautes Etudes, a post for which Claude Lévi-Strauss and Louis Althusser have intervened on his behalf.

21 June Lacan founds the *Ecole Freudienne de Paris* (EFP).

October final issue (8) of *La Psychanalyse*.

1965   *19 January* dissolution of the SFP.

1966   *January* first issue of the journal *Cahiers pour l'analyse*.

February–March Lacan presents six lectures in the US on the topic of 'desire and demand', organized by Roman Jakobson (1896–1982) (Columbia University, MIT, Harvard University, The University of Detroit, The University of Michigan, The University of Chicago).

18–21 October Lacan attends an international symposium at the Johns Hopkins University in Baltimore, MD on 'The Languages of Criticism and the Sciences of Man', where he presents 'Of Structure as an Inmixing of an Otherness Prerequisite to Any Subject Whatever'.

November publication of *Ecrits*. Lacan sends a copy to Heidegger.

	December marriage of Judith Lacan and Jacques-Alain Miller.
1967	*9 October* Lacan proposes the procedure of the pass as a means to verify the end of analysis and to recruit new 'analysts of the school'.
1968	*Autumn* publication of the first issue of the journal *Scilicet*. *December* opening of the Department of Psychoanalysis at the Centre Expérimental Universitaire de Vincennes. Serge Leclaire is appointed director of the department.
1969	*January* lectures in the Department of Psychoanalysis commence. *March* the introduction of the pass provokes a schism within the EFP, leading to the creation of the *Organisation Psychanalytique de Langue Française* (OPLF). *November* Lacan moves his seminar to the Faculté de Droit (Place du Panthéon) in Paris.
1970	*September* Leclaire resigns as director of the Department of Psychoanalysis, and is succeeded by Jean Clavreul.
1973	Publication of *Seminar XI, The Four Fundamental Concepts of Psychoanalysis* in French, transcribed and edited by Jacques-Alain Miller. *30 May* death of Caroline Lacan-Roger.
1974	The Department of Psychoanalysis at Vincennes is reorganized and Jacques-Alain Miller becomes its new director.
1975	First issue of the journal *Ornicar?*. *16 June* Lacan opens the 5th International James Joyce Symposium in Paris. *November–December* lecture tour in the US (Yale University 24–25 November; Columbia University 1 December; MIT 2 December 1975).
1977	Publication of *Ecrits: A Selection* and *Seminar XI: The Four Fundamental Concepts of Psychoanalysis* both translated by Alan Sheridan. Lacan writes a new preface for the English translation of *Seminar XI*.
1979	Creation of Fondation du Champ Freudien, directed by Judith Miller.
1980	*5 January* Lacan dissolves the EFP. *12–15 July* Lacan presides the first international conference of the Fondation du Champ Freudien in Caracas. *October* creation of the *Ecole de la Cause Freudienne* (ECF). *10 October* Lacan conducts his final case-presentation.

1981	*9 September* death of Lacan in Paris. Buried at Guitrancourt.
1983	Death of Marie-Louise Blondin.
1985	Twenty psychoanalytic organizations exist in France, nineteen of which have their roots in Lacan's teachings.
	Jacques-Alain Miller wins a legal battle over the rights to edit and publish Lacan's seminars.
1986	Death of Laurence Bataille.
1993	Death of Sylvia Maklès-Lacan.
1994	Death of Marc-François Lacan.

Bibliography of works by Jacques Lacan in English

The most exhaustive bibliography of Jacques Lacan's books, seminars, articles and ephemera is *Bibliographie des travaux de Jacques Lacan* (Paris: InterEditions, 1983), compiled by Joël Dor. An updated version of this landmark work of reference was published in 1993 as *Nouvelle bibliographie des travaux de Jacques Lacan* (Paris: E.P.E.L). The second most comprehensive bibliography is *Jacques Lacan: An Annotated Bibliography* (New York NY and London: Garland, 1988), a two-volume work compiled by Michael Clark, which provides references to Lacan's works and their translations, as well as to numerous secondary sources. Clark's bibliography also includes excellent annotations for all published materials. The contents of each of Lacan's unpublished seminars (seventeen volumes in French) has been summarized by Marcelle Marini in her *Jacques Lacan: The French Context* (New Brunswick NJ: Rutgers University Press, 1992[1986]). A bibliography of Lacan's works in English, compiled by Richard G. Klein, is available on the world wide web at http://www.lacan.com/bibliography.htm

In compiling my own bibliography I have tried to give complete references for all of Lacan's works in English (both original works and translations, complete texts and excerpts, first publications and reprints) that were available at the time of my cut-off point (Autumn 1999). I have only included published source materials, thus leaving aside translations that have been produced for private use only, such as Cormac Gallagher's ongoing translations of Lacan's unpublished seminars. Because the bibliography is addressed primarily at an English-speaking readership, I have provided the information for the English texts first, and subsequently the original French edition, if it exists, in its most accessible format. Dates in square brackets do not refer to the year in which Lacan's text was first published, but to the year in which it was originally composed. In some cases, this date coincides with Lacan's presentation of the text at a conference or scientific meeting; sometimes it represents the date of editing.

(1953[1951]) 'Some Reflections on the Ego', *The International Journal of Psycho-Analysis*, 34(1), pp. 11–17.

(1956) 'Fetishism: The Symbolic, the Imaginary and the Real', co-authored with Wladimir Granoff, in Sándor Lorand (ed.) *Perversions: Psychodynamics and Therapy*, New York NY: Gramercy Books, pp. 265–276. Second edition, London: Ortolan Press, 1965.

(1966[1957]) 'The Insistence of the Letter in the Unconscious', trans. Jan Miel, *Yale French Studies*, 36/37, pp. 112–147. Reprinted in Jacques Ehrmann (ed.) (1970) *Structuralism*, New York NY: Anchor Books, pp. 101–137. Also reprinted in Richard and Fernande De George (eds) (1972) *The Structuralists from Marx to Lévi-Strauss*, Garden City NY: Anchor Books, pp. 287–323. New translation: (1977g[1957]). 'L'instance de la lettre dans l'inconscient ou la raison depuis Freud', *Ecrits*, Paris: du Seuil, 1966, pp. 493–528.

(1968a[1949]) 'The Mirror-phase as Formative of the Function of the I', trans. Jean Roussel, *New Left Review*, 51, pp. 71–77. Reprinted in Slavoj Žižek (ed.) (1994) *Mapping Ideology*, London and New York NY: Verso, pp. 93–99. New translation: (1977c[1949]). 'Le stade du miroir comme formateur de la fonction du Je telle qu'elle nous est révélée dans l'expérience psychanalytique', *Ecrits*, Paris: du Seuil, 1966, pp. 93–100.

(1968b[1953]) 'The Function of Language in Psychoanalysis', trans. with notes and commentary Anthony Wilden, in Anthony Wilden, *The Language of the Self – The Function of Language in Psychoanalysis by Jacques Lacan*, Baltimore MD and London: The Johns Hopkins University Press, pp. 1–156. This is a translation of Lacan's 'Rome Discourse' without the preface, reissued in 1981 as Jacques Lacan, *Speech and Language in Psychoanalysis*, trans. with notes and commentary Anthony Wilden, Baltimore MD and London: The Johns Hopkins University Press, pp. 1–156. For a new translation of the entire 'Rome Discourse', see (1977e[1953]). 'Fonction et champ de la parole et du langage en psychanalyse', *Ecrits*, Paris: du Seuil, 1966, pp. 237–322.

(1970[1966]) 'Of Structure as an Inmixing of an Otherness Prerequisite to Any Subject Whatever', in Richard Macksey and Eugenio Donato (eds) *The Languages of Criticism and the Sciences of Man: The Structuralist Controversy*, Baltimore MD and London: The Johns Hopkins University Press, pp. 186–200. Reprinted in Richard Macksey and Eugenio Donato (eds) (1972) *The Structuralist Controversy: The Languages of Criticism and the Sciences of Man*, Baltimore MD and London: The Johns Hopkins University Press, pp. 186–200. These volumes comprise the proceedings of a 1966 conference, also including Lacan's comments on papers presented by Charles Morazé (pp. 41–44) and Lucien Goldmann (pp. 120–122).

(1971[1966]) 'Réponse à des étudiants en philosophie sur l'objet de la psych-analyse' [Responses to Students of Philosophy Concerning the Object of Psychoanalysis], trans. Anthony Rudolf and Annette Lavers, in Annette Lavers, 'Some Aspects of Language in the Work of Jacques Lacan', *Semiotica*, 3(3), pp. 269–279. This is a translation of one paragraph from Lacan's 1966 address. For a full translation, see (1987f[1966]). 'Réponse à des étudiants en philosophie sur l'objet de la psychanalyse', *Cahiers pour l'analyse*, 1966, 3, pp. 5–13.

(1972[1956]) 'Seminar on "The Purloined Letter"', trans. Jeffrey Mehlman, *Yale French Studies*, 48, pp. 38–72. Reprinted as 'Jacques Lacan, Seminar on "The Purloined Letter,"' in John P. Muller and William J. Richardson (eds) (1988) *The Purloined Poe: Lacan, Derrida and Psychoanalytic Reading*, Baltimore MD and London: The Johns Hopkins University Press, pp. 28–54. Also reprinted in Morris Philipson and Paul J. Goodall (eds) (1980) *Aesthetics Today*, Readings selected, edited and introduced by Morris Philipson and Paul J. Goodall, New York NY: New American Library, pp. 383–412; Robert Con Davis and Ronald Schleifer (eds) (1989) *Contemporary Literary Criticism: Literary and Cultural Studies*, 2nd edition, New York NY: Longman, pp. 300–320; Emanuel E. Berman (ed.) (1993) *Essential Papers on Literature and Psychoanalysis*, New York NY: New York University Press, pp. 270–299. This translation does not include Lacan's three appendices to the text. 'Le séminaire sur "La Lettre volée"', *Ecrits*, Paris: du Seuil, 1966, pp. 11–61.

(1977a[1959]) 'Desire and the Interpretation of Desire in Hamlet', Edited by Jacques-Alain Miller, trans. James Hulbert, *Yale French Studies*, 55/56, pp. 11–52. Reprinted in Shoshana Felman (ed.) (1982) *Literature and Psychoanalysis – The Question of Reading: Otherwise*, Baltimore MD and London: The Johns Hopkins University Press, pp. 11–52. This is a translation of three sessions from Lacan's unpublished *Séminaire VI, Le désir et son interprétation*. 'L'objet Ophélie – Le désir et le deuil – Phallophanie', texte établi par Jacques-Alain Miller, *Ornicar?*, 1983, 26/27, pp. 7–44.

(1977b[1964]) *The Four Fundamental Concepts of Psychoanalysis*, Edited by Jacques-Alain Miller, trans. Alan Sheridan, London: The Hogarth Press and the Institute of Psycho-Analysis. *Le Séminaire, Livre XI, Les quatre concepts fondamentaux de la psychanalyse*, texte établi par Jacques-Alain Miller, Paris: du Seuil, 1973. The English translation of *Séminaire XI* contains a new preface by Lacan, published in French in *Ornicar?*, 1977, 12/13, pp. 124–126, but includes neither Lacan's postface, nor his summary of the seminar printed on the back cover of the French edition. For this summary, see (1995d[1965]).

(1977c[1949]) 'The Mirror Stage as Formative of the Function of the I as Revealed in Psychoanalytic Experience', *Ecrits: A Selection*, trans. Alan Sheridan, London: Tavistock, pp. 1–7. Previous translation: (1968a[1949]). Reprinted in Dan Latimer (ed.) (1989) *Contemporary Critical Theory*, New York NY: Harcourt Brace, pp. 500–509. Also reprinted in Robert Con Davis and Ronald Schleifer (eds) (1994) *Contemporary Literary Criticism: Literary and Cultural Studies*, 3rd edition, New York NY and London: Longman, pp. 381–386. 'Le stade du miroir comme formateur de la fonction du Je telle qu'elle nous est révélée dans l'expérience psychanalytique', *Ecrits*, Paris: du Seuil, 1966, pp. 93–100.

(1977d[1948]) 'Aggressivity in Psychoanalysis', *Ecrits: A Selection*, trans. Alan Sheridan, London: Tavistock, pp. 8–29. 'L'agressivité en psychanalyse', *Ecrits*, Paris: du Seuil, 1966, pp. 101–124.

(1977e[1953]) 'The Function and Field of Speech and Language in Psychoanalysis', *Ecrits: A Selection*, trans. Alan Sheridan, London: Tavistock, pp. 30–113. Previous partial translation: (1968b[1953]). 'Fonction et champ de la parole et du langage en psychanalyse', *Ecrits*, Paris: du Seuil, 1966, pp. 237–322.

(1977f[1955]) 'The Freudian Thing, or the Meaning of the Return to Freud in Psychoanalysis', *Ecrits: A Selection*, trans. Alan Sheridan, London: Tavistock, pp. 114–145. 'La chose freudienne ou Sens du retour à Freud en psychanalyse', *Ecrits*, Paris: du Seuil, 1966, pp. 401–436.

(1977g[1957]) 'The Agency of the Letter in the Unconscious or Reason since Freud', *Ecrits: A Selection*, trans. Alan Sheridan, London: Tavistock, pp. 146–178. Previous translation: (1966[1957]). 'L'instance de la lettre dans l'inconscient ou la raison depuis Freud', *Ecrits*, Paris: du Seuil, 1966, pp. 493–528.

(1977h[1957–58]) 'On a Question Preliminary to Any Possible Treatment of Psychosis', *Ecrits: A Selection*, trans. Alan Sheridan, London: Tavistock, pp. 179–225. 'D'une question préliminaire à tout traitement possible de la psychose', *Ecrits*, Paris: du Seuil, 1966, pp. 531–583.

(1977i[1958]) 'The Direction of the Treatment and the Principles of its Power', *Ecrits: A Selection*, trans. Alan Sheridan, London: Tavistock, pp. 226–280. 'La direction de la cure et les principes de son pouvoir', *Ecrits*, Paris: du Seuil, 1966, pp. 585–645.

(1977j[1958]) 'The Signification of the Phallus', *Ecrits: A Selection*, trans. Alan Sheridan, London: Tavistock, pp. 281–291. New translation: (1982b [1958]). 'La signification du phallus', *Ecrits*, Paris: du Seuil, 1966, pp. 685–695.

(1977k[1960]) 'The Subversion of the Subject and the Dialectic of Desire in the Freudian Unconscious', *Ecrits: A Selection*, trans. Alan Sheridan, London: Tavistock, pp. 292–325. 'Subversion du sujet et dialectique du désir dans l'inconscient freudien', *Ecrits*, Paris: du Seuil, 1966, pp. 793–827.

(1977l[1969]) 'Preface', in Anika Lemaire, *Jacques Lacan*, trans. David Macey, London: Routledge and Kegan Paul, pp. vii–xv. 'Préface', in Anika Rifflet-Lemaire, *Jacques Lacan*, Bruxelles: Pierre Mardaga, 1970, pp. 9–20.

(1977m[1969]) 'Appendix: General Purport of a Conversation with Lacan in December 1969', in Anika Lemaire, *Jacques Lacan*, trans. David Macey, London: Routledge and Kegan Paul, pp. 249–253. 'Teneur de l'entretien avec J. Lacan', in Anika Rifflet-Lemaire, *Jacques Lacan*, Bruxelles: Pierre Mardaga, 1970, pp. 401–407.

(1977n[1972]) 'On Jakobson', trans. Louise Vasvari Fainberg, *Gradiva: A Journal of Contemporary Theory and Practice*, 1(2/3), pp. 152–160. This is one session from Lacan's *Seminar XX*. New translation: (1998a[1972–73]:

14–25). 'A Jakobson', in Jacques Lacan, *Le Séminaire, Livre XX, Encore*, texte établi par Jacques-Alain Miller, Paris: du Seuil, 1975, pp. 19–27.

(1979[1953]) 'The Neurotic's Individual Myth', trans. Martha Noel Evans, *The Psychoanalytic Quarterly*, 48(3), pp. 405–425. Reprinted in Laurence Spurling (ed.) (1989) *Sigmund Freud: Critical Assessments, Vol. II: The Theory and Practice of Psychoanalysis*, London and New York NY: Routledge, pp. 223–238. 'Le mythe individuel du névrosé ou poésie et vérité dans la névrose', texte établi par Jacques-Alain Miller, *Ornicar?*, 1979, 17/18, pp. 289–307.

(1980a[1976]) 'A Lacanian Psychosis: Interview by Jacques Lacan', trans. Stuart Schneiderman, in Stuart Schneiderman (ed.) *Returning to Freud: Clinical Psychoanalysis in the School of Lacan*, New Haven CT and London, Yale University Press, pp. 19–41. Reprinted in Stuart Schneiderman (ed.) (1993) *How Lacan's Ideas are Used in Clinical Practice*, Northvale NJ and London: Jason Aronson Inc., pp. 19–41. 'Entretien de Jacques Lacan avec M. Gérard Lumeroy', *Le discours psychanalytique*, 1992, 7, pp. 55–92.

(1980b) 'Lacan's letter', trans. Oscar Zentner, *Papers of the Freudian School of Melbourne*, 1, pp. 2–5. New translation: (1987j[1980]). 'Lettre de dissolution', *Ornicar?*, 1980, 20/21, pp. 9–10.

(1980c[1938]) 'The Oedipus Complex', trans. Andrea Kahn, *Semiotext(e)*, 4(1), pp. 190–200. This is the final part of Lacan's 1938 encyclopaedia essay on the family. *Les complexes familiaux dans la formation de l'individu. Essai d'analyse d'une fonction en psychologie*, Paris: Navarin, 1984, pp. 88–112.

(1980d[1972]) 'Ste Anne . . . ', trans. Denise Green, *Semiotext(e)*, 4(1), pp. 208–218. This is one session (3 March 1972) from Lacan's unpublished *Séminaire XIX, . . . ou pire/Le savoir du psychanalyste*.

(1981a) 'The Seminar, Paris, June 10th 1980', trans. Oscar Zentner, *Papers of the Freudian School of Melbourne*, 2, pp. 97–101. Reprinted in *Papers of the Freudian School of Melbourne*, 1998, 19, pp. 13–17. 'Le malentendu', *Ornicar?*, 1981, 22/23, pp. 11–14.

(1981b) 'The Seminar, Caracas, July 12th 1980', trans. Oscar Zentner, *Papers of the Freudian School of Melbourne*, 2, pp. 103–106. Reprinted in *Papers of the Freudian School of Melbourne*, 1998, 19, pp. 19–22. 'Le séminaire de Caracas', *L'Ane*, 1981, 1, pp. 30–31.

(1982a[1951]) 'Intervention on Transference', trans. Jacqueline Rose, in Juliet Mitchell and Jacqueline Rose (eds) *Feminine Sexuality: Jacques Lacan and the école freudienne*, New York NY and London: W. W. Norton and Company, pp. 61–73. Reprinted in Charles Bernheimer and Claire Kahane (eds) (1985) *In Dora's Case: Freud – Hysteria – Feminism*, New York NY: Columbia University Press, pp. 92–104. 'Intervention sur le transfert', *Ecrits*, Paris: du Seuil, 1966, pp. 215–226.

(1982b[1958]) 'The Meaning of the Phallus', trans. Jacqueline Rose, in Juliet Mitchell and Jacqueline Rose (eds) *Feminine Sexuality: Jacques Lacan and the école freudienne*, New York NY and London: W. W. Norton and

Company, pp. 74–85. Previous translation: (1977j[1958]). Reprinted in Sue Vice (ed.) (1998) *Psychoanalytic Criticism: A Reader*, Cambridge: Polity Press, pp. 120–129. 'La signification du phallus', *Ecrits*, Paris: du Seuil, 1966, pp. 685–695.

(1982c[1958]) 'Guiding Remarks for a Congress on Feminine Sexuality', trans. Jacqueline Rose, in Juliet Mitchell and Jacqueline Rose (eds) *Feminine Sexuality: Jacques Lacan and the école freudienne*, New York NY and London: W. W. Norton and Company, pp. 86–98. 'Propos directifs pour un Congrès sur la sexualité féminine', *Ecrits*, Paris: du Seuil, 1966, pp. 725–736.

(1982d[1973]) 'God and the Jouissance of The Woman – A Love Letter', trans. Jacqueline Rose, in Juliet Mitchell and Jacqueline Rose (eds) *Feminine Sexuality: Jacques Lacan and the école freudienne*, New York NY and London: W. W. Norton and Company, pp. 137–161. This translation consists of two sessions from Lacan's *Seminar XX*. New translation: (1998a [1972–73]:64–89). 'Dieu et la jouissance de La Femme – Une lettre d'âmour', in Jacques Lacan, *Le Séminaire, Livre XX, Encore*, texte établi par Jacques-Alain Miller, Paris: du Seuil, 1975, pp. 61–82.

(1982e[1975]) 'Seminar of 21 January 1975', trans. Jacqueline Rose, in Juliet Mitchell and Jacqueline Rose (eds) *Feminine Sexuality: Jacques Lacan and the école freudienne*, New York NY and London: W. W. Norton and Company, pp. 162–171. This is one session from Lacan's *Le Séminaire XXII, R.S.I.* 'Séminaire du 21 janvier 1975', *Ornicar?*, 1975, 3, pp. 104–110.

(1982f) 'Freud in the Century', trans. Stuart Schneiderman and Helena Schulz-Keil, *Lacan Study Notes*, 1(1), pp. 1–3. This is a translation, with omissions, of the second section of Lacan's centenary address on Freud's influence in the 20th century, included in *Seminar III*. For a new translation, see Lacan (1993[1955–56]:235–237). *Le Séminaire, Livre III, Les psychoses*, texte établi par Jacques-Alain Miller, Paris: du Seuil, 1981, pp. 267–270.

(1982–83[1961]) 'Merleau-Ponty: In Memoriam', trans. Wilfried Ver Eecke and Dirk De Schutter, *Review of Existential Psychology and Psychiatry*, 18 (1/2/3), pp. 73–81. Reprinted in Keith Hoeller (ed.) (1993) *Merleau-Ponty and Psychology*, Atlantic Highlands NJ: Humanities Press, pp. 73–81. 'Maurice Merleau-Ponty', *Les temps modernes*, 1961, 184/185, pp. 245–254.

(1985a[1970]) 'Sign', trans. Stuart Schneiderman, in Marshall Blonsky (ed.) *On Signs*, Baltimore MD: The Johns Hopkins University Press, pp. 203–206. This is a translation of the first three pages of Lacan's 1970 text 'Radiophonie'. 'Radiophonie', *Scilicet*, 1970, 2/3, pp. 55–58.

(1985b[1955]) 'Symbol and Imaginary', trans. Stuart Schneiderman, in Marshall Blonsky (ed.) *On Signs*, Baltimore MD: The Johns Hopkins University Press, pp. 206–209. This is a translation of a passage from Lacan's *Seminar II*. New translation: (1988c[1954–55]:304–308). *Le Séminaire, Livre II, Le moi dans la théorie de Freud et dans la technique de la psychanalyse*, texte établi par Jacques-Alain Miller, Paris: du Seuil, 1978, pp. 350–354.

(1987a[1953]) 'Letter to Rudolph Loewenstein', trans. Jeffrey Mehlman,

October, 40, pp. 55–69. Reprinted in Joan Copjec (ed.) (1990) *Television/A Challenge to the Psychoanalytic Establishment*, New York NY: W. W. Norton and Company, pp. 53–67. 'Lettre de Jacques Lacan à Rudolph Loewenstein', in Jacques-Alain Miller (ed.) (1976) *La scission de 1953. La communauté psychanalytique en France – 1*, supplément au numéro 7 d'*Ornicar?*, Paris: Navarin, pp. 120–135.

(1987b[1953]) 'Letter to Heinz Hartmann', trans. Jeffrey Mehlman, *October*, 40, pp. 70–71. Reprinted in Joan Copjec (ed.) (1990) *Television/A Challenge to the Psychoanalytic Establishment*, New York NY: W. W. Norton and Company, pp. 69–70. 'Lettre de Jacques Lacan à Heinz Hartmann', in Jacques-Alain Miller (ed.) (1976) *La scission de 1953. La communauté psychanalytique en France – 1*, supplément au numéro 7 d'*Ornicar?*, Paris: Navarin, pp. 136–137.

(1987c[1960]) 'Letter to D. W. Winnicott', trans. Jeffrey Mehlman, *October*, 40, pp. 76–78. Reprinted in Joan Copjec (ed.) (1990) *Television/A Challenge to the Psychoanalytic Establishment*, New York NY: W. W. Norton and Company, pp. 75–77. 'Lettre à D. W. Winnicott', *Ornicar?*, 1985, 33, pp. 7–10.

(1987d[1963]) 'Introduction to the Names-of-the-Father Seminar', Edited by Jacques-Alain Miller, trans. Jeffrey Mehlman, *October*, 40, pp. 81–95. Reprinted in Joan Copjec (ed.) (1990) *Television/A Challenge to the Psychoanalytic Establishment*, New York NY: W. W. Norton and Company, pp. 81–95. 'Séminaire du 20 novembre 1963', *Bulletin de l'Association freudienne*, 1985, 12, pp. 3–5; 13, pp. 3–6.

(1987e[1964]) 'Founding Act', trans. Jeffrey Mehlman, *October*, 40, pp. 96–105. Reprinted in Joan Copjec (ed.) (1990) *Television/A Challenge to the Psychoanalytic Establishment*, New York NY: W. W. Norton and Company, pp. 97–106. 'Acte de fondation de l'Ecole freudienne de Paris', in Jacques-Alain Miller (ed.) (1977) *L'excommunication. La communauté psychanalytique en France – 2*, supplément au numéro 8 d'*Ornicar?*, Paris: Navarin, pp. 149–152.

(1987f[1966]) 'Responses to Students of Philosophy Concerning the Object of Psychoanalysis', trans. Jeffrey Mehlman, *October*, 40, pp. 106–113. Reprinted in Joan Copjec (ed.) (1990) *Television/A Challenge to the Psychoanalytic Establishment*, New York NY: W. W. Norton and Company, pp. 107–114. Previous partial translation: (1971[1966]). 'Réponse à des étudiants en philosophie sur l'objet de la psychanalyse', *Cahiers pour l'analyse*, 1966, 3, pp. 5–13.

(1987g[1969]) 'A Letter to Le Monde', trans. Jeffrey Mehlman, *October*, 40, pp. 116–117. Reprinted in Joan Copjec (ed.) (1990) *Television/A Challenge to the Psychoanalytic Establishment*, New York NY: W. W. Norton and Company, pp. 115–116. 'Lettre du Dr. Jacques Lacan', *Le Monde*, 5 juillet 1969.

(1987h[1969]) 'Impromptu at Vincennes', trans. Jeffrey Mehlman, *October*, 40, pp. 117–127. Reprinted in Joan Copjec (ed.) (1990) *Television/A Challenge to the Psychoanalytic Establishment*, New York NY: W. W. Norton and Company, pp. 117–128. 'L'impromptu de Vincennes', *Magazine littéraire*, 1977, 121, pp. 21–25.

(1987i[1973]) 'Television', trans. Denis Hollier, Rosalind Krauss and Annette Michelson, *October*, 40, pp. 5–50. Reprinted in Joan Copjec (ed.) (1990) *Television/A Challenge to the Psychoanalytic Establishment*, New York NY: W. W. Norton and Company, pp. 1–46. *Télévision*, Paris: du Seuil, 1974.

(1987j[1980]) 'Letter of Dissolution', trans. Jeffrey Mehlman, *October*, 40, pp. 128–130. Reprinted in Joan Copjec (ed.) (1990) *Television/A Challenge to the Psychoanalytic Establishment*, New York NY: W. W. Norton and Company, pp. 129–131. Previous translation (1980b) 'Lettre de dissolution', *Ornicar?*, 1980, 20/21, pp. 9–10.

(1987k[1980]) 'The Other is Missing', trans. Jeffrey Mehlman, *October*, 40, pp. 131–133. Reprinted in Joan Copjec (ed.) (1990) *Television/A Challenge to the Psychoanalytic Establishment*, New York NY: W. W. Norton and Company, pp. 133–135. 'L'autre manque', *Ornicar?*, 1980, 20/21, pp. 11–12.

(1987l[1980]) 'Letter to *Le Monde*', trans. Jeffrey Mehlman, *October*, 40, p. 133. Reprinted in Joan Copjec (ed.) (1990) *Television/A Challenge to the Psychoanalytic Establishment*, New York NY: W. W. Norton and Company, p. 135. 'Lettre de Jacques Lacan au journal *Le Monde*', *Ornicar?*, 1980, 20/21, p. 13.

(1987m[1960]) 'From *The Ethics of Psychoanalysis*', trans. Dennis Porter, *Newsletter of the Freudian Field*, 1(1), pp. 11–13. This is a translation of the second section of the fourteenth session of Lacan's *Seminar VII*. New translation: (1992[1959–60]:182–184). *Le Séminaire, Livre VII, L'éthique de la psychanalyse*, texte établi par Jacques-Alain Miller, Paris: du Seuil, 1986, pp. 214–216.

(1987n[1932]) 'The Case of Aimée, or Self-punitive Paranoia', in John Cutting and Michael Shepherd (eds) *The Clinical Roots of the Schizophrenia Concept: Translations of Seminal European Contributions on Schizophrenia*, Cambridge and New York NY: Cambridge University Press, pp. 213–226. This is a translation, with omissions, of the central case of Lacan's doctoral thesis. 'De la psychose paranoïaque dans ses rapports avec la personnalité' (1932), in *De la psychose paranoïaque dans ses rapports avec la personnalité, suivi de Premiers écrits sur la paranoïa*, Paris: du Seuil, 1975, pp. 149–205.

(1987o[1965]) 'Homage to Marguerite Duras, on *Le ravissement de Lol V. Stein*', trans. Peter Connor, in Marguerite Duras, *Marguerite Duras*, San Francisco CA: City Lights Books, pp. 122–129. 'Hommage fait à Marguerite Duras, du Ravissement de Lol V. Stein', *Cahiers Renauld-Barrault*, 1965, 52, pp. 7–15.

(1988a[1945]) 'Logical Time and the Assertion of Anticipated Certainty: A New

Sophism', trans. Marc Silver and Bruce Fink, *Newsletter of the Freudian Field*, 2(2), pp. 4–22. 'Le temps logique et l'assertion de certitude anticipée. Un nouveau sophisme', *Ecrits*, Paris: du Seuil, pp. 197–213.

(1988b[1953–54]) *The Seminar, Book I, Freud's Papers on Technique*, Edited by Jacques-Alain Miller, trans. with notes John Forrester, Cambridge: Cambridge University Press. *Le Séminaire, Livre I, Les écrits techniques de Freud*, texte établi par Jacques-Alain Miller, Paris: du Seuil, 1975.

(1988c[1954–55]) *The Seminar, Book II, The Ego in Freud's Theory and in the Technique of Psychoanalysis*, Edited by Jacques-Alain Miller, trans. Sylvana Tomaselli, notes John Forrester, Cambridge: Cambridge University Press. *Le Séminaire, Livre II, Le moi dans la théorie de Freud et dans la technique de la psychanalyse*, texte établi par Jacques-Alain Miller, Paris: du Seuil, 1978.

(1988d[1933]) 'The Problem of Style and the Psychiatric Conception of Paranoiac Forms of Experience', trans. Jon Anderson, *Critical Texts*, 5(3), pp. 4–6. 'Le problème du style et la conception psychiatrique des formes paranoïaques de l'expérience', in *De la psychose paranoïaque dans ses rapports avec la personnalité, suivi de Premiers écrits sur la paranoïa*, Paris: du Seuil, 1975, pp. 383–388.

(1988e[1933–34]) 'Motives of Paranoiac Crime: The Crime of the Papin Sisters', trans. Jon Anderson, *Critical Texts*, 5(3), pp. 7–11. 'Motifs du crime paranoïaque: le crime des sœurs Papin', in *De la psychose paranoïaque dans ses rapports avec la personnalité, suivi de Premiers écrits sur la paranoïa*, Paris: du Seuil, 1975, pp. 389–398.

(1988f[1938]) 'The Family Complexes', trans. Carolyn Asp, *Critical Texts*, 5(3), pp. 12–29. This is a partial translation of Lacan's 1938 text on the family. *Les complexes familiaux dans la formation de l'individu: Essai d'analyse d'une fonction en psychologie*, Paris: Navarin, 1984, pp. 21–25 and pp. 75–112.

(1989a[1962]) 'Kant with Sade', trans. James B. Swenson Jr, *October*, 51, pp. 55–75. 'Kant avec Sade', *Ecrits*, Paris: du Seuil, 1966, pp. 765–790.

(1989b[1965]) 'Science and Truth', trans. Bruce Fink, *Newsletter of the Freudian Field*, 3(1/2), pp. 4–29. 'La science et la vérité', *Ecrits*, Paris: du Seuil, 1966, pp. 855–877.

(1989c[1975]) 'Geneva Lecture on the Symptom', trans. Russell Grigg, *Analysis*, 1, pp. 7–26. 'Conférence à Genève sur le symptôme', *Le bloc-notes de la psychanalyse*, 1985, 5, pp. 5–23.

(1990a[1969]) 'Note on the Child', trans. Russell Grigg, *Analysis*, 2, pp. 7–8. 'Deux notes sur l'enfant', *Ornicar?*, 1986, 37, pp. 13–14.

(1990b[1964]) 'Presence of the Analyst', trans. Alan Sheridan, in Aaron H. Esman (ed.) *Essential Papers on Transference*, New York NY and London: New York University Press, pp. 480–491. This is a reprint of Chapter 10 from (1977b[1964]).

(1991[1961]) 'Metaphor of the Subject', trans. Bruce Fink, *Newsletter of the Freudian Field*, 5(1/2), pp. 10–15. 'Appendice II. La métaphore du sujet', *Ecrits*, Paris: du Seuil, 1966, pp. 889–892.

(1992[1959–60]) *The Seminar, Book VII, The Ethics of Psychoanalysis*, Edited by Jacques-Alain Miller, trans. with notes Dennis Porter, New York NY and London: W. W. Norton and Company. *Le Séminaire, Livre VII, L'éthique de la psychanalyse*, texte établi par Jacques-Alain Miller, Paris: du Seuil, 1986.

(1993[1955–56]) *The Seminar, Book III, The Psychoses*, Edited by Jacques-Alain Miller, trans. with notes Russell Grigg, New York NY and London: W. W. Norton and Company. *Le Séminaire, Livre III, Les psychoses*, texte établi par Jacques-Alain Miller, Paris: du Seuil, 1981.

(1995a[1964]) 'Position of the Unconscious', trans. Bruce Fink, in Richard Feldstein, Bruce Fink and Maire Jaanus (eds) *Reading Seminar XI: Lacan's Four Fundamental Concepts of Psychoanalysis*, Albany NY: State University of New York Press, pp. 259–282. 'Position de l'inconscient', *Ecrits*, Paris: du Seuil, 1966, pp. 829–850.

(1995b[1967]) 'Proposition of 9 October 1967 on the Psychoanalyst of the School', trans. Russell Grigg, *Analysis*, 6, pp. 1–13. 'Proposition du 9 octobre 1967 sur le psychanalyste de l'Ecole', *Scilicet*, 1968, 1, pp. 14–30.

(1995c[1974]) 'Spring Awakening', trans. Silvia Rodríguez, *Analysis*, 6, pp. 32–34. 'L'éveil du printemps', *Ornicar?*, 1986, 39, pp. 5–7.

(1995d[1965]) 'Lacan's Summary of Seminar XI', trans. Cormac Gallagher, *The Letter: Lacanian Perspectives on Psychoanalysis*, 5, pp. 1–17. 'Résumé rédigé pour l'annuaire de l'Ecole pratique des Hautes Etudes', in Jacques Lacan, *Le Séminaire, Livre XI, Les quatre concepts fondamentaux de la psychanalyse*, texte établi par Jacques-Alain Miller, Paris: du Seuil, 1973, back cover. Although translated in full, Lacan's summary has been cut and amalgamated with the translator's comments.

(1996a[1964]) 'On Freud's "Trieb" and the Psychoanalyst's Desire', trans. Bruce Fink, in Richard Feldstein, Bruce Fink and Maire Jaanus (eds) *Reading Seminars I and II: Lacan's Return to Freud*, Albany NY: State University of New York Press, pp. 417–421. 'Du "Trieb" de Freud et du désir du psychanalyste', *Ecrits*, Paris: du Seuil, 1966, pp. 851–854.

(1996b[1966]) 'Presentation of the *Memoirs* of President Schreber in French Translation', trans. Andrew J. Lewis, *Analysis*, 7, pp. 1–4. 'Présentation des *Mémoires* du Président Schreber en traduction française', *Ornicar?*, 1986, 38, pp. 5–9.

(1996c[1950]) 'A Theoretical Introduction to the Functions of Psychoanalysis in Criminology', in collaboration with Michel Cénac, trans. Mark Bracher, Russell Grigg and Robert Samuels, *Journal for the Psychoanalysis of Culture and Society*, 1(2), pp. 13–25. 'Introduction théorique aux fonctions de la psychanalyse en criminologie', en collaboration avec Michel Cénac, *Ecrits*, Paris: du Seuil, 1966, pp. 125–149.

(1996d[1963–69]) 'Correspondence with Jacques Lacan', trans. Jeffrey Mehlman, in Olivier Corpet and François Matheron (eds) *Louis Althusser: Writings on Psychoanalysis – Freud and Lacan*, New York NY: Columbia University Press, pp. 145–173. 'Correspondance avec Jacques Lacan', in

Olivier Corpet and François Matheron (eds) (1993) *Louis Althusser. Ecrits sur la psychanalyse. Freud et Lacan*, Paris: Stock/IMEC, pp. 267–305.

(1996e[1973?]) 'A Man and a Woman', trans. Carolyn Jane Henshaw, *Papers of the Freudian School of Melbourne*, 17, pp. 79–97. 'Un homme et une femme', *Bulletin de l'Association freudienne internationale*, 1993, 54, pp. 13–21.

(1998a[1972–73]) *The Seminar, Book XX, On Feminine Sexuality, the Limits of Love and Knowledge (Encore)*, Edited by Jacques-Alain Miller, trans. with notes Bruce Fink, New York NY and London, W. W. Norton and Company. *Le Séminaire, Livre XX, Encore*, texte établi par Jacques-Alain Miller, Paris: du Seuil, 1975.

(1998b[1976]) 'A Propos of Transsexualism: Interview with Michel H.', trans. Philip Anderson, *Papers of the Freudian School of Melbourne*, 19, pp. 153–192. 'Entretien avec Michel H.', in Marcel Czermak and Henry Frignet (eds) *Sur l'identité sexuelle: A propos du transsexualisme*, Paris: Editions de l'Association freudienne internationale, 1996, pp. 311–353.

(1998c[1973]) 'L'étourdit', in Alan Sokal and Jean Bricmont, *Intellectual Impostures: Postmodern Philosophers' Abuse of Science*, London: Profile Books, p. 20 and pp. 29–32. This is a translation of three excerpts from Lacan's text. 'L'étourdit', *Scilicet*, 1973, 4, p. 40, pp. 14–15 and p. 22.

(1999[1966–67]) 'Jacques Lacan's Summary of the Seminar of 1966–1967', trans. Cormac Gallagher, *The Letter: Lacanian Perspectives on Psychoanalysis*, 15, pp. 90–96. 'La logique du fantasme', *Ornicar?*, 1984, 29, pp. 13–18.

General bibliography

Abraham, K. (1979[1908]) 'The Psycho-Sexual Differences between Hysteria and Dementia Praecox', *Selected Papers*, London: The Hogarth Press and the Institute of Psycho-Analysis, pp. 64–79.

Actes de l'Ecole de la Cause freudienne (1984) *Transfert et interprétation dans les névroses et les psychoses*, 6.

—— (1985) *Clinique des névroses et hystérie*, 8.

—— (1987) *L'expérience psychanalytique des psychoses*, 13.

Alexandris, A. and Vaslamatzis, G. (eds) (1993) *Countertransference: Theory, Technique, Teaching*, London: Karnac Books.

Alquier, J., Grimaud, J., Lévy, M., Mallassagne, G., Menard, A., Michel-Petersen, D., Poirot-Hubler, Cl. and Szulzynger, A. (1992) 'Quelle issue pour le transfert chez le psychotique?', in Association de la Fondation du Champ freudien (ed.) *Les stratégies du transfert en psychanalyse*, Paris: Navarin, pp. 169–174.

André, Serge (1984) 'Transfert et interprétation dans un cas de perversion', *Actes de l'Ecole de la Cause freudienne*, 6, pp. 15–19.

—— (1993) *L'imposture perverse*, Paris: du Seuil.

Aparicio, D., Aromí, A., Bardón, C., Bordenave, V., Calderón de la Barca, A., d'Angelo, L., Eldar, S., Gómez Musso, L., Grisolía, A., Molas, D., Monné, A., Soto, M. and Tizio, H. (1990) 'La perversion comme limite', in Fondation du Champ freudien (ed.) *Traits de perversion dans les structures cliniques*, Paris: Navarin, pp. 331–337.

Aparicio, S. (1984) 'La forclusion, préhistoire d'un concept', *Ornicar?*, 28, pp. 83–106.

Apollon, W., Bergeron, D. and Cantin, L. (1990) *Traiter la psychose*, Québec: GIFRIC.

Aristotle (1963) *Aristotle's Categories and De Interpretatione*, trans. with notes J. L. Ackrill, Oxford: Clarendon Press.

—— (1996) *Physics*, trans. Robin Waterfield, Oxford: Oxford University Press.

Association de la Fondation du Champ freudien (ed.) (1992) *Les stratégies du transfert en psychanalyse*, Paris: Navarin.

Association Mondiale de la Psychanalyse (ed.) (1996) *Les pouvoirs de la parole*, Paris: du Seuil.

Atkins, P. (1995) 'Science as Truth', *History of the Human Sciences*, 8(2), pp. 97–102.

Attié, J. (1985) 'La passe', *Quarto*, 19, pp. 35–42.

Aulagnier-Spairani, P., Clavreul, J., Perrier, F., Rosolato, G. and Valabrega, J.-P. (1967) *Le désir et la perversion*, Paris: du Seuil.

Baas, B. (1992) *Le désir pur. Parcours philosophiques dans les parages de J. Lacan*, Louvain: Peeters.

Baas, B. and Zaloszyc, A. (1988) *Descartes et les fondements de la psychanalyse*, Paris: Navarin Osiris.

Balint, M. (1952) *Primary Love and Psycho-Analytic Technique*, London: Tavistock.

Baton, Y., Fajersztajn, R., Fressy-Meunier, M.-L., de Halleux, B., Kusnierek, M., Le Boulangé, Ch., Lysy Stevens, A., Stevens, A., de Villers, G. and Zenoni, A. (1992) 'Note sur la "liquidation" du transfert', in Association de la Fondation du Champ freudien (ed.) *Les stratégies du transfert en psychanalyse*, Paris: Navarin, pp. 428–438.

Benvenuto, B. and Kennedy, R. (1986) *The Works of Jacques Lacan: An Introduction*, London: Free Association Books.

Bernheimer, C. and Kahane, C. (eds) (1985) *In Dora's Case: Freud – Hysteria – Feminism*, New York NY: Columbia University Press.

Bibring, E. (1937) 'Therapeutic Results of Psycho-Analysis', *The International Journal of Psycho-Analysis*, 18(1), pp. 117–126.

—— (1954) 'Psychoanalysis and the Dynamic Psychotherapies', *Journal of the American Psychoanalytic Association*, 2(4), pp. 745–770.

Bonaparte, M. (1938[1936]) 'Some Palaeobiological and Biopsychical Reflections', *The International Journal of Psycho-Analysis*, 19(2), pp. 214–220.

—— (1952) *Psychanalyse et biologie*, Paris: Presses Universitaires de France.

Boothby, R. (1991) *Death and Desire: Psychoanalytic Theory in Lacan's Return to Freud*, London and New York NY: Routledge.

Borch-Jacobsen, M. (1992) *The Emotional Tie: Psychoanalysis, Mimesis, and Affect*, Stanford CA: Stanford University Press.

—— (1996) *Remembering Anna O.: A Century of Mystification*, London and New York NY: Routledge.

Bouvet, M. (1967–68) *Œuvres psychanalytiques* (2 vols), Paris: Payot.

Bowie, M. (1991) *Lacan*, London: Fontana.

Brabant, E., Falzeder, E. and Gampieri-Deutsch, P. (eds) (1993) *The Correspondence of Sigmund Freud and Sándor Ferenczi, Volume 1: 1908–1914*, Cambridge MA and London: The Belknap Press of Harvard University Press.

Bracher, M., Alcorn, M. W. Jr, Corthell, R. J. and Massardier-Kenney, F. (eds) (1994) *Lacanian Theory of Discourse: Subject, Structure and Society*, New York NY and London: New York University Press.

Braunstein, N. and Saal, F. (1990) 'Façade de la perversion: le fantasme écran d'un sujet supposé savoir jouir', in Fondation du Champ freudien (ed.) *Traits de perversion dans les structures cliniques*, Paris: Navarin, pp. 282–284.

Broca, R. (1984) 'Sur l'érotomanie du transfert', *Actes de l'Ecole de la Cause freudienne*, 6, pp. 47–52.

—— (1985) 'La psychanalyse, un nouveau mode de lien social?', *Quarto*, 20/21, pp. 5–9.

—— (1988) 'Le psychanalyste face à la psychose sous transfert', in GRAPP (ed.) *Les psychiatres et la psychanalyse aujourd'hui*, Paris: Navarin, pp. 179–183.

Brooks, P. (1992[1984]) *Reading for the Plot: Design and Intention in Narrative*, Cambridge MA and London: Harvard University Press.

Brousse, M.-H. (1988) 'Question de suppléance', *Ornicar?*, 47, pp. 65–73.

Burgoyne, B. (1997) 'Interpretation', in Bernard Burgoyne and Mary Sullivan (eds) *The Klein–Lacan Dialogues*, London: Rebus Press, pp. 45–58.

Cassin, J., Cassin, R., Guéguen, P.-G., Maleval, J.-C., Mérian, R., Monnier, J.-L., Robert, P. and Sauvagnat, F. (1992) 'Le débat sur la liquidation du transfert', in Association de la Fondation du Champ freudien (ed.) *Les stratégies du transfert en psychanalyse*, Paris: Navarin, pp. 103–108.

Cassirer Bernfeld, S. (1952) 'Freud and Archaeology', *The Yearbook of Psychoanalysis*, 8, pp. 39–55.

Castanet, Hervé (1999) *La perversion*, Paris: Anthropos.

Cathelineau, P.-C. (1998) *Lacan, lecteur d'Aristote. Politique, Métaphysique, logique*, Paris: Editions de l'Association Freudienne Internationale.

Chadwick, T. (1999) 'Come Again? Some Observations on Bruce Fink's Translation of *Seminar XX: Encore*', Paper presented at the 5th Lacan Symposium in Australia, Melbourne, 8 August 1999, unpublished.

Clausewitz, C. von (1976[1832]) *On War*, trans. Michael Howard and Peter Paret, Princeton NJ: Princeton University Press.

Clavreul, J. (1977[1964]) 'Exposé introductif – Réunion GEP', in Jacques-Alain Miller (ed.) *L'excommunication. La communauté psychanalytique en France – 2*, supplément au numéro 8 d'*Ornicar?*, Paris: Navarin, pp. 138–148.

Clervoy, P. (1997) *Henri Ey (1900–1977): Cinquante ans de psychiatrie en France*, Le Plessis-Robinson: Synthélabo.

Colby, K. M. (1951) *A Primer for Psychotherapists*, New York NY: Ronald Press.

Cottet, S. (1996[1982]) *Freud et le désir du psychanalyste*, Paris: du Seuil.

Cusanus, N. (Cardinal Nicholas of Cusa) (1985[1449]) *On Learned Ignorance*, trans. with an appraisal by Jasper Hopkins, Minneapolis MN: Arthur J. Banning Press.

Damourette, J. and Pichon, E. (1928) 'Sur la signification psychologique de la négation en français', *Journal de psychologie normale et pathologique*, 25, pp. 229–253.

Daumal, R. (1972a[1938]) 'Les pouvoirs de la parole dans la poétique hindoue',

Les pouvoirs de la parole. Essais et Notes, II (1935–1943), Edition établie par Claudio Rugafiori, Paris: Gallimard, pp. 44–73.

Daumal, R. (1972b[1940]) 'Pour approcher l'art poétique hindou', *Les pouvoirs de la parole. Essais et Notes, II (1935–1943)*, Edition établie par Claudio Rugafiori, Paris: Gallimard, pp. 83–97.

David-Ménard, M. (1989[1983]) *Hysteria from Freud to Lacan: Body and Language in Psychoanalysis*, trans. Catherine Porter, Ithaca NY and London: Cornell University Press.

Decker, H. S. (1991) *Freud, Dora, and Vienna 1900*, New York NY: The Free Press.

Devereux, G. (1951) 'Some Criteria for the Timing of Confrontations and Interpretations', *The International Journal of Psycho-Analysis*, 32(1), pp. 19–24.

Dolar, M. (1998) 'Cogito as the Subject of the Unconscious', in Slavoj Žižek (ed.) *Cogito and the Unconscious*, Durham NC and London: Duke University Press, pp. 11–40.

Dor, J. (1987) *Structure et perversions*, Paris: Denoël.

—— (1997[1995]) *The Clinical Lacan*, Edited by Judith Feher Gurewich in collaboration with Susan Fairfield, Northvale NJ and London: Jason Aronson Inc.

Eidelstein, A., Lombardi, G. and Mazzuca, R. (1990) 'Une décision éthique', in Fondation du Champ freudien (ed.) *Traits de perversion dans les structures cliniques*, Paris: Navarin, pp. 375–385.

Eisler, M. J. (1921[1920]) 'A Man's Unconscious Phantasy of Pregnancy in the Guise of Traumatic Hysteria: A Clinical Contribution to Anal Erotism', trans. F. R. Winton, *The International Journal of Psycho-Analysis*, 2(3/4), pp. 255–286.

Eissler, R. S. (ed.) (1954) '106th Bulletin of the International Psycho-Analytical Association', *The International Journal of Psycho-Analysis*, 35(1), pp. 267–290.

Eliot, T. S. (1974[1922]) 'The Waste Land', *Collected Poems 1909–1962*, London and Boston MA: Faber and Faber, pp. 61–86.

Esman, A. H. (ed.) (1990) *Essential Papers on Transference*, New York NY and London: New York University Press.

Etchegoyen, R. H. and Miller, J.-A. (1996) *Silence brisé. Entretien sur le mouvement psychanalytique*, Paris: Agalma.

Evans, D. (1998) 'From Kantian Ethics to Mystical Experience: An Exploration of Jouissance', in Dany Nobus (ed.) *Key Concepts of Lacanian Psychoanalysis*, London: Rebus Press, pp. 1–28.

Favez-Boutonnier, J. (1977[1961]) 'Lettre au Président de l'IPA', in Jacques-Alain Miller (ed.) *L'excommunication. La communauté psychanalytique en France – 2*, supplément au numéro 8 d'*Ornicar?*, Paris: Navarin, p. 25.

Fenichel, O. (1941[1938–39]) *Problems of Psychoanalytic Technique*, trans. David Brunswick, Albany NY: The Psychoanalytic Quarterly Inc.

—— (1945) *The Psychoanalytic Theory of Neurosis*, New York NY: W. W. Norton and Company.

Ferenczi, S. (1980[1909]) 'Introjection and Transference', *First Contributions to Psycho-Analysis*, New York NY: Brunner/Mazel, pp. 35–93.

Fink, B. (1990) 'Alienation and Separation: Logical Moments of Lacan's Dialectic of Desire', *Newsletter of the Freudian Field*, 4(1/2), pp. 78–119.

—— (1995a) *The Lacanian Subject: Between Language and Jouissance*, Princeton NJ and London: Princeton University Press.

—— (1995b) 'Science and Psychoanalysis', in Richard Feldstein, Bruce Fink and Maire Jaanus (eds) *Reading Seminar XI: Lacan's Four Fundamental Concepts of Psychoanalysis*, Albany NY: State University of New York Press, pp. 55–64.

—— (1996a) 'The Nature of Unconscious Thought or Why No One ever Reads Lacan's Postface to the Seminar on "The Purloined Letter"', in Richard Feldstein, Bruce Fink and Maire Jaanus (eds) *Reading Seminars I and II: Lacan's Return to Freud*, Albany NY: State University of New York Press, pp. 173–191.

—— (1996b) 'Logical Time and the Precipitation of Subjectivity', in Richard Feldstein, Bruce Fink and Maire Jaanus (eds) *Reading Seminars I and II: Lacan's Return to Freud*, Albany NY: State University of New York Press, pp. 356–386.

—— (1997) *A Clinical Introduction to Lacanian Psychoanalysis: Theory and Technique*, Cambridge MA and London: Harvard University Press.

—— (1998) 'The Master Signifier and the Four Discourses', in Dany Nobus (ed.) *Key Concepts of Lacanian Psychoanalysis*, London: Rebus Press, pp. 29–47.

Fondation du Champ freudien (ed.) (1986) *Hystérie et obsession. Les structures cliniques de la névrose et la direction de la cure*, Paris: Navarin.

—— (1988) *Clinique différentielle des psychoses*, Paris: Navarin.

—— (1990) *Traits de perversion dans les structures cliniques*, Paris: Navarin.

Freud, A. (1966[1936]) 'The Ego and the Mechanisms of Defense', *The Writings of Anna Freud, Vol. 2*, New York NY: International Universities Press.

Freud, S. (1894a) 'The Neuro-Psychoses of Defence', *Standard Edition*, 3, pp. 45–61.

—— (1896b) 'Further Remarks on the Neuro-Psychoses of Defence', *Standard Edition*, 3, pp. 157–185.

—— (1896c) 'The Aetiology of Hysteria', *Standard Edition*, 3, pp. 191–221.

—— (1900a) 'The Interpretation of Dreams', *Standard Edition*, 4/5.

—— (1901b) 'The Psychopathology of Everyday Life', *Standard Edition*, 6.

—— (1905a[1904]) 'On Psychotherapy', *Standard Edition*, 7, pp. 257–268.

—— (1905d) 'Three Essays on the Theory of Sexuality', *Standard Edition*, 7, pp. 135–243.

—— (1905e[1901]) 'Fragment of an Analysis of a Case of Hysteria', *Standard Edition*, 7, pp. 7–122.

Freud, S. (1906a[1905]) 'My Views on the Part played by Sexuality in the Aetiology of the Neuroses', *Standard Edition*, 7, pp. 271–279.

—— (1909b) 'Analysis of a Phobia in a Five-Year-Old Boy', *Standard Edition*, 10, pp. 5–147.

—— (1909d) 'Notes upon a Case of Obsessional Neurosis (The "Rat Man")', *Standard Edition*, 10, pp. 155–249.

—— (1910a[1909]) 'Five Lectures on Psycho-Analysis', *Standard Edition*, 11, pp. 7–55.

—— (1910d) 'The Future Prospects of Psychoanalytic Therapy', *Standard Edition*, 11, pp. 139–151.

—— (1911c[1910]) 'Psycho-Analytic Notes Upon an Autobiographical Account of a Case of Paranoia (Dementia Paranoides)', *Standard Edition*, 12, pp. 3–82.

—— (1912b) 'The Dynamics of Transference', *Standard Edition*, 12, pp. 97–108.

—— (1912e) 'Recommendations to Physicians Practising Psycho-Analysis', *Standard Edition*, 12, pp. 109–120.

—— (1913c) 'On Beginning the Treatment (Further Recommendations on the Technique of Psycho-Analysis I)', *Standard Edition*, 12, pp. 121–144.

—— (1913i) 'The Disposition to Obsessional Neurosis', *Standard Edition*, 12, pp. 317–326.

—— (1914b) 'The Moses of Michelangelo', *Standard Edition*, 13, pp. 209–236.

—— (1914g) 'Remembering, Repeating and Working-Through (Further Recommendations on the Technique of Psycho-Analysis II)', *Standard Edition*, 12, pp. 145–156.

—— (1915a[1914]) 'Observations on Transference-Love (Further Recommendations on the Technique of Psycho-Analysis III)', *Standard Edition*, 12, pp. 159–171.

—— (1915c) 'Instincts and their Vicissitudes', *Standard Edition*, 14, pp. 109–140.

—— (1915d) 'Repression', *Standard Edition*, 14, pp. 141–158.

—— (1915e) 'The Unconscious', *Standard Edition*, 14, pp. 166–204.

—— (1916–17a[1915–17]) 'Introductory Lectures on Psycho-Analysis', *Standard Edition*, 15/16.

—— (1918b[1914]) 'From the History of An Infantile Neurosis (The "Wolf Man")', *Standard Edition*, 17, pp. 7–122.

—— (1919a[1918]) 'Lines of Advance in Psycho-Analytic Therapy', *Standard Edition*, 17, pp. 157–168.

—— (1919e) '"A Child is Being Beaten" – A Contribution to the Study of the Origin of Sexual Perversions', *Standard Edition*, 17, pp. 175–204.

—— (1920a) 'The Psychogenesis of a Case of Homosexuality in a Woman', *Standard Edition*, 18, pp. 145–172.

—— (1920g) 'Beyond the Pleasure Principle', *Standard Edition*, 18, pp. 1–64.

—— (1921c) 'Group Psychology and the Analysis of the Ego', *Standard Edition*, 18, pp. 65–143.

—— (1922b[1921]) 'Some Neurotic Mechanisms in Jealousy, Paranoia and Homosexuality', *Standard Edition*, 18, pp. 221–232.

—— (1923b) 'The Ego and the Id', *Standard Edition*, 19, pp. 1–66.

—— (1923c[1922]) 'Remarks on the Theory and Practice of Dream-Interpretation', *Standard Edition*, 19, pp. 109–121.

—— (1924d) 'The Dissolution of the Oedipus Complex', *Standard Edition*, 19, pp. 173–179.

—— (1925f) 'Preface to Aichhorn's *Wayward Youth*', *Standard Edition*, 19, pp. 271–275.

—— (1925h) 'Negation', *Standard Edition*, 19, pp. 235–239.

—— (1925j) 'Some Psychical Consequences of the Anatomical Distinction between the Sexes', *Standard Edition*, 19, pp. 241–258.

—— (1926d[1925]) 'Inhibitions, Symptoms and Anxiety', *Standard Edition*, 20, pp. 87–172.

—— (1926e) 'The Question of Lay Analysis', *Standard Edition*, 20, pp. 177–250.

—— (1927e) 'Fetishism', *Standard Edition*, 21, pp. 152–157.

—— (1930a[1929]) 'Civilization and its Discontents', *Standard Edition*, 21, pp. 57–145.

—— (1933a[1932]) 'New Introductory Lectures on Psycho-Analysis', *Standard Edition*, 22, pp. 5–182.

—— (1937c) 'Analysis Terminable and Interminable', *Standard Edition*, 23, pp. 216–253.

—— (1937d) 'Constructions in Analysis', *Standard Edition*, 23, pp. 255–269.

—— (1939a[1937–39]) 'Moses and Monotheism', *Standard Edition*, 23, pp. 1–137.

—— (1940a[1938]) 'An Outline of Psycho-Analysis', *Standard Edition*, 23, pp. 144–207.

—— (1950a[1895]) 'Project for a Scientific Psychology', *Standard Edition*, 1, pp. 281–397.

—— (1954) *Cinq psychanalyses*, trans. Marie Bonaparte and Rudolph M. Loewenstein, Paris: Presses Universitaires de France.

—— (1955a[1907–8]) 'Original Record of the Case', *Standard Edition*, 10, pp. 251–318.

—— (1974[1907–8]) *L'homme aux rats. Journal d'une analyse*, trans. with an introduction Elza Ribeiro Hawelka, Paris: Presses Universitaires de France.

—— (1987[1907–8]) 'Originalnotizen zu einem Fall von Zwangsneurose (Rattenmann)', *Gesammelte Werke*, Nachtragsband, Frankfurt am Main: S. Fischer Verlag, pp. 503–569.

Freud, S. and Breuer, J. (1895d) 'Studies on Hysteria', *Standard Edition*, 2.

Frie, R. (1997) *Subjectivity and Intersubjectivity in Modern Philosophy and Psychoanalysis: A Study of Sartre, Binswanger, Lacan and Habermas*, New York NY and London: Rowman and Littlefield.

Gamwell, L. and Wells, R. (eds) (1989) *Sigmund Freud and Art: His Personal Collection of Antiquities*, New York NY: Abrams.

Gardiner, M. (ed.) (1972) *The Wolf-Man and Sigmund Freud*, London: The Hogarth Press and the Institute of Psycho-Analysis.

Garrabé, J. (1997) *Henri Ey et la pensée psychiatrique contemporaine*, Le Plessis-Robinson: Synthélabo.

Georgin, R. (1973) *Le temps freudien du verbe*, Lausanne: L'Age d'homme.

—— (1977) *Lacan. Théorie et pratiques*, Lausanne: L'Age d'homme.

Ginzburg, C. (1980) 'Morelli, Freud and Sherlock Holmes: Clues and Scientific Method', trans. Anna Davin, *History Workshop: A Journal of Socialist Historians*, 9, pp. 5–36.

Giroud, F. (1990) *Leçons particulières*, Paris: Fayard.

Glover, Edward (1931) 'The Therapeutic Effect of Inexact Interpretation: A Contribution to the Theory of Suggestion', *The International Journal of Psycho-Analysis*, 12(4), pp. 399–411.

Godin, J.-G. (1990) *Jacques Lacan, 5, rue de Lille*, Paris: du Seuil.

Gorkin, M. (1987) *The Uses of Countertransference*, Northvale NJ and London: Jason Aronson Inc.

Granoff, W. and Perrier, F. (1991[1960]) 'Le problème de la perversion chez la femme et les idéaux féminins', *Le désir et le féminin*, Paris: Aubier, pp. 21–110.

Greenson, R. R. (1965) 'The Working Alliance and the Transference Neurosis', *The Psychoanalytic Quarterly*, 34(1), pp. 155–181.

Grigg, R. (1991) 'Signifier, Object, and the Transference,' in Ellie Ragland-Sullivan and Mark Bracher (eds) *Lacan and the Subject of Language*, New York NY and London: Routledge, pp. 100–115.

—— (1998) 'From the Mechanism of Psychosis to the Universal Condition of the Symptom: On Foreclosure', in Dany Nobus (ed) *Key Concepts of Lacanian Psychoanalysis*, London: Rebus Press, pp. 48–74.

Grinstein, A. (1983) *Freud's Rules of Dream Interpretation*, Madison CT: International Universities Press.

Grosz, E. (1990) *Jacques Lacan: A Feminist Introduction*, London and New York NY: Routledge.

Grünbaum, A. (1984) *The Foundations of Psychoanalysis: A Philosophical Critique*, Berkeley/Los Angeles CA and London: University of California Press.

—— (1993) *Validation in the Clinical Theory of Psychoanalysis: A Study in the Philosophy of Psychoanalysis*, Madison CT: International Universities Press.

Gueguen, P.-G. (1995) 'Transference as Deception', in Richard Feldstein, Bruce Fink and Maire Jaanus (eds) *Reading Seminar XI: Lacan's Four Fundamental Concepts of Psychoanalysis*, Albany NY: State University of New York Press, pp. 77–90.

Guyomard, P. (1992) *La jouissance du tragique. Antigone, Lacan et le désir de l'analyste*, Paris: Aubier-Flammarion.

—— (1998) *Le désir d'éthique*, Paris: Aubier.

Hesnard, A. (1959) 'Letter to Pearl King', in Jacques-Alain Miller (ed.) *L'excommunication. La communauté psychanalytique en France* – 2, supplément au numéro 8 d'*Ornicar?*, Paris: Navarin, p. 9.

Horowitz, M. J. (1998) *Cognitive Psychodynamics: From Conflict to Character*, New York NY: John Wiley and Sons.

Israel, L. (1996[1974]) *La jouissance de l'hystérique. Séminaire 1974*, Paris and Strasbourg: Arcanes.

Jackson, S. W. (1999) *Care of the Psyche: A History of Psychological Healing*, New Haven CT and London: Yale University Press.

Jacobs, T. J. (1999) 'Countertransference Past and Present: A Review of the Concept', *International Journal of Psycho-Analysis*, 80(3), pp. 575–594.

Jalley, E. (1998) *Freud, Wallon, Lacan. L'enfant au miroir*, Paris: E.P.E.L.

Jones, E. (1950[1927]) 'The Early Development of Female Sexuality', *Papers on Psycho-Analysis*, 5th edition, London: Baillière, Tindall, and Cox, pp. 438–451.

Judson, L. (1991) 'Chance and "Always or for the Most Part" in Aristotle', *Aristotle's Physics: A Collection of Essays*, Oxford: Clarendon Press, pp. 73–99.

Julien, P. (1994[1981]) *Jacques Lacan's Return to Freud: The Real, the Symbolic and the Imaginary*, trans. Devra Beck Simiu, New York NY and London: New York University Press.

—— (1995) *L'étrange jouissance du prochain. Ethique et psychanalyse*, Paris: du Seuil.

Kant, I. (1996[1788]) 'Critique of Practical Reason', trans. Mary J. Gregor, *The Cambridge Edition of the Works of Immanuel Kant: Practical Philosophy*, New York NY: Cambridge University Press, pp. 133–258.

Kernberg, O. (1993) 'The Current Status of Psychoanalysis', *Journal of the American Psychoanalytic Association*, 41(1), pp. 45–62.

Khiara, B. (1996) 'Une référence de Lacan à l'esthétique Indienne', *La cause freudienne*, 32, pp. 144–150.

King, P. (ed.) (1960) '117th Bulletin of the International Psycho-Analytical Association', *The International Journal of Psycho-Analysis*, 41(2/3), pp. 167–211.

Kirk, G. S. and Raven, J. E. (1957) *The Presocratic Philosophers*, Cambridge: Cambridge University Press.

Kitcher, P. (1992) *Freud's Dream: A Complete Interdisciplinary Science of the Mind*, Cambridge MA and London: MIT Press.

Klotz, J.-P. (1993) 'Pour une réforme de l'Ecole', *La lettre mensuelle*, 116, pp. 7–12.

Kojève, Alexandre (1969[1933–39]) *Introduction to the Reading of Hegel*, trans. James H. Nichols Jr, Edited by Allan Bloom, New York NY and London: Basic Books.

Kris, E. (1951) 'Ego Psychology and Interpretation in Psychoanalytic Therapy', *The Psychoanalytic Quarterly*, 20(1), pp. 15–30.

Kuspit, D. (1989) 'A Mighty Metaphor: The Analogy of Archaeology and Psychoanalysis', in Lynn Gamwell and Richard Wells (eds) *Sigmund Freud and Art: His Personal Collection of Antiquities*, New York NY: Abrams, pp. 133–151.

Lacan, J. (1958–59) *Le Séminaire VI, Le désir et son interprétation* [Desire and its Interpretation], unpublished.

—— (1961–62) *Le Séminaire IX, L'identification* [Identification], unpublished.

—— (1962–63) *Le Séminaire X, L'angoisse* [Anxiety], unpublished.

—— (1965–66) *Le Séminaire XIII, L'objet de la psychanalyse* [The Object of Psychoanalysis], unpublished.

—— (1966a[1946]) 'Propos sur la causalité psychique' [Remarks on Psychical Causality], *Ecrits*, Paris: du Seuil, pp. 151–193.

—— (1966b[1955]) 'Variantes de la cure-type' [Variations of the Standard Treatment], *Ecrits*, Paris: du Seuil, pp. 323–362.

—— (1966c[1957]) 'La psychanalyse et son enseignement' [Psychoanalysis and its Teaching], *Ecrits*, Paris: du Seuil, pp. 437–458.

—— (1966d[1956]) 'Situation de la psychanalyse et formation du psychanalyste en 1956' [The Situation of Psychoanalysis and the Training of the Psychoanalyst in 1956], *Ecrits*, Paris: du Seuil, pp. 459–491.

—— (1966e[1960]) 'Remarque sur le rapport de Daniel Lagache: "Psychanalyse et structure de la personnalité"' [Remark on the Report by Daniel Lagache: "Psychoanalysis and the Structure of Personality"], *Ecrits*, Paris: du Seuil, pp. 647–684.

—— (1966f[1954]) 'Réponse au commentaire de Jean Hyppolite sur la "Verneinung" de Freud' [Reply to Jean Hyppolite's Commentary on Freud's "Negation"], *Ecrits*, Paris: du Seuil, pp. 381–399.

—— (1966–67) *Le Séminaire XIV, La logique du fantasme* [The Logic of the Fantasy], unpublished.

—— (1967–68) *Le Séminaire XV, L'acte psychanalytique* [The Psychoanalytic Act], unpublished.

—— (1968a[1967]) 'De la psychanalyse dans ses rapports avec la réalité' [On Psychoanalysis in its Relations with Reality], *Scilicet*, 1, pp. 51–59.

—— (1968b[1967]) 'La méprise du sujet supposé savoir' [The bungled action of the supposed subject of knowing], *Scilicet*, 1, pp. 31–41.

—— (1968c[1967]) 'De Rome 53 à Rome 67: La psychanalyse – Raison d'un échec' [From Rome 53 to Rome 67: Psychoanalysis – The Reason of a Failure], *Scilicet*, 1, pp. 42–50.

—— (1968–69) *Le Séminaire XVI, D'un Autre à l'autre* [From an Other to the other], unpublished.

—— (1970) 'Radiophonie' [Radiophony], *Scilicet*, 2/3, pp. 55–99.

—— (1970–71) *Le Séminaire XVIII, D'un discours qui ne serait pas du semblant* [Of a Discourse that Would not be of Semblance], unpublished.

—— (1971–72) *Le Séminaire XIX, . . . ou pire/Le savoir du psychanalyste* [. . . or worse/The Psychoanalyst's Knowledge], unpublished.

—— (1972[1956]) 'Seminar on "The Purloined Letter"', trans. Jeffrey Mehlman, *Yale French Studies*, 48, pp. 38–72.

—— (1973[1972]) 'L'étourdit' [The amasaid], *Scilicet*, 4, pp. 5–52.

—— (1973–74) *Le Séminaire XXI, Les non-dupes errent* [The non-duped err/The Names of the Father], unpublished.

—— (1975a[1931]) 'Ecrits "inspirés": Schizographie' ["Inspired" Writings: Schizography], in *De la psychose paranoïaque dans ses rapports avec la personnalité, suivi de Premiers écrits sur la paranoïa*, Paris: du Seuil, pp. 365–382.

—— (1975b[1932]) 'De la psychose paranoïaque dans ses rapports avec la personnalité' [On Paranoid Psychosis in its Relations with Personality], in *De la psychose paranoïaque dans ses rapports avec la personnalité, suivi de Premiers écrits sur la paranoïa*, Paris: du Seuil, pp. 13–362.

—— (1975c[1974–75]) 'Le Séminaire XXII, R.S.I.' [R.S.I.], *Ornicar?*, 2, pp. 87–105; 3, pp. 95–110; 4, pp. 91–106; 5, pp. 15–66.

—— (1975d[1973]) 'Introduction à l'édition allemande d'un premier volume des Ecrits' [Introduction to the German Edition of a First Volume of the Ecrits], *Scilicet*, 5, pp. 11–17.

—— (1975e) ' . . . ou pire' [. . . or worse], *Scilicet*, 5, pp. 5–10.

—— (1976a[1949]) 'Règlement et doctrine de la Commission de l'enseignement' [Regulations and Doctrine of the Teaching Committee], in Jacques-Alain Miller (ed.) *La scission de 1953. La communauté psychanalytique en France – 1*, supplément au numéro 7 d'*Ornicar?*, Paris: Navarin, pp. 29–36.

—— (1976b[1953]) 'Projet d'amendement aux statuts proposés par le docteur Sacha Nacht pour l'Institut de Psychanalyse' [A Project of Amendment to the Statutes proposed by doctor Sacha Nacht for the Institute of Psychoanalysis], in Jacques-Alain Miller (ed.) *La scission de 1953. La communauté psychanalytique en France – 1*, supplément au numéro 7 d'*Ornicar?*, Paris: Navarin, pp. 52–63.

—— (1976–77[1975–76]) 'Le Séminaire XXIII, Le sinthome' [The Symptom/The Holy Man], *Ornicar?*, 6, pp. 3–20; 7, pp. 3–18; 8, pp. 6–20; 9, pp. 32–40; 10, pp. 5–12; 11, pp. 2–9.

—— (1977a[1959]) 'Desire and the Interpretation of Desire in Hamlet', ed. Jacques-Alain Miller, trans. James Hulbert, *Yale French Studies*, 55/56, pp. 11–52.

—— (1977b[1964]) *The Four Fundamental Concepts of Psychoanalysis*, ed. Jacques-Alain Miller, trans. Alan Sheridan, London: The Hogarth Press and the Institute of Psycho-Analysis.

—— (1977c[1949]) 'The Mirror Stage as Formative of the Function of the I as Revealed in Psychoanalytic Experience', *Ecrits: A Selection*, trans. Alan Sheridan, London: Tavistock, pp. 1–7.

—— (1977d[1948]) 'Aggressivity in Psychoanalysis', *Ecrits: A Selection*, trans. Alan Sheridan, London: Tavistock, pp. 8–29.

—— (1977e[1953]) 'The Function and Field of Speech and Language in

Psychoanalysis', *Ecrits: A Selection*, trans. Alan Sheridan, London: Tavistock, pp. 30–113.

Lacan, J. (1977f[1955]) 'The Freudian Thing, or the Meaning of the Return to Freud in Psychoanalysis', *Ecrits: A Selection*, trans. Alan Sheridan, London: Tavistock, pp. 114–145.

—— (1977g[1957]) 'The Agency of the Letter in the Unconscious or Reason since Freud', *Ecrits: A Selection*, trans. Alan Sheridan, London: Tavistock, pp. 146–178.

—— (1977h[1957–58]) 'On a Question Preliminary to Any Possible Treatment of Psychosis', *Ecrits: A Selection*, trans. Alan Sheridan, London: Tavistock, pp. 179–225.

—— (1977i[1958]) 'The Direction of the Treatment and the Principles of its Power', *Ecrits: A Selection*, trans. Alan Sheridan, London: Tavistock, pp. 226–280.

—— (1977j[1958]) 'The Signification of the Phallus', *Ecrits: A Selection*, trans. Alan Sheridan, London: Tavistock, pp. 281–291.

—— (1977k[1960]) 'The Subversion of the Subject and the Dialectic of Desire in the Freudian Unconscious', *Ecrits: A Selection*, trans. Alan Sheridan, London: Tavistock, pp. 292–325.

—— (1977l) 'Ouverture de la section clinique' [Opening of the Clinical Section], *Ornicar?*, 9, pp. 7–11.

—— (1977m[1973]) 'Sur l'expérience de la passe' [On the Experience of the Pass], *Ornicar?*, 12/13, pp. 117–123.

—— (1978[1973]) 'La psychanalyse dans sa référence au rapport sexuel' [Psychoanalysis in its Reference to the Sexual Relationship], in Giacomo B. Contri (ed.) *Lacan in Italia/En Italie Lacan 1953–1978*, Milan: La Salamandra, pp. 58–77.

—— (1979[1953]) 'The Neurotic's Individual Myth', trans. Martha Noel Evans, *The Psychoanalytic Quarterly*, 48(3), pp. 405–425.

—— (1980a[1976]) 'A Lacanian Psychosis: Interview by Jacques Lacan', trans. Stuart Schneiderman, in Stuart Schneiderman (ed.) *Returning to Freud: Clinical Psychoanalysis in the School of Lacan*, New Haven CT and London, Yale University Press, pp. 19–41.

—— (1980b) 'Lacan's letter', trans. Oscar Zentner, *Papers of the Freudian School of Melbourne*, 1, pp. 2–5.

—— (1981a) 'The Seminar, Paris, June 10th 1980', trans. Oscar Zentner, *Papers of the Freudian School of Melbourne*, 2, pp. 97–101.

—— (1981b) 'The Seminar, Caracas, July 12th 1980', trans. Oscar Zentner, *Papers of the Freudian School of Melbourne*, 2, pp. 103–106.

—— (1982a[1951]) 'Intervention on Transference', trans. Jacqueline Rose, in Juliet Mitchell and Jacqueline Rose (eds) *Feminine Sexuality: Jacques Lacan and the école freudienne*, New York NY and London: W. W. Norton and Company, pp. 61–73.

—— (1982b[1974]) 'Note italienne' [Italian Note], *Ornicar?*, 25, pp. 7–10.

—— (1984[1969]) 'L'acte psychanalytique' [The Psychoanalytic Act], *Ornicar?*, 29, pp. 18–25.

—— (1985[1970]) 'Sign', trans. Stuart Schneiderman, in Marshall Blonsky (ed.) *On Signs*, Baltimore MD: The Johns Hopkins University Press, pp. 203–206.

—— (1986[1967]) 'Une procédure pour la passe' [A Procedure for the Pass], *Ornicar?*, 37, pp. 7–12.

—— (1988a[1945]) 'Logical Time and the Assertion of Anticipated Certainty: A New Sophism', trans. Marc Silver and Bruce Fink, *Newsletter of the Freudian Field*, 2(2), pp. 4–22.

—— (1988b[1953–54]) *The Seminar, Book I, Freud's Papers on Technique*, ed. Jacques-Alain Miller, trans. with notes John Forrester, Cambridge: Cambridge University Press.

—— (1988c[1954–55]) *The Seminar, Book II, The Ego in Freud's Theory and in the Technique of Psychoanalysis*, ed. Jacques-Alain Miller, trans. Sylvana Tomaselli, notes John Forrester, Cambridge: Cambridge University Press.

—— (1988d[1933]) 'The Problem of Style and the Psychiatric Conception of Paranoiac Forms of Experience', trans. Jon Anderson, *Critical Texts*, 5(3), pp. 4–6.

—— (1988e[1933–34]) 'Motives of Paranoiac Crime: The Crime of the Papin Sisters', trans. Jon Anderson, *Critical Texts*, 5(3), pp. 7–11.

—— (1989a[1962]) 'Kant with Sade', trans. James B. Swenson Jr, *October*, 51, pp. 55–75.

—— (1989b[1965]) 'Science and Truth', trans. Bruce Fink, *Newsletter of the Freudian Field*, 3(1/2), pp. 4–29.

—— (1989c[1951–52]) 'Seminario su "L'uomo dei lupi"' [Seminar on the Wolf Man], trans. Alberto Turolla, *La psicoanalisi*, 6, pp. 9–12.

—— (1990a[1953]) 'Letter to Rudolph Loewenstein', trans. Jeffrey Mehlman, in Joan Copjec (ed.) *Television/A Challenge to the Psychoanalytic Establishment*, New York NY: W. W. Norton and Company, pp. 53–67.

—— (1990b[1963]) 'Introduction to the Names-of-the-Father Seminar', ed. Jacques-Alain Miller, trans. Jeffrey Mehlman, in Joan Copjec (ed.) *Television/A Challenge to the Psychoanalytic Establishment*, New York NY: W. W. Norton and Company, pp. 81–95.

—— (1990c[1964]) 'Founding Act', trans. Jeffrey Mehlman, in Joan Copjec (ed.) *Television/A Challenge to the Psychoanalytic Establishment*, New York NY: W. W. Norton and Company, pp. 97–106.

—— (1990d[1973]) 'Television', trans. Denis Hollier, Rosalind Krauss and Annette Michelson, in Joan Copjec (ed.) *Television/A Challenge to the Psychoanalytic Establishment*, New York NY: W. W. Norton and Company, pp. 1–46.

—— (1990e[1980]) 'Letter of Dissolution', trans. Jeffrey Mehlman, in Joan Copjec (ed.) *Television/A Challenge to the Psychoanalytic Establishment*, New York NY: W. W. Norton and Company, pp. 129–131.

—— (1991a[1969–70]) *Le Séminaire, Livre XVII, L'envers de la psychanalyse*

[The Other Side of Psychoanalysis], texte établi par Jacques-Alain Miller, Paris: du Seuil.

Lacan , J. (1991b[1960–61]) *Le Séminaire, Livre VIII, Le transfert* [Transference], texte établi par Jacques-Alain Miller, Paris: du Seuil.

—— (1991c[1961]) 'Metaphor of the Subject', trans. Bruce Fink, *Newsletter of the Freudian Field*, 5(1/2), pp. 10–15.

—— (1992[1959–60]) *The Seminar, Book VII, The Ethics of Psychoanalysis*, ed. Jacques-Alain Miller, trans. with notes Dennis Porter, New York NY and London: W. W. Norton and Company.

—— (1993[1955–56]) *The Seminar, Book III, The Psychoses*, ed. Jacques-Alain Miller, trans. with notes Russell Grigg, New York NY and London: W. W. Norton and Company.

—— (1994[1956–57]) *Le Séminaire, Livre IV, La relation d'objet* [Object-relations], texte établi par Jacques-Alain Miller, Paris: du Seuil.

—— (1995a[1964]) 'Position of the Unconscious', trans. Bruce Fink, in Richard Feldstein, Bruce Fink and Maire Jaanus (eds) *Reading Seminar XI: Lacan's Four Fundamental Concepts of Psychoanalysis*, Albany NY: State University of New York Press, pp. 259–282.

—— (1995b[1967]) 'Proposition of 9 October 1967 on the Psychoanalyst of the School', trans. Russell Grigg, *Analysis*, 6, pp. 1–13.

—— (1996a[1964]) 'On Freud's "*Trieb*" and the Psychoanalyst's Desire', trans. Bruce Fink, in Richard Feldstein, Bruce Fink and Maire Jaanus (eds) *Reading Seminars I and II: Lacan's Return to Freud*, Albany NY: State University of New York Press, pp. 417–421.

—— (1996b[1966]) 'Presentation of the *Memoirs* of President Schreber in French Translation', trans. Andrew J. Lewis, *Analysis*, 7, pp. 1–4.

—— (1996c[1950]) 'A Theoretical Introduction to the Functions of Psychoanalysis in Criminology', in collaboration with Michel Cénac, trans. Mark Bracher, Russell Grigg and Robert Samuels, *Journal for the Psychoanalysis of Culture and Society*, 1(2), pp. 13–25.

—— (1998a[1972–73]) *The Seminar, Book XX, On Feminine Sexuality, the Limits of Love and Knowledge (Encore)*, ed. Jacques-Alain Miller, trans. with notes Bruce Fink, New York NY and London, W. W. Norton and Company.

—— (1998b[1957–58]) *Le Séminaire, Livre V, Les formations de l'inconscient* [The Formations of the Unconscious], texte établi par Jacques-Alain Miller, Paris: du Seuil.

—— (1998c[1976]) 'A Propos of Transsexualism: Interview with Michel H.', trans. Philip Anderson, *Papers of the Freudian School of Melbourne*, 19, pp. 153–192.

Lachaud, D. (1995) *L'enfer du devoir. Le discours de l'obsessionel*, Paris: Denoël.

Laforgue, R. (1926) 'Verdrängung und Skotomisation', *Internationale Zeitschrift für Psychoanalyse*, 12, pp. 54–65.

Lagache, D. (1952) 'Le problème du transfert', *Revue française de psychanalyse*, 16(1/2), pp. 5–115.

—— (1953[1951]) 'Some Aspects of Transference', *The International Journal of Psycho-Analysis*, 34(1), pp. 1–10.

—— (1993[1954]) 'Freudian Doctrine and the Theory of Transference', *The Work of Daniel Lagache: Selected Papers 1938–1964*, trans. Elisabeth Holder, London: Karnac Books, pp. 131–151.

Laurent, E. (1994) 'Psychanalyse et Science: le vide du sujet et l'excès des objets', *Quarto*, 56, pp. 31–35.

—— (1995) 'Alienation and Separation I/II', in Richard Feldstein, Bruce Fink and Maire Jaanus (eds) *Reading Seminar XI: Lacan's Four Fundamental Concepts of Psychoanalysis*, Albany NY: State University of New York Press, pp. 19–38.

Lebovici, R. (1956) 'Perversion sexuelle transitoire au cours d'un traitement psychanalytique', *Bulletin d'activités de l'Association des Psychanalystes de Belgique*, 25, pp. 1–16.

Leclaire, S. (1990) 'Entretien avec Serge Leclaire sur l'Instance Ordinale', *L'Ane*, 43, pp. 28–32.

Lee, J. S. (1990) *Jacques Lacan*, Boston MA: Twayne.

Le Gaufey, G. (1998) *Anatomie de la troisième personne*, Paris: E.P.E.L.

Lévi-Strauss, C. (1969[1949]) *The Elementary Structures of Kinship*, trans. James Harle Bell and John Richard von Sturmer, London: Eyre and Spottiswoode.

Liart, M. (1985) 'Le psychanalyste ne s'autorise que de lui-même', *Quarto*, 19, pp. 3–6.

—— (1988) 'La suppléance comme tentative de guérison', *Actes de l'Ecole de la Cause freudienne*, 15, pp. 17–20.

Libbrecht, K. (1998) 'The Original Sin of Psychoanalysis: On the Desire of the Analyst', in Dany Nobus (ed.) *Key Concepts of Lacanian Psychoanalysis*, London: Rebus Press, pp. 75–100.

Little, M. I. (1951) 'Counter-Transference and the Patient's Response to it', *The International Journal of Psycho-Analysis*, 32(1), pp. 32–40.

—— (1990) *Psychotic Anxieties and Containment: A Personal Record of an Analysis with Winnicott*, Northvale NJ and London: Jason Aronson Inc.

Loewenstein, R. M. (1951) 'The Problem of Interpretation', *The Psychoanalytic Quarterly*, 20(1), pp. 1–14.

Luborsky, L. (1984) *Principles of Psychoanalytic Psychotherapy: A Manual for Supportive-Expressive Treatment*, New York NY: Basic Books.

Macalpine, I. (1950) 'The Development of the Transference', *The Psychoanalytic Quarterly*, 19(4), pp. 501–539.

Macalpine, I. and Hunter, R. (1988[1955]) 'Translators' Introduction', in Daniel Paul Schreber, *Memoirs of My Nervous Illness* (1903) trans. Ida Macalpine and Richard Hunter, 2nd edition with a new introduction by Samuel M. Weber, Cambridge MA and London: Harvard University Press, pp. 1–28.

Macey, D. (1988) *Lacan in Contexts*, London and New York NY: Verso.

McGuire, W. (ed.) (1974) *The Freud/Jung Letters: The Correspondence between Sigmund Freud and C. G. Jung*, trans. Ralph Manheim and R. F. C. Hull, Princeton NJ: Princeton University Press.

Macmillan, M. (1997) *Freud Evaluated: The Completed Arc*, Cambridge MA and London, MIT Press.

Mahler, M. S. (1968) *On Human Symbiosis and the Vicissitudes of Individuation: Infantile Psychosis*, New York NY: International Universities Press.

Mahler, M. S., Pine, F. and Bergman, A. (1975) *The Psychological Birth of the Human Infant: Symbiosis and Individuation*, London: Hutchinson.

Mahony, P. J. (1986) *Freud and the Rat Man*, New Haven CT and London: Yale University Press.

—— (1996) *Freud's Dora: A Psychoanalytic, Historical, and Textual Study*, New Haven CT and London: Yale University Press.

Mann, D. (1997) *Psychotherapy, an Erotic Relationship: Transference and Countertransference Passions*, London and New York NY: Routledge.

—— (ed.) (1999) *Erotic Transference and Countertransference: Clinical Practice in Psychotherapy*, London and New York NY: Routledge.

Marcus, S. (1984) *Freud and the Culture of Psychoanalysis: Studies in the Transition from Victorian Humanism to Modernity*, Boston MA and London: George Allen and Unwin.

Marinelli, L. (ed.) (1998) *'Meine . . . alten und dreckigen Götter'. Aus Sigmund Freuds Sammlung*, Frankfurt am Main: Stroemfeld.

Maslow, A. H. and Mittelmann, B. (1951[1941]) *Principles of Abnormal Psychology: The Dynamics of Psychic Illness*, New York NY and London: Harper and Row.

Masson, J. M. (ed.) (1985) *The Complete Letters of Sigmund Freud to Wilhelm Fließ 1887–1904*, trans. Jeffrey Moussaieff Masson, Cambridge MA and London: The Belknap Press of Harvard University Press.

Mauss, M. (1988[1925]) *The Gift: Forms and Functions of Exchange in Archaic Societies*, trans. Ian Cunnison, London: Routledge.

Melman, C. (1984) *Nouvelles études sur l'hystérie*, Paris: Joseph Clims.

Meyer, N. (1974) *The Seven-per-cent Solution*, New York NY: E.P. Dutton and Co.

Miller, J.-A. (1977) 'Introduction aux paradoxes de la passe', *Ornicar?*, 12/13, pp. 105–112.

—— (1983[1982]) 'Schizophrénie et paranoia', *Quarto*, 10, pp. 18–38.

—— (1984a) 'C.S.T.', *Ornicar?*, 29, pp. 142–147.

—— (1984b) 'Transfert et interprétation', *Actes de l'Ecole de la Cause freudienne*, 6, pp. 33–37.

—— (1987) 'Sur la leçon des psychoses', *Actes de l'Ecole de la Cause freudienne*, 13, pp. 142–144.

—— (1990) 'Entretien sur la Cause Analytique avec Jacques-Alain Miller', *L'Ane*, 42, pp. 26–30.

—— (1992) 'La refonte de 1992', *La lettre mensuelle*, 112, pp. 1–2.

—— (1993) 'Clinique ironique', *La cause freudienne*, 23, pp. 7–13.

—— (1994[1992]) 'Love's labyrinths', trans. Tom Radigan, *Lacanian Ink*, 8, pp. 7–13.

—— (1995a[1994]) 'Come iniziano le analisi', *La cause freudienne*, 29, pp. 7–15.

—— (1995b[1994]) 'E=UWK: Towards the 9th International Encounter of the Freudian Field', trans. Vicente Palomera, *Analysis*, 6, pp. 14–31.

—— (1996a[1989]) 'On Perversion', in Richard Feldstein, Bruce Fink and Maire Jaanus (eds) *Reading Seminars I and II: Lacan's Return to Freud*, Albany NY: State University of New York Press, pp. 306–320.

—— (1996b[1994]) 'Commentary on Lacan's Text', trans. Bruce Fink, in Richard Feldstein, Bruce Fink and Maire Jaanus (eds) *Reading Seminars I and II: Lacan's Return to Freud*, Albany NY: State University of New York Press, pp. 422–427.

—— (1996c[1989]) 'A Discussion of Lacan's "Kant with Sade"', in Richard Feldstein, Bruce Fink and Maire Jaanus (eds) *Reading Seminars I and II: Lacan's Return to Freud*, Albany NY: State University of New York Press, pp. 212–237.

—— (1996d) 'L'interprétation à l'envers', *La cause freudienne*, 32, pp. 9–13.

—— (1998) 'Les contre-indications au traitement psychanalytique', *Mental: Revue internationale de santé mentale et psychanalyse appliquée*, 5, pp. 9–17.

Milner, J.-C. (1995) *L'Œuvre claire. Lacan, la science, la philosophie*, Paris: du Seuil.

Mordier, J.-P. (1981) *Les débuts de la psychanalyse en France 1895–1926*, Paris: Maspéro.

Mourgue, R. and Von Monakow, C. (1928) *Introduction biologique à l'étude de la neurologie et de la psychopathologie*, Paris: Alcan.

Muller, J. P. (1996) *Beyond the Psychoanalytic Dyad: Developmental Semiotics in Freud, Peirce and Lacan*, New York and London: Routledge.

Muller, J. P. and Richardson, W. J. (1988) 'Lacan's Seminar on "The Purloined Letter": Overview', *The Purloined Poe: Lacan, Derrida and Psychoanalytic Reading*, Baltimore MD and London: The Johns Hopkins University Press, pp. 55–98.

Nasio, J.-D. (1997[1990]) *Hysteria: The Splendid Child of Psychoanalysis*, trans. Susan Fairfield, Northvale NJ and London: Jason Aronson Inc.

Nobus, D. (1998) 'Life and Death in the Glass: A New Look at the Mirror Stage', *Key Concepts of Lacanian Psychoanalysis*, London: Rebus Press, pp. 101–138.

—— (forthcoming) *Choosing Sexuality: A Lacanian Inquiry into the Laws of Sexual Diversity*, Albany NY: State University of New York Press.

Nunberg, H. (1951) 'Transference and Reality', *The International Journal of Psycho-Analysis*, 32(1), pp. 1–9.

Nunberg, H. and Federn, E. (eds) (1962) *Minutes of the Vienna Psychoanalytic Society. Vol. I: 1906–1908*, New York NY: International Universities Press.

Ofshe, R. and Watters, E. (1994) *Making Monsters: False Memories, Psychotherapy, and Sexual Hysteria*, New York NY: Charles Scribner's Sons.

Ogden, C. K. and Richards, I. A. (1923) *The Meaning of Meaning: A Study of the Influence of Language upon Thought and of The Science of Symbolism*, London: Henley.

Ohayon, A. (1999) *L'impossible rencontre. Psychologie et psychanalyse en France 1919–1969*, Paris: La Découverte.

Orr, D. W. (1954) 'Transference and Countertransference: A Historical Survey', *Journal of the American Psychoanalytic Association*, 2(4), pp. 621–670.

Pandey, K. C. (1950) 'Indian Aesthetics', *Comparative Aesthetics Vol. 1*, Benares: Varansasi.

Paul, L. (1963) 'The Logic of Psychoanalytic Interpretation', in Louis Paul (ed.) *Psychoanalytic Clinical Interpretation*, New York NY: The Free Press of Glencoe, pp. 249–272.

Plato (1951) *The Symposium*, trans. Walter Hamilton, Harmondsworth: Penguin.

Porge, E. (1997) *Les noms du père chez Jacques Lacan. Ponctuations et problématiques*, Ramonville Saint-Agne: Erès.

Porge, E. and Soulez, A. (eds) (1996) *Le moment cartésien de la psychanalyse. Lacan, Descartes, le sujet*, Strasbourg and Paris: Arcanes.

Quackelbeen, J. (1994) 'The Psychoanalytic Discourse Theory of Jacques Lacan: Introduction and Application', *Studies in Psychoanalytic Theory*, 3(1), pp. 21–43.

Rabinovitch, S. (1998) *La forclusion. Enfermés dehors*, Ramonville Saint-Agne: Erès.

Radhakrishnan, S. (ed.) (1953) *The Principal Upanisads*, London: George Allen and Unwin Ltd.

Ragland, E. (1995) *Essays on the Pleasures of Death: From Freud to Lacan*, New York NY and London: Routledge.

Rank, O. (1923[1922]) 'Perversion and Neurosis', *The International Journal of Psycho-Analysis*, 4(3), pp. 270–292.

Rapport Turquet (1977[1963]) in Jacques-Alain Miller (ed.) *L'excommunication. La communauté psychanalytique en France – 2*, supplément au numéro 8 d'*Ornicar?*, Paris: Navarin, pp. 41–45.

Reagan, C. E. (1996) *Paul Ricoeur: His Life and His Work*, Chicago IL and London: The University of Chicago Press.

Regnault, F. (1995) 'The Name-of-the-Father', in Richard Feldstein, Bruce Fink and Maire Jaanus (eds) *Reading Seminar XI: Lacan's Four Fundamental Concepts of Psychoanalysis*, Albany NY: State University of New York Press, pp. 65–74.

Reich, A. (1951) 'On Counter-Transference', *The International Journal of Psycho-Analysis*, 32(1), pp. 25–31.

Reik, T. (1935) *Surprise and the Psychoanalyst*, London: G. Routledge and Sons.

—— (1948) *Listening with the Third Ear: The Inner Experience of a Psychoanalyst*, New York NY: Farrar, Straus and Company.

Reinhard, K. (1996) 'The Freudian Things: Construction and the Archaeological Metaphor', in Stephen Barker (ed.) *Excavations and Their Objects: Freud's Collection of Antiquity*, Albany NY: State University of New York Press, pp. 57–79.

Rey, P. (1989) *Une saison chez Lacan*, Paris: Robert Laffont.

Rey-Flaud, H. (1996) *L'éloge du rien. Pourquoi l'obsessionel et le pervers échouent là où l'hystérique réussit*, Paris: du Seuil.

Rickman, J. (1957[1951]) 'Methodology and Research in Psycho-pathology', *Selected Contributions to Psycho-Analysis*, London: The Hogarth Press and the Institute of Psycho-Analysis, pp. 207–217.

Ricoeur, Paul (1970[1965]) *Freud and Philosophy: An Essay on Interpretation*, trans. Denis Savage, New Haven CT and London: Yale University Press.

Rodríguez, S. A. and Rodríguez, L. S. (1989) 'On the Transference', *Analysis*, 1, pp. 165–185.

Roublef, Irène (1994[1964]) 'Le désir de l'obsessionel dans la perspective de Jacques Lacan', *Esquisses psychanalytiques*, 20, pp. 5–24.

Roudinesco, E. (1982) *La bataille de cent ans. Histoire de la psychanalyse en France.1 (1885–1939)*, Paris: Ramsay.

—— (1990[1986]) *Jacques Lacan & Co.: A History of Psychoanalysis in France 1925–1985*, trans. Jeffrey Mehlman, London: Free Association Books.

Roudinesco, E. and Plon, M. (1997) *Dictionnaire de la psychanalyse*, Paris: Fayard.

Ryle, A. and Brockman, B. J. (1992) *Cognitive-Analytic Therapy: Active Participation in Change – A New Integration in Brief Psychotherapy*, New York NY: John Wiley and Sons.

Sachs, J. (1995) *Aristotle's Physics: A Guided Study*, New Brunswick NJ: Rutgers University Press.

Safouan, M. (1983) *Jacques Lacan et la question de la formation des analystes*, Paris: du Seuil.

—— (1988) *Le transfert et le désir de l'analyste*, Paris: du Seuil.

Saks, E. R. (1999) *Interpreting Interpretation: The Limits of Hermeneutic Psychoanalysis*, New Haven CT and London: Yale University Press.

Scheidhauer, M. (1985) *Le rêve freudien en France (1900–1926)*, Paris: Navarin.

Schmideberg, M. (1934) 'Intellektuelle Hemmung und Eßstörung', *Zeitschrift für Psychoanalytische Pädagogik*, 8, pp. 109–116.

—— (1935) 'Reassurance as a Means of Analytic Technique', *The International Journal of Psycho-Analysis*, 16(2), pp. 307–324.

Schneiderman, S. (1983) *Jacques Lacan: The Death of an Intellectual Hero*, Cambridge MA and London: Harvard University Press.

Schneiderman, S. (ed.) (1993[1980]) *How Lacan's Ideas are Used in Clinical Practice*, Northvale NJ and London: Jason Aronson Inc.

Schreber, D. P. (1988[1903]) *Memoirs of My Nervous Illness*, trans. Ida Macalpine and Richard A. Hunter, with a new introduction by Samuel M. Weber, Cambridge MA and London: Harvard University Press.

Shengold, L. (1989) *Soul Murder: The Effects of Childhood Abuse and Deprivation*, New Haven CT and London: Yale University Press.

Shepherd, M. (1985) *Sherlock Holmes and the Case of Dr Freud*, London and New York NY: Tavistock.

Silvestre, M. (1984) 'Transfert et interprétation dans les psychoses: une question de technique', *Actes de l'Ecole de la Cause freudienne*, 6, pp. 53–56.

—— (1993[1984]) 'Transfert et répétition', *Demain la psychanalyse*, Paris: du Seuil, pp. 145–154.

Sipos, J. (1994) *Lacan et Descartes. La tentation métaphysique*, Paris, Presses Universitaires de France.

Skriabine, P. (1993) 'Où en est-on avec le transfert?', in Marie-Hélène Brousse, Serge Cottet, Jean-Pierre Klotz, Pierre Skriabine, Alexandre Stevens and Marc Strauss (eds) *Commentaire de 'La direction de la cure et les principes de son pouvoir'*, Lille: Association la Cause freudienne, pp. 26–37.

Soble, A. (1990) *The Structure of Love*, New Haven CT and London: Yale University Press.

Soler, C. (1987) 'Quelle place pour l'analyste?', *Actes de l'Ecole de la Cause freudienne*, 13, pp. 29–31.

—— (1995) 'The Subject and the Other I/II', in Richard Feldstein, Bruce Fink and Maire Jaanus (eds) *Reading Seminar XI: Lacan's Four Fundamental Concepts of Psychoanalysis*, Albany NY: State University of New York Press, pp. 39–53.

—— (1996a) 'The Symbolic Order I/II,' in Richard Feldstein, Bruce Fink and Maire Jaanus (eds) *Reading Seminars I and II: Lacan's Return to Freud*, Albany NY: State University of New York Press, pp. 39–55.

—— (1996b) 'Transference', in Richard Feldstein, Bruce Fink and Maire Jaanus (eds) *Reading Seminars I and II: Lacan's Return to Freud*, Albany NY: State University of New York Press, pp. 56–60.

—— (1996c[1989]) 'Hysteria and Obsession', in Richard Feldstein, Bruce Fink and Maire Jaanus (eds) *Reading Seminars I and II: Lacan's Return to Freud*, Albany NY: State University of New York Press, pp. 248–282.

—— (1996d) 'Silences', *La cause freudienne*, 32, pp. 26–30.

Solms, M. (1995) 'New Findings on the Neurological Organization of Dreaming: Implications for Psychoanalysis', *The Psychoanalytic Quarterly*, 64(1), pp. 43–67.

—— (1997) *The Neuropsychology of Dreams: A Clinico-Anatomical Study*, Hillsdale NJ: Lawrence Erlbaum.

—— (1998) 'Before and After Freud's *Project*', in Robert M. Bilder and F. Frank LeFever (eds) *Neuroscience of the Mind: On the Centennial of Freud's*

Project for A Scientific Psychology, New York NY: The New York Academy of Sciences, pp. 1–10.

Solms, M. and Saling, M. (1986) 'On Psychoanalysis and Neuroscience: Freud's Attitude to the Localizationist Tradition', *International Journal of Psycho-Analysis*, 67(2), pp. 397–416.

Sorabji, R. (1980) *Necessity, Cause and Blame: Perspectives on Aristotle's Theory*, London: Duckworth.

Spence, D. P. (1982) *Narrative Truth and Historical Truth: Meaning and Interpretation in Psychoanalysis*, New York NY and London: W. W. Norton and Company.

—— (1987) *The Freudian Metaphor: Toward Paradigm Change in Psychoanalysis*, New York NY and London: W. W. Norton and Company.

Stevens, A. (1987) 'L'holophrase', *Ornicar?*, 42, pp. 45–79.

—— (1988) 'Aux limites de la psychose', *Ornicar?*, 47, pp. 74–79.

Stockreiter, K. (1998) 'Am Rand der Aufklärungsmetapher: Korrespondenzen zwischen Archäologie und Psychoanalyse', in Lydia Marinelli (ed.) *'Meine . . . alten und dreckigen Götter'. Aus Sigmund Freuds Sammlung*, Frankfurt am Main: Stroemfeld, pp. 81–93.

Stone, L. (1961) *The Psychoanalytic Situation: An Examination of Its Development and Essential Nature*, New York NY: International Universities Press.

—— (1967) 'The Psychoanalytic Situation and Transference: Postscript to an Earlier Communication', *Journal of the American Psychoanalytic Association*, 15(1), pp. 3–57.

Strachey, J. (1934) 'The Nature of the Therapeutic Action of Psycho-Analysis', *The International Journal of Psycho-Analysis*, 15(1), pp. 127–159.

Strindberg, A. (1968[1887]) 'Soul Murder', *Drama Review*, 13, pp. 113–118.

Tannenbaum, S. A. (1917) 'Some Current Misconceptions of Psychoanalysis', *Journal of Abnormal Psychology*, 12, pp. 390–422.

Tausk, V. (1919) 'Über die Entstehung des "Beeinflußungsapparates" in der Schizofrenie', *Internationale Zeitschrift für ärztliche Psychoanalyse*, 5(1), pp. 1–33.

Thompson, M. G. (1994) *The Truth about Freud's Technique: The Encounter with the Real*, New York NY: New York University Press.

Timpanaro, S. (1976[1974]) *The Freudian Slip: Psychoanalysis and Textual Criticism*, trans. Kate Soper, London: New Left Books.

Van het Reve, K. (1994[1987]) 'Dr Freud und Sherlock Holmes', *Dr Freud und Sherlock Holmes*, trans. Gerd Busse, Frankfurt am Main: S. Fischer Verlag, pp. 16–24.

Vanier, A. (1990) 'Lacan et la Laienanalyse', *Revue internationale d'histoire de la psychanalyse*, 3, pp. 275–288.

Verhaeghe, P. (1995) 'From Impossibility to Inability: Lacan's Theory of the Four Discourses', *The Letter: Lacanian Perspectives on Psychoanalysis*, 4, pp. 76–99.

Verhaeghe, P. (1997[1987]) *Does the Woman Exist? From Freud's Hysteric to Lacan's Feminine*, trans. Marc du Ry, London: Rebus Press.

—— (1998) 'Causation and Destitution of a Pre-ontological Non-entity: On the Lacanian Subject', in Dany Nobus (ed.) *Key Concepts of Lacanian Psychoanalysis*, London: Rebus Press, pp. 164–189.

Wachsberger, H. (ed.) (1992) *La passe à l'entrée de l'Ecole? La question de Madrid*, Paris: Eolia.

Wajeman, G. (1982) *Le maître et l'hystérique*, Paris: Navarin.

Weatherill, R. (1998) *The Sovereignty of Death*, London: Rebus Press.

Weiß, C. and Weiß, H. (1989) 'Dem Beispiel jener Forscher folgend . . . Zur Bedeutung der Archäologie im Leben Freuds', *Luzifer-Amor. Zeitschrift zur Geschichte der Psychoanalyse*, 2(3), pp. 45–71.

Wells, F. L. (1913–14) 'On Formulation in Psychoanalysis', *Journal of Abnormal Psychology*, 8, pp. 217–227.

Welsh, A. (1994) *Freud's Wishful Dream Book*, Princeton NJ and London: Princeton University Press.

Wilde, O. (1990[1893]) 'Lady Windermere's Fan', *The Complete Works of Oscar Wilde*, London and Glasgow: Collins, pp. 385–430.

Wohlgemuth, A. A. (1923) *A Critical Examination of Psycho-Analysis*, London: Allen and Unwin.

Wolstein, B. (ed.) (1988) *Essential Papers on Countertransference*, New York NY and London: New York University Press.

Young, R. J. C. (1999) 'Freud's Secret: The Interpretation of Dreams was a Gothic Novel', in Laura Marcus (ed.) *Sigmund Freud's The Interpretation of Dreams: New Interdisciplinary Essays*, Manchester and New York NY: Manchester University Press, pp. 206–231.

Zeigarnik, B. (1927) 'Über das Behalten von erledigten und unerledigten Handlungen', *Psychologische Forschung*, 9, pp. 1–85.

Zetzel, E. R. (1956) 'Current Concepts of Transference', *The International Journal of Psycho-Analysis*, 37(4), pp. 369–376.

—— (ed.) (1962) '120th Bulletin of the International Psycho-Analytical Association', *The International Journal of Psycho-Analysis*, 43(4/5), pp. 362–375.

Žižek, Slavoj (1996) 'Hegel with Lacan, or The Subject and its Cause', in Richard Feldstein, Bruce Fink and Maire Jaanus (eds) *Reading Seminars I and II: Lacan's Return to Freud*, Albany NY: State University of New York Press, pp. 397–413.

—— (1997) *The Plague of Fantasies*, London and New York NY: Verso.

—— (1999) 'Kant with (or against) Sade', in Elizabeth Wright and Edmond Wright (eds) *The Žižek Reader*, Oxford: Blackwell, pp. 283–301.

Zupančič, A. (1995) *Die Ethik des Realen: Kant mit Lacan*, Wien: Turia und Kant.

—— (1998) 'The Subject of the Law', in Slavoj Žižek (ed.) *Cogito and the Unconscious*, Durham NC and London: Duke University Press, pp. 41–73.

Index